A COLLECTION
OF GAELIC PROVERBS
AND FAMILIAR PHRASES

A COLLECTION OF GAELIC PROVERBS AND FAMILIAR PHRASES

Edited by Alexander Nicolson

Birlinn

This edition first published in 1996 by
Birlinn Limited
West Newington House
10 Newington Road
Edinburgh
EH9 1QS

www.birlinn.co.uk

Reprinted 2003

First published in 1881
Revised and reprinted 1882
Third edition with index 1951

ISBN 1 874744 14 9

Typeset in Plantin by Westkey Ltd, Falmouth
Printed and bound by WS Bookwell, Finland

CONTENTS

Alexander Nicolson
and his Collection

Alexander Nicolson—later always known as Sheriff Nicolson—was for many years among the most popular of nineteenth century Gaels in public life. He was born on 27th September 1827 at Husabost, an estate in the north of Skye where his father, Malcolm Nicolson, was proprietor. After an education from private tutors in his native parish, he went to Edinburgh University with a view to entering the ministry of the Free Church of Scotland. A highly successful student, Nicolson graduated BA in 1850 and was later awarded the Honorary Degree of MA 'in respect of services rendered as assistant to several of the Professors'.

At some point, however, he had changed his mind about the ministry and decided on a legal career. He worked as a sub-editor on the *Encyclopaedia Britannica* and did some newspaper work before being called to the Scottish Bar in 1860. Work as a reporter for *The Scottish Jurist* brought in a small income, but he found it difficult to advance in the legal profession in the capital.

In 1865 he was appointed as Assistant Commissioner by the Scottish Education Commission, which involved him in the congenial task of inspecting schools in the Scottish islands, his report being described by Lord Ardmillan as 'the most readable blue-book ever printed'.

In 1872, his hopes of a successful legal career in Edinburgh at an end, he accepted the office of Steward-substitute (later Sheriff-substitute) of Kirkcudbright. In 1885 he moved to a similar post in Greenock, but he retired because of ill-health in 1889. Other activities during those years included work as a member of the Committee appointed in 1881 by the SSPCK for the revision of the Gaelic Bible and as a member of the Napier Commission, appointed in 1883 to enquire into crofting conditions in the Highlands.

Alexander Nicolson was considered to be one of the best Gaelic scholars of his day, and he was urged by Professor John Stuart Blackie to accept the new Chair of Celtic at Edinburgh University, which Blackie himself had laboured so strenuously to have endowed. By then, however, Nicolson was installed elsewhere, and could not be persuaded. There appears to be a general consensus that he lacked the energy to fulfil his undoubted potential. Even the kindly Henry Whyte, in his 'Gaelic Men of Letters' series in *The Celtic Monthly*, says that he was 'a man of intellectual power and high literary ability, but his energy was somewhat crippled by a lethargic constitution'.

While this may have been so in the intellectual field, his climbing exploits show another side to Sheriff Nicolson. He is regarded as one of the pioneers of mountain climbing in his beloved Cuillins, one of whose peaks, Sgurr Alasdair, was named after him after he had climbed it. The name had been insisted on by members of the Alpine Club, Nicolson himself having suggested Sgurr Lagain.

Of his popularity during his own time there is little doubt. Sir Archibald Geikie was a student of Nicolson's and speaks of a 'big-boned Celt with a look of strength and kindliness', while the Lochaber poet Mary MacKellar has this description of him at a meeting arranged to discuss the proposed Chair of Celtic:

'S bha 'n Siorra MacNeacail am breacan bha grinn,
Gaisgeach rìoghail nam buadh sheinneadh duanag gu binn;
Cridh' fearail an t-saighdeir, 's mar mhaighdinn e ciùin;
Sùil mar lainnir nan leug bhios air èideadh mo rùin.

Sealgair an daimh chràcaich san àrd-chreachann ghlas,
'S bheireadh bradan gu bruaich às an fhuar-linne chais;
Bidh ceartas is tròcair triall còmhl' riut tren t-saogh'l,
Is claon-bhreith gu bràth cha toir àrmann mo ghaoil.

(*Oran mun Choinnimh-Chòmhraidh . . . airson Cathair Ghàidhlig . . .*)

'And Sheriff Nicolson was there in tartan that was elegant,
Kingly talented hero who could melodiously sing a song;
Manly of heart as a soldier, and gentle as a maiden;
An eye like the shine of the jewels in my beloved one's apparel.

Hunter of the antlered stag on the grey mountain-top,
He'd bring a salmon to the bank of the cold, fast-flowing river;
Justice and mercy will accompany you through life,
And my dear hero will never give an unjust judgment.'

Visits to Skye were common, and his love of the island was constantly expressed in his writings. His best known poem is perhaps *The Isle of Skye*, with its frequently quoted quatrain:

Jerusalem, Athens and Rome,
I would see them before I die;
But I'd rather not see any one of the three
Than be exiled forever from Skye!

He himself later translated the poem into Gaelic.

In Henry Whyte's judgment, 'He wrote Gaelic and English with equal grace, and was no mean poet in either language'. Another of his better known pieces is his marching song in praise of the exploits of Highland regiments, with its chorus (borrowed from Mac Mhaighstir Alasdair) of *Agus hò, Mhòrag*. Some of his pieces were anthologised, but much of his writing is still uncollected, both original work and translations. However, the marching song and the poem on Skye are two of fifteen romantic and mildly satirical pieces collected in *Verses*, published by David Douglas of Edinburgh in 1893, very shortly after Nicolson's sudden and unexpected death on 13th January of that year. They were edited by Walter Smith, D.D., who also contributed an occasionally critical memoir.

Nicolson's retiral had not been a long one—less than four years with his sister in Edinburgh. He had not married. He had published *A Life of the Late Adam Black* and edited *Edinburgh Essays*, but the nearest thing to a magnum opus is undoubtedly *A Collection of Gaelic Proverbs and Familiar Phrases. Based on Macintosh's Collection*, which was published in Edinburgh by Maclachlan and Stewart in 1881. The collection has never been superseded.

Work on it appears to have started in Kirkcudbright, as Nicolson wrote the following letter to the editor of the magazine *An Gàidheal* from there on 16th June 1873.

Dear Sir,—Having in view the preparation of a new edition of 'Mackintosh's Gaelic Proverbs,' now a scarce book, I shall be obliged to any of
your readers who will kindly send me any additions *(sop as gach seid)* to
the unpublished stock of Gaelic proverbs, in order to make the collection
as complete as possible.—I am, yours truly,

ALEX. NICOLSON

Nicolson later adopted the spelling Macintosh, a form he defends
in his note on the original compiler.

As he indicates in his Preface, the first edition appeared in 1785,
and there was no reprint in Macintosh's lifetime. The second edition
was prepared by Alexander Campbell and published by William
Stewart of Edinburgh in 1819. Nicolson's collection may be said, in
a sense, to be a third edition, but it contained three times as many
proverbs and phrases as the first edition—close to 4,000 in all—and
it is not unreasonable to consider it a new work in its own right. It
was published in 1881 by Maclachlan and Stewart, and both its
title-page and its dedication to the Rev. Norman MacLeod ('Caraid
nan Gàidheal') are reproduced elsewhere. A revised edition appeared in 1882, and in 1885 Maclachlan and Stewart published *A
Birthday Book: in Gaelic and English*, edited by M.C. Clerk, a
miscellany in which some of the proverbs appeared among extracts
from various literary works, with those of James 'Ossian' Macpherson being the most prominent. Thereafter, and perhaps surprisingly,
Nicolson's collection was not reprinted until 1951.

That edition was published by the Caledonian Press in Glasgow
for Malcolm MacInnes, another native of Skye, who reproduced
Nicolson's list almost totally unaltered (although reset), even following the pagination of the original, but gave each proverb a
number—the numbering starting anew on each page—and added a
comprehensive English index at the end of the book. In his Foreword
MacInnes thanked Mr Neil Macleod of Staffin in Skye for assistance
with the index and noted that it contained over 8,000 references. In
the present edition that index has been adapted by Marion Sinclair.

This book is the third edition—or, if preferred, the third reprint—
of the original 1881 publication. Since the text has been reset once
again, the opportunity has been taken to include in the main text
those proverbs and phrases that Nicolson 'got too late for insertion
in their alphabetical places, or omitted' and that he listed as a
supplement at the end of the collection. However, the sayings in

verse that he also included in that supplement have been left in their original position.

The only other difference between this edition and its predecessors is in the orthography. The spelling of Gaelic has been modified and modernised very considerably even since 1951, to say nothing of 1881. It therefore seemed essential that the spelling in this reprint should be updated, the main guide followed being the Scottish Certificate of Education Examination Board's *Gaelic Orthographic Conventions* . . . (1981). The punctuation has been revised and modern conventions have been adopted in matters such as the use of capital letters and italics, while some misprints have been corrected. Some revision of the spelling of Irish, Scots and English versions of proverbs given has also been carried out. However, none of the proverbs or translations or other versions has been altered in any other way. This means, for example, that the gender of a small number of Gaelic nouns, although not the expected one, has not been changed. But a few proverbs do appear in a slightly different order as the result of a spelling change, or for other reasons.

One of the recent changes in Gaelic spelling is the use of one accent instead of two, and because of this and because of other changes in the way accents are used, Nicolson's own separate note on accents has not been reprinted here. However, the paragraphs on spelling in his Preface have been reproduced as they were, even although they no longer apply one hundred per cent. (Absolute uniformity of spelling has not, in fact, been imposed, but there is a greater degree of it than in the original work.) In addition, Nicolson's usage when quoting the sources of proverbs in the Preface has been left unaltered, although elsewhere in the work some modifications have been made in that area.

There have been other selections of proverbs published since Nicolson's work first appeared, some of them highly interesting and attractive, but this still remains the standard work, and it is hoped that its re-issue will be welcomed. Alexander Nicolson was good company, and the actual commentary is sometimes as rewarding as its subject.

Ian MacDonald

Malcolm MacInnes

Most of those who are familiar with Nicolson's collection of proverbs nowadays will know it through the red-bound edition of 1951 published by the Caledonian Press for Malcolm MacInnes. What was new about that edition was its painstakingly compiled index, of which the index in this edition is an abridged version.

Interestingly, although Nicolson's junior by over forty years, MacInnes was cut from not dissimilar cloth. Both men were natives of Skye, both had brilliant academic careers at the University of Edinburgh, both became advocates and both were of a literary bent. Each of them, too, was of striking appearance and large of frame. MacInnes, in fact, was one of the best all-round athletes of his time in Scotland, displaying his prowess first at the Skye Games, later becoming Great Britain and Ireland Inter-University champion for both hammer and shot-putt and, in 1901, competing for Scotland at the International Games and winning the shot.

Born at Drumfearn, in Sleat, in 1871, MacInnes attended the Raining School in Inverness (while Dr. Alexander MacBain was Headmaster), and then took the M.A. and LL.B. at Edinburgh, where he was also Medallist or Prizeman in Philosophy, English Literature, Scots Law and Public Law, MacPherson Scholar in Latin and Greek and Thomson Scholar in Law. He was also an athletics Blue and captain of the shinty team.

In 1901 he emigrated to South Africa, where he laboured in the mines, studied privately, graduated LL.B. in Dutch-Roman Law at Capetown and became a member of the Faculty of Advocates of South Africa. In 1907 he was appointed Permanent Secretary for Education in the newly instituted Transvaal School Board in Johannesburg.

Meanwhile, he kept up his athletic interests and was at one point champion for hammer and for shot for the whole of South Africa. He retired from the post in 1926, having done 'valuable work which did much to ensure the success of the new education scheme in the Transvaal'. Returning to Scotland, MacInnes farmed at Ostaig in Skye for a while but later settled in Inverness. He was a member of Inverness County Council for some time, and for some years before his death was honorary piper to the Gaelic Society.

Described in one of his obituaries as 'one of the most notable and versatile intellects of his generation', Malcolm MacInnes was also active as a writer and editor. He was the author of two Gaelic operettas (*Iseabail na h-Airigh* and *Suiridhe Ruairidh*) and of four English blank verse dramas (*Massacre of Glencoe, The Forty-Five, Mary Queen of Scots* and *The Appin Murder*), and he also compiled and edited musical works (*Traditional Airs of Skye and the West, Gaelic and English Songs of Skye* and *120 Bag Pipe Tunes*, this last being a collection of pipe music which also draws on family tradition).

MacInnes had come of a Sleat family which had a particularly rich tradition in song, story, piping and dancing. His father and several of his brothers played musical instruments, particularly the pipes. His brother Myles, himself a noted athlete, was one of the foremost members of the Highland Land League and a vice-president of the Scottish Home Rule Association. One of Malcolm MacInnes's collateral ancestors was said to have been instructed by the MacArthurs, hereditary pipers to the MacDonalds of Sleat, and he himself was an accomplished piper and wrote extensively on the subject of pibroch.

He was said to be a 'very severe critic of musical developments and arrangements which violated the native structure of traditional Gaelic melodies'. It is also interesting that he proposed at one time to re-edit the famous collection of songs published in the *Journal of the Folk-Song Society* in 1911 by Frances Tolmie, whom he knew personally.

Unlike the man whom he had honoured by his own devotion to the collection of proverbs, Malcolm MacInnes was long-lived, dying in Inverness on 2nd December 1951 at the age of eighty. He is still remembered by an older generation, and, as with Nicolson, his life was full of achievement and interest and would repay much closer study. Ironically, he did not live to see the proverb collection in its expanded form published, but many have had cause to be grateful for his efforts since then, and at this juncture it is appropriate to place this small stone on his cairn.

                                                            Ian MacDonald

A COLLECTION

OF

GAELIC PROVERBS

AND

FAMILIAR PHRASES.

BASED ON
MACINTOSH'S COLLECTION.

EDITED BY

ALEXANDER NICOLSON, M.A., LL.D.,

ADVOCATE.

An sean-fhacal gu fada fìor,
Cha bhriagaichear an sean-fhacal.

EDINBURGH:
MACLACHLAN AND STEWART.

LONDON: SIMPKIN, MARSHALL, & CO.

—

1881.

THIS BOOK IS DEDICATED

TO THE MEMORY OF

THE REV. NORMAN MAC LEOD, D.D.,

MINISTER OF ST. COLUMBA CHURCH, GLASGOW;

A MAN WORTHY TO BE REMEMBERED

WITH AFFECTIONATE VENERATION

BY ALL LOVERS OF THE SCOTTISH HIGHLANDS,

THEIR PEOPLE, AND THEIR LANGUAGE;

WHOSE PERFECT KNOWLEDGE OF GAELIC PROVERBS,

AND HAPPY USE OF THEM,

GAVE A SPECIAL CHARM TO

HIS HIGHLAND DIALOGUES,

WHICH IN WISDOM, HUMOUR, TENDERNESS,

IN HEIGHT OF AIM, PURENESS OF SPIRIT,

AND SIMPLE BEAUTY OF STYLE,

HAVE NOT BEEN SURPASSED

IN THE LITERATURE OF ANY COUNTRY.

PREFACE

The collection of Gaelic Proverbs and Phrases, on which the present collection is based, was first published at Edinburgh in 1785. Some account of the compiler and the publication will be found at the end of this volume. Though small in bulk, and in several respects defective, Macintosh's collection was a valuable contribution to Celtic Literature. It was at that time, and has continued to be, the only collection of Celtic Proverbs gathered into a book, and translated for the benefit of the world. It had the still greater merit of being a genuine product of the past, the editor's share in the compilation of which consisted in simply giving as correctly as he could the words of sayings familiar to the people among whom he lived, rendering them into English, and occasionally illustrating them by an explanation, an anecdote, or a parallel.

Macintosh contemplated a new edition some time before his death, which took place in 1808, and a new dedication, to Sir John Macgregor Murray of Lanrick, was found among his papers. But the second edition, which did not appear till 1819, shows no other mark of his hand. The additions to the collection were probably found among his papers, but the new editor, Alexander Campbell (author of *The Grampians Desolate* and other works), says nothing on the subject. A short memoir of Macintosh forms the Preface, and may fairly be characterised as a curiosity in Biography. The title-page says that the collection is 'Englished anew,' and the claim is well founded, much of the English being of a very novel kind. The ignorance of the elements of Gaelic displayed in some of the new translations is still more extraordinary, often so ludicrous as to make it matter of

wonder and regret that Campbell ventured on the task.[1] Macintosh's
translations are on the whole creditable, sometimes happy; the new
ones substituted for them are rarely changes for the better; much
oftener they give nonsense for sense, and turgid commonplace for
pithiness. A few specimens are given below.[2] The spelling in the new
edition is far worse than in the old, which, for the period when it
appeared, may be considered very respectable.

A more remarkable defect in both editions is the omission of many
of the most familiar and popular proverbs and phrases, such as, *An
là a chì 's nach fhaic, Am fear a bhios air dheireadh beiridh a' bhiast air,
An gad air an robh 'n t-iasg, Am fear a bhios gun mhodh, saoilidh e,* &c.,
Aisling caillich, &c., *Gach dìleas gu deireadh, Is treasa tuath na tighearna, Saoilidh am fear a bhios 'n a thàmh,* &c., *Tarruing am bleidir'
ort,* &c., &c.

These various defects in both editions, and the comparative rarity
of the book, suggested the present edition. The whole original
collection has been translated anew, so far as that seemed necessary,
and the additions to it, through the kind assistance of numerous
friends, have trebled the number of proverbs and phrases given by
Macintosh. The number in the first edition was 1305; in the second,
1538; in this edition it exceeds 3900.

The coming in of fresh materials from time to time, and the desire
to make the collection as complete and correct as possible, have
delayed the publication to a degree requiring some apology. *Cha bhi
luathas agus grinneas,* a very Celtic sentiment, has perhaps been too

---

[1]   It is with compunction that one speaks thus of a man for whom both Burns and
Scott had some regard, and to whom we are in that respect indebted not a little.
Several of Scott's best songs, 'Jock of Hazeldean,' 'Pibroch of Donald Dhu,' 'Mac-
Gregor's Gathering,' 'MacCrimmon's Lament,' 'Donald Caird's come again,' were
written for *Albyn's Anthology,* a collection of Scottish Songs and Music, edited by
Campbell.

[2]   'A lion beagan 'us beagan,' is rendered *Fill little and little;* 'B'e sin seangan toirt
greim a gearran,' *That were the emmet's bite bewailing;* 'Cha ghille mur umhailt,' *He is
not a disobedient man-servant;* 'Lèintibh farsuin,' &c., *Narrow shirts;* 'Cha d' ith na coin
an aimsir,' *The dogs did not worry the wether;* 'Dalt arain-eòrna Mhic Philip,' *MacGillip's
oat-cake foster-child;* 'Gheibh bean bhaoth dlùth gun cheannach, 's cha 'n fhaigh i
inneach,' *A wizard's wife will get retribution without buying it, and she will not get a cure;*
'Leigheas air leth a' losgadh, *Burning is half cure;* Leann dubh air mo chridhe,
Black-beer at my heart; 'Trod nam ban mu 'n scarbh,' *The wife's scolding about the heron*
(this is one of the comparatively few mistranslations of Macintosh); 'Tha 'n uaill an
aghaidh an tairbh,' *Pride is in the bull's front.* One specimen of Campbell's grandilo-
quence may suffice. 'Cha 'n ann do 'n ghuin an gàire' is fairly rendered by Macintosh,
Smiles are not companions of pain. Campbell's improved version is *The laugh is not
excited by the sharp lancinating pain of a stitch.*

influential. But the alphabetical arrangement was decided on from the beginning, as the most useful and feasible; and some of the best additions came at the very last.[1]

It is fair also to state that the most of these valuable new materials were received without translations, in most cases without note or comment, and not always in the most legible handwriting. Nor will it be new to any one who has meddled with Proverbs to hear that the most diverse interpretations of the same saying are sometimes given, by persons of the most competent qualifications as judges of Folk-lore. This fact consoles one somewhat under the certainty that all the translations and explanations will not please everybody.

We have as yet no absolute standard of Gaelic orthography, and it is no disgrace, considering that William Shakespeare spelled his own great name in several ways, and that even Samuel Johnson's English spellings are not all followed now. Our Gaelic version of the Bible is generally accepted by all reasonable persons as our grammatical standard, but being a human production it cannot claim infallibility, and it was from the beginning too much regulated by deference to the practice of Irish grammarians, and a slight dread of anything too vernacular and simple. The latest edition of it, an admirable one,[2] proves that it is possible to get three Gaelic scholars to agree in orthography. But Mr. J. F. Campbell does not exaggerate when he questions whether 'there are ten men now living who would write a hundred lines of Gaelic offhand, and spell them in the same way'. I have been very desirous to make this book in that respect as correct as possible, and in general accordance with the best authorities. But an occasional divergence from the canonical norm, and even varied spellings of the same word, have seemed to me not only excusable but desirable. The phrases in which these words occur belong to the simplest vernacular forms of speech, and ought to be so given as to represent faithfully the varieties of phrase and pronunciation found among Gaelic-speaking people. The greater part of the two thousand three hundred sayings here first collected were received in MS, mostly from good Gaelic scholars, who spelled sometimes in different ways.

Among these varieties of spelling are *béul* and *bial*, *bréug* and *briag*, *féur* and *fiar*, *sgéul* and *sgial*, *rìs* and *rithist*, &c. To adhere uniformly

---

[1] There are still a good many Gaelic sayings which have never got into print. The present Editor will be glad to get any such.
[2] Published for the Edinburgh National Bible Society, 1880.

to any of these would sometimes spoil the rhyme or rhythm on which the charm of a proverb often depends. The only positive innovation in this volume, so far as I know, is a very small one, *seo* for *so*, chosen because it more correctly represents the sound 'sho', the common pronunciation of the word in the Highlands. For the same reason I have invariably substituted *sid* for *sud*, and *dhaibh* for *dhoibh*, the former being the pronunciation of Inverness-shire, which I naturally preferred to that of Argyllshire. The addition of the acute accent to such words as *béul* and *lóm* is not an innovation, having the sanction of such a Gaelic scholar as James Munro. It is difficult to see why *féin* and *mór* should be always accented, and *béul* and *lóm* left without it. The use of accents might well be limited to ambiguous words, such as *lon*, *lón* and *lòn*, all of different sound and meaning. Except for this purpose, they are useless alike to those who know the language, and to those who do not. They are all the more confusing, when it is found that the Irish use of them entirely differs from ours, and that, with us, some people write *mór*, and others *mòr*, the one sounding like *mould*, the other like *more*. Having adhered to the use of accents in this book, I have chosen the former of these, as representing what I consider the better pronunciation; and following the example of Munro, I have given the same accent to *lóm*, *dónn*, *tóm*, &c. The words *ceard*, *fearr*, &c., I have purposely left without accent, because there are two pronunciations of them, equally correct. Some say *kyard* and *fyarr*, accented *ceàrd* and *feàrr*; others say *kyaird* and *fare*, spelled *cèard* and *fèarr*. For the same reason the accent is omitted over *fhein*, when preceded by the first personal or possessive pronoun. It is a singular peculiarity of speech, in a part of the North Western Highlands and most of the Islands, that they say *ay-hain (e-fhéin)*, himself, but *mee-heen (mi-fhein)*, myself. This curious variety may not be defensible, but the fact has been taken into consideration.

In many cases the vowel in a word is sounded long or short, according to the apposition of the word, and, as in Greek, the presence or absence of the accent should mark this, *e.g., Féill*, where the *e* is long, *Feill-Brighde* where it is short. This has generally been kept in view, but occasional slips will be found.

In addition to some misplacings or omissions of accents, there are a few omissions of apostrophes, chiefly after the article *a*, contracted for *an*. Probably they will never be noticed, except by some very critical eyes.

As to the matter of the book, I have followed, and I hope improved upon, the example of Macintosh, in giving such illustrative notes and comments as seemed necessary or suitable. In this respect my original intention, merely to give an improved translation, with a few additions, has been greatly changed, and I found at last that the collection could no more be called 'Macintosh's Collection'. He rightly included Familiar Phrases as well as Proverbs, and I have followed the example, giving a large number of vernacular phrases which, though not proverbs, are household Highland words, all the more worthy to be preserved, that the use of the Gaelic language in its native land is slowly but surely passing away. The venerable creature dies hard,[1] but the process is going on, some of her heartless children doing their little best to hasten her end. I have included phrases and sayings which may seem of small value, but if that be an error, it is on the safe side. Good Macintosh was not afraid to give some specimens of Gaelic maledictions, and a considerable number has been added in this volume. To very strait-laced people this may seem objectionable; but it is an interesting peculiarity of these Gaelic imprecations that they are neither coarse nor blasphemous. They never take the divine name in vain; and though not commonplace, there is not one of them to be compared for a moment in malignity with the dreadful ingenuity of Ernulphus.

I have taken all due pains to translate correctly, and, so far as possible, to preserve the pith of the original, which is sometimes as difficult with Proverbs as it is with Poetry. A good many sayings are given of which the meaning is ambiguous or obscure. I have not excluded them on that account, as it sometimes happens that an old saying may have some recondite meaning, or local reference, which the words do not convey on the surface. That the interpretations I have given are always correct is too much to assume. In the case of some of the *dubh-fhacail* or dark sayings, I have thought it better to give no comment than to offer an unsatisfactory guess. Comments or illustrations have been necessarily limited to such sayings as seemed most to require them, or to invite them. They might have been multiplied indefinitely; but the line had to be drawn somewhere; and it seemed not too much to take for granted that the readers of this book would be of a class not requiring explanations of things comparatively obvious.

---

[1] 'S e 'm bial a dh'obas mu dheireadh—*The mouth gives in last.*

The only improvement in the second edition of Macintosh, excepting in paper and print, was the increased number of parallel proverbs given in the notes, which greatly added to the interest of the book. That practice, of which Erasmus showed such a wonderful example in his *Adagia*, has been followed in this volume to an extent which to some may seem excessive, to others inadequate. It has added seriously to the labour and time spent on the work, but the labour has been a pleasant one, and the time has not been wasted, if the result be found to have increased the value of the collection, from the point of view of what may be called 'Comparative Parœmiography'. Lest the array of languages sometimes cited might suggest an ostentation of learning, it is right to mention that my acquaintance with some of them is of a very slender kind, but that I have used all available means, and got help from more competent persons, to give the words in these languages correctly.[1] A few errors will be found, but none of them, I believe, of importance.

The value of Proverbs, as condensed lessons of wisdom, 'abridgements of knowledge,' as Mr. Disraeli calls them, has been recognised by the wisest of men, from Solomon to Aristotle, from Aristotle to Bacon, from Bacon to Benjamin Franklin. The interest attaching to them as an index of the character of a nation is equally great. They are an unintentional, and all the more truthful, revelation of a people's peculiarities, habits and ideas. In both these respects the proverbs embraced in this collection are entitled to a high place in the unwritten Philosophy of nations. Some of them are common to various countries; others of them are borrowed, gaining oftener than losing in their new form. But a large proportion of them is of native

[1]   The principal works that have been used in citing these parallel proverbs are, *Erasmi Adagia*, 1646; *Corpus Parœmiographorum Græcorum*, Ed. *Leutsch et Schneidewin*, 1839–51; *Ray's English Proverbs*, Ed. 1813; *Fuller's Gnomologia*, 1817; *Hazlitt's English Prov.*, 1869; *Kelly's Scottish Prov.*, 1721; *Ramsay's Scot. Prov.* (*Works*, Oliver & Co., N.D., Vol. III.); *Henderson's Scot. Prov.* (Ed. *Donald*), 1876; *Hislop's Scot. Prov.*, 1862; *Cregeen's Manks Dict.*, 1835; *Kelly's Manx Dict.*, 1866; *Bourke's Irish Grammar*, 1867; *R. McAdam's Irish Prov.* in *Ulster Arch. Journ.*, Vols. VI and VII; *Pughe's Welsh Dict.* (Ed. *Pryse*), 1866; *Myvirian Archaiology*, Vol. III, 1807; *Prov. et Dictons de la Basse-Bretagne, par L. F. Sauvé, Revue Celtique*, Vols. I, II, III; *Pineda's Spanish Dict.*, 1740; *Burke's Spanish Salt*, 1877; *Roux de Lincy's Prov. Français*, 1859; *Méry's Hist. Generale des Prov.*, 1829; *Giusti's Prov. Toscani*, 1871; *Castagna's Prov. Italiani*, 1869; *Bonifacio's Prov. Lombardi*, 1860; *Dict. of Danish Proverbs* (*Danish and French*), 1759; *Sandvoss's So Spricht das Volk*, 1860; *Sprichwörter und Spruchreden von Deutschen*, Leipzig, N.D.; *Bohn's Polyglot of Prov.*, 1857; *Bohn's Handbook of Prov.*, 1855; *Kelly's Prov. of all Nations*, 1859; *Burckhardt's Arabic Proverbs*, 1830; *Negris' Mod. Greek Prov.*, 1831; *Disraeli's Philos. of Prov.*, in *Cur. of Eng. Lit.*; *Trench on Proverbs*, 3rd ed., 1854.

growth, as certainly as is the heather on Ben Nevis, or the lichen on
Cape Wrath; and as a reflex of the ways of thinking and feeling, the
life and manners, the wisdom or superstition, the wit or nonsense
of the Celtic race in Scotland, they are interesting alike to the
historian, the philologist and the student of human nature.

In speaking of them as a representation of the sentiments of a
nation or people, it must be borne in mind that, though the Gaelic-
speaking population of Scotland is now but a small part of the whole,
their mother-tongue was up to the time of Malcolm III (1057–1093)
the vernacular speech of the greater part of the people of North
Britain, not excepting their native king, whose name alone would
have bewrayed him as such.[1] These Gaelic proverbs, therefore, so
far as they are truly ancient, must be regarded as not merely
Highland but Scottish. Where they are found in identical terms in
Gaelic and Broad Scotch or English, the presumption is, unless they
are on the face of them modern, that the Gaelic is the original,
instead of being a translation, that language having been the common speech, not only of the Scotia of the time, but of the Western
Coast and Isles, and of Galloway, centuries before either of the other
two had come into existence. To some people this statement may
be surprising, but to all competent scholars it is the mere expression
of a now well-established fact in our Scottish history.[2]

The growth of Proverbs, like that of Ballad Poetry, is one of the
most singular phenomena in the history of Literature. They are
universally admitted to embody a great deal of wit and wisdom,
artistically expressed. They must have been composed by persons
of no ordinary ability; and yet, with the exception of a small fraction
out of many thousands, their authorship is utterly unknown. This
undoubtedly has added to their influence, for the same reason that
anonymous leading articles are so much more powerful than if they
were signed. When to this are added the sanctions of antiquity and
association, these old sayings seem to address us like impersonal
oracles, the voices, not of individuals, but of many generations, like
the 'ancestral voices' heard by Kubla Khan. And yet it seems very
probable that a great many of the best of them were composed by
persons in humble life, poor in position and in culture, rich only in
mother-wit. Many of them, doubtless, were composed by gentlemen

[1] 'Calum Ceann-mór,' generally rendered 'Canmore,' Big-head Malcolm. See Note
on 'Ceann mór air duine glic,' p. 86.
[2] See Skene's *Celtic Scotland*, Vol. I.

and scholars, some by persons of high degree, at a time when Gaelic was familiar to all the Highland nobility, and when the intercourse between high and low was constant, free and kindly. Among the aristocracy of intellect, the name of one may be specially mentioned, as a Celt by birth, to whom Gaelic was his mother-tongue, our greatest scholar, George Buchanan. The most of these proverbs, however, so far as native, came from thatched cottages, and not from baronial or academic halls. They expressed the thoughts and feelings of hardy, frugal, healthy-minded and healthy-bodied men, who spent most of their time in the fields, in the woods, on the moors and on the sea. So considered, they do great credit to the people whose thoughts and manners they represent, proving that there was and is a civilisation in Celtic Scotland, much beyond the imagination even of such a brilliant Celt as Lord Macaulay. The Irish Book of Kells, and the Scottish Hunterston Brooch, reveal to the eye of the artist and the archaeologist a degree of artistic taste and skill among our Celtic ancestors which modern art can imitate, but scarcely equal. Not less plainly do these old Gaelic sayings reflect a high moral standard, an intelligence shrewd and searching, a singular sense of propriety and grace, and, what may be considered one of the tests of intellectual rank and culture, a distinct sense of humour, never found among savages or clod-hoppers.

The special relations of Scotland to some of the continental nations will account for the close similarity of some of these proverbs to foreign ones. A few of the Hebridean ones have a strong resemblance to some of the sayings of our Norse ancestors. Our old and intimate connection with France is well known. For many generations we sent soldiers and students to that country. Some Scottish priests are still educated at Douay, as in days of yore, and a Scots College was long maintained for their special benefit at Paris. From a very remote date they were in the habit of finding their way to Rome, as a verse by one of our oldest Gaelic poets, Murdoch the Scot, bears record (see p. 424). There is still a Scottish College at Rome, and some Scottish students are regularly trained in the Propaganda College. A Scottish College was founded at Madrid in 1627, translated to Valladolid in 1771, where a considerable proportion of our Roman Catholic clergy now complete their education. These facts will help to account for the similarity of many Gaelic Proverbs to French, Italian and Spanish ones. Our old military connection with Denmark and the Netherlands will help in like

manner to account for any borrowed from these countries and from
Germany. The few survivors of our much-prized contribution to the
ranks of Gustavus Adolphus very probably carried back with them
to Sutherland more proverbs than dollars.

The resemblance of our Gaelic proverbs to Irish ones, especially
Ulster ones, is what might be expected. The only wonder is that the
number of Irish ones hitherto given to the world is so small, and that
those given are so remarkably deficient in that unpremeditated airy
wit for which our Hibernian cousins are specially distinguished. The
resemblance to Manx sayings is more remarkable. In that interesting
island, with which our Celtic connection has for centuries been very
slight, sayings are still found in words almost identical with ours
which must have originated in a prehistoric period, when the Isle of
Man, the north of Ireland, the south-west of Scotland and the
Hebrides spoke the same Gaelic tongue, and had constant intercourse. The resemblance between Gaelic and Welsh proverbs, as
between the two languages, is very remote. Of the latter, unfortunately, the outside world has never been able to judge, our Cymric
relatives not having thought it worth their while to give the benefit
of their ancestral wisdom to anybody who did not understand their
own beautiful language. A great deal of it is embodied in proverbs
remarkable for brevity.

These Gaelic proverbs give very little indication of those ferocious
traits which ignorance or prejudice is apt to regard as specially
characteristic of our Celtic ancestors. They express very few sentiments of which any muscular English Christian can disapprove.
Burckhardt makes a melancholy note on one of the Egyptian
Proverbs, of which he has rendered several hundreds into English.
He says it is the *only one* of them known to him expressing any faith
in human nature. What a comment on the history of that people! Of
these Gaelic sayings, on the contrary, almost the very opposite can
be said. Their view of human nature is keen but kindly, critical but
not contemptuous. The number of them that can be condemned,
on the score of morals or of taste, is singularly small, more than can
be said of the Proverbs of several great nations. They represent very
much the character that is still found among our unadulterated
Highland people, which undoubtedly they contributed much to
form. That character is a mixture of diverse qualities, some admirable, some not so, but on the whole very respectable, seldom
repulsive, oftener attractive, most rarely of all indicating selfishness,

stupidity, heartlessness or treachery. These special faults have ever been regarded among Highlanders with antipathy, pity, contempt and abhorrence.

In these Gaelic Proverbs there is plain and consistent inculcation of the virtues of Truthfulness, Honesty, Fidelity, Self-restraint, Self-esteem, Sense of Honour, Courage, Caution, in word and deed, Generosity, Hospitality, Courtesy, Peaceableness, Love of Kindred, Patience, Promptness, Industry, Providence. There are none to be found excusing or recommending Selfishness, Cunning, Time-serving or any other form of vice or meanness. *A salmon from the stream, a deer from the forest, a wand from the wood, three thefts that no man ever blushed for*, is the only saying expressive of any looseness of sentiment in regard to the rights of property, and it is not a very shocking one, coming as it does from times when the lifting of cattle was not considered disgraceful even to men of high degree. *I would give him a night's quarters, though he had a man's head under his arm*, may sound ferocious, but it might still be used, simply as an emphatic expression of regard, by a person quite incapable of aiding or abetting a homicide.

The specimens now to be given are selected almost exclusively from the purely native proverbs.

RELIGION.—The Scottish Celts are naturally disposed to be religious, but not to speak much or familiarly of sacred things. There is a religion of old date indicated in some of these proverbs, the creed of which is very short and simple, but good so far as it goes. It combines the chief articles of the primitive Hebrew and Greek religion. It is distinctly a Necessitarian system, implying a fixed belief that there is a Fate or Providence that shapes our ends, rough hew them how we will. Here are some examples:

> *The fated will happen. For whom ill is fated, him it will strike. No man can avoid the spot where birth or death is his lot. Where folk's fate is to go, ford or hill won't prevent. You can't give luck to a luckless man. Who is born to be hanged cannot be drowned. The man of long life will escape danger. He whose destiny is cast sits on a sharp cope. His hour was pursuing him.*

This belief in Fate is associated, as in the Augustinian and Calvinistic theology, with belief in an almighty and just God. The number of proverbs in which the divine name is mentioned is small, but they are good. Here are a few:

> *All will be as God wills. What God has promised man cannot baulk. What God bestowed not won't be long enjoyed. Short-lived is all rule but the rule of*

God. All things have an end but the goodness of God. When God teaches not man cannot. God comes in distress, and distress goes. Not less in God's sight is the end of the day than the beginning. Two days alike ill God to poor men doth not will.

The certainty that evil has its reward is distinctly taught in these proverbs:

Do evil and wait the end. There is no hiding of evil but not to do it. Wrong cannot rest, nor ill deed stand. Though there be delay, the evil-doer is not forgotten. As a man makes his bed, so must he lie. What's got at the Devil's head will be lost at his tail. Repentance won't cure mischief. Death-bed repentance is sowing seed at Martinmas.

With much natural reverence for religion, our Celts have combined a wholesome spirit of inquiry and a freedom of criticism on the ministers of religion:

God has not said all thou hast said. It is not the priest's first story that should be believed. It is his own child the priest baptizes first. The priest drank only what he had. The justice of the clergy to each other. The friendship of the clergy, scraping and scratching one another. Hard as is the factor's rule, no better is the minister's. It's a fine day when the fox preaches.

There is no Gaelic proverb making any worse reflection on the clerical character than the above. The proverbs of Italy and France specially abound in insinuations against priests and women. In both respects, the Gaelic ones form a contrast to them, which testifies equally to the character of the people, their priests, and their women.

The Gaelic idea of the Devil is very different from Milton's. One of the commonest terms for that personage is *Muisean*, literally, 'the mean rascal'.

MORALS—General.

Avoid the evil, and it will avoid thee. Love the good, and forgive the bad. Do good against the ill. Every creature but man can bear well-being. He gets no ease who suffers not. Better wear than rust. A bad man makes his own fate. Pity him who makes a bad habit. Do what becomes you, and you'll see what pleases you. Going to ruin is silent work. Better the long clean road than the short dirty road. He thinks no evil who means no evil. Better the little bannock with a blessing than the big one with a curse. Good is not got without grief. A good name is sooner lost than won. It's easier to go down than to climb. One should salute with a clean hand. Good comes from sadness, and happiness from quietness.

SELF-RESPECT and SENSE OF HONOUR

As thou valuest thyself, others will esteem thee. He who lies in the mud will rise dirty. Pity him whose birthright is to eat dirt. A man's will is his kingdom. A man is king in his own house. Dead is the dependent. The dependent is timid. When a man goes down, his own back is his support. A king's son is no nobler than his company. Were the wealth of the world yours, weigh it not against your shame. A man may survive distress, but not disgrace. A man will die to save his honour. Honour is a tender thing. Honour can't bear patching. Honour is nobler than gold. Remember those you came from. Follow close the fame of your fathers. (This is Ossianic—Fingal to Oscar.)

TRUTH, JUSTICE, FIDELITY

Truth is pleasing to God. Truth is better than gold. Better be poor than a liar. Whose word is no word, his luck is no luck. Woe to him that fears not to lie. Blister on the lying tongue, padlock on the hemless mouth! A lie has but one leg. A lie needs a prop. A lie can't last long. None lied that would not steal. The lying mouth will be shut.

Counsel of the bell of Scone, touch not what is not thine own. Ill for him whose goods are another man's. The reaver's goods are ill to keep. The thief is brother to the hound. A mouthful of meat and a townful of shame. He that hides the thief is worse. Put not your sickle without leave into another's corn. Don't put your spoon into kail that's not yours. The wrongful should not be litigious. Don't lend the loan. The loan should be sent laughing home.

He that promises must pay. A promise is a debt. Willing pays no debt. There is no greater fraud than promise unfulfilled. The betrayer is the murderer. Let the knave be kept down! Forsake not a friend in the fray.

COURAGE

The weak shall not win. Assurance is two-thirds of success. The bashful won't be brave. Fear is worse than fighting. He that flees not will be fled from. Weak is the grasp of the downcast. Neither seek nor shun the fight. (This admirable saying is Ossianic.) *Swift goes the rear that's pricked by fear.*

TEMPERANCE

A man may live though not full. One may live on little, though not on nothing. Tighten your belt till you get food. Eat less and buy it. Only dogs eat to surfeit. Hunger is a good cook. Hungry birds fight best. Big belly was never bountiful. A sweet mouth will send you to beggary. Take your thirst to the stream, as the dog does. I like not the drinking fellowship. The uneasy seat in the alehouse is best. Leave the fag-end of a fair.

INDUSTRY, PUNCTUALITY, PROMPTNESS, EARLY RISING

Better knot straws than do nothing. Will is a good worker. Better try than hope. Long sleeping makes hot rowing. Lazy is the hand that ploughs not. Who won't plough when it is cold shall not reap when it is hot. He who neither works nor pushes won't get food among the bushes. The diligent weak will beat the lazy strong. The silly body builds the dyke when the corn is eaten. Take the good day early. Get bait while the tide is out. Dry shoes won't get fish. The sea won't wait for a load. Keep the fair on its day. You can't to-day recall yesterday. Time won't wait, nor tide show mercy. The late watcher never overtook the early riser. Lively is the early riser. He that lies long in bed will be all day hard bestead. Give your 'thank you' to the cock.

COURTESY, HOSPITALITY.—Highland courtesy and hospitality are so well known that a very few out of many sayings will suffice under these heads.

He that is courteous will be courteous to all. The goodman's advice ought to be taken. Forwardness spoils manners. A dog goes before his company. Courtesy never broke man's crown. The rude jester is brother to the fool.

He's a bad guest whom the house is the worse of. House with closed door can't be kept. Happy is that which is shared—pity him who fares alone. A thing is the bigger of being shared. The scarcer the food, the more bounty to share it. Welcome the coming, speed the parting guest. A feast is nothing without its conversation. The first story from the host, and tales till morning from the guest.

BENEVOLENCE

Sense hides shame. Love hides ugliness. Woe to him who won't maintain his own poor one. Woe to him who vexes the weak. None ever did violence but suffered violence. Woe to him who would wish a ruined home to any one.

PATIENCE

Better weary foot than weary spirit. The day is longer than the brae, we'll be at the top yet. Patience overcomes trouble. Patience never hurt a man. Patience wins victory. Patience wears out stones.

HUMILITY

The heaviest ear of corn bends its head lowest. Sit lowly, and pay nobly.

SILENCE, CAUTION, WORDS AND DEEDS, APPEARANCES

It's a big word that the mouth can't hold. A word is big when it's lessened. It's good manners to be silent. Choose thy speech. Say little and say well. It's well that the teeth are before the tongue. Shut mouth incurs no debt. If you tell all you see, you'll tell what will shame you. If you hear a hueless tale, don't repeat it. Believe not the bad report till proved. A man's smile is not his own. Not words prove, but deeds. The worst cow lows loudest. Puffing won't make piping. Fulsome talk won't make help. The nodding of heads doesn't row the boat. A rotten stick is often nice to look at. The Devil is often attractive. A rich heart may be under a poor coat. Good sword has often been in poor scabbard.

Fools

It's difficult to give sense to a fool. Who won't take advice is worthless, who takes every advice is so. It's bad flesh that won't take salt, worse is the body that won't take warning. As crooked as the fool's furrow.

Boors

The clown is known at morning—he breaks his shoe-tie. If you hit a dog or a clown, hit him well. Give the impudent fellow an inch and he'll take an ell. He that is rude thinks his rudeness good manners. Don't provoke a barbarian.

WOMEN, MARRIAGE.—I don't know any other Proverbs that speak of women so respectfully as the Gaelic ones do. They are not wanting in humour, but they never regard women as inferior creatures and mere causes of mischief, which is the point of view of the Proverbs of several great nations.

Meal is finer than grain, women are finer than men. There was never good or ill but women had to do with. Modesty is the beauty of women. I like not pullets becoming cocks. Take no woman for a wife in whom you cannot find a flaw. Choose your wife as you wish your children to be. Take a bird from a clean nest. Choose the good mother's daughter, were the Devil her father. If you take a wife from Hell, she'll bring you home there. When you see a well-bred woman, catch her, catch her; if you don't do it, another will match her. Their own will to all men, all their will to women. What a woman knows not she'll conceal. Harsh is the praise that cannot be listened to; dark are the dames that cannot be dallied with. Where a cow is, a woman will be, where a woman is, temptation will be. (This is attributed to St. Columba.) *A man's wife is his blessing or bane. If you wish to be praised, die; if you wish to be decried, marry. You are too merry, you ought to marry. Who speaks ill of his wife dishonours himself. True or false, it will injure a woman. Warm is the mother's breath.*

Children

Pity those who have them, pity more those who haven't. Better no children than luckless children. The crow likes her greedy blue chick. A house without dog or cat or child, a house without mirth or smile. The motherless child has many faults.

EDUCATION

Better be unborn than untaught. When the twig is tender, it is easiest bent. The child you teach not at your knee, you won't teach at your ear (i.e., when grown up). *The early learning is the pretty learning. A child is known by his manners. The child that's left to himself will put his mother to shame. Ignorance is a heavy burden. Blind is the ignorant. He that knows is strong.*

KINDRED, FOSTERHOOD, CLANNISHNESS

Blood is hotter than water. Blood is stronger than breeding. Blood will withstand the rocks. Flesh will warm to kin against a man's will. All the water in the sea won't wash out our kindred. Bare is shoulder without brother, bare hearth without sister. Pity him who turns his back on his people. Trews like to be among clothes, I like to be among my people. Throw reproach on your kinsman, it will rest on your family. The Clans of the Gael shoulder to shoulder! Dear is a kinsman, but the pith of the heart is a foster-brother. Pity him who has few foster-friends.

FRIENDSHIP

Friendship is as it's kept. Friends are lost by calling often, and by calling seldom. It's poor friendship that needs to be constantly bought. Two crossing the ford are best near each other. A friend's eye is a good looking-glass. Better coldness of a friend than warmth of an enemy. A silly friend is more troublesome than a wise enemy. A friend can't be helped without trouble. He is not my friend that hurts me. Pity him who has weak friends. Don't say you know a man till you divide a spoil with him.

LANDLORD AND TENANT.—Some of these sayings are remarkable, and worthy of attention, all the more that the people whose thoughts they express are naturally contented, quiet, tractable, averse to innovation, agitation, or violence.

Tenantry are stronger than laird. (In its original sense this would be *Tribe is stronger than Chief.* See Skene's *Celtic Scotland*, Vol. III, chap. iv and vi.) *A farmer on his feet is taller than a gentleman on his knees. Woe to him that forsakes the tenantry without winning the laird. An alder lord will twist an oak tenant. Ill for them that have a weak lord. He that quarrels with the gentry is a miserable man. It's easy to put him out whose own the house is not. Slippery is the flagstone at the great house door. The yield of the land is according to the laird. But for fear of double rent, Tiree would yield a double crop. It's little we complain, though we suffer much. One teat of a cow is better than a quarter of oats. Tenant after tenant makes the lands dear. The sheep's jaw will put the plough on the shelf. Where there are no boys in arms, there will be no armed men.*

HUSBANDRY, FOOD.—There are a great many sayings under these heads. They belong to a time when the cultivation of the soil, though of a rude and primitive kind, supplied the chief source of living to the population, and was done with ploughs and not with spades, when the great majority of the peasantry had horses, cows and sheep of their own. Their food consisted chiefly of oatmeal cakes, porridge, and gruel, butter and cheese, occasionally fish, very rarely meat. One Gaelic word peculiarly indicates the dependence of the Gael on the soil—*teachd-an-tìr*, 'the yield of the land', the most common term for 'living, sustenance'. Scarcity of food, sometimes dearth, was not confined to the Highlands two centuries ago, but it was naturally more common in the remoter and least cultivated parts. One of the sayings very exactly expresses the Highland character in reference to food. *A man can live on little, but not on nothing.* Moderation in meat and drink has always been a Highland characteristic. The use of whisky is comparatively modern. Among the sayings here collected it is only once mentioned by name, while references to ale and wine are numerous.

SAYINGS THAT REFER TO PREHISTORIC TIMES

The number of sayings that refer to Fionn or Fingal, and the people of whom he was head, the *Féinne*, whom we prefer not to call 'Fenians' (see Note on 'Cha tug Fionn,' p. 109), is considerable; and there is no class of sayings more frequently quoted in the Highlands and referred to, since time immemorial. *The Fingalian fairplay, As strong as Cuchullin, Like Ossian after the Feinne, Conan's life among the devils,* and many others, are still among the familiar phrases in every Celtic household in Scotland. Very curiously, not one of them is included in the Irish Proverbs hitherto published. This does not of course imply that they are unknown in Ireland. It would be inexplicable if they were not; and Canon Bourke (who, it is to be hoped, will yet publish the collection of Irish Proverbs of which he gave a specimen in his Grammar) informs me that he has been familiar with some of them from his childhood. But it strengthens the belief that the whole story and poetry of Fionn and the *Féinne* have been more deeply implanted, and better preserved, whatever the reason be, among the Scottish than among the Irish Gael.

Of Druidism, which some excessively knowing and critical writers, far in advance of the Venerable Bede, and even of Julius Cæsar, have treated as a mere myth, there are at least two curious relics among these Gaelic sayings: *As clever as Coivi the Druid. Though near the stone be to the ground, nearer is the help of Coivi* (see Note, p. 157). Such sayings as 'Deiseal air gach nì' belong to the same period.

HUMOROUS SAYINGS.—The notion of most Sassenachs anent 'Scotch Wut' is derived at second-hand from our dear Elia and Sydney Smith, both of whom, though exquisitely clever and delightful, were quite fallible men. Any one who thinks the Scottish people inferior in humour to the English had better contrast the Proverbs of the one nation with those of the other. At the risk of being considered partial or parochial, the present editor has no hesitation in saying that the Sassenach is incarnate prose compared with the Scot, that the Northern sayings greatly surpass the Southern in humour, felicity and love of artistic form. He cannot claim for the Scottish Celts a greater sense of humour than is found among the Lowlanders, but he does claim for them a very delicate edge, with a cut not less severe. As for their being a melancholy people, there could be nothing more absurd imagined. One can be thoughtful, even pensive, and yet very fond of fun, *in loco*. Irony and satire, more than humour strictly so called, are characteristic of the Scottish Gael.

Here follow some specimens:

Twenty-one captains over twenty soldiers. The birds live, though not all hawks. It's the bigger of that, as the wren said, when it dropped something in the sea. Big egg never came from wren. 'Where art thou, wren? said the eagle: 'Far above thee,' said the wren (on the eagle's back). Howling is natural to dogs. He's a fine man if you don't ask of him. The wren spreads his feet wide in his own house. The highway is wide, and may be trod. Better a lobster than no husband. Better peace with a hen than strife. You would be a good messenger to send for death. The longest lay will end at last. The old woman is the better of being warmed, but not of being burned. It would be thick water that would wash his face. Bold is the puppy in the lap of strength. He sat very awry when he did that. You were born far from the house of good manners. You were not in when sense was being shared. Your grandmother's death is long in your memory. Better 'Heyday!' than 'Alas!' Pity him who would put you in the ship's bow! It's a big beast that there isn't room for outside. An inch off a man's nose is a great deal. He is lucky to whom you would promise the gallows. Geese understand each other. 'There's meat and music here,' as the fox said when he ran away with the bagpipe. The fish in the sea like us mortals be. You spoiled a dwarf, and didn't make a man. Even a haggis will run downhill. Two will have peace to-night, myself and the white horse, as the wife said when her husband died. Like the white horse at the mill-door, thinking more than he

said. Like the old cow's tail, always last. It's not easy to put trews on a cat.
You may be a good man, as Neil of the Mountain said to the cat, but you
haven't the face of one. Pity your sweet mouth should ever go under ground.
Women's patience—up to three. The sod is a good mother-in-law. The sea will
settle when it marries.

POETICAL SAYINGS.—Among purely poetical and pretty sayings,
the Gaelic ones take a high place. Here are a few examples, in
addition to some already given.

Blue are the hills that are far from us. Night is a good herd-man; she brings
all creatures home. The three prettiest dead, a child, a salmon, and a
black-cock. The sea likes to be visited. Thy heart's desire to thy pulse! There is
no smoke in the lark's house. Black is the berry but sweet; black is my lassie
but bonnie. 'I will keep to my sweetheart,' said the girl, 'a mouth of silk, and
a heart of hemp.' High is the stag's head on the mountain crags. Pretty is the
mouse in the corn-plat. The ocean hides much. Like stone sent uphill is the long
Spring evening, like stone running down glen is soft Autumn evening.

It now becomes me to mention those to whom I have been most
indebted for their contributions to this collection, and their help
in other ways. The largest and best collections were received from
the Rev. J. G. Campbell of Tiree and Mr. A. A. Carmichael, North
Uist. Both came unasked, and were supplemented, as occasion
required, by illustrations out of the rich stores of Gaelic Folk-lore,
Poetry and Tradition which both these gentlemen are ever ready
generously to communicate to those interested in them. Mr.
Archibald Sinclair, Glasgow, gave me a valuable collection made
by his worthy father, a great part of which had been got from Mr.
Carmichael. He also lent me a copy of the second edition of
Macintosh, which had belonged to the late Mr. Ewen MacLean,
a good Gaelic scholar, who had contemplated a new edition, to be
dedicated to his friend James Munro. I am indebted to it for several
emendations, and two or three very good additional proverbs. To
the Rev. J. W. MacIntyre, Kilmodan, I am indebted for a copy of
a good collection dated so long ago as 1769 by a certain Ewen
MacDiarmid, which came into the possession of Mr. John Shaw,
Kinloch Rannoch. From the Rev. M. MacPhail, Kilmartin, I
received an excellent collection, made by himself in his native
island, Lewis. To my dear old friend, the Rev. A. MacGregor,
Inverness, I am indebted for several interesting illustrations, and
some good sayings, recovered from memory, out of a large collec-

tion made by him long ago in the Isle of Skye, the MS of which had unfortunately been lost.

To the late Donald C. MacPherson, of the Advocates' Library, a special tribute is due. He was a Lochaber man, steeped in Gaelic lore and sentiment, a scholar, chiefly self-taught, and a genius. He supplied me with a considerable number of proverbs found among the Gaelic MSS of the Library, besides many fresh additions and illustrations from his own remarkable memory. Some of his contributions to the *Gael*[1] are such as no other man could have given. Much as I have been assisted in this work by other friends, I received most help from him, and of a constant and ever ready kind. By his early death Gaelic Literature has sustained a great loss, and no one has more cause to lament it than I have.

Of others to whom I have been indebted for contributions of Proverbs are Mr. Donald McLaren, Loch Earn, Mrs. Mary Mac-Kellar, Mr. Alex. Mackay and Mr. Murdo MacLeod, of Edinburgh, both from Sutherland.

Mr. Donald Mackinnon, M.A., Edinburgh, whose papers on Gaelic Proverbs in the *Gael* showed exceptional knowledge of the subject, and power to deal with it, has given me valuable assistance in many ways. To the Rev. Dr. Clerk of Kilmallie, and the Rev. Mr. Stewart of 'Nether Lochaber,' I am much bound for kind help and suggestions. Of friends who helped me in regard to foreign proverbs, I have specially to thank Mr. A. L. Finlay, Dumfries, and Mr. J. A. Hjaltalin, Iceland.

In addition to the various sources above acknowledged, I found a considerable number of proverbs in the interesting columns of the *Highlander*, some in the *Gael*, and a few in the Dictionaries of Armstrong, the Highland Society and MacAlpine. I carefully searched, and not in vain, in the pages of the *Teachdaire Gaelach* (1829–31), *Teachdaire Ur Gaidhealach* (1835–36), *Cuairtear nan Gleann* (1840–43) and *Fear-tathaich nam Beann* (1848), four Gaelic Periodicals, the best contributions to which were made by Dr. Norman Mac Leod, to whose memory this book is dedicated. He was the Editor, the life and soul, of the *Teachdaire* and the *Cuairtear*. Of all men that ever wrote Gaelic prose, he wrote the best and raciest, the language, not of mere propriety and elegance, but of natural

---

[1] A well conducted Gaelic Magazine, which lasted longer than any of its predecessors—six years. Its stoppage in December 1877 was much to be regretted.

genius, equally incomparable in moving laughter or tears. His Gaelic Dialogues, 'Còmhradh nan Cnoc,' and his answers to correspondents, are spiced with proverbial phrases and allusions, of which no one else could make such happy, sometimes such crushing use. His command of them seemed inexhaustible; his quiver never was emptied, and his arrows never missed.

One other friend I must mention, who has given me neither proverbs nor explanations, but whose assistance, in the shape of stimulus and example, has been quite unique—Professor Blackie. His appreciation of Gaelic proverbs is as great and natural as his love of the Highlands; and if any living man specially deserved to have this book dedicated to him, as a mark of gratitude from a Highlander, on behalf of the people and language for whom he has done so much, that man is he. *Buaidh 'us piseach air a cheann!*

KIRKCUDBRIGHT,
December, 1880

GAELIC PROVERBS AND
FAMILIAR PHRASES

A

A' bheairt sin nach fhaighear ach ceàrr, 's e foighidinn as fheàrr a dhèanamh rithe—*The loom that's awry is best handled patiently.*

The word *beairt* has various meanings, but in its primary use seems to have been equivalent to the word 'loom,' which meant other tools or engines, as well as weaving looms. In the above proverb, however, the weaving loom seems to have been in view, and the meaning to be that if it be found to be out of gear, it is better to handle it patiently than to try to put it right, at the risk of breaking the threads. 'What can't be cured must be endured' expresses nearly the same idea, but not exactly.

A' bheinn as àirde tha san tìr, 's ann oirre 's trice chì thu 'n ceò—*The highest hill is oftenest covered with clouds.*

So is it with those who tower above the common level of mankind.

A' bhèist as mò ag ithe na bèist' as lugha, 's a' bhèist as lugha 'dèanamh mar a dh'fhaodas i—*The bigger beast eating the lesser one, and the lesser one doing as it may.*

It is interesting to find Modern Science anticipated in an old Gaelic story. This graphic expression of a great physical and moral truth occurs in a description of ocean life, common to several of those West Highland Tales on the collection and editing of which Mr. J. F. Campbell has bestowed so much generous care. See Vol. II, pp 201, 210.

A bhith gu dàna modhail, sin lagh na cùirte—*To be bold and courteous is the court rule.*

This is a good description of the manner best suited for securing attention in courts of all kinds.

A' bhò as miosa th' anns a' bhuaile, 's i 's cruaidhe geum.—*The worst cow in the field lows the loudest.*

> *Al.*—A' bhò as lugha feum, 's i 's mò geum. See also 'Chan i bhò' and 'Geum mòr'.

A' buain nan àirneagan searbha, 's a' saltairt air na cìrean-meala.—*Plucking the bitter sloes, and trampling on the honeycomb.*

A' call làn na lèidhe air imlich a màis.—*Losing the ladle-full licking its outside.*

A' call nam boitean a' cruinneachadh nan sop.—*Losing the bundles gathering the wisps.*

> See 'A' sgaoileadh nan sguab'.

A' caoidh nam buideal falamh.—*Bewailing the empty casks.*

A chailleach, an gabh thu 'n rìgh? Cha ghabh, 's nach gabh e mi.—*Crone, will you have the king? I won't, as he won't have me.*

> There is a humorous philosophy in this.

A' chaor' a thèid anns a' chreig, chan eil aic' ach tighinn aiste mar a dh'fhaodas i.—*The sheep that gets into the rock must get out as best she can.*

A' chiad sgeul air fear an taighe, 's gach sgeul gu lath' air an aoigh.—*The first story from the host, and tales till morning from the guest.*

> This is one of the sayings most purely characteristic of the old manners and customs of the Highlands, carrying one back without difficulty to the Arabian Nights' Entertainments, traces of which survive in some of the Gaelic tales.

A' chlach nach tachair ri m'chois, cha chiùrr i mi.—*The stone that doesn't meet my foot won't hurt me.*

> See 'An rud nach laigh'.
> The stane that lies not in yir gait breaks not yir taes.—*Scot. P.*

A' chorc an ionad a' chuinnseir.—*The knife in the place of the sword.*

A chuid de Phàrras da!—*His share of Paradise to him!*

> *Al.*—de Fhlaitheanas—*of Heaven.* The word F., still in common use as the Gaelic for Heaven, has been interpreted by good authorities (Armstrong, Highl. Soc. *Dict.* &c.) as *Flath-innis*, the Isle of Heroes, an etymology which is both poetical and probable. A simpler and more scientific etymology (Eber's *Celt. Stud.*, p. 116) makes it *Flaithemnas*, or *Flaitheamhnas*, sovereignty, dignity, glory. In Bedell's Irish Bible, *Flaitheamhnas* and *Flaitheasa* are used in the Old Test. to denote Heaven and Heavens; but *Neamh* and *Neamhdha* more commonly. In the New Test., *Neamh* only is used for the singular. In our Gaelic Bible the latter alone is used in both sing. and plur.

A' chuid nach gabh na leanaban gabhaidh an t-seann-bhean fhèin.—*What the children won't take the old woman will.*

A' chùil a bhios fosgailte, thèid na coin innte.—*The dogs will go into the corner that's open.*

A' chuirm as luaithe bhios ullamh, suidheamaid uile ga gabhail.—*The feast that's soonest ready let us all sit down to.*

A' chuiseag ruadh a dh'fhàsas san òtraich, 's i 's àirde thogas a ceann.—*The red weed from the dunghill lifts its head the highest.*

> The proudest nettle grows on a midden.—*Scot.*

A chur a ruith na cuthaig.—*Sending him to chase the cuckoo.*

> Literally a 'gowk's errand.'

A' cromadh air na beaga.—*Stooping to the little.*

A' cunntas shlat gun aodach.—*Counting yards without cloth.*

A' cur a' bhodaich às a thaigh fhèin.—*Putting the old man out of his own house.*

A' cur an eich 's e 'na fhallas.—*Urging on the sweating horse.*

A' cur an sgileam air an sgoileam.—*Making a noise about a trifle.*

> This is a specimen of unmeaning words used to express something.

A' cur bruic à ladhran.—*Kicking badgers out of his heels.*

> Said of one in a great rage.

A' cur na snàthaid air a' choltar.—*Putting the needle on the coulter.*

A' cur shnaim air na suip.—*Knotting straws.*

A' dèanamh cuain mhòir de chaolas cumhang.—*Making a great ocean of a narrow strait.*

A dh'aindeoin cò theireadh e!—*Gainsay who dare!*
> The Clanranald motto.

A' dol sna h-eachaibh deiridh.—*Going among the hindmost horses.*
> Said of persons when their failing powers disqualify them for leading places, as in a team of horses.

A' ghaoth 'g iarraidh nam port.—*The wind seeking harbours.*
> Said of an unsteady wind.

A h-uile cù air a' chù choimheach.—*All the dogs down on the strange dog.*
> *Al.*— Gach olc an tòin a' choimhich.

A h-uile fear a thèid a dholaidh, gheibh e dolar o MhacAoidh.—*Every man that's down in luck will get a dollar from Mackay.*
> This refers to the enlisting for the Highland regiment raised by Lord Reay for service under the King of Denmark (1626–29) and Gustavus Adolphus (1629–32), in which Scots so greatly distinguished themselves.

> A h-uile latha sona dhut,
> Gun latha idir dona dhut!—
>
> *Every day good luck to thee,*
> *And no day of sorrow be!*

A h-uile nì thun a' bheòil.—*Everything to the mouth.*
> This is primarily true of infants, but has a much wider application.

A h-uile rud a thèid san lìon, 's iasg e.—*All is fish that goes into the net.*

A leisgeul sin dhaibh fhèin.—*It's theirs to excuse that.*

A lìon beagan is beagan, mar a dh'ith an cat an sgadan.—*Little by little, as the cat ate the herring.*

> Little and little the cat eats the stickle.—*Eng. P.*

A mhic a' chait dam bu dual am bainne òl!—*Son of the cat, born to drink milk!*

A rèir do mheas ort fhèin, measaidh càch thu.—*As thou valuest thyself, others will esteem thee.*

> Autant vaut l'homme comme il s'estime.—*Fr.* Him who makes chaff of himself the cows will eat.—*Arab.* Wer nichts aus sich macht, ist nichts.—*Germ.*

A' ruith fear an taighe 'na thaigh fhèin.—*Taking the goodman's right in his own house.*

A' ruith na seiche air a bruaich.—*Keeping to the edge of the hide.*

> Applied to persons in straitened circumstances. A man with plenty of hides would help himself out of the best part; a poor man would need to begin at the outside.

A' sgaoileadh nan sguab 's a' trusadh nan siobhag.—*Scattering the sheaves and gathering the straws.*

A shalchar fhèin leis gach rubha.—*To every headland its own foul ground.*

As t-Earrach nuair a bhios a' chaora caol, bidh am maorach reamhar.—*In Spring when the sheep is lean, the shellfish is fat.*

A thoil fhèin do gach duine, 's an toil uile do na mnathan.—*Their will to all men, and all their will to the women.*

> Nought's to be had at woman's hand,
> Unless ye gie her aa the plea.—*Scot. song.*
> Ce que femme veut Dieu le veut.—*Fr.*

Abair rium mun abair mi riut.—*Speak to me ere I speak to thee.*

Abhsadh a' chromain-luch.—*Shortening sail kite-fashion.*

> A Hebridean phrase, applied to awkward handling of a sail—letting it down too suddenly, like the descent of a kite.

Adharc na bà maoile 's duilich a toirt dith.—*It's hard to take the horn off the hornless cow.*

Adharc 'na chliathaich!—*A horn in his side!*

> *Al.*—An dunaidh ad chliathaich!—*The mischief in your side!*
> These are forms of malediction, undoubtedly of native origin. Those which are so are generally less offensive in expression than those of more 'civilised' nations.

Ag itheadh na cruaiche fon t-sìoman.—*Eating the stack under the rope.*

Aicheadh na caillich air an sgillinn—nach e sgillinn idir a bh' ann ach dà bhonn-a-sia.—*The old wife's denial of the penny—it was not a penny but two half-pence.*

Aig bainnsean 's aig tòrraidhean aithnichear càirdean is eòlaich.—*At weddings and at funerals relatives and friends are known.*

> At marriages and burials, friends an kinsfolk be known—*The Booke of Merry Riddles*, 1629.

Aig deireadh a' chluiche chìtear cò bhuinnigeas.—*At the end of the game the winner is seen.*

> Al fin del giuoco si vede chi guadagna.—*Ital.*

Air a' ghabhail sin fhèin.—*On that footing, be it so.*

Air a làimh fhèin, mar a bha 'n ceàrd sa chaonnaig.—*For his own hand, as the smith was in the fight.*

> This seems to be the original of the Scottish proverb 'For his ain hand, as Henry Wynd fought,' referred to by Sir Walter Scott in *The Fair Maid of Perth*, ch. xxxiv. The word *ceàrd*, now applied only to tinkers, was originally applied to artificers in all kinds of metals—gold, silver, iron &c.; and the word *ceàrdach* still means a smithy.

Air an doras air an tig amharas a-steach, thèid gràdh a-mach.—*Where doubt comes in, love goes out.*

> Hvor Mistanke gaaer ind, gaaer Kjærlighed ud.—*Dan.*

Air cheart lomaidh, 's air èiginn.—*Very barely and with difficulty.*

Air do shlàinte, ghoistidh ùir, sop air sùil an t-seann ghoistidh!—
Here's thy health, my new gossip, farewell the old one!

> 'Sop air sùil' is a curious expression, literally 'A wisp on the eye'. The
> meaning is that the old friend is to be hidden away, out of sight, out
> of mind.

Air fhad 's ge 'n tèid thu mach, na toir droch sgeul dhachaigh ort
fhèin.—*However far you go abroad, bring home no ill tale of yourself.*

Air ghaol an leanaibh, pògar a' bhanaltram.—*The nurse is kissed for
the sake of the child.*

> 'Kissing the child for the sake of the nurse' is the more common
> English phrase, but there is a German saying identical with the above.

Air ghlainead an tobair, bidh salchar ann.—*Be the fountain ever so
clean, some dirt in it will be seen.*

Air mheud 's a their na slòigh, cha ghlòir a dhearbhas ach gnìomh.—
For all the world can say, not words but deeds are proof.

> *Al.*—Beul a labhras, ach gnìomh a dhearbhas. Gwell es eun oberer
> evit kant lavarer.—*Breton.* I fatti son maschi, le parole femmine.—*Ital.*
> Obras son amores, que no buenas razones.—*Span.* Worte sind gut,
> wenn Werke folgen.—*Germ.*

Air mheud 's ge 'm faigh thu gu math, 's lughaid a gheibh thu gu
h-olc.—*The more you find of good, the less you'll get of ill.*

Airson mo chuid-sa den ghràn, leigidh mi 'n àth 'na teine.—*For my
share of the grain, the kiln may go on fire.*

> For my peck of malt, set the kiln on fire—Cheshire &c.

Aireamh na h-Aoine air caoraich a bhail' ud thall!—*Friday's numbering on the neighbouring sheep!*

> 'Aireamh na h-Aoin' ort!' is simply another form of 'Bad luck to you!'
> On the supposed unluckiness of Friday, see App. I.

Aisigidh leannanachd an tochradh.—*Sweethearting brings the tocher.*

Aisling caillich mar a dùrachd.—*An old wife's dream as her desire.*

> Ὅ τι εἶχεν ἡ γρῃὰ 'ς τὸν νουν της, τὄβλεπε 'ς τὸ ὄνειρον
> της.—*Mod. Gr.*

Aiteamh na gaoithe tuath, sneachd is reothadh anns an uair.—*After thaw with northern blast, snow and frost follow fast.*

Aithghearr an fhidhleir dhuibh on taobh tuath.—*The black fiddler's short-cut from the north.*

> A roundabout way. *Al.*—Aithghearr an tàilleir dhuibh do Ghleann Cuaich, mun cuairt an saoghal—*The black tailor's short cut to Glen Quoich—round the world.*

Aithne an Leòdhasaich mhòir air an Leòdhasach eile.—*The big Lewisman's recognition of the other Lewisman.*

> The big man is supposed to say, 'Tha aithne gun chuimhn' agam ort'—*'I recognise, but don't remember, you.'*

Aithneachadh bò badhail, no fàilt' a' chruidh.—*The wandering cow's welcome, or the kine's salute.*

> Macintosh's explanation of this saying is that, when a strange beast joins a herd, the rest attack it. An ingenious commentator suggests as the proper reading 'Aithnichidh bò a badhail'—*A cow knows her own stall*—which makes good sense. But the noun *badhail* is Irish; *buabhail* is our word for stall.

Aithnichear air a' bheagan ciamar a bhiodh am mòran.—*From the little may be seen what the big might have been.*

Aithnichear am balach sa mhadainn—bristidh e barrall a bhròige.—*The clown is known at morning—he breaks his shoe-tie.*

> This is a curious illustration of the general amenity of manners characteristic of the Celts. The *balach* is a combination of 'bully' and 'snob,' and it is meant he is so rude and impatient that he can't even tie his shoe without showing his roughness. Curiously enough, a word expressing much the same thing in modern Greek is βλάχος.

Aithnichear an leòmhann air sgrìob de ionga.—*The lion is known by a scratch of his claw.*

> Ex ungue leonem—*Lat. P.* Dall' unghia si conosce il leone.—*Ital.* A l'ongle on connait le lion.—*Fr.*

Aithnichear fear doimeig air fàire.—*The slattern's husband can be known afar.*

> The Ulster version is 'Aithnighear fear na cuaróige ar faithche i measc cháich.' A South Uist saying is 'Is luath fear na droch mhnà air a' mhachair Uibhistich'—*'Swift goes the bad wife's husband on the Uist plain'.*

Aithnichear leanabh air a bheusaibh.—*A child is known by his manners.*

> Even a child is known by his doings.—*Prov.* xx, 11.

Aithnichear searrach seann làrach ann an greigh.—*An old mare's foal is known in a herd.*

> Supposed, whether truly or not, to be more lively than others. See 'Mac bantraich'.

Aithnichidh an truaighe a daoine fhèin.—*Misery knows its own people.*

Aithnichidh na leth-chiallaich a chèile.—*Half-wits recognise each other.*

> This is a touching fact, of which observant persons must have seen many instances.

Albainn bheadarrach!—*Beloved Scotland!*

> *Beadarrach* is perhaps oftener used to mean 'playful', but the above appears to be an expression of simple affection.

Am biadh a dh'ithear anns a' chùil, thig e thun an teine.—*The food that's eaten in the corner will come to the hearth.*

Am biadh a theachdas os cionn gach bìdh—snaoisein.—*The food that can go on the top of all food—snuff.*

> The once general use of snuff has given place, in the Highlands as elsewhere, to smoking. A snuff-mull is now rarely to be seen.

Am beul a' phoca tha 'n caomhnadh.—*The saving is at the mouth of the bag.*

> See 'Am fear nach dèan bail'.

Am bolla air an sgillinn, 's gun an sgillinn ann.—*The boll at a penny, and no penny to buy it.*

> The Scotch boll is a measure of grain, sixteen pecks. There is a Danish saying, 'When it rains porridge, the beggar has no spoon.'

Am brèid ga thomhas air an toll.—*Measuring the patch on the hole.*

Am brògach beag 's an cuaranach mòr.—*The boy with shoes, the man with socks.*

> Brought up to wear shoes, and reduced when grown to wearing the *cuaran* (Welsh *cwaran*), a kind of sock made of untanned leather—the ancient foot-gear, which every man made for himself.

Am bronnach Geamhraidh, 's an seang Earraich.—*Squabby in Winter, and skinny in Spring.*

> The reference is to young cattle.

Am fac' thu rud 's a chùl riut?—*Saw you aught with its back to you?*

> This was reckoned a bad omen. See 'Chuala mi chuthag'.

Am facal a thig à Ifrinn, 's e gheibh, mas e 's mò bheir.—*The word that comes from Hell will get if it bid well.*

> The howlet was screamin', while Johnnie cried, 'Women
> Wad marry auld Nick, if he'd keep them aye braw!'
>
> H. McNeill

Am fear a bhios a bharra-mhanadh a-mach, suidhidh e air fàil chorraich.—*He whose destiny is cast sits on a sharp cope.*

> There is something very awful in this saying, reminding of that of the Psalmist: 'Their foot shall slide in due time.' The belief in Fate, expressed by such words as *dàn, manadh, sona* &c., was as strong in the Celts, as many of these proverbs show, as in any ancient Greek or modern Islamite. The word *fàl* is found in the Scottish *fail dyke*.

Am fear a bhios a' riarachadh na maraig, bidh an ceann reamhar aige fhèin.—*The man that divides the pudding will have the thick end to himself.*

> Puddings, in the sense familiar to John Bull, were not known to the hardy Celts. But several kinds of pudding more akin to the sausage, in which oatmeal and suet, blood and various other savoury ingredients formed the chief elements, were and still are well known, both in the Highlands and Lowlands of Scotland. To such dainties reference is made in the well-known song *The Barrin o the Door*:
>
> > An first they ate the white puddings,
> > An then they ate the black.

Am fear a bhios air deireadh, bidh na coin comaidh ris.—*He that comes last will have the dogs as messmates.*

> Chi tardi arriva mal allogia.—*Ital.*

Am fear a bhios air dheireadh, beiridh a' bhiast air.—*Him that's last the beast will catch.*

> This saying seems to have originated in a children's game, but like many such things it has a serious moral. 'Deil tak the hinmost' conveys the same idea.

Am fear a bhios air thoiseach, thèid a stobadh anns an fhèith.—*He that goes first will get stuck in the mud.*

Am fear a bhios an-diugh an uachdar, car mu char a-nuas e màireach.—*He that's uppermost today, turn over turn he's down tomorrow.*

> This refers, of course, to the wheel of Fortune.

Am fear a bhios ann, nìtear clann ris.—*Such a man as there is, children will be got by.*

> This is susceptible of more than one interpretation. See 'Am fear nach tèid'.

Am fear a bhios beudach e fhèin, cha sguir e dh'èigneachadh chàich.—*He that is guilty himself will always be urging others.*

> See 'Miann an droch dhuine'.

Am fear a bhios carach sa bhaile seo, bidh e carach sa bhail' ud thall.—*He who is tricky in this farm will be tricky yonder.*

Am fear a bhios fad' aig an aiseag, gheibh e thairis uaireigin.—*He that waits long at the ferry will get over some time.*

> Tout vient à point, à qui sait attendre.—*Fr.* Chi aspettar puote, ha ciò che vuole.—*Ital.*

Am fear a bhios fearg air a ghnàth, 's coltach a ghnè ris an dris.—*He who is always angry is of nature like the bramble.*

Am fear a bhios fada gun èirigh, bidh e 'na leum fad an latha.—*He who lies long in bed will be all day hard bestead.*

> Uomo lento non ha mai tempo.—*Ital.*

Am fear a bhios gun each gun eathar, 's fheudar dha coiseachd.—*He who has neither horse nor boat must go on foot.*

Am fear a bhios gun mhodh, saoilidh e gur modh am mì-mhodh.—*He that is rude thinks his rudeness good manners.*

Am fear a bhios modhail, bidh e modhail ris a h-uile duine.—*He that is courteous will be courteous to all.*

> This shows a knowledge of true courtesy, and of the highest breeding.

Am fear a bhios 'na thàmh, cuiridh e 'n cat san teine.—*The idle man will put the cat in the fire.*

Am fear a bhios san fhèithe, cuiridh a h-uile fear a chas air.—*Every foot will tread on him who is in the mud.*

> Wer am Boden liegt, über den läuft Jedermann.—*Germ.*

Am fear a bhios tric an gàbhadh, thèid a bhàthadh uaireigin.—*The man who often is in danger will be some day drowned.*

> This is undoubtedly Hebridean.

Am fear a bhios tric anns a' mhuileann, leanaidh an sadach ris.—*He that's often in the mill will be dusty.*

> Chi va al mulino, s' infarina.—*Ital.*

Am fear a bhrathas, 's e mharbhas.—*He that betrays is the murderer.*

Am fear a bhuaileadh mo chù, bhuaileadh e mi fhèin.—*He that would strike my dog would strike me.*

Am fear a cheanglas, 's e shiùbhlas.—*He that ties best travels best.*

> He that fastens his knapsack or bundle most carefully will go with
> least interruption—so of all human affairs.
> See 'Ceangail teann'. Fast bind, fast find.—*Eng.* Quien bien ata, bien
> desata.—*Span.*

Am fear a cheannaicheas am fath-each, ceannaichidh e an t-ath
each.—*He that buys an old hack will have to buy another horse.*

> *Al.*—Ceannaich seann rud, 's bi gun aon rud.—*Buy an old thing, and
> have nothing.*

Am fear a chriomas, ionnlaideadh.—*Let him that picks wash.*

> He that soils his fingers must clean himself.

Am fear a chuireadh a chorrag am shùil, chuirinn mo ghlùn 'na
chliabh.—*Who would put his finger in my eye, I would put my knee on
his chest.*

> This looks as if the Transatlantic practice of 'gouging' had been at
> one time known in the Highlands. If it were so, it must have been very
> long ago.

Am fear a dh'imich an cruinne, cha d'fhiosraich co-dhiù b'fheàrr
luathas no maille; ach thug e 'n t-urram do dh'fhear na moch-èirigh.—*He who went round the globe couldn't tell which was best, speed
or slowness; but he gave the palm to the early riser.*

Am fear a dh'itheas a sheanmhair, faodaidh e h-eanraich òl.—*He
that eats his grandmother may sup her broth.*

> When Farquhar the Leech had tasted the 'bree' of the serpent, his
> master, who knew that his apprentice now had his eyes opened to see
> the secrets of nature, and his ears to understand the language of birds,
> threw the pan at him in wrath, crying, 'Ma dh'òl thu an sùgh, ith an
> fheòil'—'If you have supped the juice, eat the flesh!' See Campbell's
> *W. H. T.*, II, 262. *Al.* Ge b'e dh'ith an fheòil, òladh e 'm brochan. An
> té d'ith an fheoil, óladh sé an brot.—*Irish.* As good eat the devil as the
> broth he is boiled in.—*Eng.* Chi ha mangiato il diavolo, mangia anche
> le corna.—*Ital.* 'Seanmhair' is also a playful term applied to a pig in
> some parts of the Highlands.

Am fear a dh'itheas an t-ìm, togadh e 'n tobhta.—*He that's to eat the butter, let him build the walls.*

> The meaning here is that the man who is to reap the profit should erect the necessary buildings. Butter appears, from several old sayings, to have been one of the chief products of the primitive Highlands. A keg of butter containing about 2 cwt., in good preservation, found in May 1879 at some depth in a peat-moss, in Kingairloch, is now preserved in the Museum of the Scot. Soc. of Antiquaries. The keg was hollowed out of a solid piece of tree. Several such have been found in Irish bogs. See *Ulster Journ. of Arch.*, Vol VII, p. 288.

Am fear a dh'itheas an ceann, dathadh e 'm bus.—*He that eats the (sheep's) head, let him singe it himself.*

Am fear a gheibh ainm na moch-èirigh, faodaidh e laighe anmoch.—*He that gets the name of early rising may lie in bed late.*

> Acquista buona fama, e mettiti à dormire.—*Ital.* Cobra buena fama, y échate á dormir.—*Span.* Get the word o soon risin, an ye may lie in bed aa day.—*Scot.*

Am fear a gheallas, 's e dh'ìocas.—*He that promises must pay.*

> Promise is debt.—*Engl.* Zusagen macht Schuld.—*Germ.* Belofte maakt schuld, en schuld maakt belofte.—*Dutch.* Quien promete, en deuda se mete.—*Span.*

Am fear a ghleidheas a chuid, gleidhidh e chàirdean.—*He that keeps his means will keep his friends.*

> See *Timon of Athens.*

Am fear a ghleidheas a theanga, gleidhidh e charaid.—*Who keeps his tongue will keep his friend.*

> Better lose a jest than a friend.—*Eng.* Better tine joke than friend.—*Scot.* Gjem din Mund og gjem din Ven.—*Dan.*

Am fear a ghoideadh an t-ugh-circe, ghoideadh e 'n t-ugh-geòidh.—*Who would steal the hen egg would steal the goose egg.*

Am fear a ghoideas an t-snàthad bheag, goididh e 'n t-snàthad mhòr.—*He that steals the little needle will steal the big one.*

Am fear a ghoideadh an t-snàthad, ghoideadh e 'm meuran.—*He who would steal the needle would steal the thimble.*

> He that steals a preen will steal a better thing.—*Scot.*
> He who steals an egg would steal an ox.—*Eng.*

Am fear a labhras olc mu mhnaoi, tha e cur mì-chliù air fhèin.—*Who speaks ill of his wife dishonours himself.*

> Quien á su muger no honra, á si mismo deshonra.—*Span.*

Am fear a laigheas sa pholl, togaidh e 'n làthach.—*He who lies in the mud will rise dirty.*

> Gin ye faa doun i the dub, ye'll rise up fylt wi glaur.—*Scot.*

Am fear a mharbhadh a mhàthair a chianamh, bheireadh e beò a-nis i.—*The man who would have killed his mother a little ago would bring her alive now.*

> Said when a good day appears after a heavy storm, or in any similar circumstances.

Am fear a nì dìorras, is iomadh a nì dìorras ris.—*He that is obstinate will often meet his match.*

Am fear a nì obair 'na thràth, bidh e 'na leth-thàmh.—*He that does his turn in time sits half idle.*—*Scot.*

Am fear a phòsas airson earrais, tha e reic a shaorsa.—*Who wives for dower resigns his power.*

> Argentum accepi, dote imperium vendidi.—*Plautus.*
> Qui prend une femme pour sa dot,
> A la liberté tourne le dos.—*Fr.*

Am fear a phòsas bean, pòsaidh e dragh.—*He that marries a wife marries trouble.*

> Have wife, have strife.—*Engl.* Qui femme a, noise a.—*Fr.*
> I have found no Gaelic proverb expressing anything more unfavourable to marriage and to women than this one; which is more than can be said for any of the greater nations of Europe.

Am fear a ruitheas an eathar shalach, thèid e air sgeir-mhara uair-eigin.—*He that sails a foul-bottomed boat will some day run on a rock.*

> This saying smells strongly of the Hebridean sea.

Am fear as fhaide bha beò riamh, fhuair e 'm bàs.—*He who lived longest died at last.*

Am fear as fhaide chaidh on taigh, 's e 'n ceòl bu bhinne chual' e riamh 'Tiugainn dachaigh'.—*To him that farthest went away the sweetest music he ever heard was 'Come home'.*

> East or West, home (hame) is best.—*Engl. and Scot.* Ost und West, daheim das Best.—*Germ.* Oost, West, t'huis best.—*Dutch.*
> These are all characteristically brief and plain. More tender and poetic are the Italian 'Casa mia, casa mia, per piccina que tu sia, tu mi sembri una badia' and 'Casa mia, mamma mia'.

Am fear as fhaide chaidh riamh on taigh, bha cho fad' aige ri tighinn dachaigh.—*The man that went farthest from home had as far to come back.*

Am fear as fhaide saoghal, 's e 's mò a chì.—*He that lives longest sees most.*

Am fear as fheàrr a chuireas, 's e 's fheàrr a bhuaineas.—*He who sows best reaps best.*

> Chi mal semina mal raccoglie.—*Ital.* Quien bien siembra, bien coge.—*Span.*

Am fear as fliche, rachadh e don allt.—*Let him that is wettest go to the burn.*

> It is said that, a young wife having made this response to her husband, who asked for some water on coming home wet, he went and fetched a bucketful which he straightway emptied over her head, adding, 'Cò 's fliche a-nis?'—*'Who is wettest now?'* There is a Breton story exactly to the same effect.

Am fear as luaithe làmh, 's e 's fheàrr cuid.—*Quickest hand gets biggest share.*

> See 'Ge b'e 's luaithe làmh,' 'Bidh a' chuid as miosa' &c.

Am fear as lugha toinisg, 's e 's àirde mòthar.—*The man of least sense makes most noise.*

> A fool also is full of words.—*Eccles.* x, 14.

Am fear as luime, 's e as luaithe.—*He that is barest runs best.*

> Let us lay aside every weight . . . and run with patience the race that is set before us.—*Heb.* xii, 1. A sillerless man gangs fast through the market.—*Scot.*

Am fear as mò a gheallas, 's e as lugha cho-gheallas.—*He that promises most will perform least.*

Am fear as mò a gheibh, 's e as mò a dh'iarras.—*He that gets most will ask most.*

Am fear as treas' an uachdar, 's am fear as luaith' air thoiseach.—*The strongest above and the swiftest in front.*

Am fear a th' anns a' chùil, biodh a shùil air an teine.—*He that's in the corner, let him watch the fire.*

> This is a pleasant reminiscence of the old Highland life, calling up a picture of a cosy gathering round the central peat fire, when stories were told, riddles proposed or songs sung. The person in the corner, where a heap of peats was piled, was bound to keep his eye on the fire and throw on peats when required.

Am fear a thèid a dh'iarraidh an iasaid, thèid e dh'iarraidh a' bhròin.—*He that goes a-borrowing goes a-sorrowing.—Eng.*

> Agent emprunté porte tristesse.—*Fr.* Borgen maakt zorgen.—*Dutch.* Debts make the cheeks black.—*Arab.*

Am fear a thèid a ghnàth a-mach le lìon, gheibh e iasg uaireigin.—*He that goes out regularly with his net will get fish sometime.*

> The word in Macintosh was *eun*, not *iasg*, but the latter is the more common form of the saying, the use of nets for catching birds having long ago ceased in the Highlands.

Am fear a thèid a-mach air na h-uaislean, is duine truagh am measg chàich e.—*He that quarrels with the gentry is a miserable man.*

> A very Celtic sentiment, and painfully true.

Am fear a thèid don taigh mhòr gun ghnothach, bheir e gnothach às.—*He that goes without business to the great house will get something there to do.*

> *Al.*—Am fear nach toir gnothach a-mach, bheir e gnothach dhachaigh *and* Am fear nach toir gnothach don bhaile mhòr, bheir e gnothach às.

Am fear a thèid san dris, fimridh e tighinn aiste mar a dh'fhaodas e.—*He that goes among the briars must come out as best he can.*

Am fear a thèid san droigheann domh, thèid mi san dris da.—*Who goes through the thorns for me, I'll go through the briars for him.*

> Am fear a thig anmoch Disathairne
> 'S a dh'fhalbhas moch Diluain—
> B'fheàrr leam airson a chuideachaidh
> An duine sin a dh'fhuireach bhuam.
>
> —*Who comes late on Saturday night*
> *And early on Monday goes away,*
> *For any help I get from him,*
> *I'd rather like him at home to stay.*

Am fear a thig gun chuireadh, suidhidh e gun iarraidh.—*He that comes unbidden will sit down unasked.*

Am fear a thug buaidh air fhèin, thug e buaidh air nàmhaid.—*He that conquers himself conquers an enemy.*

> He that ruleth his spirit is better than he that taketh a city.—*Prov.* xvi, 32. Iracundiam qui vincit hostem superat maximum.—*P. Syrus.* Wer seinen Zorn bezwingt, hat einen Feind besiegt.—*Germ.*

Am fear aig am beil, cumadh e, 's am fear om bi, tarraingeadh e.—*He who has, let him hold; he who wants, let him pull.*

> The good old rule, the simple plan,
> That they should take who have the power,
> And they should keep who can.—*Wordsworth.*

Am fear aig am bi an Ròimh, bidh an Ròimh aige ri chumail suas.—*He that has Rome must keep Rome up.*

Am fear aig am bi ìm, gheibh e ìm.—*He that has butter will get more.*

> He that hath, to him shall be given.—*Mark* v, 25.

Am fear aig am bi maighstir, bidh fios aig' air.—*He that has a master will know it.*

Am fear air am bi an uireasbhaidh, biodh an t-saothair.—*The man that wants must take the trouble.*

> Am fear air am bi an t-ànradh,
> Chan ann as t-Samhradh as fhas' e.
>
> —*He whose portion is distress*
> *In Summer finds its weight no less.*

Am fear air am bi beul, bidh sporan.—*He that has a mouth will also have a purse.*

> This seems to mean that the power of asking and of keeping go together.

Am fear air nach tàinig, thig.—*He that has escaped misfortune will meet it yet.*

Am fear dan dàn a' chroich, cha tèid gu bràth a bhàthadh.—*Who is born to be hanged will never be drowned.*

> *Al.*—Cha mheall an t-uisg' a' chroich.—*The water will never waur the widdie.*—*Scot.* I have great comfort from this fellow: methinks he hath no drowning mark upon him: his complexion is perfect gallows.—*The Tempest*, Act I, Sc. 1. Chi è nato per la forca mai s' annegherà.—*Ital.* Wer hängen soll ersäust nicht.—*Germ.* Die geboren is om te hangen, behoeft geen vrees te hebben van verdrinken.—*Dutch.* Han drukner ikke der hænges skal, uden Vandet gaaer over Galgen.—*Dan.*

Am fear dan dàn an donas, 's ann da a bheanas.—*For whom ill is fated, him it strikes.*

> Am fear falamh, 's e gun nì,
> Suidhidh fada shìos bho chàch;
> Air mheud nam beus a bhios 'na chorp,
> 'S ioma lochd a gheibhear dha.
>
> —*He that is poor and bare*
> *Must not sit his betters near;*
> *Be his virtues e'er so rare,*
> *Many will his faults appear.*

> *Al.* 'Suidheadh e' in line 2, and 'na cèille' in line 3. See *James* ii, 2, 3.

Am fear leis am fuar, fuaigheadh e.—*He that's cold, let him sew (make clothes)*.

Am fear leis nach lèir a leas, 's mòr de chèill a chailleas e.—*He that does not see his good loses much the use of sense.*

Am fear nach bi 'n aodann na creige, cha bhi eagal air gun tuit e.—*He that is not in the face of the rock will not be afraid of falling.*

Am fear nach bi olc 'na aire, cha smaoinich e olc fir eile.—*He who means no evil thinks no evil.*

Am fear nach biath a chù, cha stuig.—*Who does not feed his dog will not set him on.*

Am fear nach cluinn gu math, cha toir e freagairt mhath.—*He that hears badly will answer badly.*

> *Al.*—freagraidh e gu mì-mhail. En döv Hörer giör en galen Svarer.— *Dan.*

Am fear nach cluinn ceart, chan innis ach cearbach.—*He that does not hear well will report badly.*

Am fear nach cuir a chuid an cunnart, cha dèan e call no buinnig.— *He who hazards not will neither lose nor win.*

> Naught venture, naught have.—*Eng.* Chi non s' arrischia non guadagna.—*Ital.* Quien no se aventura, no ha ventura.—*Span.*

Am fear nach cuir a shnaim, caillidh e chiad ghrèim.—*He that doesn't knot his thread will lose his first stitch.*

> Said to have been communicated for a consideration by a tailor to his apprentice, as the most valuable secret in the trade. There is a legend that the Devil once took to learning the trade of tailor but quite failed, because he could never put a knot on the thread. This may have suggested the title of the popular air *The Deil amang the Tailors.*

Am fear nach cuir sa Mhàrt, cha bhuain e as t-Fhoghar.—*He that doesn't sow in March will not reap in Autumn.*

Am fear nach cuir ri latha fuar, cha bhuain ri latha teth.—*Who won't sow when it is cold shall not reap when it is hot.*

> *Per con.* 'S fhearr curachd anmoch na bhith gun churachd idir.—*Better sow late than not sow at all.*

Am fear nach cùm, cuireadh e mach.—*He that cannot keep, let him deliver.*

Am fear nach cunntadh rium, cha chunntainn ris.—*I'll keep no reckoning with him that keeps no reckoning with me.*

> The saying of the *Gobha Crom*, Harry Wynd, at the combat on the Inch of Perth. The story goes that Harry, having killed his man, sat down to rest. The chief of the Clan Chattan came up and demanded the reason. Harry said he had fulfilled his bargain, and earned his money. 'Him that serves me without counting his hours,' said the chief, 'I reward without reckoning wages.' Whereupon Harry made the above reply, rose up, and resumed the fight.—See *The Fair Maid of Perth*, ch. xxxiv.

Am fear nach dèan bail air beul a' bhuilg, nì an t-ìochdar bail air fhèin.—*If you don't spare the mouth of the bag, the bottom will spare itself.*

> Better spare at brim than at bottom.—*Engl. and Scot.*
> Bedre at spare paa Bredden, end paa Bunden.—*Dan.*

Am fear nach dèan Nollaig le dheòin, nì e Càisg a dh'aindeoin.—*He who won't keep Christmas must keep Easter.*

> The Church of Rome requires communion at least once a year, and that at Easter. He who omits it at Christmas can't avoid it then. Another proverb, however, throws a different light on this one: Am fear nach dèan Nollaig shunndach, nì e Chàisg gu tùrsach deurach.— *He who hasn't a merry Christmas will have a sad and tearful Easter,* i.e., he whose family circumstances prevent him from enjoying Christmas will have greater grief before Easter.

> Am fear nach dèan obair no gnìomh,
> Chan fhaigh e biadh feadh nam preas.
>
> —*He that neither works nor pushes*
> *Won't find food among the bushes.*

Am fear nach dèan toil a' Phàpa, fàgadh e an Ròimh.—*He that won't obey the Pope, let him leave Rome.*

> Qui veut vivre à Rome, ne doit pas se quereller avec le Pape.—*Fr.*

Am fear nach do chleachd an claidheamh, fàgaidh e air a thom e.—*He that's not used to the sword will leave it where he sat.*

Am fear nach do thàrr gu bhogha, thàrr gu chlaidheamh.—*He that did not get at his bow got at his sword.*

> This alludes to a sudden attack followed by confusion, and probable panic, as is suggested by another saying:

Am fear nach fhanadh ri bhogha, chan fhanadh ri chlaidheamh.—*He who wouldn't wait for his bow wouldn't wait for his sword.*

> A still deeper stage of cowardice is indicated in the saying

Am fear nach d'fhuair toll, dh'iarr e doras.—*He that couldn't find a hole sought a door.*

Am fear nach eil math air aoigheachd na h-oidhche thoirt seachad, tha e math air saodachadh an rathaid.—*He that is not good at giving a bed is good at showing the road.*

> See 'Easgaidh mun rathad mhòr'.
> He that is ill o his harboury is guid at the way-kenning.—*Scot.*

Am fear nach èisd ris na 's olc leis, chan fhaic e na 's ait leis.—*He who won't listen to what he dislikes won't see what he likes.*

Am fear nach fhosgail a sporan, fosglaidh e bheul.—*The man who won't open his purse will open his mouth.*

> Words costing nothing.—See *James* ii,15.

Am fear nach freagair athair no mhàthair, freagraidh nì 's tàire, craiceann an laoigh.—*He that won't listen to his father or mother will listen to a meaner thing, the calf's skin.*

> Macintosh interprets this as referring to 'neer-do-weels' who enlist and follow the drum. But drum-heads are not made of calf-skin.

Am fear nach gabh comhairle, gabhaidh e cam-lorg.—*He who won't take counsel will take a roundabout way.*

> The Irish version of this substitutes *comhrac* for *cam-lorg*, which makes good sense. *Cam-lorg* also means 'a crooked stick', and the proverb may be rendered accordingly.

Am fear nach gabh nuair a gheibh, chan fhaigh nuair as àill.—*He that will not when he may, when he wills he shall have nay.*—*Eng.*

Am fear nach glèidh na h-airm san t-sìth, cha bhi iad aige 'n àm a' chogaidh.—*He that keeps not his arms in time of peace will have none in time of war.*

> This is a sound maxim of State policy.
>
> Weapons bode peace.—*Scot.* One sword keeps another in the sheath.—*Eng., Germ., Dan.* L'armi portan pace.—*Ital.*

Am fear nach guth a ghuth, cha rath a rath.—*Whose word is no word, his luck is no luck.*

> This is one of the testimonies to the value of truthfulness in which these Gaelic proverbs are not wanting.

Am fear nach marcaich ach anmoch, caillidh e a spuir.—*He who rides but late will lose his spurs.*

> Seldom ride, tine the spurs.—*Scot.*

Am fear nach meudaich an càrn, gu meudaich e chroich!—*Who won't add to the cairn may add to the gibbet!*

> It was an ancient Celtic custom to erect a cairn, or pile of stones, as a memorial to the good fame or infamy of the person buried beneath it. In either case it was considered the duty of every passer-by to add a stone to the cairn. The above proverb seems to refer specially to the case of a criminal's cairn. The term 'fear air chàrn,' 'a man on a cairn', is still known in Gaelic as signifying an outlaw, or person whose life is forfeited to public justice. Sayings having a similar reference are 'B'fhearr leam e bhith fo chàrn chlach'—*I should rather he were under a cairn of stones*; ' 'S oil leam nach robh do luath fo chàrn'—*I'm sorry your ashes are not under a cairn*; and the Welsh 'Carn ar dy ben!' (or 'wyneb')—*A cairn on thy head (or face)!*' A common saying, on the other hand, referring to cairns erected in testimony of respect is 'Cuiridh mi clach ad charn'—*I'll add a stone to your cairn*. See Smith's *Galic Antiquities*, pp 49–53, and Rowlands's *Mona Antiqua*, p. 49.

Am fear nach misnich, cha bhuannaich.—*Who won't venture shall not win.*

> Fortuna favet fortibus.—*Lat.* Faint heart never won fair lady.—*Eng. and Scot.* Le couard n'aura belle amie.—*Fr.* A los osados ayuda la fortuna.—*Span.*

Am fear nach seall roimhe, seallaidh e 'na dhèidh.—*He that won't look before him must look behind him.*

Am fear nach teagaisg Dia, cha teagaisg duine.—*Whom God teaches not, man cannot.*

Am fear nach teich, teichear roimhe.—*He that flees not will be fled from.*

Am fear nach tèid e fhèin gu mhnaoi, tuigeadh e gun tèid fear eile.—*He that visits not his wife, wot he that another will.*

Am fear nach toir an air' air a' bheagan, chan airidh air a' mhòran.—*He that is not careful with the little is not worthy of much.*

> He that is faithful in that which is least is faithful also in much.—*Luke* xvii, 10. Die 't klein versmaad, is 't groot niet waard.—*Dutch.*

Am fear nach toir an aire dha fhèin, bidh càch a' fanaid air.—*He that cares not for himself will be made a mock of.*

Am fear nach treabh aig a' bhaile, cha treabh e às.—*He that won't plough at home won't plough abroad.*

Am fear nach treabh air muir, cha treabh e air tìr.—*He that will not plough at sea, neither will he plough on land.*

> This does not bear out the opinion of some who have represented the Highlander as essentially averse to seafaring.

Am fear tha grad gu gealladh, 's tric leis mealladh.—*Quick to promise often deceives.*

Am feur a thig a-mach sa Mhàrt, thèid e staigh sa Ghiblean.—*The grass that comes out in March shrinks away in April.*

> Cito maturum, cito putridum.—*Lat.* Presto maturo, presto marzo.—*Ital.* Soon ripe, soon rotten.—*Eng.*

Am fitheach a' cur a-mach a theanga leis an teas.—*The raven putting out his tongue for heat.*

Am fitheach a dh'èireas moch, 's ann leis a bhios sùil a' bheathaich a tha sa pholl.—*The raven that rises early gets the eye of the beast in the bog.*

> Am foinne mun iadh a' ghlac,
> Is niarachd mac air am bi;
> Am foinne mun iadh a' bhròg,
> Is niarachd bean òg air am bi.

> —*Wart on the palm is luck to lad,*
> *Wart on instep luck to lass.*

Am mac air an spàrr 's an t-athair gun bhreith.—*The son on the roost and the father unborn.*

This is one of many ingenious Gaelic riddles, and means the smoke of a fire which has not yet kindled. It is applied as a proverb to the case of anything loudly heralded before it has come into existence.

Am mìos buidh.—*The yellow month*—July.

Am mìos dubh.—*The black month*—November.

Am mìos marbh.—*The dead month*—December to January.

Am port as fheàrr a ghabh Ruairidh riamh, ghabhte seirbhe dheth.—*The best tune Rory ever played might tire one.*

Al.—Fàsar sgith den cheòl as binne.

Roderick Morrison, called Ruairidh Dall, Blind Rory, a celebrated harper, and bard to MacLeod of MacLeod. See App. II.

Amadan an dà fhichead bliadhna, cha bhi e ciallach ri bheò.—*The fool of forty will never be wise.*

Quien á veinte no es galan, ni á treinta tiene fuerza, ni á quarenta riqueza, ni á cincuenta esperiencia, ni será galan, ni fuerte, ni rico, ni prudente.—*Span.*

Amadan na mì-thoirt, bhiodh meas duine ghlic air nam biodh e 'na thosd.—*The poor fool would pass for a wise man if he held his tongue.*

> *Al.*—Saoilidh iad gum beil e glic, ma bhios e tric 'na thosd. Doeth dyn tra tawo.—*Wise is man while silent.*—*Welsh.* Even a fool when he holdeth his peace is counted wise.—*Prov.* xvii, 28. A wise look may secure a fool, if he talk not.—*Eng.* Nichts sieht einem gescheidten Mann ähnlicher, als ein Narr der das Maul hält.—*Germ.* El bobo, si es callado, por sesudo es reputado.—*Span.* Narren er andre Folk liig saa længe han tier.—*Dan.*

Amaisidh an dall a bheul.—*The blind can hit his mouth.*

Amas roghainn.—*Chance choice.*

Amhairc romhad mun toir thu do leum.—*Look before you leap.*

Amharas a' mhèirlich air Ailean.—*The thief's suspicion of honest Allan.*

Amhlaireachd Chlann MhicPhilip.—*The rude absurd play of the MacKillops.*

> The word *amhlaireachd* is very difficult to translate, and probably nobody will be satisfied with the translation, least of all the Mac-Killops. The saying is given for what it is worth, which is perhaps little. Other clans, still more notable than the MacKillops, are characterised in sayings which the editor has thought proper to give, such as they are.

An car a bhios sa mhàthair, 's gnàth leis a bhith san nighinn.—*The twist of the mother is natural to the daughter.*

An car a bhios san t-seana mhaide, 's duilich a thoirt às.—*The crook in the old stick is ill to take out.*

An car a nìtear a dh'aindeoin, bidh e cam no carrach.—*What is done unwillingly will be done with a twist or roughly.*

An ceann 's na casan a' chuid as fhasa roinn; bidh an ceann aig fear an taighe, 's na casan aig a' chloinn.—*The head and trotters are the easiest shared; the head to the goodman, the trotters to the bairns.*

> An ciad latha den ghaoith deas,
> An dara latha den ghaoith 'n iar,
> An treas latha den ghaoith tuath,
> 'S a' ghaoth 'n ear gach uair is ial.

> —*First day south wind,*
> *Second day west wind,*
> *Third day north wind,*
> *East wins always.*

This is meant to indicate the order in which the wind generally goes round the compass on the West coast in Summer, when it blows oftenest from the East.

An ciad Mhàrt, leig seachad; an dara Màrt, mas fheudar; an treas Màrt, ged nach rachadh clach ceanna-mheòir an aghaidh na gaoithe tuath, cuir an sìol san talamh.—*The first Tuesday let pass; the second if need be; the third, though you couldn't send a stone a nail's breadth against the north wind, sow your seed.*

> *Al.*—ged nach cuireadh tu dòirneag.
> Other proverbs, such as 'Cuir do shìol sa Mhàrt,' indicate that the month of March was formerly considered the right time for sowing in the Highlands. The third week of March, Old Style, would be the first week of April, New Style, which would now be considered too early. The reason for naming Tuesday seems to be that Monday was considered an unlucky day for beginning any work of importance.

An cleachdadh a bh' aig Niall, bha e riamh ris.—*The habit Neil had he always stuck to.*

> Iann eo, Iann e vo—*John he is, John he will be.*—Breton.

An cleachdadh a bhios aig duine staigh, bidh e aig' air chèilidh.—*As his habits are at home, so they are with strangers.*

'An cnocan, an cnocan,' ars a' chailleach gu leòdach, 'far an do chaill mi mo Ghàidhlig, 's nach d'fhuair mi mo Bheurla'.— *The hillock, the hillock,' said the old woman, lisping, 'where I lost my Gaelic, and did not find my English.'*

> This is given as a known saying in one of Dr. MacLeod's racy contributions to *An Teachdaire Gàidhealach*. No man had a keener appreciation of the absurd conceit which leads some weak-minded Celts to affect ignorance of their mother-tongue after a few months' absence in the Lowlands, from which they bring home a kind of English so fine as to be unintelligible.

An co-dhalta nach dearbh àite, 's mairg a dh'àraich duine riamh.— *The foster-child that proves it not, pity him that reared.*

> The closeness of relationship established by fosterage among the Celts is almost without parallel; and the sayings and stories illustrative of this are numerous. 'Co-dhaltas gu ceud, is càirdeas gu fichead.'— *'Fostership to a hundred, blood-relation to twenty degrees'*—is perhaps the strongest expression of Highland feeling on this point.

An coinneamh roghainn.—*Facing choice.*

> Prepared for any alternative.

An crann ron damh.—*The plough before the ox.*

> The cart before the horse.

An cron a bhios san aodann, chan fhaodar a chleith.—*The fault that's in the face cannot be concealed.*

An dall air muin a' chrùbaich.—*The blind on the back of the cripple.*

An dèidh cogaidh thig sìth.—*After war comes peace.*

An dèidh gaoithe thig uisge.—*After wind comes rain.*

An deireadh an latha is math na h-eòlaich.—*At the close of the day acquaintances are good.*

> At the end of a day's journey, or of life, it is good to get among friends.

An dubhan an aghaidh a' chròcain.—*The hook against the crook.*

An dubh-liath cuid an amadain, 's an sgamhan cuid na h-òinsich.— *The spleen the fool's part, the lights the silly woman's.*

An duine 's miosa càradh, an duine gun chinneadh thaobh athar no màthar.—*The man of worst condition, he who has no kin by father or mother.*

An Fhèinn air a h-uilinn.—*The Feinn on its elbow.*

> The *Fèinn* (i.e., Fionn or Fingal and his men) were laid spellbound, *fo gheasaibh,* in a cave which no man knew of. At the mouth of the cave hung a horn, *dùdach,* which if any man ever should come and blow three times, the spell would be broken, and the *Fèinn* would rise alive and well. A hunter one day, wandering in the mist, came on this cave, saw the horn, and knew what it meant. He looked in and saw the *Fèinn* lying asleep all round the cave. He lifted the horn and blew one blast. He looked in again and saw that the *Fèinn* had wakened, but lay still with their eyes staring, like those of dead men. He took the horn again, blew another blast, and instantly the *Fèinn* all moved, each resting on his elbow. Terrified at their aspect, the hunter turned and fled homewards. He told what he had seen and, accompanied by friends, went to search for the cave. They could not find it, it has never again been found; and so there still sit, each resting on his elbow, waiting for the final blast to rouse them into life, the spellbound heroes of the old Celtic world!—See *Gael,* Vol. II, p. 241.
>
> Another version of this fine legend lays the scene in the heart of that beautiful hill called Tomnahurich near Inverness. A man found himself one evening at the entrance of a cave leading into the bowels of the hill. He entered, and saw the *Fèinn* lying all around. From the roof of the cave hung a chain that would ring when shaken—*slabh-raidh-èisdeachd*—'audience-chain'. He shook it and it sounded a ringing peal, at which the sleeping heroes awoke, and turned their great cold eyes on the man. The poor creature instantly took to his heels, and rushed out of the cave and down the hill, hearing behind him, amid the howling of wakened deerhounds, a voice that cried, 'A dhuine dhona ghòraich, is miosa dh'fhàg na fhuair thu'!—*'Thou wretched foolish man, that worse left than thou foundest!'*

An gad air an robh 'n t-iasg.—*The withe on which the fish was.*

An gad as faisge don sgòrnan, 's e 's còir a ghearradh an toiseach.—
The withe next the windpipe should be cut first.

> Before hemp was used in this country the commonest kind of rope
> was made of twisted twigs of osier or birch, as it was in the days of
> Samson and the Philistines. When a criminal was hanged with one of
> these rude ropes (whence the Scottish term *widdie* & *withy*), anyone
> wishing to save his life would cut the withe round his throat, or if a
> horse fell and was in danger of being strangled by his harness, the
> same rule would follow.—See Note by R. MacAdam on Irish proverb
> 'Gearr an gad is foisce don sgórnach'.—*Ulster Journal of Archaeol.*,
> Vol. VI, p. 178. Lord Bacon, in his Essays ('Of Custom'), says he
> remembers that "an Irish rebel condemned put up a petition to the
> deputy that he might be hanged in a wyth, and not in an halter,
> because it had been so used with former rebels."

An gog mòr 's an t-ugh beag.—*Loud cackle, little egg.*

> Great cry and little wool.—*Eng.* Grand vanteur, petit faiseur.—*Fr.*

An gràn as luaith' a thèid don mhuileann, 's e 's luaith' a thig
às.—*The grain that soonest goes to mill will come soonest out.*

> Ante molam primus qui venit non molat imus.—*Lat.* Chi primo arriva
> al molino primo macina.—*Ital.* Quien primero viene primero
> muele.—*Span.* Hvo der kommer först til Mölle faaer först malet.—
> *Dan.* Qui premier arrive au moulin premier doit mouldre.—*Fr.*

An Inid, an ciad Mhàrt den t-solas Earraich.—*Shrovetide, the first
Tuesday of the Spring moon.*

An Inid bheadaidh, thig an latha ron oidhche.—*The forward Shrove-
tide, day comes before the night.*

> This means that the Feast comes before the Vigil.

An inisg ga cur, 's a bun aig a' bhaile.—*The reproach getting spread,
and its root at home.*

An là a chì 's nach fhaic.—*Every day—present or absent.*

> This is one of the most frequently used of familiar sayings—usually
> added to a farewell, e.g. 'Beannachd leat, an là chì 's nach fhaic' or
> 'A h-uile latha'. Curiously enough, this favourite phrase was not
> included in either edition of Macintosh.

An lagh a rinn Solamh, fuilingeadh e leis.—*Solomon should suffer by his own law.*

An là bhios sinn ri òrach, biomaid ri òrach; ach an là bhios sinn ri maorach, biomaid ri maorach.—*When we are after gold, let us be at it; but when we are after shellfish, let us be at it.*

The chiefs of the Macleods and of the Macdonalds each kept a fool, and laid a bet which of the two was the greater fool. Both were ordered to go to the shore and gather shellfish. A piece of gold was placed where it would attract their notice. "Look here," said the Macdonald fool to his companion, "here's gold." "Yes, yes," said the other, "when we are after gold, let us be" &c. It is a question, from the point of view of the highest wisdom, which of the two was the greater fool.

An làmh a bheir, 's i a gheibh.—*The hand that gives is the hand that gets.*

The liberal soul shall be made fat.—*Prov.*vi, 25.

An làrach nam bonn.—*On the spot.*

Literally 'in the print of the soles'.

An leanabh a dh'fhàgar dha fhèin, cuiridh e mhàthair gu nàire.—*The child that's left to himself will put his mother to shame.*

An leanabh nach foghlaim thu ri d'ghlùn, chan fhoghlaim thu ri d'chluais.—*The child whom you teach not at your knee you won't teach at your ear.*

Al.—Am fear nach lùb ri glùn, cha lùb ri uilinn.
Betwixt three and thirteen thraw the woodie while it's green.—*Scot.*

This wise Scottish maxim is now substantially embodied in an Act of Parliament (35 & 36 Vict., c. 62), Sect. 69 of which enacts that "It shall be the duty of every parent to provide elementary education in reading, writing and arithmetic for his children between five and thirteen years of age."

An leann a nì duine dha fhèin, òladh e a leòr dheth.—*The ale a man makes for himself let him have his fill of.*

> The use and brewing of ale in the Highlands in former times, before any stronger drink was common, is indicated by several proverbs. The application of this proverb, and of the next, is very much the same as that in reference to a man's choice of a bed to lie on.

An leann a rinn thu ad dhèoin, òlaidh tu ad dh'aindeoin deth.—*The ale you made willingly you'll drink against your will.*

An lon-dubh, an lon-dubh spàgach! Thug mise dha coille fhasgach fheurach, 's thug esan dhomh am monadh dubh fàsach.—*The blackbird, the sprawling blackbird! I gave him a sheltered grassy wood, and he gave me the black desolate moor.*

> Supposed by some (note in the second edition of Macintosh) to refer either to the Roman or to the Scandinavian invader. It seems more applicable to some recent invaders, but the meaning is obscure.

An luibh nach fhaighear, chan i choibhreas.—*The herb that can't be found can never heal a wound.*

An naidheachd as mò am bliadhna, 's i 's lugha an ath-bhliadhna.—*The greatest news this year will be least the next.*

An neach a ghèilleas do ghiseagan, gèilleadh giseagan da.—*Him that yields to spells, let spells yield to.*

> *Al.*—Na gèill do ghis, 's cha ghèill gis dhut.
> He that follows freets, freets will follow him.—*Scot.*

An neach a shìneas a làmh, sìneadh e chas.—*He that stretches his hand must stretch his foot.*

> There are two interpretations of this: the one is that he that 'lifts' had better run; the other that the too liberal may some day need to go dunning or begging.

An neach as tàire bhios a-staigh, 's ann leis as àird' a mhuinntir.—*The meanest person in the house brags most of his kindred.*

> 'We hounds slew the hare,' quo the blear-eyed messan.—*Scot.*

An neach nach cinn 'na chadal, cha chinn e 'na fhaireachadh.—*He that grows not in his sleep will not grow when he's awake.*

An nì chì na big, 's e nì na big.—*What the little ones see, the little ones do.*

An nì chluinneas na big, 's e chanas na big.—*What the little ones hear, the little ones say.*

> As the old cock crows, so crows the young.—*Eng.* Wie die Alten singen, so zwitschern auch die Jungen.—*Germ.* Som de Gamle synge, saa tviddre de Unge.—*Dan.*

An nì chuir na maoir a dh'Ifrinn, farraid an nì a b'fheàrr a b'aithne dhaibh.—*What sent the officers to hell, asking what they knew full well.*

> The *maor* (a name generally applied to bailiffs and other inferior civil officers) was, and perhaps still is, a person inveterately disagreeable to the Celtic mind.

An nì a chùm an eidheann o na gobhair.—*What kept the goats from the ivy.*

> The inaccessibility of the rock or wall. Goats are said to be very fond of ivy.

An nì a gheall Dia, cha mheall duine.—*What God has promised man cannot baulk.*

> What God will, no frost can kill.—*Eng.* Wham God will help nane can hender.—*Scot.* L'homme propose, et Dieu dispose.—*Fr.* El hombre propone, y Dios dispone.—*Span.* Mennesket spaaer, Gud raa'er.—*Dan.*

An nì a tha 'n dàn, tachraidh e.—*The fated will happen.*

> Che sarà, sarà.—*Ital.* Det kommer vel der skee skal.—*Dan.*

An nì a thig leis a' ghaoith, falbhaidh e leis an uisge.—*What comes with the wind will go with the rain.*

> Lightly come, lightly go.—*Eng.* Come wi the wind and gang wi the water.—*Scot.* Ligt gekomen, ligt gegaan.—*Dutch.* Cha daink lesh y gheay nach ragh lesh yn ushte.—*Manx.*

An nì nach cluinn thu 'n-diugh, chan aithris thu màireach.—*What you do not hear today you will not report tomorrow.*

> *Al.*—Mur cluinneadh tu sin, chan abradh tu e.

An nì nach eil caillte, gheibhear e.—*What is not lost can be got.*

An nì nach fios do na mnathan ceilidh iad.—*What the women don't know they'll conceal.*

>Women conceal all that they know not.—*Eng.*

>I well believe
>Thou wilt not utter what thou dost not know—
>And so far will I trust thee, gentle Kate.
>*Henry IV*, Part I.

An nì nach gabh nighe, cha ghabh e fàsgadh.—*What will not wash will not wring.*

An nì nì subhach an dàrna h-aba, nì e dubhach an t-ab' eile.—*What makes one abbot glad makes another abbot sad.*

>Ce qui nuit à l'un, duit à l'autre.—*Fr.* Non pianse mai uno che non ridesse un altro.—*Ital.*

An obair a thòisicheas Diluain, bidh i luath no bidh i mall.—*The work that begins on Monday will be either quick or slow.*

>Monday, being the first free day of the week, gives a good chance for getting on with work, but if one relies too much on having abundance of time, the work will probably be put off.

An oidhch' a mharbhar am mult, agus an oidhch' a theirgeas e.—*The night the wedder is killed, and the night it's finished.*

>The suggestion is that the repast should be liberal on both occasions.

An òrdag an aghaidh na glaice.—*The thumb against the palm.*

An ràmh as faisg' iomair.—*Pull the oar that's nearest.*

An ràn mòr agus an gal tioram.—*Great cry and weeping dry.*

An rathad fada glan, 's an rathad goirid salach.—*The long clean road and the short dirty road.*

>Short cuts often lead into mire. So is it also with those who hasten to 'get on' in the world.

An rud a bhios 'nad bhroinn, cha bhi e 'nad thiomnadh.—*What's in yir wame's no in yir testament.—Scot.*

> Fat housekeepers make lean executors.—*Eng.* Fette Küche, magere Erbschaft.—*Germ.* Grand chère, petit testament.—*Fr.* Grassa cucina, magro testamento.—*Ital.*

An rud a bhios sàmhach, cha chluinn na luchain e.—*What is silent the mice won't hear.*

An rud a chinneas sa chnàimh, cha tig e às an fheòil.—*What's bred in the bane will bide in the flesh.—Scot.*

> An rud fhásas sa chnáimh, ní féidir a dhíbirt as an bhfheoil.—*Ir.* Wat in 't gebeente gegroeid is, wil uit het vleesch niet.—*Dutch.*

An rud a chuir an earb air an loch—an èiginn.—*What made the roe take the loch—necessity.*

An rud a chuireas duine, 's e bhuaineas e, mar a thuirt an òinseach a bha cur na mine.—*What man sows, that will he reap, as the silly woman said when she sowed meal.*

An rud a chuireas e 'na cheann, cuiridh e 'na chasan e.—*What he puts into his head goes to his feet.*

An rud a dh'fhalbhas, chan e a dh'fhòghnas.—*That which goes won't suffice.*

An rud a gheibhear aig ceann an Deamhain, caillear e aig earball.—*What is got at the Devil's head will be lost at his tail.*

> What's gotten ower the Deil's back is spent below his belly.—*Scot.* Male partum, male disperit.—*Plaut.* Ill gotten, ill spent.—*Eng.* Hvad man med Synd faaer, det med Sorg gaaer.—*Dan.*

An rud a nì e le chrògan, millidh e le spògan, coltach ri d'sheana bhrògan Gàidhealach.—*What he does with his hands he spoils with his feet, like your old Highland brogues.*

An rud a nì math do bhàillidh Dhiùra, cha dèan e cron don Rùsgan MacPhàil.—*What's good for the Jura factor will do no harm to Fleecy MacPhail.*

> There was a small Jura farmer of the name of MacPhail, nicknamed 'Rùsgan,' whom the factor liked but took pleasure in chaffing. One day when R. came to pay his rent, the factor helped himself from the bottle which always stood on the table, and said to R., 'I think you are better without this,' to which R. replied as above, and proceeded to help himself. This saying, trivial as was its origin, has survived for two centuries.

An rud a nìtear gu math, chìtear a bhuil.—*What is done well, its effect will tell.*

An rud a nìtear sa chùil, thig e dh'ionnsaigh an teine.—*What's done in the corner will come to the hearth.*

An rud as fheudar, 's fheudar e.—*What must be must.*

An rud a thèid sa bhrù, thèid a shùgh do na casan.—*What goes into the belly sends its sap to the feet.*

An rud a their a h-uile duine, bidh e fìor.—*What everybody says must be true.*

> There is no proverb of such general acceptance as this with so little truth in it.

An rud anns an tèid dàil, thèid dearmad.—*Delay brings neglect.*

An rud nach bi air an t-slinnean, bidh e air an t-sliasaid.—*What is not on the shoulder will be on the loin.*

An rud nach binn le duine cha chluinn duine.—*What is not pleasant to his ear a man will not hear.*

An rud nach cluinn cluas cha ghluais cridhe.—*What the ear hears not the heart moves not.*

> Faith cometh by hearing.—*St Paul.*

An rud nach do bhuilich Dia, chan fhada mhealar e.—*What God bestowed not won't be long enjoyed.*

> Ill-won gear winna enrich the third heir.—*Scot.* Unrecht Gut thut nicht gut.—*Germ.*

An rud nach laigh ann ad ròd, cha bhrist e do lurg.—*What doesn't lie in your way won't break your leg.*

An rud nach tig 's nach tàinig dhachaigh, grùthan na h-earba gun bhrachadh.—*What never came nor will come home, the roe's liver untainted.*

An ruith air an ruaig, 's an ruaig air an ruith.—*The chase retreating, and the rout running.*

An rùn nam biodag dha chèile.—*At daggers' drawing.*

An saoghal a' dol mu seach, 's an t-each air muin a' mharcaiche.—*The world going upside down, the horse mounted on the horseman.*

An seanfhacal gu fada fìor, cha bhreugaichear an seanfhacal.—*The old saying long proved true shall never be belied.*

> Paréceme, Sancho, que no hay refran que no sea verdadero.—*Don Quixote.*

An searrach bu chòir a bhith san làir, 's ann a dh'fhàs e 'na ghearran.—*The foal that should have been in the mare grew into a gelding.*

> Said of an over-presumptuous youth.

An sinead 's an donad, mar a bha cuilean a' mhadaidh-ruaidh.—*The older the worse, like the fox's whelp.*

> *Al.*—Piseach cuilean a' mhadaidh-ruaidh—mar as sin' e, 's ann as miosa.

An sneachd nach tig mu Shamhain thig gu reamhar mu Fhèill Brìghde.—*The snow that comes not at Hallowmas will come thick at Candlemas.*

An solas ùr 's a chùl ri làr.—*The new moon with her back downwards.*

An t-ainm gun an tairbhe.—*The name without the profit.*

An taobh a bheir thusa do chùl, nam bu tig an t-aon là a bheir thu t'aghaidh!—*Where you turn your back, may you never turn your face!*

An taobh a bhios an dàn don droing dol, cha bhac àth no aonach.— *Where folk's fate is to go, ford or hill won't prevent.*

Fram eru feigs götur.—*The 'fey' man's road is straight.*—*Icel.*

An taobh a chuir thu 'n gruth, cuir 'na shruth am meug.—*Where you made the curds to go, you may set the whey a-flow.*

An taobh a thèid an fheannag, bheir i feaman leatha.—*When the craw flees her tail follows.*—*Scot.*

An taobh as bòidhche den chòmhla.—*The prettiest side of the door.*

> The outside of a main door is meant, but not in a metaphorical sense. The outside was usually planed, and sometimes painted, the inside left rough.

An taoman nas mò na 'n long.—*The baler bigger than the boat.*

An t-each a bhuailear sa cheann, bidh e sgàthach.—*The horse that is struck in the head will be full of fear.*

> He will start at every movement of his master, anticipating another stroke. This extreme sensitiveness, painful to see, as the result of brutal treatment, is still more painful to see among schoolchildren, as it sometimes, though happily not often, is.

An teine nì duine dha fhèin, 's e chòir a gharadh ris.—*The fire one makes for himself he has a right to be warmed at.*

An tì a shireas air gach aithneach.—*The one that asks of every acquaintance.*

An t-iasg a chriomas gach boiteag, thèid a ghlacadh uaireigin.—*The fish that bites every worm (i.e., bait) will be caught sometime.*

An tinneas as fheàrr na 'n t-slàinte.—*The illness that's better than health.*

> This is a euphemistic Celtic form of describing childbirth.

An tìr don tigear, is i ghabhar.—*The land that's come to will be taken.*

An tobar nach traoigh.—*The fountain that dries not up.*

> This is one of the *dubh-fhacail* or 'dark sayings' the meaning of which can only be conjectured. It probably refers to the goodness of God.

An toiseach an t-saic tha 'n riaghailt.—*In the mouth of the sack is the measure.*

An triùir nach fuiling an cniadachadh—seann bhean, cearc agus caora.—*The three that won't bear caressing—an old woman, a hen and a sheep.*

An t-strathair an àite na dìollaid.—*The pack-saddle in place of the saddle.*

An t-suirghe chnaparra.—*The sturdy wooing.*

> This means, of course, what is called 'Scotch wooing'.

An tuagh an dèidh an tàil, 's an tàl an dèidh an locair.—*The axe after the adze, and the adze after the plane.*

An t-uasal Leathaineach, 's an ceatharnach Raghnallach.—*The gentleman of Clan MacLean, and the warrior of Clan Ranald.*

> The MacLeans have generally got credit for a certain high-bred polish, on which they rather plume themselves. 'An cinne mòr, 's am pòr mì-shealbhach'—*'The great race, and the unfortunate seed'*—is one of their sayings of themselves. Another is 'Ged tha mi bochd, tha mi uasal—buidheachas do Dhia, 's ann de Chlann Illeathain mi!'— *'Though I am poor, I am well-born—God be thanked, I am a MacLean!'* The MacDonalds, on the other hand, bear the character of manliness and force, with a tendency to swagger. 'Spagada-gliog Chlann Dòmh-naill agus leòm Leathaineach'—*'The MacDonald ostentation and the MacLean affectation'*—is a saying of this import.

An t-ugh a thoirt às a' ghog.—*Guessing the egg from the cackle.*

An uair a bhios a' bhrù làn, 's miann leis an t-sùil tàmh.—*When the belly is full, then the eye waxes dull.*

> *An uair* is always pronounced *nuair* colloquially, and is generally so written. It is sometimes even degraded into *dar*.

An uair a bhios a' ghaoth air chall, iarr à deas i.—*When there is no wind, seek it in the south.*

> Yn chiuney smoo erbee, geay jiass sniessy j'ee.—*Manx.*

An uair a bhios a' mhuc sàthach, cinnidh an drabh goirt.—*As the sow fills the draff sours.—Eng., Scot.*

An uair a bhios am poball dall, nì an gille cam ministear.—*When the congregation's blind, the one-eyed lad will suit their mind.*

'The one-eyed is king among the blind.' See 'Is rìgh an cam'.

An uair a bhios am port a' fàs fada, bidh e fàs searbh.—*When the tune gets tiresome, it gets harsh.*

An uair a bhios an cupan làn, cuiridh e thairis.—*When the cup is full, it will overflow.*

An uair a thig rìgh ùr, thig lagh ùr.—*When a new king comes, new laws come.*

An uair as làine 'n cupan, 's ann as dorr' a ghiùlan.—*When the cup is fullest it is most difficult to carry.*

Al.—Is duilich cupan làn a ghiùlan.
A fu cup is ill to carry. When the cup is fu, carry it even.—*Scot.*

Plenitude of power or wealth is difficult to bear without overbearing. The saying is meant to correct that tendency, specially developed in upstarts.

An uair a bhios an deoch a-staigh, bidh an ciall a-mach.—*When drink's in, wit's oot.—Scot.*

Vino dentro, senno fuora.—*Ital.* Do entra beber, sale saber.—*Span.* Als de wijn ingaat, gaat de wijsheid uit. Wanneer de wijn is in de man, dan is de wijsheid in de kan.—*Dutch.* Naar Ollet gaaer ind, da gaaer Viddet ud.—*Dan.*

An uair a bhios càch air an eathar, bidh siubhal nan taighean aig Loiream.—*While the rest are with the boat, Trifler goes from house to house.*

This is a Lewis saying, applied to contemptible fellows who stay at home while proper men go hazarding their lives at sea. Similar is 'Bog-a-loireag, math air tir, is diblidh air muir'.

An uair a bhios gill' agad, tarraing a chluas.—*When you have a servant, pull his ear.*

An uair a bhios mise thall, geàrr an drochaid.—*When I am over, cut down the bridge*.

An uair a bhios Murchadh 'na thàmh, bidh e ruamhar.—*When Murdoch takes rest, he delves*.

> This is said to have been spoken by a farmer's wife in Jura of her husband, who was of a type rather rare in the Highlands. When in to dinner from ploughing in the fields, he would say to his men, 'Nach toir sinn làmh air a' chàl, fhad 's a bhios sinn 'na ar tàmh'—'*Let us take a turn at planting the kale while we are idle.*'

An uair a bhios an sgadan mu thuath, bidh Murchadh Ruadh mu dheas.—*When the herring is in the north, Red Murdoch is in the south*.

> Red Murdoch is the restless, unlucky man, always out of the way when something good is to be got.

An uair a bhios nì aig a' chat, nì e crònan.—*When the cat has something, she purrs*.

> 'Applied to such mean persons as are too noisy and insufferable when they once become rich.'—*Note by Macintosh*.

An uair a bhios rud a dhìth air Dòmhnall, gheibh e fhèin e.—*When Donald wants anything, he'll get it himself*.

> Donald represents the pushing man who will not be over-nice in helping himself to what he wants. 'Dòmhnall da fhèin,' '*Donald for himself*,' is a somewhat similar phrase.

An uair a bhuaileas tu cù, buail gu math e.—*When you strike a dog, strike him well*.

An uair a chailleas an saor a riaghailt, claonaidh na clàir.—*When the carpenter loses his rule, the boards will go awry*.

An uair a chailleas duin' a stòras, chan fhiù a sheòladh no chomhairle.—*When a man loses his means, his direction and advice go for nothing*.

> Ffol pob tlawd—*Foolish is every poor one.*—*Welsh*. Arme lui wijsheid gaat meest verloren.—*Dutch*. In armer Leute Mund verdirbt viel Weisheit.—*Germ*.

An uair a chì thu bean oileanach, beir oirre, beir oirre; mur beir thus' oirre, beiridh fear eile oirre.—*When you see a well-bred woman, catch her, catch her; if you don't do it, another will match her.*

An uair a dh'èireas Iain Dubh, laighidh am ministear.—*When Black John rises, the minister lies down.*

> The 'minister's man'—an important functionary in Scotland.—See Dean Ramsay's *Reminiscences.*

An uair a dh'ithear an t-arbhar, is ann a thogas am bodach an gàrradh.—*When the corn is eaten, the silly body builds the dyke.*

An uair a gheibh an leibidean a-staigh, 's e fear an taighe 'n truaghan.—*When the trifler gets in, pity the goodman of the house.*

An uair a lasas sin, nì e teine.—*When that lights, it will make a fire.*

> Fire, quoth the fox, when he — on the ice.—*Eng.*
>
> The Gaelic proverb is connected with the same parable as the English one, coarse but comical.

An uair a gheibh sinn biadh, gheibh sinn poit.—*When we get food, we'll get a pot.*

> A good maxim for young couples intent upon furnishing a house. Be sure of your living first.

An uair a leumas e an Fhèill Brìghde, chan earb an sionnach earball ris an deigh.—*When Candlemas is past, the fox won't trust his tail to the ice.*

> There may be hard frost at that season, but it cannot be depended on.

An uair a laigheas a' ghaoth, 's maoth gach sian.—*No weather's ill, if the wind be still.*—*Eng., Scot.*

An uair a mhìosaicheas an t-Earrach, tha e sìos is suas tuille.—*When the Spring is past a month, it's up and down thenceforth.*

> The husbandman after that can go on steadily with his work.

An uair as àirde sheòlas an ceàrd-dubhan, 's ann san làthaich a thuiteas e.—*When the dung-beetle flies highest, it's in the dirt it falls.*

An uair as Ciadaineach an t-Samhain, is iargaineach fir an domhain.—*When Hallowmass falls on Wednesday, all men are uneasy.*

> Supposed, no one knows why, to portend a severe winter.

An uair as fheàrr an cluich, 's fheàrr sgur.—*When the play is best, 'tis
best to cease.*

> *Al.*—Am beadradh—*the daffing.* Tra s' reaie yn chloie, share faagail
> jeh.—*Manx.* Lascia la burla quando più piace.—*Ital.* A la burla,
> dejarla quando mas agrada.—*Span.* Wenn der Scherz am besten ist,
> soll man aufören.—*Germ.* Naar Legen er feirest, er han bedst at lade
> fare.—*Dan.*

An uair as lugha 'n naidheachd, 's ann as mò an t-sìth.—*Least news,
most peace.*

> No news is good news.—*Eng.*

An uair as mò an èiginn, dearbhar an caraid dìleas.—*A friend in need
is a friend indeed.*—*Eng.*

An uair as truim' an t-uisge, 's ann as giorr' e.—*When the rain is
heaviest, 't will be soonest over.*

An uair as teinne air duine, 's e cheann a cheart mhuineal.—*When
a man is most in straits, his head is his best support.*

> Literally, 'his head is his real neck,' i.e., he must rely on his own brains
> to hold up his head. See 'An uair a thèid duine'.

An uair as teinn' an taod, 's ann as dòch' e bristeadh.—*When the rope
is tightest, it is nearest breaking.*

> Po tynaf fo'r llinyn cynt af y tyr.—*Welsh.* Naar Strængen er stindest,
> da brister han snarest.—*Dan.*

An uair a sguireas am meur de shileadh, sguiridh am beul de
mholadh.—*When the finger ceases to distil, the mouth ceases to
praise.*

> Irish and Manx nearly in same words, *làmh* for *meur.*

An uair a shaoil leat a bhith air muin na muice, 's ann a bha thu làmh
rithe san làib.—*When you thought you were on the sow's back, you were
beside her in the puddle.*

An uair a thàinig e gus a h-aon 's gus a dhà.—*When it came to one and two.*

An uair a tharraingeas gach duin' a chuid thuige, 's mairg a bhios gun chuid aige.—*When every man draws his share, pity him who has none at all.*

An uair a thèid a' chailleach 'na ruith, thèid i 'na deann-ruith.— *When the old wife runs, she runs with a vengeance.*

An uair a thèid duine gu luim, 's e dhruim as taice dha.—*When a man goes down, his own back is his support.*

> Selbst ist der Mann.—*Germ.*

An uair thèid bior san losgann, nì e sgreuch.—*When the toad is pierced, he screeches.*

An uair a thèid na mèirlich a throd, thig daoin' ionraic gu 'n cuid.—*When thieves fall out, honest men come to their own.*

> When thieves reckon, leal folk come to their gear.—*Scot., Eng.* Wanneer dieven kijven bekomen, vrome lieden hare goederen.— *Dutch.* Naar Tyvene trættes, faaer Bonden sine Koster.—*Dan.* Les larrons s'entrebattent, et les larchins découvrent.—*Fr.* Pelean los ladrones, y descubrense los hurtos.—*Span.*

An uair a thèid thus' air d'each mòr, thèid thu thairis air.—*When you mount your high horse, you'll tumble over.*

> Vaulting ambition, which o'erleaps its self,
> And falls on the other.—*Macbeth.*

An uair a theirigeas gach meas, 's math na mucagan.—*When all fruit is done, hips are good.*

An uair a theirigeas gual, sguiridh obair.—*When coal is done, work ceases.*

> The work referred to is the smith's, the coal a kind of charcoal or coke, called *eala-ghual*, which used to be made of peat.

An uair thig an Samhradh, togaidh sinn taigh: thig an Samhradh, 's cha tog taigh no taigh—'s fheàrr a bhith muigh na bhith staigh.— *When Summer comes, we'll build a house; Summer comes, and house or no house, it's better to be out than in.*

An uair a thig air duine, thig air uile.—*When anything comes on a man, everything comes.*

> *Al.*—An uair a thig aon nì, thig gach aon nì.—*Misfortunes seldom come alone.* It never rains but it pours.—*Eng.* Ill comes upon waur's back.—*Scot.* Een ongeluk komt zelden alleen.—*Dutch.* Malheur ne vient jamais seul.—*Fr.* Le disgrazie non vengon mai sole.—*Ital.* Adonde vas, mal? Adonde mas hay.—*Span.*

An uair a thig an latha, thig comhairle.—*With day counsel will come.*

> Tra hig y laa, hig eh choyrle lesh.—*Manx.* 'Εν νυκτὶ βουλή.—*Gr.* La nuit porte conseil.—*Fr.* La notte è la madre di pensieri.—*Ital.* Dormiréis sobre ello, y tomaréis acuerdo.—*Span.* Guter Rath kommt über Nacht.—*Germ.* Take counsel of your pillow.—*Eng.*

An uair a thig tionndadh na h-aimsir, tillidh gach eun ri ealtainn.—*When the change of season comes, each bird returns to his flock.*

An uair a thrèigeas na dùthchasaich Ile, beannachd le sìth Alba!—*When the natives forsake Islay, farewell the peace of Scotland!*

> The population of Islay has decreased much by emigration, but it is to be hoped the peace of Scotland is safe notwithstanding.

An uair a thughas e cheann, tughaidh e thaigh.—*When he thatches his head, he will thatch his house.*

An uaisle ga cumail suas a dh'aindeoin.—*Keeping up gentility in spite of everything.*

> A man down on his back, after a wrestle with a *tannasg*, was asked by the spectre if this was the worst plight he ever was in? 'Not at all,' said he. 'What then?' said the ghost. 'An càs as cruaidhe anns an robh mise riamh, an uair a bha mi eadar an fhèile agus an aimbeairt, agus a' cumail na h-uaisle suas a dh'aindeoin'—*'The worst plight I ever was in was when I was between hospitality and want, and keeping up gentility in spite of all'.* 'That was hard work,' said the ghost, 'but get up, you'll never encounter these two again'; and so let him go.
>
> The conflict between hospitality and want is prettily illustrated in one of Fingal's questions to the daughter of King Cormac. 'What is hotter than fire?' said F. 'A good man's cheek,' said the lady, 'to whom visitors come, and no food to give them'—'Gnùis dhuine mhath don tig aoighean, gun bhiadh aige dhaibh'. Fingal's greatest strait was when he was between want and denial, 'eadar an t-euradh is aimbeairt,' *q.v.*

Anail a' Ghàidheil—air a' mhullach.—*The Gael's breathing-place—on the summit.*

> Right up Ben Lomond could he press,
> And not a sob his toil confess.—*Scott.*

Anmoch gu loch, moch gu abhainn, 's mu mheadhan-latha na h-uillt.—*Late to the loch, early to the river, and about noon to the burns.*

> This is an angler's advice.

Ann am mullach nam meall.—*At the top of the heights.*

> At the height of passion. [MacInnes has 'quarrel'.]

Ann an coileach an t-sruth.—*In the eddy of the stream.*

> Applied to persons in extreme difficulty.

Aon a dh'iarras 's a dhà dheug a dh'òlas, no pathadh na caorach.—*One asking and twelve drinking, or the sheep's thirst.*

Aon bhò a bhristeas an gàrradh, 's a dhà dheug a leumas.—*One cow breaks the dyke, and a dozen leap it.*

Aon lath' as t-Earrach, naoi as t-Fhoghar.—*One day in Spring, nine in Autumn.*

Aon mhac caillich, 's aon mhart muilleir.—*An old woman's only son, and a miller's one cow.*

Aon mhacan na truaighe, is dualach gun tèid e dholaidh.—*The unfortunate little only son, 'tis natural for him to go to the dogs.*

Aon nighean caillich, aon eun teallaich.—*The old wife's only daughter, the one hearth-chicken.*

Aontachadh bradaig le breugaig, 's aontachadh breugain le braidean.—*The thief's assent to the liar, and the liar's to the thief.*

> *Al.*—Ceist bradaig air breugaig.
> Ask Jock Thief gif I be a leear.—*Scot.* Domanda al mio caro se sono ladro.—*It.*

Ar taigh tughta, 's ar talla tàirngte.—*Our house thatched, and our hall nailed.*

> All ready for occupation.

Aran is uighean tioram, culaidh-mharbhaidh MhicSamhain; am fear as math le mhnaoi e bhith diombuan, chaoidh cha dual da bhith fallain.—*Dry bread and eggs would be the death of a savage; he whose wife wishes him short life can't be in good health.*

> This refers to one of the Highland notions about certain food which are often fanciful. See 'Ugh gun ìm'. An English saying, 'After an egg drink as much as after an ox,' is to the same effect. 'MacSamhain' is the name for a kind of mythical savage.

Ardan na poite bige, cha tig e seach an luath.—*The pride of the little pot won't go beyond the ashes.*

> *Al.*—Onfhadh na poite bige.

As a' choire anns an teine.—*Out of the kettle into the fire.*

As an dris anns an droigheann.—*Out of the briars into the thorns.*

As an teine don ghrìosaich.—*Out of the fire into the embers.*

> 'Εἰς τὸ πυρ ἐκ του καπνου.—*Lucian.* De fumo in flammam.—*Lat.* Cader dalla padella nelle bragie.—*Ital.* Andar de zocos en colodros.— *Span.* Fugir do fumo, e cahir no fogo.—*Port.* Sauter de la poêle sur la braise.—*Fr.* Out of the frying-pan into the fire.—*Eng.*

At a' bhuinn-duibh, agus bàs an aon mhic.—*The swelling of the heel, and the death of the only son.*

> Said by a Lewis woman who suffered under both pains at once. 'Losgadh buinn-duibh, losgadh gu cnàimh' is another saying expressive of the agony caused by a sore heel.

Atach seann seòladair, an t-atach as miosa th' ann.—*An old sailor's cast-off things, worst of all cast-offs.*

> This is equally applicable to an old sailor's garments or his used-up craft. *Atach = Ath-aodach.*

Athair na Dìlinn!—*Father of the Flood!*

> An interjection not unnatural in a rainy climate.

Athais an dàrna cuir air a' char eile.—*The reproach of the one twist against the other.*

    Al.—An dàrna curra—*the one heron* &c.

B

Badhbh sam bith a nì guidhe, far an teoth' an gaol, 's ann as truim' am buille.—*When a wicked woman curses, where the love is hottest, there the blow is heaviest.*

Bagair 's na buail.—*Threaten and strike not.*

There is something of the Bombastes character in this advice, but its discretion cannot be denied.

Baile Dhubhthaich bhòidheach, 's Dòrnach na gorta,
Sgiobal nan ùbhlan, 's Bil an arain-choirce;
Euraboll nan adagan, Dùn Robain a' chàil,
Goillspidh nan sligean dubha, is Druim Muighe 'n t-sàil.

—Bonnie Tain, and hungry Dornoch,
Skibo for apples, and Beil for oatcakes;
Eriboll for haddocks, Dunrobin for kail,
Golspie for black shells, Drumuie for brine.

All these places, with the exception of Tain, are on the coast of Sutherlandshire.

B'ainmig leis a' chirc adhartan a bhith aice.—*It is not common for hens to have pillows.*

Applied to persons affecting luxuries unsuitable to them.

Balach is balgaire tighearna,
Dithis nach bu chòir leigeil leo—
Buail am balach air a' charbad
'S buail am balgaire san t-sròin.

—A laird's flunkey and his dog,
These are two one should not spare—
Slap the flunkey on the cheek,
Hit the hound upon the nose.

This verse is said to have been composed by John Morrison of Bragar in Lewis, who lived during the latter half of the 17th century and was held in high repute for his administrative talent and ready wit. Having come on one occasion to Seaforth Lodge at Stornoway, to explain his refusal to pay an overcharge made by the factor, he was assailed at the door by a big dog, which barked furiously at him. Morrison hit him in the nose with his stick, and sent him away howling. Next came out a flunkey, who addressed himself to Morrison in no polite terms, and got in reply a good whack on the jaw. More noise followed, which at last brought Seaforth himself. Morrison explained the whole thing to the laird's satisfaction, and finished his story, it is said, with the above verse. For an account of him and his family, see Captain Thomas's 'Traditions of the Morrisons,' *Proc. of Scot. Soc. of Ant.*, Vol. XII, pp 526–531.

Bainne nan gobhar fo chobhar 's e blàth, 's e chuir an spionnadh sna daoine a bha.—*Goat milk foaming and warm—that gave their strength to our fathers.*

B'àlainn a' ghnùis, nam b'iùlmhor am beus.—*The face were lovely were the 'haviour good.*

B'amhail mura b'fhìor.—*Probable if it were not true.*

This resembles, but wants the point of, 'Se non è vero è ben trovato'.

Barail a' bhruic air a ladhran, barail bhochd.—*The badger's opinion of his own claws, a poor opinion.*

Bàs an fhithich ort!—*The raven's death to you!*

This is much the same as 'Droch bhàs ort!'—a very common phrase. It was a popular belief among the Gael that the young raven kills the old one. Not less emphatic is 'Bàs gun sagart ort!'—'*Death without priest to you!*'

Bata 's treasa na 'n cuaille, gille 's uaisle na mhaighstir.—*Cane stronger than club, servant finer than master.*

Bàthadh mòr aig oirthir.—*A great drowning near the land.*

> Margr druknar nœrri landi.—*Icel.*

Bàthaidh toll beag long mhòr.—*A little hole will sink a big ship.*

Bàthaidh uisge teth teine.—*Hot water will quench fire.*

> Foul water will sloken fire.—*Scot.*

B'e sin a bhith cur iomchoire 'n deaghaidh Chaluim.—*That were blaming Malcolm after he's away.*

B'e sin a bhith cur na caora air theadhair làmh ri taigh a' mhèirlich.—*That were tethering the sheep near the thief's house.*

B'e sin a bhith dol eadar a' chraobh 's a rùsg.—*That were to go between the tree and its bark.*

> Il ne faut mettre le doigt entre l'arbre et l'écorce.—*Fr.*

B'e sin a bhith tàladh seangain air crios.—*That were hushing an ant to sleep on a girdle.*

> Trying to do an absurd thing. Somewhat to the same effect is 'Cala seangain air crios'—'*An ant's harbour on a girdle*'.

B'e sin a' chearc a' gairm ron choileach.—*That were the hen crowing before the cock.*

> Triste es la casa, donde la gallina canta, y el gallo calla.—*Span.*

B'e sin ainmeachadh bà air buachaille, 's a toirt uaithe feasgar.—*That were to name a cow on a herd, and take her from him at evening.*

> It was usual, and still is, to allot one of the cows of a herd to the cowherd for his own supply of milk.

B'e sin am màm air muin an t-saic.—*That were the heap above the sack.*

B'e sin an dà latha.—*That were the change of days.*

> It is common to hear ''S ann air a thàinig an dà latha' said of a person who has suffered a change of circumstances. See 'Cha robh duine gun dà latha'.

B'e sin an deur ga iarraidh air a' chat, 's e fhèin san dian-mhiamh-ail.—*That were asking a drop from the cat, and the cat mewing clamorously.*

B'e sin an dìol dubh air a' ghruth gheal.—*That were the black usage of the white curds.*

> Unnatural treatment of a thing or person.

B'e sin an ealain gun rath.—*That was the skill without luck.*

> Many of the proverbs inculcate the dangerous doctrine that luck is better than skill or effort. There is a story about two carpenters who got their choice from a certain witch or *glaistig* between 'ealain gun rath' and 'rath gun ealain'. The one chose the former, became a perfect artificer, and yet never prospered. The other chose the latter, never rose above being a botcher, and yet 'got on' in the world. So much for luck! See a story of the same sort in Campbell's *W. H. T.*, II, 86, where *rath* is mistaken for *ràdh*—'speech'.

B'e sin an gille 'chur an àit' an duin'-uasail.—*That were putting the servant in place of the gentleman.*

B'e sin an gràdh luath 's am fuath clis.—*That was the hasty love and the quick hate.*

> *Al.*—Cha tug gaol luath nach tug fuath clis.
> Soon hot, soon cold.—*Eng.*

B'e sin an reul san oidhche dhoilleir.—*That was the star in the dark night.*

> *Al.*—B'e sin an rionnag san oidhche fhrasaich. Often said ironically of a pretentious person.

B'e sin an salann ga chur sa mhuir.—*Putting salt into the sea.*

> Bwrw heli yn y môr.—*Welsh.*

B'e sin fiodh a chur do Loch Abar.—*That were sending wood to Lochaber.*

B'e sin ìm a chur do thaigh àirich.—*That were sending butter to a dairyman's house.*

> Sending owls to Athens.—*Gr.* Sending pines to Norway.—*Dan.* Carrying coals to Newcastle.—*Eng.* Caain saut to Dysart, and puddins to Tranent.—*Scot.* Taking blades to Damascus.—*Arab.* Pepper to Hindostan.—*Pers.* Cockles to St. Michel.—*Fr.*

B'e sin an seangan a' toirt grèim' à gearran.—*That were the ant biting the gelding.*

B'e sin an tuagh a thoirt à làimh an t-saoir.—*That were to take the axe out of the carpenter's hand.*

B'e sin buille sa cheann is seachain am muineal.—*That were hitting the head and avoiding the neck.*

B'e sin cead iarraidh òrd a bhualadh air bàirnich.—*That were asking leave to lift a limpet.*

> Literally, 'to strike a hammer on a limpet'. Limpets, which are much used as bait in the Highlands and Islands, are naturally considered free to all mankind. The tool used for detaching them is called *òrd-bàirnich*, though generally it is a chisel rather than a hammer. A huge block of trap which has slipped from the face of a cliff in one of the islands of Loch Bracadale in Skye is called 'Ord-bàirnich Fhinn,' 'Fingal's limpet-hammer'.

B'e sin fair' a' chlamhain air na cearcan.—*That were the kite's watch over the hens.*

> Such protection as vultures give to lambs.—*Pizarro.*

B'e sin grèim den easgainn air a h-eàrr.—*That were taking the eel by the tail.*

B'e sin 'Hò!' fada bhon chrodh.—*That were a call far from the cows.*

> Out of place, or before the time.

B'e sin iasad an Deamhain don mhuileann.—*That were the Devil's loan to the mill.*

> Bleùd an Diaoul—*the Devil's meal.—Breton.*
> There are proverbs of various nations implying a disbelief in the honesty of millers, and this seems to be one of them.

B'e sin latha thogail do shaic, 's cha b'ann don mhuileann.—*That was the day for lifting your sacks, but not to the mill.*

> This refers either to a *creach*, or 'lifting' of property against the owner's will, or to a flitting.

B'e sin marag earbsa ris a' chù dhubh.—*That were trusting a pudding to the black dog.*

B'e sin na smeuran-dubha san Fhaoilleach.—*That were the bramble-berries in February.*

> Said of anything out of season.

B'e sin saoradh air ceann a' choin bhradaich.—*That were absolving the thievish dog.*

B'e sin urras gun earras, mise dhol an urras ortsa.—*That were the security without substance, were I to warrant thee.*

Beag agus beag èisg seo, ach tuilleadh agus tuilleadh às an t-seilbh chiadna.—*Little fish this, but there's more and more in the same store.*

> Said when one gets a small fish to begin with. Somewhat similar is 'Fuil air iasg! Mharbh mi sgiollag.'

Beag àigh ort!—*Small luck to you!*

> *Al.*—Beagan pisich.

Bean à taigh-mòr, is bò à baile, cha fhreagair an duine bochd.—*A wife from the big house, and a cow from a farm, won't suit the poor man.*

> The wife accustomed to the style of a gentleman's house might probably be ill to please in a poor thatched cottage; and a fine Ayrshire cow would be more difficult to keep than a hardy Highland one.

Bean fhada, chaol, dhìreach—miann Dhòmhnaill Amadain.—*The fool Donald's fancy—a tall, slender, straight wife.*

> Probably the fancy of the wise man who invented this saying was a stout, strong and what is called in the Lowlands a 'wise-like' woman.

Bean ga bhuain, dall ga mheangadh, curaidh ga shnìomh—'s figh an reamhar air a' chaol, mas math leat an taod a bhith buan.—*A woman to pluck it, a blind man to lop it, a strong man to twist it—and weave the thick on the thin, if you wish your rope to last.*

> This refers to the making of a rope of birch or willow twigs. A woman would choose nice twigs, and a blind man would use his knife cautiously.

Bean ga thrèigsinn, is stiùir ga dhiùltadh.—*Wife forsaking him, and helm disobeying.*

> A very sad predicament.

Bean ruadh dhubh-shùileach, cù lachdann las-shùileach, fear an fhuilt dhuibh 's na feusaige ruaidhe—na trì còmhlaichean as mios' air bith.—*A red-haired black-eyed woman, a dun fiery-eyed dog, a black-haired red-bearded man—the three unluckiest to meet.*

> Another Gaelic saying about the red beard and the black head is 'Fear a' chinn duibh 's na feusaige ruaidhe, cò thuig riamh a nàdar?' Still more emphatic are 'Fear a' chinn duibh, &c., na teirg eadar e 's a' chreag' and the old English rhyme:
>
> A red beard and a black head—
> Catch him with a good trick and take him dead.

Beannachd a shaoid 's a shiubhail leis! Biodh e nochd far an robh e raoir.—*The blessing of his state and his journey be with him! Let him be tonight where he was last night.*

> This is like an Oriental expression of hospitality.

Beannachd Chaluim Ghobha: 'Mo thogair ged nach till'.—*Smith Malcolm's blessing: 'I care not if he come not back'.*

Beannachd dhut fhèin, ach mallachd do d'oid'-ionnsachaidh!—*Blessing to thyself, but a curse on thy teacher!*

Beannachd 'nan siubhal 's 'nan imeachd! 'S e 'n-diugh Dihaoine, cha chluinn iad sinne.—*Blessing on their going and way! This is Friday, they won't hear us.*

> A charm against fairies. Friday was the day on which they were believed to visit Fairyland.

Beatha Chonain am measg nan deamhan: 'Mas olc dhomh, chan fheàrr dhaibh.'—*Conan's life among the demons: 'If bad for me, for them no better.'*

> Conan is one of the principal characters celebrated in the Fenian legends, and the only disagreeable one. He is called 'aimlisg na Fèinne,' 'the mischief of the Fenians,' and is described as rash, quarrelsome and meddlesome. He visited *Ifrinn* (Hell) in search of some of his departed friends, and gave as good as he got there to the fiends. Sir Walter Scott picked up this story, and made use of it in *Waverley*, where Mrs Flockhart asks, "And will ye face thae tearing chields, the dragoons, Ensign Maccombich?" "Claw for claw, as Conan said to Satan, Mrs Flockhart, and the deevil tak the shortest nails."

> "Is olc do bheatha, Chonain!" is another saying in reference to this legend.

Beathaich thusa mis' an-diugh, is beathaichidh mis' thus' a-màireach.—*Feed thou me today, and I'll feed thee tomorrow.*

Beinn Nibheis mhòr a' glaodhaich 'na laighe-siùbhla, 's cha tàinig aiste ach an luchag fheòir.—*Great Ben Nevis crying in travail, and nothing came of it but a field-mouse.*

> This, no doubt, is a mere version of 'Parturiunt montes,' but it has the merit of local colouring.

Beiridh am beag tric air a' mhòr ainmig.—*The short quick will overtake the long slow.*

Beiridh bean mac; 's e Dia a nì an t-oighre.—*A woman may bear a son, but God makes the heir.*

> Hæredem Deus facit, non homo.—*Coke.*

Beiridh tu air a bhith gu math nuair a thig d'fheusag.—*You will be a good one by the time your beard grows.*

> Said ironically to forward young people.

Beò bochd gun airgead, mar a bha 'n t-Albannach roimhe.—*Poor living without money, as the Scot of old had.*

Beul a labhras, ach gnìomh a dhearbhas.—*The mouth speaks but the deed proves.*

> See 'Air mheud 's a their'.

Beul gun fhàitheam.—*A mouth without hem.*

> *Al.*—A bheul air a ghualainn.—*His mouth on his shoulder* = his heart on his sleeve.

Beul sìos air na mnathan, mur faighear 's gach àit' iad!—*Confound the women, if they are not found everywhere!*

> Women's work is never done.—*Eng. and Scot.*
>
> The phrase 'Beul sìos ort!'—'*Down mouth to you!*'—probably means 'May you be laid upside-down', i.e., dead. 'Beul seachad ort!' is sometimes used instead.

Beus na tuath far am bìtear, is e a nìtear.—*The manners of the folk one lives among will be followed.*

> Thy neighbour is thy teacher. Live with him who prays, and thou prayest. Live with the singer, and thou singest.—*Arab.* He who herds with the wolves will howl.—*Fr., Ital., Span., Germ., Dan.* When you are at Rome, do as Rome does.—*Eng.*

B'fhada bho chèile crodh-laoidh an dà sheanar.—*Far apart were the milk-cows of their grandfathers.*

> Said of persons whose ancestors were far removed from each other in place or position—e.g., marrying out of one's sphere.

B'fhaide bhiodh donas à droch mhnaoi na bhithinn-sa dèanamh sin.—*A shrew's ill nature would be longer out of her than I would be about that.*

> In other words, "I should do it in no time".

B'fhasa Eòghann a chur air each.—*'Twere easier to put Ewen on horseback.*

> In A. Campbell's note on this, he says it alludes to MacNeil of Barra, but that is doubtful. Macintosh, in his note on another proverb, 'Chan ann a h-uile là a thèid MacNèill air each,' says, "There is an ingenious sarcastical description, of setting MacNeil on horseback, in Gaelic, in my hands setting forth the grandeur, antiquity, and valour of MacNeil of Barra." A version of that curious composition, got in 1859 from the recitation of a man in Blair Atholl, is given in Mr J. F. Campbell's *Leabhar na Féinne*, pp 210, 211. After an elaborate description of the dressing and arming of Ewen, the extraordinary virtues of his steed and the splendour of his harness, the ignominious fiasco is thus briefly told: "S chaidh e trì uairean timcheall an òtraich, 's ghabh e eagal mòr, 's phill e.'—'*He went three times round the dunghill, took a great fright, and returned!*'

> Another version, called 'Cliù Eobhain,' curiously differing from the above, is given by Mr D. C. Macpherson in the *Gael*, Vol. IV, pp 112, 113. It was copied from a MS in the Irish character apparently about a century old.

B'fheàrr a bhith gun bhreith na bhith gun teagasg.—*Better unborn than untaught.*

> The English is that of Heywood, given in Hazlitt's English Proverbs, with this old rhyme:

> > A chyld were better to be unbore
> > Than to be untaught, and so be lore.

B'fheàrr a bhith gun fhàinne na fàinne luachrach.—*Better no ring than a rush ring.*

> This proverb is both English and Scotch.

B' fheàrr a bhith sàmhach na droch dhàn a ghabhail.—*Better be silent than sing a bad song.*

> Macintosh translates the last three words 'receive an affront'.

B'fheàrr a' chreach a thighinn don tìr na madainn mhìn san Fhaoill-
leach fhuar.—*Better foray coming to the land than mild morning in the
cold month of storms.*

> Share craght ve sy cheer na mee ny mannan (*month of kids*) cheet stiagh
> meein.—*Manx.*

> The *Faoilleach*, or *Faoillteach*, was the name given to the time of year
> nearly corresponding to the present month of February, usually a time
> of storms and cold. Mild weather at this time was and is regarded as
> unseasonable, and not to be desired. Some other proverbs to the same
> effect as the above will be found further on. See *Faoilleach*. Of old
> English and Scottish ones are the following:

> > February fill the dike
> > Either with the black or white,
> > But if it be white it's the better to like.

> > The hind had as lief see his wife on the bier
> > As that Candlemas Day should be pleasant and clear.

> > Aa the months o the year
> > Curse a fair Februeer.

B'fheàrr a leth an-dè na gu lèir an-diugh.—*Better the half yesterday
than the whole today.*

> Ὤκειαι χάριτες γλυκύτεραι—*Gr. Anth.* Bis dat qui cito dat.—*Lat.*
> The best generosity is the quick.—*Arab.* One today is worth two
> tomorrow.—*Eng.* En Skilling er i Tide saa god som en Daler.—*Dan.*
> E meglio aver oggi un uove che domani una gallina.—*Ital.* Mas vale
> un 'toma' que dos 'te daré'.—*Span.*

B'fheàrr cumail a-muigh na cur a-mach.—*Better keep out than put
out.*

B'fheàrr dha bonnach is toll am bruicheadh e e.—*Better for him were
a cake and a hole to bake it in.*

> 'Than think of such a thing' is understood.

B'fheàrr do MhacDhòmhnaill còmhdach a bhith aige dha fhèin.—
Better were it for MacDonald to have as much as would cover himself.

> I have not been able to ascertain the origin of this saying.

B'fheàrr gun tòiseachadh na sgur gun chrìochnachadh.—*Better not begin than stop without finishing.*

B'fheàrr leam fhaicinn na chluinntinn.—*I would rather see it than hear it.*

> Seeing is believing.—*Arab., Eng., Scot.* Chi con l' occhio vede, col cuor crede.—*Ital.* Die Augen glauben sich selbst, die Ohren an den Leuten.—*Germ.* Hooren zeggen is half gelogen.—*Dutch.*

B'fheàrr suidhe làmh ri fear-cuthaich na làmh ri fear lomnochd.—*Better sit next a madman than next a naked man.*

> 'Naked' here means needy. It may be intended to signify that a destitute man is apt to be dangerous, as another proverb indicates, "S ionann fear 'na èiginn 's fear a' chuthaich,' and the Latin, 'Esurienti ne occurras'.

B'fhialaidh an coileach mu chuid an eich.—*The cock was very bountiful with the horse's corn.*

> *Al.*—Fialachd mhath mu chuid chàich.
> Hens are free of horse corn.—*Scot.*

Bha 'beir 's cha bheir' aige.—*It was 'catch and won't catch' with him.*

> Said of one who just misses, or all but misses, a thing.

Bha caochladh clòimhe 'n clò Chaluim.—*There were various wools in Malcolm's cloth.*

> Said of persons whose character or works are inconsistent or heterogeneous.

Bha doras Fhinn don ànrach fial.—*Fingal's door was free to the needy.*

> In the ballad called 'Urnaigh Oisein' (*Leabhar na Féinne*, pp 41–46; *Gael*, I, 83), consisting of a dialogue between Ossian and St Patrick, Patrick says:
>
> > Ge beag a' chuil chrònanach
> >   Is mònaran na grèine,
> > Gun fhios don Righ mhòralach,
> >   Cha tèid fo bhil' a sgèithe.

> —*Small as is the humming gnat*
> *And the mote in sunbeam,*
> *Unknown to the majestic King,*
> *They pass not 'neath his wing.*

To this Ossian replies:

> 'N saoil thu 'm b'ionann e 's Mac Cumhail,
> An rìgh bh' againn air na Fiannaibh?
> Dh'fhaodadh gach neach bha air thalamh
> Teachd 'na thalla-san gun iarraidh.

> —*Think'st thou then to equal him*
> *To our King, the son of Cüal?*
> *All the world might enter in*
> *To his hall unbidden.*

Bha e 'na dhlùth 's 'na inneach air.—*He was both warp and woof to it.*

He was the body and soul of the thing.
'Dlùth glic agus inneach gòrach' is said of a person who seems foolish but is really wise.

Bha gnothaichean mòr an Aoraisge.—*There were great doings at Eriska.*

Eriska is a small island in Loch Creran. The story goes that the wife of the laird of Airds (long ago) kept a paramour on this island whom she treated luxuriously. The family fool got wind of it, and went on repeating "Great doings at Eriska" till his master inquired into the matter.

Bha iasad a ghabhail 's a thoirt riamh air feadh an t-saoghail.—*Borrowing and lending were always in fashion.*

Bha là eile aig fear na bracha.—*The maltman had other days.*

Said of people in reduced circumstances. See 'Bu là eile'.

Bha là eile ann.—*There was a different day.*

Al.—'Bha là dha sin' or 'Bha 'n là sin ann', phrases generally used by old people recalling the days when they could perform feats to be done no more.

Bha mis' an ceàrdaich gobha roimhe seo.—*I have been in a smithy before now.*

> The allusion is probably to the common practice of testing men's strength and agility, in a smithy, with the big hammer, and the meaning is something equivalent to "I am no greenhorn."

Bha 'n t-àm ann.—*It was high time.*

Bha sìneadh saoghail aige.—*He had a new lease of life.*

Bha 'n uair ga ruith.—*His hour was pursuing him.*

> There is something impressive in the picture this suggests, of a man pursued by the 'shadow feared of man'.

Bha rudeigin de dh'uisge far na bhàthadh an gamhainn.—*There's aye some water whaur the stirkie drouns.—Scot.*

Bha siud an dàn da.—*That was fated for him.*

Bha thu 'd shlàint' an uair a chaidh do chòta dhèanamh.—*You were in good health when your coat was made.*

> Said to one whose coat is too wide.

Bheir a h-uile Didòmhnaich seachdain leis.—*Every Sunday brings a week with it.*

Bheir aon duine triùir bhàrr an rathaid.—*One man will lead three off the road.*

Bheir aon fhear each gu uisge, ach cha toir dà fhear dheug air òl.—*One man may lead a horse to water, but twelve won't make him drink.*

> A man may lead a horse to the water, but four and twenty winna gar him drink.—*Scot.*

Bheir duine beath' air èiginn, ach cha toir e rath air èiginn.—*A man may force a livelihood, but cannot force fortune.*

> Here again appears the belief in Fate as a power superior to human will.

Bheir ao-dòchas misneach do ghealtair.—*Desperation drives on cowards.*

> Put a coward to his metal, and he'll fight the Deil.—*Scot.*
> A man who would like to run away sometimes fights like a lion when escape is impossible.

Bheir duine glic breith bliadhna air fear na h-aon oidhche.—*A wise man will from one night's knowledge judge another for a year.*

> He can judge in a night, from a man's conversation and manners, as much as a person less sagacious could do in a year.

Bheir fear na moch-èirigh buaidh air fear na fionnairidh.—*The early riser will beat the late watcher.*

Bheir fòid a bhreith 's a bhàis fear gu 'àit' air èiginn.—*No man can avoid the spot where birth or death is his lot.*

Bheir mis' ort nach òl thu bainne bhàrr spàin.—*I'll make you so that you can't drink milk from a spoon.*

> This forcible form of threat comes from the Hebrides.

Bheir na daoine beaga rud às an speur cho luath ris na daoine mòra.—*Little people will bring things from the sky as soon as big ones.*

> A hint to big people that they need not aim at things too high even for them. A similar saying is 'Thoir thusa rionnag às an speur, 's bheir mise nuas tèile'—*'Bring you a star down from the sky, and I'll bring another.'*

Bheir sin an teang' às a' chlag.—*That will take the tongue out of the bell.*

Bheireadh e gàir' air gamhainn.—*It would make a stirk laugh.*

Bheireadh e mac-tall' às na creagan.—*He would make the rocks re-echo.*

> Said of a loud-voiced person.

Bheireadh e snìomh air cridhe na cloiche.—*It would wrench the heart of a stone.*

Bheireadh seillean math mil à sin.—*A good bee could get honey out of that.*

Bheireadh tu cho fad' a' gleusadh do phìoba 's a bheireadh fear eil' a' cluich puirt.—*You would take as long to tune your pipe as another would to play a tune.*

Ye're as lang tuning yir pipes as anither wad play a spring.—*Scot.*

Bheirear comhairle seachad, ach cha toirear giùlan.—*Counsel can be given, but not conduct.*

Bheirinn cuid oidhche dha ged a bhiodh ceann fir fo achlais.—*I would give him a night's quarters though he had a man's head under his arm.*

Nothing could be more expressive than this of the Highland virtues of hospitality and clannishness in excess.

Bhiodh sonas aig an t-stròdhaire nam faigheadh mar a sgapadh e.—*The spendthrift were happy, could he get as he scatters.*

> Bheirinn m'fhalt a-mach Diardaoin
> 'S dhèanainn m'ìnean maol Diluain;
> 'S shiùbhlainn an sin bho chuan gu cuan.

> —*I would cut my hair on Thursday*
> *And pare my nails on Monday;*
> *Then I'd sail from sea to sea.*

Friday being an unlucky day, a man going on a voyage, for which Saturday or Sunday would be preferred, would get his hair cut on Thursday. Why Monday should be preferred for paring nails it is hard to see, except that doing it on Sunday was unlucky.

> Bhith fadadh teine fa loch,
> Bhith tiormachadh cloich an cuan—
> Comhairle thoirt air mnaoi bhuirb,
> Mar bhuill' ùird air iarann fuar.

> —*As kindling a fire on a loch,*
> *As drying a stone in the ocean,*
> *Like stroke of hammer on cold iron*
> *Is counsel to a shrewish woman.*

An Irish version of this is slightly different:

> Coigilt teine le loch,
> No cathamh cloch le cuan,

Comhairle thabhairt do mhnaoi bhoirb,
No buille de ribe air iarann fuar.—Bourke's *Ir. Gram.*, p.279.

This verse was given as part of a song picked up in S. Uist by Mr
Carmichael which appeared in the 'Nether Lochaber' column of the
Inverness Courier. It has also been ascribed, but without sufficient
warrant, to John Morrison of Bragar. He may have said it to his wife,
but it does not follow that he composed it.

Bhith umhail da thighearna, 's e dligh' an òglaich.—*To obey his master
is the servant's duty.*

Bho bhrògan àrd gu brògan ìosal, 's bho bhrògan ìosal gu breabanan.—*From high shoes to low shoes, and from low shoes to half-soles.*

Bhon a rinn mi 'n òirleach, nì mi 'n rèis.—*As I have made the inch,
I'll make the span.*

> Tra tou jannoo yn trie (*troigh*), jean yn oarlagh.—*Manx.* Gie ye an
> inch, and ye'll tak a span.—*Scot.* Give him an inch, and he'll take an
> ell.—*Eng.*

Bhon as e 's nì do Chlann Nèill na dòirneagan, gabhadh iad don
ionnsaigh.—*Since the property of the MacNeils consists of pebbles, let
them take to them.*

> Probably said on the occasion of a fight between the MacNeils and
> some other clan. The beach at Castlebay in Barra, where the chief
> resided, abounds in sea-worn stones piled up by the Atlantic waves.

Bhon as tu mharcaich an t-each, crùdh e.—*Since you have ridden the
horse, shoe him.*

Bhon làimh gus am beul, cuibhreann as fheàrr air bith.—*From hand
to mouth, the best of all portions.*

> This saying, inconsistent with modern wisdom but not with primitive
> Christianity, is neutralised by the following one.

Bhon làimh gus am beul, cha dèan e duine còir am feasda.—*From
hand to mouth will never make a worthy man.*

Bho nach banachag mi, cha bhi mi trod mun fheur.—*As I am not a
dairymaid, I won't quarrel about the grass.*

> I won't dispute about what is not in my province.

Bho nach fhaod mi beantainn don ghèadh mhòr, pronnaidh mi na h-iseanan.—*As I cannot touch the big goose, I'll pound the goslings.*

> If I canna kep guse, I'll kep gaislin.—*Scot.* Very probably said first by a fool, who got bitten by a gander. See Lover's 'Essay on Fools,' in *Legends of Ireland.* But there is much of human nature in the sentiment. Even kings and statesmen have exemplified it.

Bho nach leam, cha tarraing.—*Since it is not mine, I won't draw it.*

> This, if referring to a rope, is selfish. But it is susceptible of a better interpretation, as a caution to mind one's own business.

Bhrist thu air gàrradh an t-sagairt.—*You have broken the priest's wall.*

> Said to children when they lose teeth in their seventh year, at which time they are supposed in the Roman Church to become responsible.

Bhuail iad a ceann air an àmraidh.—*They struck her head against the ambry.*

> Said of a servant who looks like her food. *Ambry* or *amry*, old English and Scotch for cupboard, originally *almerie*, or place for keeping alms in. 'He has broken his face on the ambry,' says Kelly, 'is spoken of bluff, fat-cheek'd boys.'

Bhuail thu 'n tarrang air a ceann.—*You have hit the nail on the head.*

Bhuain e maorach an uair a bha 'n tràigh ann.—*He gathered shellfish while the tide was out.*

> Same as making hay while the sun shone.

Bi 'd thosd 's ad chuimhne.—*Be silent and mindful.*

> In the story of Fingal's enchantment in the house of the Blàr Buidhe (*Celt. Rev.*, Vol. I, p. 197; *Gael*, IV, 10), it is said of him, 'Bha Fionn 'na thosd 's 'na chuimhne' while he was undergoing dreadful torture.

Bi 'd thosd 's bi 'd chomaidh.—*Be silent, and take your share.*

> Ask no questions for conscience's sake.

Bi gu subhach, geamnaidh,
Moch-tràthach as t-Samhradh;
Bi gu curraiceach, brògach,
Brochanach sa Gheamhradh.

—In Summer time be cheerful, chaste
And early out of bed;
In Winter be well-capped, well-shod
And well on porridge fed.

Dr. John Smith, in his *Galic Antiquities*, attributes the first half of this excellent advice to the Druids. A more probable opinion ascribes it to the *Ollamh Muileach*, Dr. John Beaton, one of a family famous in the Highlands for medical skill. He was family physician to the MacLeans, and died in 1657, as a Latin inscription on his tomb in Iona still bears.

Brochan means both 'porridge' and 'gruel'. In most parts of the Highlands it is or was applied equally to both, while in some parts, such as Skye, porridge is always called *lite* and gruel alone *brochan*. Gruel undoubtedly is more for Winter than for Summer, while porridge is equally for all the year round.

Bi thusa bruidhinn, 's bidh na h-uighean agamsa.—*You talk away, and I'll have the eggs.*

Biadh a thoirt don fhearann mun tig an t-acras air; fois a thoirt da mum fàs e sgìth; a ghart-ghlanadh mum fàs e salach—comharran an deagh thuathanaich.—*To feed the land before it get hungry; to give it rest before it grow weary; to weed it well before it get dirty—the marks of a good husbandman.*

Biadh-gràineachaidh aig seana chù.—*Food of loathing to an old dog.*

Biadh math monaidh maragan-dubha.—*Black puddings are good food for the moors.*

Bidh a' chuid as miosa aig a' bhus as taise.—*The modest mouth gets the smallest share.*

Beidh nídh ag an sárachán nuair a bheas an náireachán falamh.—*Ir.*
A modest beggar's bag is empty.—*Hungar.*

Bidh adhaircean fad' air a' chrodh tha fada uainn.—*Far-off cows have long horns.*

>Omne ignotum pro magnifico.—*Lat.*
>*Al.*—Adhaircean fad' air a' chrodh tha 'n Eirinn *or* a th' anns a' cheò. The same idea is more prettily expressed in the saying 'Is gorm na cnuic tha fada uainn' (*Scot.* and *Ir.*—*glas* for *gorm, Ir.*), of which Campbell's beautiful lines are a paraphrase:

>>'Tis distance lends enchantment to the view
>>And robes the mountain in its azure hue.

Bidh an coileach-circe 'g obair fad an latha, ach cha bhi nì 'na sgròban am beul na h-oidhche.—*The barn-door cock works all day, but his crop is empty at night.*

>Gallo bom nunco foi gordo—*Good cock was never fat.*—*Port.*

Bidh an duine foghainteach beò, ge b'e 'n clobh' a chòir.—*The able man will make a living, had he but the tongs to start with.*

>The tongs are mentioned as belonging specially to the wife's province, and not an implement likely to be chosen by the man.

Bidh an iall ruighinn gu leòr gus am brist i.—*The thong is tough enough till it breaks.*

Bidh an iomchoire 'n lorg a' challa.—*The blame will follow the loss.*

Bidh an luaireagan-luatha 'na uallachan gille.—*The child that grovels in the ashes will be a jaunty lad.*

Bidh an osna dheireannach cràidhteach.—*The last sigh will be grievous.*

Bidh an tubaist a' ruith nan clibistean.—*Mishap follows upon misadventure.*

Bidh an t-ubhal as fheàrr air a' mheangan as àirde.—*The best apple is on the highest bough.*

>Die süssesten Trauben hängen am höchsten.—*Germ.*

>"Happy would that nation be," says Macintosh in the Dedication of his collection to the Earl of Buchan, "where every person of distinguished rank would endeavour to distinguish himself still more essentially, by being beneficial to the public, and thereby confirm our old Gaelic saying 'Bithidh meas is fearr,' &c."

Bidh bean-mhuinntir aig an fheannaig as t-Fhoghar.—*The crow has a maidservant in Autumn.*

> Said of people who keep more servants than they need.

Bidh boladh a' mhairbh den làimh fhalaimh.—*The empty hand will smell like the dead.*

> This is one of the most emphatic sayings on the evils of poverty.

Bidh breith luath lochdach.—*A hasty judgment will be hurtful.*

> *Al.*—Cha tug breith luath nach tug dà uair.—*He who judges hastily must judge twice.*
> De fol juge brève sentence.—*Fr.*

Bidh cas an eòin ghòraich san ribe.—*The silly bird's foot will go into the snare.*

Bidh cnothan aig Iain fhathast: 'Ma bhitheas, cnagadh Iain iad,' arsa Muisean.—*John will have nuts yet: 'If he has, let him crack them,' said the mean devil.*

> Bithidh e cho mòr ri cnoc
> Mum faic duine fhèin a lochd.

> *—Ere a man his fault can see,*
> *Big as mountain it will be.*

> *Al.*—Bidh cron duine cho mòr ri beinn mun lèir dha fhèin e.

Bidh cuid an amadain am beul a bhuilg.—*The fool's share is in the mouth of his bag.*

Bidh Dihaoine an aghaidh na seachdain.—*Friday will be contrary to the week.*

> Selde is the Friday all the weke y-like.—*Chaucer.*
> This groundless fancy is perhaps connected with the supposed un-luckiness of Friday.

Bidh dòrn aig fear na h-eadraiginn.—*The interposer will get struck.*

> Cha táinig fear an eadargáin saor a riamh.—*Ir.*

Bidh dùil ri fear-fairge, ach cha bhi ri fear-reilige.—*There is hope of the man at sea, but none of the man in the churchyard.*

Bidh dùil ri fear-feachda, ach cha bhi ri fear-lice.—*The man of war may return, but not the buried man.*

> *Al.*—Bidh dùil ri beul cuain, ach cha bhi ri beul uaigh. Bíonn súil le muir, ach cha bhíonn súil le cill.—*Ir.*

Bidh e geal nuair a thiormaicheas e, mun duirt an droch bheannighe.—*It will be white when it dries, as the bad washerwoman said.*

Bidh fear na foille fodha.—*The deceitful will be down.*

Bidh fear na h-aon bhò uair gun bhainne.—*The man of one cow will sometimes want milk.*

Bidh fonn air gille nan lùb—'s e h-uile rud ùr as fheàrr.—*The volatile youth's desire—all that's new is best.*

> Changes are lichtsome, and fules are fond of them.—*Scot.*

Bidh gach fear a' tarraing uisge gu mhuileann fhèin.—*Each draws water to his own mill.*

> Chacun tire l'eau à son moulin.—*Fr.* Ognun tira l'acqua al suo molino.—*Ital.*

Bidh gach nì mar as àill le Dia.—*All will be as God wills.*

Bidh iteagan bòidheach air na h-eòin tha fad' às.—*Far awa fowls hae fine feathers.—Scot.*

Bidh latha ga dhìoladh, 's latha ga phàigheadh.—*A day will require and a day repay.*

Bidh meas air math nuair a chaillear e.—*The good is esteemed when lost.*

> Extinctus amabitur idem.—*Hor.* Bien perdu, bien connu.—*Fr.* Ben perduto è conosciuto.—*Ital.* Bien perdido y conocido.—*Span.*

Bidh mìr a' ghill' èasgaidh air gach mèis.—*The smart lad's share is on every dish.*

Bidh nàdar a' choin mhòir sa chuilean.—*The big dog's nature will be in the pup.*

Bidh na gobhair bodhar as t-Fhoghar.—*The goats are deaf in Harvest.*

> Harvest ears thick of hearing.—*Eng.*

Bidh rud aig fear na coise fliche.—*The man of wet foot will get something*.

> This refers to fishing. See 'Cha dèan brògan tioram'.

Bidh rud uime nach robh mun chùl-chàise.—*Something will come of it more than of the cheese-back*.

> Three parties of the Macdonalds of Glencoe went in different directions on a *Faoigh Nollaig*, or 'gentle begging' expedition for the Christmas of 1543. They met by appointment at the Black Mount, and proceeded to divide the proceeds, when it was found, after everything else had been divided, that the remnant of a cheese was still to be disposed of. From words on the subject the claimants came to blows—not with fists, alas, but with dirks; and, if the story be true, only one man out of eighteen was left to tell the tale! A small loch at the spot where this happened is still known as 'Lochan na Fala,' 'The Bloody Tarn.'—*Cuairtear*, Vol. I, p. 211.

Bidh sannt naoinear air aon mhnaoi gun sliochd.—*A childless woman has the greed of nine*.

> *Al.*—Bidh sannt nan seachd sagart anns a' mhnaoi gun laogh gun luran.—*A childless woman has the greed of seven priests*.

Bidh sonas an lorg na caithimh.—*Luck follows spending*.

> This is doubtful doctrine, unless in the sense of Solomon's proverb, 'There is that scattereth, and increaseth'.

Bidh sùilean ghobhar aig na mnathan a' gleidheadh am fear dhaibh fhèin.—*Wives have goats' eyes in keeping their husbands to themselves*.

> *Al.*—ag iarraidh fir. Goats are very sharp-sighted.

Bidh teine math an sin nuair a ghabhas e.—*That will be a good fire when it kindles*.

> See 'An uair a lasas'.

Bidh tu beò am bliadhna.—*You will survive this year*.

> Said to a person who suddenly appears when being spoken of.

Bidh uan dubh aig caora bhàin, 's uan bàn aig caora dhuibh.—*A white sheep may have a black lamb, and a black sheep a white one*.

Biodh aice an rubha a bheir i mach.—*Let her take the point she can clear.*

> Said of a boat, and applicable to human beings.

Biodh e dubh no odhar no donn, 's toigh leis a' ghobhair a meann.—*Be it black or dun or brown, the goat likes her own kid.*

> Every craw thinks her ain bird white.—*Scot.* Jeder Mutter Kind ist schön.—*Germ.*

Biodh e reamhar no caol, 's mairg nach beathaicheadh laogh dha fhèin.—*Be it fat or lean, pity the man that won't rear a calf for himself.*

> This was said of a fairy changeling, which turned out such a miserable object that someone seriously proposed that it should be thrown into the burn. The father made the above answer.

Biodh earalas mèirlich agad air gach neach, ach na dèan mèirleach de neach idir.—*Be cautious with everyone as if with a thief, but make a thief of no-one.*

> The doctrine of suspicion here inculcated is not to be admired.

Biodh gach fear a' toirt sgairbh à creagan dha fhèin.—*Let every man take scarts out of rocks for himself.*

> Alleged to have been said by a St Kilda man to his comrade, who was holding the rope above, and asked if he had secured the birds for them both. On hearing the answer above quoted, the holder of the rope is said to have replied, "Let every man hold the rope for himself"—and let him go! The story is probably a fiction. Scarts are certainly not the birds sought after by these bold cragsmen.

Biodh mionach ar n-èisg aig ar n-eòin fhèin.—*Oor ain fishguts to oor ain sea-maws.—Scot.*

Blàth nan deur mun tig an dìle.—*The look of drops before the flood.*

Bò a' bhuabhaill-thulchainn.—*The cow of the end-stall.*

> The saying in Lochaber is 'Am mart a bhios sa bhuabhaill-thulchainn, is toigh leath' e'—'*The cow in the end-stall likes it.*'

> The original meaning of the word *tulchann* is simply 'gable', 'end', 'stern'. The *buabhall-thulchainn* or end-stall was the innermost in the row, and was used for the accommodation of a cow that had lost her calf, in place of which a stuffed imitation-calf was brought in whenever she was to be milked. Hence came the application of the word *tulchann* to the imaginary calf, and of the term 'tulchan-bishop' to persons appointed to that office in Scotland after the Reformation, simply as receivers-general of the temporalities, for the benefit of the baron or his creatures. 'The Bishop had the title, but my Lord got the milk or commoditie.'—Calderwood's *Hist. of the Ch. of Scotland*, cited in Jamieson's Dict. *s.v. Tulchane.*

Bò mhaol am buaile choimhich.—*A hornless cow in a strange fold.*

Bò mhaol odhar, 's bò odhar mhaol.—*A polled dun cow, and a dun polled cow.*

> Six and half a dozen.

Bò mhòr 'na h-aon atha-grùthain.—*A big cow all liver.*

> An old woman in Lewis, living with her married son, went out to look at the weather on a snowy night. Her son asked her when she came in what sort of night it was. "Tha," ars ise, "oidhche rionnagach, reulach, gun turadh, gun ghaoith, gun uisge." "Seadh, gu dearbh!" ars esan, " 's iongantach da-rìreadh an oidhch' i." "Seadh," ars ise, "ach 's iongantaiche na sin bò mhòr a bhith 'na h-aon atha-grùthain." Her daughter-in-law had been for days serving up the liver of a lately killed cow, and nothing else, till the old woman could stand it no longer. A similar story is told, in Lochaber, of a deaf and dumb girl and her step-mother. The girl spoke for the first and last time on being asked what sort of night it was: "Tha oidhche ghaothar, ghaothar, 's i gu fèathail, fèathail, i gu soilleir, soilleir, 's i gu doilleir dorcha; a' ghaoth à shìos 's an t-uisg' à shuas." Her stepmother said it was strange. "Seadh," ars ise, "ach 's iongantaiche na sin gur h-àinean uil' am mart!"—*Yes, but more strange is it that the cow is all liver!*" And she spoke never more.

Bochd 's rud agam, bochd 's mi falamh; bidh mi bochd ri m'bheò.—
Poor when I have, poor when I haven't, poor I'll ever be.

Boght, boght dy bràgh.—*Manx.*

Bodach eadar dha cheathairne.—*An old man between two bands.*

An odd man in a game, such as shinty, who, after each leader has
chosen his side, gets the unenviable position of assisting the losing
side. "Bodach leth-bharrach" is another term of the same meaning.

> Bogha dh'iubhar Easragain,
> Ite fìrein Locha Trèig,
> Cèir bhuidhe Bhaile na Gailmhinn,
> 'S ceann bhon cheàrd MacPheidearain.

> —*Bow from yew of Esragin,*
> *Eagle feather from Loch Treig,*
> *Yellow wax from Galway town,*
> *Arrow-head by MacPhederan.*

This verse, descriptive of the best kind of bow and arrows, is quoted
by Dr. Smith in his *Sean Dana*, p. 4. Esragin is on the N. side of Loch
Etive, Loch Treig to the E. of Ben Nevis. The MacPhederans were
celebrated smiths.

Bodachan beag an taobh taigh' a mhnà.—*A little old body at the side
of his wife's house.*

Bòid a' bhàird ris a' chaisteal, 's an caisteal ga thrèigsinn.—*The bard's
vow to the castle, when the castle turned its back on him.*

Al.—Mionnan a' bhàird &c.—'Cha tèid mi fhèin don chaisteal
bhreun—cha tèid, cha leig iad ann mi!'—'*I won't go to the vile
castle—no, they won't let me!*'

Bòid ciaraig ris na fearaibh, 's bòid nam fear ri ciaraig.—*The swarthy
maid's vow against the men, and the men's vow against her.*

Never to marry one of them! See 'Is dubh'.

Boinn' am beul na gaoithe.—*A drop in the wind's mouth.*

Al.—Uisg' am bun an t-soirbheis—*A wind prophesying rain.* A
counter-saying is 'Chan e fead a bhainn' a th' ann'—'*It is not the
milk-whistle,*' i.e., the sound of the wind does not prognosticate rain,
which makes the grass to grow and the milk to flow.

Boinne snighe 'n ceann na leapadh.—*A drop from the roof at the bed-head.*

One of the ideals of discomfort.

Bonnach a mhealladh cloinne—oir thiugh is cridhe tana.—*A cake to cozen children—thick edge and thin heart.*

Bonnach air bois cha bhruich 's cha loisg.—*A cake on the palm won't toast or burn.*

B'olc an airidh gun dèanadh an turadh dolaidh.—*'Twere a pity that dry weather should do harm.*

It's a pity fair weather should e'er do harm.—*Scot.*

Breac à linne, slat à coille 's fiadh à fireach—mèirle nach do ghabh duine riamh nàir' aiste.—*A fish from the pool, a wand from the wood, a deer from the mountain—thefts no man ever was ashamed of.*

Al.—Slat à coille, fiadh à doire, breac à buinne—trì rudan às nach do ghabh Gàidheal nàire riamh.
The free doctrine of this old saying is still held in the Highlands, but there is very little poaching, notwithstanding.

Breac a' mhuiltein air an adhar; latha math a-màireach.—*A dappled sky today; a good day tomorrow.*

Breunan is Fudaidh an cuideachd a chèile.—*Dirty and Rubbishy going together.*

A Lewis proverb, taken from a verse by John Morrison of Bragar, on having sent two servants to pull heather:

Chuir mise Breunan is Fudaidh
A bhuain fraoich an cuideachd a chèile;
Thug Breunan dhachaigh an cudthrom,
'S thug Fudaidh dhachaigh na geugan.

—*I sent B. and F. to pull heather together: B. brought home the weight, and F. brought home the boughs.*

Brìgh gach cluiche gu dheireadh.—*The essence of a game is at the end.*

Bris mo chlaigeann air thùs, 's an sin ciùrr mo chorrag.—*First break my skull, then hurt my finger.*

Bristidh am ball-acrach am meadhan an t-slaodaidh.—*The anchor-rope will break in the dragging.*

Bristidh an teanga bhog an cnàimh.—*The smooth tongue breaks the bone.*

> By long forbearing is a prince persuaded, and a soft tongue breaketh the bone.—*Prov.* xxv, 15. A tongue breaketh bone, and itself hath none.—*Eng.*
> This figure is applied in the opposite sense by the son of Sirach (xxviii, 17)—The stroke of the whip maketh marks in the flesh, but the stroke of the tongue breaketh the bones.

Bristidh each gun urras cnàimhean.—*A horse without warrant will break bones.*

Bronnach an t-each, seang an làir.—*The horse big-bellied, the mare slim.*

> This is meant as an advice to buyers.

Bruidhinn bheag is fuaim dhòrn.—*Low speaking and sound of fists.*

Bu cheannach leam d'ugh air do ghloc.—*Your egg is dear for so much cackling.*

Bu cho math dol a dh'iasgach gun mhaorach 's dol a chùirt gun sporan.—*As well go fishing without bait as to court without purse.*

Bu chòir an t-iasad a chur dhachaigh a' gàireachdaich.—*The loan should be sent laughing home.*

> A loan (*or* len') should come laughing home.—*Eng. and Scot.* This pretty saying may be taken to apply to the giving of the loan and the returning of it. To lend freely is to send the borrower home smiling; to send the loan back laughing is to repay liberally.

Bu dual da sin.—*That was his birthright.*

> This is one of the most familiar and characteristic sayings in the Highlands, where the belief in blood and hereditary tendencies and claims is very strong. It is difficult to translate it literally. It might be paraphrased, 'That is what you might expect of his father and mother's son.' The four following proverbs have the same import.

Bu dual do dh'isean an ròin a dhol thun na mara.—*The young seal takes naturally to the sea.*

Bu dual do laogh an fhèidh ruith a bhith aige.—*It is natural for the fawn to be swift of foot.*

Bu dual don bhlàthaich tòchd an ime.—*It's natural that buttermilk should smell of butter.*

Bu dual don mheann meagad a dhèanamh.—*It's natural for the kid to bleat.*

Bu gheur an cù a bheireadh an t-earball uaithe.—*It would be a clever dog that would take the tail from him.*

Bu là eil' e do dh'fhear buain na mòna.—*It is change of days for him who is cutting peats.*

> Once well-to-do, now a Gibeonite.

Bu mhath an teachdair' thu shireadh an Aoig.—*You would be a good messenger to send for Death.*

> Egli è buono a mandarlo per la morte.—*Ital.*

Bu mhath an t-iasad mur h-iarrte rithist e.—*The loan were good but for the repaying.*

Bu mhath an cudaig far nach faight' an saoidhean.—*The cuddy is good when no saithe can be got.*

> The young saithe is in some parts of Scotland called 'cuddy,' in others 'podly,' in Shetland 'sillock'. It is alleged of the inhabitants of a certain island near Skye that they go even further than this proverb, and say, ''S math an sgadan nuair nach fhaighear an saoidhean'—*'The herring is good'* &c. But they now resent this as a weak invention of the enemy.

Bu mhath ìmpidh a' choilich mu shìol a thoirt do na cearcan.—*Well pleaded the cock for corn to the hens.*

Bu mhòr am beud do bheul binn a dhol gu bràth fo thalamh.— *'Twere pity thy sweet mouth should ever go under ground.*

> Said ironically of bad singers.

Bu tiugh an t-uisge nigheadh aodann.—*It would be thick water that would wash his face.*

Bu tu chuir craiceann do thòin air d'aghaidh!—*It's you that put your buttock-skin on your face!*

> Said to shameless people.

Bu tu gille mòr leth an taighe!—*What a great half-the-house lad you are!*

> Said of a manservant assuming too much authority in the house.

Buail an t-iarann fhad 's a tha e teth.—*Strike the iron while it's hot.*

> Buail an t-iarann fad is tá sé te.—*Ir.* Bwoaill choud (*cho fad*) as ta 'n yiarn cheh.—*Manx.* So in *Eng., Scot., Fr., Ital., Germ.* &c.

Buail do chuilean, agus 's ann thugad a ruitheas e.—*Beat your puppy, and it's to you he'll run.*

Buailidh e bròg ort fhèin fhathast.—*It will hurt yourself hereafter.*

> Lit., 'strike a shoe on you'. Hitting one with a shoe was a mark of humiliation, as in the East—'Over Edom will I cast out my shoe.'—Ps. lx, 8.

Buainidh aon fhacal ceud.—*One word will set loose a hundred.*

Builgean air teanga nam breug, 's brangas air beul gun fhàitheam!— *Blister on the lying tongue, and padlock for the hemless mouth!*

Buill' air gach craoibh, 's gun chraobh ga leagail.—*A stroke at every tree, without felling any.*—*Eng.*

Buille do chù mo charaide, 's mìr do chù mo nàmhaid.—*A blow to my friend's dog, a bite to my enemy's.*

Buille gach fir air ceann an fhir charraich.—*Every man's blow on the scabby man's head.*

> A scald head is soon broken.—*Eng.*

Buille mu seach, mar a bha bàta nan each.—*Stroke about, like the horse-boat.*

> A boat with horses in it is not easily rowed.

Buill' on taod, is cead dol dachaigh.—*A stroke of the rope, and leave to go home.*

Buille sa cheann, no dhà san amhaich.—*A blow on the head, or two on the neck.*

> This applies to the killing of hares and rabbits.

Buille san t-sùil, buille sa ghlùin, buille san uilinn—na trì buillean as duilich' fhulang.—*A blow in the eye, a blow on the knee, a blow on the elbow—the three hardest blows to bear.*

Buinnigear buaidh le foighidinn.—*Patience wins victory.*

Bùrn dubh ort!—*Black water on you!*

Bùrn teth don fhaochaig, is goil gu leth don fheusgan.—*Hot water for the wilk, a boil and a half for the mussel.*

C

Cadal a' chlàrsair: seachd ràithean gun fhaireach.—*The harper's sleep: seven quarters of a year without wakening.*

Cadal a' mhuilleir 's an t-uisge dol seachad.—*The miller asleep, and the water running by.*

> Meikle water gaes by when the miller sleeps.—*Scot.*

Cadal na caorach san dris ort!—*The sheep's sleep in the briars to you!*

Cadal na deargainn air a' ghreadail dhut!—*The sleep of the flea on the gridiron to you!*

Cadal nan con sa mhuileann 's na mnathan a' criathradh.—*The sleep of dogs in the mill while the women are sifting.*

> Cadley ny moddee tra ta ny mraane creearey.—*Manx.* He sleeps as dogs do when wives sift meal.—*Eng.*, i.e., wide awake, but eyes shut—'dog-watch'.

Cadal fada ri gaoith mhòir.—*High wind and long sleep.*

Cagar na ban-ghrùdair.—*The alewife's whisper.*

> Ironical—the whisper apt to become loud. The *ban-ghrùdair* has long ago died out in the Highlands. In old times most of the ale drunk in Scotland was brewed by women.

Caib air no dheth, cùm do chas air an sgonnan.—*Iron on or off, keep your foot on the peg.*

> The *caib* of the old crooked spade, *cas-chrom*, was the iron with which it was pointed; the *sgonnan* was the peg on which the right foot was pressed. The meaning is 'Keep working, even with a defective implement.'

Caidlidh duine air gach cneadh ach a chneadh fhèin.—*A man can sleep on every hurt but his own.*

> Mal d' autrui n'est que songe.—*Fr.* Let er den Byrde som en anden bær.—*Dan.*

Caillear bò an droch mhuthaich seachd bliadhna ron mhithich.—*The cow of the bad herdman is lost seven years too soon.*

Caillear bò buachaille.—*A herdman's cow may be lost.*

Càirdeas Chonain ris na deamhain.—*Conan's friendship for the devils.*

> 'Cuff for cuff.' See 'Beatha Chonain'.

Càirdeas na clèire—sgrìobadh is sgròbadh a chèile.—*The friendship of the clergy—scraping and scratching each other.*

'Càit a bheil thu, dhreathain-duinn?' ars an iolair. 'Tha mis' an seo, os do chionn,' ars an dreathan-donn.—*'Where art thou, wren?' said the eagle. 'I am here, above thee,' said the wren.*

> The wren and eagle had a trial which would soar highest. After a considerable ascent, the eagle could see the wren nowhere and made the above inquiry. The wren was all the time perched on the eagle's back!

Càit am biodh na puirt nach faigheadh na clàrsairean?—*Where would the tunes be the harpers could not find?*

Caith mar a gheibh, 's gheibh mar a chaitheas.—*Spend as you get, and you'll get as you spend.*

> There is that scattereth and yet increaseth.—*Prov.* xi, 24.

Caitheamh crìontaig air a cualaig.—*The scrub's spending of her little faggot.*

Caithidh bò ri bleoghann, agus each ri treabhadh.—*Cows wear with milking, and horses with ploughing.*

Caithidh domhan duine.—*The world wears out man.*

Call caraid tadhal tric, 's call caraid tadhal ainmig.—*Friends are lost by calling often, and by calling seldom.*

> Withdraw thy foot from thy neighbour's house, lest he be weary of thee, and hate thee.—*Prov.* xxvi, 17. A casa de tu hermano no irás cada serano.—*Span.*

Calum beag a chur a dhìth gu Murchadh mòr a reamhrachadh.—*Starving little Malcolm to fatten big Murdoch.*

> Robbing Peter to pay Paul.

Camshronaich bhog an ime.—*The soft buttery Camerons.*

> This, like most similar sayings about clans, originated, of course, among enemies. The Camerons were said to be very fond of butter; but who could deny that they were brave?

Caomhain, 's cò dha? Cuimhnich am bàs.—*Save, and for whom? Remember death.*

> It is said in *An Teachd. Gael*, Vol. I, p. 282, that this excellent saying was found engraved on a stone at the top of Ben Lawers, but no authority is given for the statement.

Caomhnadh a' chama-chnòdain, caomhnadh as miosa na caith-eamh.—*The saving of the crooked gurnet—worse than spending.*

> Applied to mean gruff persons.

Caomhnadh math air a' bheagan Bheurla, 's a' Ghalltachd gu lèir romhainn!—*Be sparing of the little English, with the whole Lowlands in front of us!*

> Said by an old man to his son on their way to the Falkirk market when the son, who had a little more English than the old man, began to air it at Dumbarton.

Caora luideagach a thèid san dris, fàgaidh i h-olainn san dos.—*The ragged sheep that goes into the briers will leave her wool there.*

Car an aghaidh cuir.—*Turn against twist.*

> Diamond cut diamond.

Car tuathal d'aimhleis ort!—*The left about unlucky turn to you!*

> This is founded on the old idea that motion in the course of the sun was lucky, and in the opposite direction unlucky. *Car tuathal* literally means 'northward turn'. See *Deiseal.*

Carghas a' chion, an Carghas as miosa th' ann.—*Lent for want is worst of Lent.*

> Fasting for sheer want of food. *Carghas,* Ir. *Carghas,* Manx *Cargys,* Welsh *Garawys* = Quadragesima.

Carraig Phàidein fo na brìdich.—*Pat's rock under pigmies.*

> This is a Tiree saying, probably of Irish origin, applied to anything venerable under foot of the unworthy. The Rev. Mr Campbell, from whom I got it, says that Pàidean is the diminutive of Pàdraig and = Pat or Paddy, whence MacFadyen. But he knows no place of the name of 'Carraig Phàidein'; neither do I. Can it possibly refer to Creag Phàdraig near Inverness? Another version, however, makes it 'Carraig Fhearghais,' Carrickfergus, a well known place.

Cas air creathaill, 's làmh an cuigeil, comharradh na deagh mhnà-taighe.—*Foot to cradle, hand to distaff, mark the good housewife.*

> The foot at the cradle, the hand at the reel, is a sign that a woman means to do weel.—*Scot.*

Cas circ' an criathar.—*A hen's foot in a sieve.*

> A bad or unpleasant fit.

Casan tioram Chlann an Tòisich.—*The dry feet of the Macintoshes.*

> This refers to some occasion when the Macintoshes were supposed by their enemies to have been unduly averse to wetting their feet. 'Fadal Chlann an Tòisich' is of the same sort.

Cat a' chinn bhig, 's bean a' chinn mhòir.—*The small-headed cat, the big-headed woman.*

> Supposed to be the best of their kind.

Càtachaidh am biadh fiadh na beinne.—*Food will tame the mountain deer.*

Cath ceann an teallaich.—*The fireside battle.*

> *Al.*—Cath bun an t. Macintosh ascribes this saying to Hay, the mythical founder of the Errol family. The story is that, being asked by Kenneth III after the battle of Loncarty, in which he decided the day, if he had ever been in a harder fight, he replied that he had a harder battle every day at home—a scolding wife, crying children, and little to give them.

Cead na caillich don laogh mhear.—*The old wife's leave to the frisky calf.*

> When she could hold it no longer.

Ceangail teann, is faigh tèarainte.—*Fast bind, fast find.*—*Eng., Scot., Fr. &c.*

> Kiangle myr noid (nàmhaid), as yiow (gheibh) myr carrey (charaid).—*Manx.*

>> Shut doors after you: fast bind, fast find,
>> A proverb never stale in thrifty mind. *Merch. of Ven.*, II, 5.

Ceangal nighean an rìgh air a leannan.—*The king's daughter's tie to her lover.*

> Easily broken.

Ceann cnòdain, 's ceann sgadain, 's ceann goibhr' air dhroch fheannadh—trì cinn nach fhiach ithe.—*A gurnet's head, a herring's head and an ill-flayed goat's head—three heads not fit to eat.*

Ceann dearg air na bheil a-muigh!—*Red head on all that's out!*

> Said for luck when the first fish is caught.

>> Ceann guin air madainn Earraich—
>> 'S mairg a chailleadh a chaomh-charaid.

>> —*A Spring morning with a stinging head.*
>> *Who would lose his well-loved friend?*

The connection of the two ideas here is far from being obvious. The meaning seems to be that, as a bitter Spring morning is often followed by a fine day, so is the displeasure of a friend not to be taken as a ground for serious quarrel.

Ceann mòr air duine glic, 's ceann circ' air amadan.—*Big head on wise man, hen's head on fool.*

> This is more correct as a general observation than the Scotch 'Muckle head and little wit,' the German 'Dickkopf, Dummkopf,' the French 'Grosse tête, peu de sens,' the Irish 'Ceann mór ar bheagán céille,' and the Manx 'Kione mooar er y beggan cheilly'.

Ceann mòr is muineal caol, aogas an droch ghamhna.—*Big head and slender neck mark the bad stirk.*

> *Al.*— casan caol .

Ceann nathrach is earball peucaig air an Earrach.—*Spring with a serpent's head and a peacock's tail.*

> March comes in with an adder's head, and goes out with a peacock's tail.—*Eng.*

> Biting cold followed by sunny weather.

Ceannach geal nuair a thig an sneachd.—*White bargains when the snow comes.*

> Snow brings the markets down.

Ceannaich mar d'fheum is reic mar d'àilgheas.—*Buy as you must, and sell as you can.*

> Oportet patremfamilias esse vendacem, non emacem.—*Cato.*

Ceannard air fhichead air fichead saighdear.—*Twenty-one captains over twenty soldiers.*

> With four and twenty men,
> And five and thirty pipers.—*Aytoun.*

Ceannsaichidh a h-uile fear an droch bhean ach am fear aig am bi i.—*Every man can rule a shrew save he that hath her.*—*Eng.*

Cearc a' dol a dh'iarraidh geòidh.—*A hen going in quest of a goose.*

> *Al.*—Ugh na circe &c. The hen's egg gaes to the haa, to bring the goose's egg awa.—*Scot.*

Cearc reamhar a' choilich chaoil.—*Fat hen and lean cock.*

Ceàrdach dùthcha, muileann sgìreachd is taigh-òsda—na tri àit-eachan as fheàrr airson naidheachd.—*A countryside smithy, a parish mill and a public house—the three best places for news.*

Ceartas na clèire ri chèile.—*The justice of the clergy to each other.*

> Impressively illustrated in many decisions of Presbyteries, Synods, Assemblies and General Councils.

Ceilidh ciall masladh.—*Sense hides shame.*

Ceilidh gràdh gràin.—*Love hides deformity.*

Ceilidh seirc aineimh.—*Love hides blemishes.*

> Love cochereth all sins.—*Prov.* x, 12. Love shall cover a multitude of sins.—1 *Pet.* iv, 8. Τυφλὸς ὁ Ἔρως.—*Gr.* Love is blind—Love sees no faults—Love makes a good eye squint.—*Eng.* Love overlooks mony fauts.—*Scot.* Falaigheann grá gráin, agus chí fuath a lán.—*Ir.*

Cèilidh nam ban Slèibhteach.—*The visiting of the Sleat women.*

> Sleat is the southernmost parish in the Isle of Skye. Whether the women there are more given now to spending their time in afternoon calls than is the fashion elsewhere, it would be hard to say. The insinuation was, I believe, that their visits were sometimes prolonged till next morning! Jealousy probably had something to do with this saying. See 'Slèibhte riabhach nam ban bòidheach'.

Ceist an fhithich air an fheannaig.—*The raven's question to the crow.*

> The sort of question sometimes asked by a 'Great Power' of another, or perhaps smaller, Power in cases of annexation, oppression &c.

Ceist bradaig air breugaig.—*The question of the thief to the liar.*

> Asking for a certificate of character. See 'Aontachadh'.

Ceithir busacha fichead an Ile, 's ceithir àrdacha fichead am Muile.—*Twenty-four 'buses' in Islay, and twenty-four 'Ards' in Mull.*

> A common termination of names of places in Islay is *bus* or *bos* (generally *bost* in Skye and Lewis), from the Norse *bolstað or bustaðr* 'a dwelling-place'. The Gaelic prefix *àrd* or *àird*, a height or promontory, is common in Mull and elsewhere.

Ceò Foghair, sneachd Earraich.—*Autumn fog, Spring snow*.

Ceum air do cheum, a chailleach, 's an ceum barrachd aig Eògh-ann.—*Step for step to thee, old woman, and the odd step to Ewen*.

> The story is that Sir Ewen Cameron of Lochiel, coming once from Inverness, was overtaken by a witch, who tried hard to pass him. 'Ceum ann, Eòghainn,' said she. He answered as above, keeping one step ahead of her, which he maintained all the way till they reached Ballachulish ferry, when he hailed the boat and got in. The ferryman wouldn't allow the witch to come in, on which she took leave of Sir E., saying, 'Dùrachd mo chridhe dhut, a ghaoil Eòghainn'!—'*My heart's desire to thee, dear Ewen!*' Sir E. knew what was what, and replied, 'Dùrachd do chridhe don chloich ghlais ud thall'—'*Thy heart's desire to that gray stone yonder.*' And at that moment the gray stone split in two! (See *Gael*, Vol. IV, p. 113.) That split stone is still pointed out on the spot where it happened.

Cha b'ann air brochan lom dubh, 's bainne chruidh mhialaich as t-Earrach, a chaidh d'àrach.—*It was not on thin black gruel and milk of lousy Spring cows you were reared*.

Cha b'ann an uchd a mhàthar a bha e.—*It was not in his mother's lap he was*.

> Said of one roughly handled.

Cha b'ann às do bhogha fhèin a thilg thu 'n t-saighead.—*It was not from your own bow you sent that arrow*.

Cha b'ann de na h-eòin thu mur biodh am bad ort.—*You wouldn't be of the birds if you hadn't the tuft*.

Cha b'ann mar a fhuair MacRùslain na mnathan.—*Not as MacRus-lan got the women*.

> This person, a kind of Celtic Eulenspiegel, figures in several stories under the various names of MacRùsgail, MacCrùislig, MacRùslaig and MacRùslan. The above saying is founded on an apocryphal story of his having found his way, disguised as a woman, into a nunnery on an island in Loch Tay, or, according to another version, in Iona. (See Campbell's *W. H. T.*, Vol. II, pp 304–27. See also Boswell's *Tour to the Hebrides*, Carruthers's ed., p. 129.)

Cha b'e cheannach a rinn e.—*It was not by purchase he got it*.

> It comes by kind, it costs him nothing.—*Eng*.

Cha b'e a' mhuileann nach meileadh ach an t-uisge nach ruith-eadh.—*It was not the mill that wouldn't grind but the water that wouldn't run.*

Cha b'e an là am fear nach tigeadh.—*The day will come, come who may.*

Cha b'e là na gaoithe là nan sgolb.—*The windy day is not the day for thatch-wattles.*

> The *sgolb* is a wattle, generally of willow, used for fastening the thatch, and the meaning is that the fastening of the thatch must not be left till the wind comes and lifts it. Ulster proverb in same words.

Cha b'e 'n clò ciar nach b'fhiach fhùcadh.—*It's not the dark home-made cloth that deserves not fulling.*

> This may be held to allude to the change of cloth, as well as of dress, which came into fashion after the despicable prohibition of tartan by Act of Parliament in 1746.

Cha b'e 'n cù mu chnàimh e.—*He was no dog over his bone.*

Cha b'e an tlàm a bh' air a chuigeil.—*That was not the stuff on his distaff.*

> I hae ither tow on my rock.—*Scot.* She hath other tow on her distaff.—*Eng.* Same as having other fish to fry.

Cha b'e sin an salann saor.—*That was no cheap salt.*

> In 1669 Charles II "appropriated an exclusive right to make salt, though only to hand it over to a courtier—the salt was consequently bad and dear. In some districts, as Galloway, the West, and the Highlands, to which the native article could not be carried, salt was wholly wanting, and the people used salt-water instead, 'by which many of them died as of plague; others being forced to buy at intolerable rates, as 16s. the boll, though they formerly had it for 4s.' "—Chambers's *Dom. Ann.* II, 332. So late as 1800, "Salt was taxed to the extent of forty times its cost."—Mackenzie's *19th Century*, p. 76.

Cha b'e sin an t-slighe 'n doras an taighe.—*That was no indoor journey.*

Cha b'e sin ciad ghlaodh-maidne bu sheirbhe leis.—*That were not the bitterest morning call to him.*

> This may refer to bagpipes or 'bitters,' both of which were at one time familiar morning heralds in Highland gentlemen's houses. If the latter, the play on words may be considered a very fair one.

Cha b'e sin deoch mhòr de dhroch cheannach.—*That was no big drink of bad bargain.*

> This seems to allude to the old practice, fortunately falling into disuse, of sealing every bargain with a good big drink.

Cha b'e sin dol don mhuileann is tighinn às.—*That was no going to the mill and returning.*

Cha b'fheàrr a' chreach air an d'fhuair.—*The spoil by which it was got was no better.*

> Said when a tenant comes to grief in land taken unmercifully from another.

Cha bheir gad air aithreachas.—*A withe won't catch repentance.*

> *Al.*—Cha leighis aithreachas breamas.—*Repentance won't cure mischief.*

Cha bheir lagh air èiginn.—*Law can't overtake necessity.*

> See 'Chan eil beart'. Angen a dydd deddf.—*Need will break law.*—*Welsh.* Nede hath no lawe.—*Eng.* Necessity has nae law.—*Scot.* Noth kennt kein Gebot.—*Germ.* Nöd bryder alle Love.—*Dan.* La necessità non ha legge.—*Ital.* Nécessité n'a pas de loi.—*Fr.*

Cha bhi am bochd sòghail saidhbhir.—*The luxurious poor will not be rich.*

Cha bhi aon duine crìonna am measg mìl' amadan.—*There is not a wise man among a thousand fools.*

Cha bhi ath-sgeul air an droch sgeul.—*Bad news is never bettered.*

Cha bhi bail air aran fuinte, no air fodar buailte.—*No sparing of baked bread or of thrashed straw.*

Cha bhi bainn' aig bò fir, 's cha bhi treabhadh an each mnatha.—*A man's cow won't yield milk, nor a woman's horse ploughing.*

> This is an exaggeration of the idea that women are the best managers of cows, and men of horses.

Cha bhi bràithreachas mu mhnaoi no mu fhearann.—*There is no partnership in women or in land.*

> Love and lordship like no fellowship.—*Eng.* Amour et seigneurie ne veulent point de compagnie.—*Fr.* Amore e signoria non soffron compagnia.—*Ital.*

Cha bhi cuimhn' air an aran nach fhan anns an sgòrnan.—*The bread is forgot that passes the throat.*

Cha bhi cuimhne air a' mhath a bha, ach cuimhnichear gu bràth am math a bhitheas.—*The good that was is forgotten, the good to come is ever in mind.*

> Ta bee eeit jarroodit—*Eaten food is forgotten.*—*Manx.* Eaten bread is forgotten.—*Eng.* Μετὰ τὴν δόσιν τάχιστα γηράσκει χάρις.—*Gr.* Rien ne viellit plus vite qu'un bien fait.—*Fr.* Val più un piacere da farsi, che cento di quelli fatti.—*It.*

Cha bhi donas toirbheartach.—*Bad won't be bountiful.*

Cha bhi dùthchas aig mnaoi no aig sagart.—*Women and priests have no birth-tie.*

> The woman that marries takes her husband's settlement, the priest's must be where the Church bids.

Cha bhi each-iasaid a chaoidh sgìth.—*A borrowed horse never tires.*

> Tw, farch benthyg!—*Gee on, hired horse!*—*Welsh.* Fremdes Pferd und eigene Sporen, haben bald den Wind verlorem.—*Germ.* Laant Hest og egne Sporer giör korte Miile.—*Dan.*

Cha bhi fios air a' chràdh gus an tig e.—*Pain is not known till it come.*

Cha bhi fear a' chiad riaraich falamh.—*The first served will not be empty.*

Cha bhi fèill air blianaich.—*Bad meat won't get market.*

Cha bhi fios air math an tobair gus an tràigh e.—*The worth of the well is not known till it dries up.*

> Ni wyddys eisiau'r ffynnon onid el yn hesp.—*Welsh.*

Cha bhi fios ciod a tha san truaill gus an tarraingear e.—*What's in the scabbard is not known till it's drawn.*

Cha bhi fòir air mnaoi gun leanabh.—*The childless woman will be helpless.*

> The Celtic philoprogenitiveness, especially as regards male offspring, is like that of the Hebrews.

Cha bhi fuachd air uallachan, air fuairead an latha.—*The fop feels no cold, however cold the day.*

> *Al.*—Cha laigh fuachd.
> Cha dennee rieaw yn voyrn feayraght.—*Pride never knew cold.*—*Manx.*
> Pride feels no cold.—*Eng.* Pride finds nae cauld.—*Scot.*

Cha bhi gean air Granndaich gus am faigh iad lite.—*Grants are not gracious till they get their porridge.*

> This is merely an alliterative version of the general observation that a man is not in such good humour before meat as after it. The same thing is said of the Campbells, the Gunns and the MacKenzies, substituting 'dìota' or 'biadh' for 'lite'.

Cha bhi luathas agus grinneas.—*Quick and fine don't combine.*

> Good and quickly seldom meet.—*Eng.* Snart og vel er sielden sammen.—*Dan.* Presto e bene non si conviene.—*Ital.*

Cha bhi miann dithis air an aon mhèis.—*Two men's desire won't be on the same dish.*

> One man's meat is another man's poison.—*Eng.*, *Scot.*

Cha bhi mo rùn gam losgadh.—*My desire (or secret) won't consume me.*

Cha bhi nàir' air a' ghortach.—*The starving man won't be bashful.*

> Rhag newyn nid oes gwyledd.—*Welsh.*

Cha bhi nàrachan treubhach, 's bidh don-bìdh air an fhear nach ith a chuid.—*The bashful won't be brave, and he'll fare ill that doesn't eat his share.*

Cha bhi sinn ga innse do na feannagan.—*We won't tell it to the crows.*

Cha bhi uaill gun dragh, 's cha bhi sinn a' draghachadh rithe.—*Pride is not without trouble, so we won't be troubled with it.*

Cha bhi 'n t-ìm sin air an roinn sin.—*That butter won't be so divided.*

Cha bhi seana ghlic òg tric fada beò.—*The early wise soonest dies.*

> Ὅν οἱ θεοὶ φιλοῦσιν ἀποθνήσκει νέος.—*Gr. (Menand).* Is cadit ante senem, qui sapit ante diem.—*Lat.* So wise, so young, they say, do ne'er live long.—*Rich. III.* Klogt Barn lever ey længe.—*Dan.*

Cha bhi suaimhneas aig eucoir, no seasamh aig droch-bheairt.—*Wrong cannot rest, nor ill deed stand.*

> There is no peace, saith my God, to the wicked.—*Isaiah* lvii, 21.

> Methought I heard a voice cry, Sleep no more!
> Macbeth does murder sleep.—*Macb.* i, 2.

Cha bhi saoithreach gun siubhal.—*The industrious must be on the move.*

Cha bhi sonas air bus lom.—*A bare mouth won't be lucky.*

> The most rational gloss for the word *lom* here seems to be one which none of the dictionaries give, but which, notwithstanding, is very applicable to the great bard Iain Lom, viz., 'curt, cutting'. The doctrine is very Celtic—politeness is better than bluntness.

Cha bhi teud rèidh san fhidhill.—*There won't be a tuned string in the fiddle.*

Cha bhi thu nas òige ri d'ionnsachadh.—*You'll never be younger to learn.*

> I.e., the sooner you know it the better.

Cha bhi Tòiseach air Tìr Inidh, 's cha bhi Tìr Inidh gun Tòiseach.—*There shall never be a Macintosh of Tirinie, nor shall Tirinie be without a Macintosh.*

> Macintosh, in a note on this, calls it 'a ridiculous prophecy concerning an ancient family in Perthshire, now extinct'; à propos of which he gives the story of their being killed by the Cummings. Tirinie is near Blair Atholl, and it is pleasant to know that a Macintosh still (1880) farms there.

> Cha bhinn teanga leam-leat,
> Cha bhithinn latha bhuat is agad;
> Cha ruiginn grinneal mo ghràidh,
> 'S cha chagnainn cùl mo chompanaich.

> —*The double tongue I love it not,*
> *I would not be now cold, now hot;*
> *Nor put my love upon the rack,*
> *Nor bite my friend behind his back.*

Cha bhi trod ach an cuid aodaich.—*Only their clothes will quarrel.*

Cha bhodach GillIosa don a h-uile fear.—*Gillies is no old man to everybody.*

> This was said by an old man at Duntulm, in Skye, to Iain Garbh, a celebrated MacLeod, who kept his galley there, where the groove is still shown, worn in the rock of the beach up and down which she was launched or drawn up. The great John wished, against the old man's advice, to set out on an expedition to Harris, and planting himself against the stem of the galley, exerted all his famed strength to shove her down, while old Gillies, with his back to the stern, resisted his efforts, and with success. When Iain Garbh gave the thing up, calling the other a 'bodach,' the old man made the above remark.

Cha bhòrd bòrd gun aran, ach 's bòrd aran leis fhèin.—*A table sans bread is no table, but bread is a table itself.*

Cha bhrìdeach air an fhaich' e.—*He is no pigmy on the battlefield.*

Cha bhrist mallachd cnàimh.—*Cursing breaks no bones.*

> See 'Cha tuit guidhe'.

Cha bhuadhaich am meata.—*The weak shall not win.*

> See 'Am fear nach misnich' and 'Cha dean tùirse'.

Cha bhuidheach gach ro dhìleas; 's mairg a dh'earbas à h-aon dìleas.—*The nearest is not always dearest; pity him whose trust is in one kinsman.*

> A little more than kin, and less than kind.—*Hamlet*, i,2.

Cha b'i an t-suirghe bean gun chosdas.—*Wooing is a costly dame.*

Cha b'ionann Ó Briain 's na Gàidheil.—*O'Brian and the Gael were not alike.*

> That O'Brian was an Irishman is all that we know of him.

Cha b'uaill gun fheum e.—*That was no useless pride.*

Cha b'uan sin air beulaibh òisge.—*That were no yearling's lamb.*

> *Al.*—laogh air beulaibh maoiseig—*a calf before a heifer.* Said of those who do something rather behind than before the time, such as marrying late.

Cha bu chòir dha cadal san fhaiche, am fear air am bi eagal nan cuiseagan.—*He that shakes at stalks should not sleep in the field.*

Cha bu dìleab air nàmhaid sin.—*That were no legacy to an enemy.*

Cha bu leis a laighe no èirigh.—*His lying down and rising up were not his own.*

> Said of one in a state of bondage, or much worried. Somewhat similar is

Cha bu shaoghal dhaibh am beatha tuille.—*Their life were life to them no more.*

Cha bu rabhadh gun leisgeul e.—*It was no unwarranted warning.*

Cha bu ruith leam ach leum.—*I would jump at it, not run.*

Cha bu tu mi, 's cha bu mhi 'n cù.—*You are not I, and I am no cur.*

> A polite Celtic form of telling a man that he is a hound.

Cha chaillear na thèid an cunnart.—*Aa 's no tint that's in hazard.*—
Scot.

> All is not lost that is in peril.—*Eng.* No se pierde todo lo que está en
> peligro.—*Span.*

Cha chall cùise sìneadh latha.—*It's not a lost cause that's adjourned.*

Cha chall na gheibh caraid.—*It's no tint what a freend gets.*—*Scot.*

Cha chaochail dubh a dhath.—*Black never changes hue.*

> *Al.*—Gabhaidh gach dath dubh, ach cha ghabh dubh dath.—*Every*
> *colour will take black, but black takes none.*
> Black will take no other hue.—*Eng.*, *Scot.* Lanarum nigræ nullum
> colorem bibunt.—*Plin.*

Cha chaoidh duin' an rud nach fhaic e.—*A man laments not what he*
does not see.

> When the eye sees not, the heart grieves not.—*Arab.* What the eye
> sees not, the heart rues not.—*Eng.*, *Scot.* Wat het oog niet en ziet, dat
> begeert het herte niet.—*Dutch.* Ojos que no ven, corazon que no
> quiebra.—*Span.*

Cha charaid ach caraid na h-airce.—*The friend in need is the only*
friend.

> I þörf skal vinar neyta.—*Icel.* Een vriend in nood is een vriend in der
> daad.—*Dutch.* Amicus certus in re incerta cernitur.—*Ennius.* Au
> besoin l'on connait l'ami.—*Fr.* A friend cannot be known in pros-
> perity.—*Eccl. (Jes.).* Câr cynwir, yn yr ing y gwelir.—*Welsh.*

Cha chat mi fhèin nach aithnich blàthach.—*I am not a cat that doesn't*
know buttermilk.

Cha cheil amadan a bheachd.—*A fool can't hide his thought.*

> Ni chêl ynfyd e feddwl.—*Welsh.* A fool uttereth all his mind.—*Prov.*
> xxix, 11. The fool's heart is in his mouth.—*Eccl. (Jes.). Arab.* A fool's
> bolt is soon shot.—*Eng.* Narren Bolzen ist bald verschossen.—*Germ.*

Cha cheil e nì a chì no chluinneas e.—*He can't hide what he sees or*
hears.

Cha cheil cearraich' a dhìsnean.—*A gamester won't conceal his dice.*

Cha cheil gruaidh cuaradh cridhe.—*The cheek hides not a hurt heart.*

Ni chêl grûdd gystudd calon.—*Welsh.*

Cha cheòl do dhuine a bhròn uile aithris.—*'Tis no music for a man to tell all his grief.*

Cha chiall saoilsinnean, 's cha ghaol ràiteannas.—*Supposing is not sense, nor is talk love.*

Stultum est dicere, putabam.—*Lat.*

Cha chinn barrag air cuid cait.—*The cat's milk makes no cream.*

Al.—Cha bhi cè air cugainn cait.
Cha dtig uachtar ar bhainne an chait.—*Ir.*

Cha chinn còinneach air clach an udalain.—*Moss grows not on the oft-turned stone.*

Al.—A' chlach a thoinndaidhear tric, cha tig còinneach oirre. This saying is found in almost every European language, ancient or modern. The usual application of it shows that a very popular saying may be founded on a very superficial analogy. It implies that the gathering of moss is a useful and meritorious function for a stone, and that the stone which innocently rolls when set in motion is not so well employed as the one that sits still and gathers moss!

The philosophy of the German proverb, 'Ein Mühlstein wird nicht moosig,' 'A millstone gets not mossy', is much better. Λίθος κυλιόμενος φυκος ὀυ ποιει.—*Gr.* Saxum volutum non obducitur musco.—*Lat.* Pietra mossa non fa musco.—*Ital.* Piedra movediza nunca moho la cubija.—*Span.* Pierre qui roule n' amasse point de mousse.—*Fr.* Wälzender Stein wird nicht moosig.—*Germ.* Een rollende steen neemt geen mos mede.—*Dutch.* Den Steen der ofte flyttes, bliver ikke mossegroet.—*Dan.* A rolling stone gathers no moss.—*Eng.* A rowin stane gathers nae fog.—*Scot.* Cha chruinnigheann cloch chasaidh caonach.—*Ir.* Y maen a dreigla ni fysygla.—*Welsh.*

Cha chinn feur air an rathad mhòr.—*Grass grows not on the high-way.*—*Eng.*

There grows nae grass at the market cross.—*Scot.* In cammino battuto erba non cresce.—*Ital.* A chemin battu ne croît pas d'herbe.—*Fr.*

Cha chluinn e glaodhaich nan còrr.—*He can't hear the crane's cry.*

>   Said of a very deaf person.

Cha chluinnte gaoir-chatha leibh.—*You would drown the battle-cry.*

>   Said to very noisy people.

Cha choileach a mhealladh am moll mi.—*I am not a cock to be caught with chaff.*

>   An old bird is not caught with chaff.—*Eng.*

Cha chòir an t-each glan a chur thuige.—*The willing horse ought not to be urged.*

>   Ní cóir gearrán éascaidh a ghréasughadh.—*Ir.* A good horse should be seldom spurred.—*Eng.* A gentle horse sud be sindle spurred.—*Scot.* Williges Pferd soll man nicht treiben.—*Germ.* Buon cavallo non ha bisogno de' sproni.—*Ital.* Cavallo que buela, no quiere espuela.—*Span.* Cavallo que voa, não quer espóra.—*Port.*

Cha chòir do dhuine a ghràdh is aithne chur a dh'aon taobh.—*One should not set his love and friendship all on one side.*

Cha chòir don chiontach a bhith reachdach.—*The wrongful should not be litigious.*

>   Ni ddyly cyfraith nis gwnel.—*Welsh.*

Cha chòir gòisinn a chur an rathad an doill.—*A snare should not be laid in the way of the blind.*

Cha chòrd muc sheasg is àl.—*A barren sow was never good to pigs.—Eng.*

Cha choisinn balbhan earrasaid, 's chan fhaigh amadan oighreachd.—*A dumby won't win a mantle, nor a fool get an inheritance.*

>   A dumb man never gets land.—*Eng.*
>   The use of the word *earrasaid* here is peculiar, the article of dress it denotes being known to us only as feminine. The second half of the proverb seems to contradict the law of primogeniture, but it means that no fool can *win* a fortune.

Cha chreach e dùthaich.—*He won't ruin a countryside.*

>   An expression of hospitality in reference to a guest.

Cha chreid an òige gun tig an aois, 's cha chreid an aois gun tig am bàs.—*Youth can't believe that age will come, nor age that death will.*

Cha chreid thu 'n t-Aog gus am faic thu 'n t-adhlac.—*You won't believe in Death till you see the burial.*

Cha chreidear an fhìrinn o bheul nam breug.—*Truth is not believed from a lying mouth.*

Cha bee breagery credit, ga dy ninsh eh y n'irriney.—*Manx.* Al bugiardo non si crede la verità.—*Ital.*

Cha chreidear fear fial gus an ruigear a chùl.—*The liberal man is not believed till his purse is drained.*

Lit., 'till his back is reached'. His difficulties are not believed so long as he has anything to give.

Cha chudthrom air loch an lach,
Cha chudthrom air each a shrian,
Cha chudthrom air caor' a h-olann,
'S cha chudthrom air colainn ciall.

—*The wild duck burdens not the loch,*
The bridle burdens not the horse,
Her wool burdens not the sheep,
And sense burdens not the body.

Al.—Cha truimid an loch *and* Cha trom leis an loch.

This fine verse is among the *Sean Fhocail* of Duncan Loudin. It was given as part of the song referred to in the note to 'Bhith fadadh teine fa loch'—*ante*, p. 65.

Cha chuimhnich an dìtheach a chù gus am bi a bhrù làn.—*The empty man doesn't remember his dog till he fills his belly.*

Cha chuir duin' a chall 'na sporan.—*A man can't put his loss into his purse.*

Cha chuir e bhuinnig air a bhrògan.—*His gain won't sole his shoes.*

Cha chuir e 'n luath mun spàrr.—*He won't send the ashes to the cross-beam.*

I.e., he won't raise a great dust.

Cha chuireadh e gad san t-srathair.—*He couldn't fix a withe in the pack-saddle.*

> Good for nothing.

Cha chuirear gad air gealladh.—*You can't put withes on promises.*

Cha chuirinn mo thuagh bheàrnach 'nad choille chrìonaich.—*I wouldn't put my notched axe into your withered wood.*

> *Al.*—'nad fhiodh carraigneach.

Cha chuirinn mo noigean air a' chial don fhear nach cuireadh deur ann.—*I wouldn't incline my noggin to him that wouldn't put a drop in it.*

> *Al.*—Na cuir do shoitheach air a chliathaich don fhear nach leasaich e.

Cha chùm an soitheach ach a làn.—*The vessel holds but its fill.*

> *Al.*—an soitheach Gàidhealach.
> Ní choinnigheann an soitheach ach a lán.—*Ir.*

Cha chùm freiteach ach deamhan.—*None but devils keep rash vows.*

Cha chumadh an Rìgh snaoisean ris a' ghaoith.—*The King himself couldn't keep the wind in snuff.*

Cha chumar cas bheò am balg.—*Living legs can't be kept in bags.*

> This *dubh-fhacal* seems to refer to the same thing as 'Cha do chuir thu do dhà chois fhathast san aon osan'—'*You haven't yet put both your legs in one hose*' = shroud.

Cha chumar taigh le beul dùinte.—*House with closed door can't be kept.*

> A very hospitable saying.

Cha daor am biadh ma gheibhear e.—*Food is not dear, if it can be got.*

Cha daoire 'n gèadh na shailleadh.—*The goose is no dearer than his salting.*

Cha deach eug no imrich nach d'fhuair moladh, 's cha do phòs nach d'fhuair càineadh.—*None died or flitted without praise, none married without blame.*

> For a more terse version, see 'Mas math leat'.

Cha deachaidh car do theadhrach mu phreas.—*Your tether didn't get round a bush.*

> Said to one who doesn't look starved.

Cha deach Theab riamh le creig.—*Almost never went over a rock.*

> Almost never was hanged.—*Eng.* Amaist was ne'er a man's life.—*Scot.*
> Nærved slaaer ingen Mand ihiel.—*Almost kills no man.—Dan.*

Cha dèan a' ghlòr bhòidheach an t-amadan sàthach.—*Fine talk won't fill the fool.*

> Fair words butter no parsnips—*Eng.* Mony words dinna fill the firlot.—*Scot.* Schöne Worte füllen den Sack nicht.—*Germ.* Belle parole non pascon i gatti.—*Ital.*

Cha dèan am balbh breug.—*Dumbie winna lee.—Scot.*

> Cha déanann balbhán bréag.—*Ir.*

Cha dèan a' phluic a' phìobaireachd.—*Puffing won't make piping.*

Cha dèan am bodach breug 's a chlann a-staigh.—*The churl won't tell lies before his children.*

> Cha déanann bodach bréag, 's a chlann i láthair.—*Ir.*
> They might innocently convict him by saying, 'O Papa'!

Cha dèan an t-òl ach am fear a dh'fhaodas.—*He only drinks who can.*

Cha dèan aon cheirean duine slàn, 's cha dèan aon sàth duine reamhar.—*One dose will not cure, nor one feed make fat.*

Cha dèan aon smeòrach Samhradh.—*One mavis makes not summer.*

> Cha déanann aon áilleog Samhradh.—*Ir.* Cha jean un ghollan-geaye Sourey, ny un chellagh-keylley Geurey.—*Manx.* Μία χελιδὼν ἔαρ ου ποιει.—*Gr.* Una hirundo non facit ver.—*Lat.* Una golondrina no hace verano.—*Span.* Une hirondelle ne fait pas le printemps.—*Fr.* Una rondine non fa primavero.—*Ital.* Eine Schwalbe macht keinen Frühling.—*Germ.* Eene zwaluw maakt geen zomer.—*Dutch.* Een Svale giör ingen Sommer—*Dan.* One swallow makes not Summer.—*Eng.*

Cha dèan brògan tioram iasgach.—*Dry shoes won't get fish.*

> No se toman truchas á bragas enjutas.—*Span.* Naõ se tomaõ trutas a bragas enxutas.—*Trouts are not taken with dry breeches.—Port.*

Cha dèan cas làidir nach ith brù mhòr.—*What strong foot earns big belly eats.*

> Ce que gantelet gagne, le gorgerin le mange.—*Fr.* Saying of Bayard. (Disraeli's *Curios. of Lit. Philosophy of Proverbs.*)

Cha dèan cas luath maorach.—*Hasty foot won't get shellfish.*

Cha dèan cat miotagach sealg.—*Cat with mittens won't catch mice.*

> The muffled cat is never good mouser.—*Eng.* Gatta inguantata non prese mai topo.—*Ital.*

Cha dèan corrag mhilis ìm, no glaimsear càise.—*Sweet finger won't make butter, nor a glutton cheese.*

Cha dean cridhe misgeach breug.—*A drunken heart won't lie.*

> *Al.*—Cha tig breug bho chridhe misgeach.
> Οἶνος, ὦ παιδες, ἀλήθεια. 'Εν οἴνω ἀλήθεια.—*Gr.* In vino veritas.—*Lat.* What soberness conceals, drunkenness reveals.—*Eng.* A fu man 's a true man.—*Scot.*

Cha dèan cù sàthach sealg.—*A full dog won't hunt.*

Cha dèan duine don' ach a dhìcheall.—*A poor fellow can do but his best.*

> Ni eill neb namyn ei allu.—*None can do but what he can.*—*Welsh.*

Cha dèan fear an sporain fhalaimh ach beag faraim san taigh-òsda.— *The man of empty purse will make but little noise in the inn.*

Cha dèan fuar bliochd.—*Cold will not make milk.*

The use of the adjective as a noun here is worthy of notice.

Cha dèan goile acrach casaid air a' bhiadh.—*A hungry stomach won't decry the food.*

Cha dèan làmh ghlan eòrna.—*Clean hand won't make barley.*

Cha dèan mi dà chliamhainn do m'aon nighinn.—*I won't make two sons-in-law for my one daughter.*

> Eigi má göra tvá mága at einne dóttur.—*Icel.*

Cha dèan minnean meann, 's cha dèan giullan clann.—*A kid begets not kids, nor a boy bairns.*

Cha dèan sinn cruit-chiùil deth.—*We won't make a harp of it.*

> *Al.*—Cha dèan sinn òran deth.—*We won't make a song of it.* Cruit,
> Scot. and Ir. Gael., a harp or fiddle; *Crwth*, Welsh; *Crowd*, Eng., a
> fiddle. The pipe, the tabor, and the trembling croud.—*Spenser.*
> Chevy-chase sung by a blind crowder.—*Sidney.*

Cha dèan thusa toll nach cuir mise cnag ann.—*You won't make a
hole that I won't put a peg in.*

> Autant de trous, autant de chevilles.—*Fr.*

Cha dèan 'Tiugainn' ceum, 's cha do chailleadh 'Theab'.—*'Come
on' does not move, and 'Almost' was never lost.*

Cha dèan sgleogaireachd ceilp.—*Fulsome talk won't make kelp.*

Cha dèan 'Tapadh leis an fhìdhlear' am fìdhlear a phàigheadh.—
'Thank you' won't pay the fiddler.

Cha dean tùirse ach truaghan, 's fear na lag-mhisnich, chan fhaigh
e bean ghlic gu Là Luain.—*None but the pitiful pine, and weak heart
will never win wise wife.*

> Faint heart never won fair lady.—*Eng., Scot.* Jamais honteux n'eut
> belle amie.—*Fr.* Verzagt' Herz freit nimmer ein schön' Weib.—*Germ.*
> Bange Hierte vandt aldrig fager Mö.—*Dan.*

Cha dèanar banas-taighe air na fraighean falamh.—*Housekeeping
can't be done with empty shelves.*

> A toom pantry makes a thriftless guidwife.—*Scot.* Bare walls make
> giddy housewives.—*Eng.* Vides chambres font femmes folles.—*Fr.*

Cha dèanar buannachd gun chall.—*No profit without loss.*

Cha dèanar duine glic ach air a chosd fhèin.—*One gets wisdom at his
own cost.*

> See 'Is fheàrr aon chiall ceannaich'.

Cha dèanar leas caraid gun saothair.—*Friend can't be helped without
trouble.*

Cha dèanar math gun mhulad.—*Good is not done without grief.*

Cha dèanar sagart gun fhoghlam, 's cha dèan foghlam sagart.—*A
priest should be learned, but learning won't make a priest.*

Cha dèanar salann gun sàl, no leas bràthar gun dìobhail.—*Salt is not made without brine, nor brother's help without loss.*

Cha dèanar seabhag den chlamhan.—*You cannot make hawks of kites.*

> A carrion kite will never make a good hawk.—*Eng.* On ne saurait faire d'une buse un épervier.—*Fr.*

Cha dèanar trèine gun triùir, 's bidh iad crùbach gun cheathrar.—*Three go to make strength, and they'll be lame without four.*

Cha deic luas na h-earba gun na coin a chur rithe.—*The swiftness of the roe is known without the loosing of the hounds.*

Cha deoch-slàint' i gun a tràghadh.—*It is no health if not drained.*

> 'No heel-taps'!

Cha d'eug duine beairteach riamh gun dìleabach.—*No rich man ever died without an heir.*

Cha d'fhàg e clach gun tionndadh.—*He left no stone unturned.*

> Char fhág sé cloch gan tiontadh.—*Ir.*

Cha d'fhàg claidheamh Fhinn riamh fuigheall beuma.—*Fingal's sword never had to cut twice.*

Cha d'fhuair am madadh-ruadh riamh teachdaire b'fheàrr na e fhèin.—*The fox never got a better messenger than himself.*

Cha d'fhuair Conan riamh dòrn gun dòrn a thoirt ga cheann.—*Conan never got a blow without returning it.*

> See 'Càirdeas Chonain'.

Cha d'fhuair droch bhuanaiche riamh deagh chorran.—*Bad reaper never got good sickle.*

> Chan fhuair droch bhuanaidhe a riamh corrán maith.—*Ir.* Cha dooar rieau drogh veaynee corran mie.—*Manx.* Never had ill workman good tools.—*Eng. Per con.* Cha d'fhuair buanaiche math droch corran riamh. Ni ddiffygion arf ar was gwych.—*Weapon to the brave won't be wanting.*—*Welsh.*

Cha d'fhuair droch iomramhaiche ràmh math riamh.—*Bad rower never got good oar.*

Cha d'fhuair duine riamh a thuarasdal gus an do choisinn e e.—*No man wages ever got until for them he had wrought.*

Cha d'fhuair sgathadh nach d'fhuiling nàire.—*Scorn comes commonly wi skaith.*—*Scot.*

> Eshyn yiow skeilley (*sgèileadh*), yiow e craid (*cnead*).—*Manx.*

Cha d'fhuair sruth leis nach d'fhuair sruth 'na aghaidh.—*None ever got tide with him that did not get against him.*

Cha d'fhuair sùil ghionach riamh cunnradh math.—*Greedy eye never got good bargain.*

Cha d'fhuaradh an Donas riamh marbh air cùl gàrraidh.—*The Devil was never found dead behind a dyke.*

> Seldom lies the Devil dead in a ditch.—*Eng.* It's lang ere the Deil dee by the dyke-side.—*Scot.*
> This well expresses the vitality of the Father of Lies.

Cha d'fhuaradh buaidh air fear na moch-èirigh.—*The early riser was never overcome.*

Cha d'fhuaradh cliath-chliata riamh air cladach.—*A harrow was never found on a shore.*

Cha d'fhuiling fuachd nach d'fhuair teas.—*None suffered cold but got heat.*

Cha dhubh grian 's cha ghealaich uisg' e.—*Sun won't blacken nor water bleach it.*

Cha dìol 'toileach' fiach.—*'Willing' pays no debt.*

> Sorrow will pay no debt.—*Eng.*

Cha d'ith na coin an aimsir.—*The time was not devoured by the dogs.*

> And yet it was wasted.
> The translation of this in the 2nd ed. of Macintosh is 'The dogs did not worry the wether'! Char ith na madaidh deireadh na bliana go fóill.—*Ir.*

Cha d'ith thu seachd cruachan-arbhair leis fhathast.—*You haven't eaten seven corn-stacks with him yet.*

> *Al.*—Cha do loisg thu seachd cruachan-mòna leis—*You haven't burnt seven peat-stacks with him.*

Cha diùlt peann breug.—*A pen won't refuse to lie.*

> Polite falsehoods are more easily written than said.

Cha dlighe do pheighinn fois.—*Penny's right is not rest.*

> Argent est rond, il faut qu'il roule.—*Fr.* I danari vanno e vengono.—
> *Ital.*

Cha do bhrist modh ceann duine riamh.—*Courtesy never broke a man's crown.*

> 'It's aye gude to be ceevil,' quo the auld wife when she beckit to the Deevil.—*Scot.*

Cha do bhrist fear riamh a bhogha nach d'fheum fear eil' an t-sreang.—*No man ever broke his bow but another needed the string.*

Cha do bhuidhinn thu air na cairtean nach do chaill thu air na dìsnean.—*You won not at the cards that you lost not at the dice.*

Cha do bhuidhinn tùs nach do bhuidhinn donas.—*Luck at first, loss at last.*

> Chi vince prima, perde il sacco e la farina.—*Ital.*

Cha do chaill 'na thoiseach nach do bhuannaich 'na dheireadh.—*Lose at first, win at last.*

Cha do chailleadh bàta riamh 's i giùlan nan seòl.—*A boat was never lost that carried her sail.*

Cha do chleachd am bodach biodag.—*The old man was not used to a dirk.*

Cha do chliath thu na threabh mise fhathast.—*You haven't harrowed yet what I have ploughed.*

Cha do chòrd dithis riamh a' cur tein' air.—*Two never agreed at the kindling of a fire.*

> See 'Cha robh dithis'.
> Char fhadaigh dís teine gan troid.—*Ir.*

Cha do chuir a bhun ris nach do chinnich leis.—*None trusted him that did not thrive.*

> [MacInnes has 'Him'.]

Cha do chuir a ghualainn nach do chuir tuar thairis.—*None ever set his shoulder to that did not what he sought to do.*

Cha do chuir Dia riamh beul thun an t-saoghail gun a chuid fa chomhair.—*God never sent the mouth but the meat with it.*—*Scot., Eng.*

> Char órdaigh Dia béal gan biadh.—*Ir.* Gud giver alle Mad, som han giver Mund.—*Dan.* Guð gefr björg með barni.—*Icel.*

Cha do dhìrich Fionn bruthach riamh, 's cha d' fhàg e bruthach gun dìreadh.—*Fingal never climbed a brae, and he left no brae unclimbed.*

> This is a puzzle more than a proverb. It means that F., being a wise man, zig-zagged up hills.

Cha do dhùin doras nach d'fhosgail doras.—*No door ever shut but another opened.*

> *Al.*—Ged dhùinear doras, fosglar doras.
> Mai si serra una porta, che non si apra un' altra.—*Ital.* Donde una puerta se cierra, otra se abre.—*Span.*
> This proverb is the one quoted by Don Quixote when he made the interesting reflection on proverbs already cited under 'An seanfhacal'.

Cha do loisg duine riamh a thaigh ron chreich ach aon duine, 's ghabh e aithreachas.—*None ever burnt his house before the foray but one, and he repented.*

> The anticipated foray never came!

Cha do mheall e ach na dh'earb às.—*He tricked but those who trusted him.*

Cha do mhill foighidinn mhath duine riamh.—*Good patience never hurt a man.*

Cha d'òl an sagart ach na bh' aige.—*The priest drank only what he had.*

Cha d'òrdaich Dia don duine bhochd an dà latha cho olc.—*Two days alike ill God to poor men doth not will.*

Cha d'rinn iad de shiùcar no de shalann thu.—*You weren't made of sugar or salt.*

> This proverb cannot claim great age.

Cha d'rinn sàr nach d'fhuiling sàr.—*None ever did violence but suffered violence.*

All they that take the sword shall perish with the sword.—*Matth.* xxvi, 52.

Cha d'rinn Theab riamh sealg.—*'Almost' never got game.*

See 'Cha deach Theab'.

Cha d'rinn uisge glan riamh leann math.—*Pure water never made good ale.*

This may be classed among 'vulgar errors'.

Cha d'rug fear na caithris riamh air fear na moch-èirigh.—*The night-watcher never overtook the early riser.*

Cha do shèid gaoth riamh nach robh an seòl cuideigin.—*No wind ever blew that did not fill some sail.*

Cha do shoirbhich dithis riamh air an aon chnoc.—*No two ever prospered on the same hill.*

Comp. with 'Cha bhi bràithreachas'.

Cha do shuidh air cloich nach duirt 'Oich!' mun d'èirich.—*None ever sat on stone that didn't sigh before he rose.*

Cha do shuidh air stiùir nach tàinig bho làimh uaireigin. *No man ever held helm that did not some time lose his hold.*

Cha leasachadh air droch obair-latha bhith fada gun tòiseachadh.—*It's no mending of a bad day's work to be long of beginning.*

Al.—gun sgur—*without stopping.*

Cha mhair a' ghrian mhaidne rè an latha.—*The morning sun won't last all day.*

Cha tàinig eun glan riamh à nead a' chlamhain.—*Clean bird never came out of kite's nest.*

Cha tàinig iasg às a' chuan nach eil cho math ann.—*There's as guid fish in the sea as ever cam oot o't.*—*Scot.*

Al.—Tha iasg cho math anns a' mhuir 's a thàinig riamh aiste. Tá iasg sa bhfairge níos fearr ná gabhadh a riamh.—*Ir.*

Cha tàinig tràigh gun mhuir-làn 'na dèidh.—*There never was ebb without flood following.*

> See 'Chan eil tuil'.

Cha tàinig ugh mòr riamh bhon dreathain-duinn.—*Large egg never came from the wren.*

> *Al.*—Cha tig.
> The Scottish version of this is applied, says Kelly, to insignificant gifts from niggardly persons.

Cha do thaisg nach d'fhimir.—*Nought was ever laid by that was not needed.*

> Keep a thing seven years, and ye'll find a use for't.—*Scot.*

Cha do thilg le leth-làimh nach do thionail le dhà làimh.—*None threw away with one hand that did not gather with both.*

> Chi butta via oro con le mani, lo cerca co' piedi.—*Ital.*

Cha do threabh thu 'n t-imir tha romhad fhathast.—*You haven't ploughed the ridge before you yet.*

> *Al.*—Treabh an t-imir a tha romhad an toiseach.
> Ars an t-each òg sa mhadainn, 'Treabhaidh sinn an t-imir ud, 's an t-imir ud eile.' Ars an seann each, 'Treabh am fear tha romhad an dràsda, 's treabhaidh sinn càch a-rithist.' Agus threabh an seann each, 's thug an t-each òg thairis.—*Said the young horse in the morning, 'We'll plough that ridge and the other one.' Said the old horse, 'Plough the one before you now, and we'll plough the rest after.' And the old horse ploughed, but the young one gave over.*

Cha do thrèig Fionn riamh caraid a làimhe deise.—*Fingal never forsook his right hand friend.*

Cha tug Fionn riamh blàr gun chumha.—*Fingal never fought a fight without offering terms.*

> This very old proverb, and the still oftener quoted one, 'Cothrom na Fèinne' (q.v.), indicate a sense of justice and generosity of which the most civilised nations of the 19th century exhibit too little in the conduct of war. Fionn or Fingal, the ideal hero-king of the Scoto-Irish race, corresponds in character, and in domestic misfortune, to King Arthur—faithful to his friends, generous to his enemies, mighty in war, gentle and wise in peace. The name Fingal, and the adjective

Fingalian, being now so generally used, are preferable, for that and
other reasons, to Finn and Fenian, though the latter are more strictly
correct. The name Fingal is not an invention of Macpherson's, as
some have imagined. It was used by Barbour in the 14th century as
the name by which the Celtic hero was then known in Scotland—

> He said, Mee thinke Martheokes sonne,
> Right as Golmakmorne was wonne,
> To have from Fyngall his menyie.
>   *The Bruce,* ed. 1620, p. 40.

Cha tug gaol luath nach tug fuath clis.—*Hasty love and sudden hate.*

Love me little, love me long.—*Eng.* Aime-moi un peu, mais continue.—*Fr.* Amami poco, ma continua.—*Ital.* Elsk mig lidt, og elsk
mig længe.—*Dan.*

Cha tug leis an truaill nach d'fhuair leis a' chlaidheamh.—*None gave
with the scabbard but got with the sword.*

Cha tug thu ach breab bheag sa ghrìosaich.—*You gave but a slight
kick to the embers.*

Cha tug thu do long fhèin gu cala fhathast.—*You haven't brought
your own ship to port yet.*

Cha tug thu ribeag à fheusaig.—*You haven't plucked a hair out of his
beard.*

Cha duirt Dia na thuirt thusa.—*God hath not said all thou hast said.*

Applicable to much theology, and other things claiming divine authority. Considering that the Celts are by nature reverential, this saying
does them great credit.

Cha dual do rath a bhith air dalta spìocaid.—*The step-child of a scrub
has a bad lot.*

Cha duine duine 'na aonar.—*A man alone is no man.*

See note to 'Bi 'd thosd'.
Al.—Chan fhiach duine 'na aonar.
It is not good that the man should be alone.—*Gen.* ii, 18. Εἰς
ἀνήρ οὐδεὶς ἀνήρ. Gr. Un homme nul homme.—*Fr.* One and none
is all one.—*Eng.* Compagnia d'uno, compagnia di niuno.—*Ital.*

Cha duine glic a dh'innseas tric anshocair.—*He is not wise who often tells his trouble.*

Cha duine glic a thèid tric don bhaile mhòr.—*He is not a wise man who goes often to the city.*

Cha ghabh fiadh gointe gaoth.—*A wounded deer won't take the wind.*

> A wounded deer always takes to the nearest water, instead of going, as usual, against the wind.

Cha ghabh i coisiche, 's cha tig marcaiche ga h-iarraidh.—*She won't take a walker, and a rider won't come for her.*

> She wadna hae the walkers, and the riders gaed by.—*Scot.*
> Dean Ramsay, in his *Reminiscences*, gives this proverb as quoted by Miss Becky Monteith, on being asked how she hadn't made a good marriage.

Cha ghabhar grèim air uisge no air teine.—*No hold can be got of water or of fire.*

Cha ghille mur h-umhailt e.—*He is no servant unless he obeys.*

Cha ghlac dòrn dùinte seabhag.—*Closed fist won't catch hawk.*

> Cha ghabhann an dorn druidte seabhac.—*Ir.* With emptie hands men may no hawkes lure.—*Chaucer.* Det er ondt at lokke Höge med tomme Hænder.—*Dan.* Met ledige handen is het kwaad havikken vangen.—*Dutch.*

Cha ghlèidh an dall an rathad mòr.—*The blind can't keep the highway.*

> This is true only in a metaphorical sense.

Cha ghleidheadh tu clach sa chladach.—*You wouldn't find a stone on the shore.*

Cha ghluais bròg no bruidhinn an droch bhean-thaighe.—*Tramping or talking won't rouse the bad housewife.*

> Ascribed to Eòghann a' Chinn Bhig. See App. III.

Cha ghruagaichean gu lèir air am bi am falt fhèin.—*All are not maidens that wear their own hair.*

> Aa arena maidens that wear bare hair.—*Scot.*
> To drop the snood, or fillet, and cover the head was formerly, both in the Highlands and Lowlands of Scotland, the sign of marriage or maternity. The old Highland head-dress of women, called *brèid*, was a square of fine linen, pinned round the head, with part hanging down behind, like some of the head-dresses in Normandy and Brittany.— Armstr. *Dict. s.v. brèid.*

Cha laigh na siantan anns na speuran.—*The storms rest not in the skies.*

> Ne caldo ne gelo resta mai in cielo.—*Ital.*

Cha le duine fhèin a ghàire.—*A man's smile is not his own.*

> I have been told by a wise counsellor that an old man advised him always to have his consulting chair set with its back to the window.

Cha leannan òinsich e.—*He is no foolish girl's fancy.*

> This and the next are generally said ironically of old or unprepossessing 'parties'.

Cha leannan baothair i.—*She is no sweetheart for a fool.*

Cha leithne Loch Obha null na nall.—*Loch Awe is no broader across than back.*

> *Al.*—Cha lugh' an uchdach na 'n leathad.—*The ascent is no less than the declivity.* 'It's as broad as it's long.'

Cha leig an leisg da deòin duin' air slighe chòir am feasd.—*If laziness but have its will, it keeps a man from virtue still.*

> For the credit of humanity, there are many proverbs of all nations directed against the vice of sloth.

Cha leig duine da dheòin a chòir-bhreith le duine beò.—*No man willingly parts with his birthright.*

Cha leigear a leas pòg a thabhairt do làimh an iasgair.—*The hand of the fisher need not be kissed.*

Cha leighis aithreachas breamas.—*Repentance won't cure mischief.*

Cha lèir dhut a' choill leis na craobhan.—*You can't see the wood for trees.—Eng.*

Cha lìon beannachd brù.—*Fair words fill not the belly.—Eng.*

> Cha líonann beannacht bolg.—*Ir.* Muckle crack fills nae sack.—*Scot.* Schoone worden vullen den zak niet.—*Dutch.*
>
> See 'Cha dèan a' ghlòr'.

Cha loisg seana chat e fhèin.—*An old cat won't burn himself.*

Cha luaithe a sguireas an tinneas diot na thòisicheas an tachas ort.—*No sooner does your sickness go than the itch attacks you.*

Cha luaithe duine gu leas na gu aimhleas.—*Man goes not faster to his good than to his ruin.*

Cha lugha air Dia deireadh an latha na thoiseach.—*Not less in God's sight is the end of the day than the beginning.*

> This is a fine sentiment, from every point of view.

Cha lugha an fhoill na 'm freiceadan.—*The treachery is not less than the guard.*

Cha lugha ceann na cèill.—*As mony heads, so mony wits.—Scot.*

> Quot homines, tot sententiae.—*Ter.* Tante teste, tanti cervelli.—*Ital.* Autant de têtes, autant d'avis.—*Fr.* So many men, so many minds.—*Eng.* Viele Köpfe, viele Sinne.—*Germ.* Zoo veel hoofden, zoo veel zinnen.—*Dutch.* Saa mange Hoveder, saa mange Sind.—*Dan.*

Cha mhac mar an t-athair thu.—*You are no son like the father.*

> 'You'll never fill your father's shoes.'

Cha mhair a' bhreug ach rè seal.—*No lie lives long.*

> A lying tongue is but for a moment.—*Prov.* xii, 19. The liar is short-lived.—*Arab.* Lügen zerschmelzen wie Schnee.—*Germ.*

Cha mhair an sionnach air a shìor-ruith.—*Reynard can't run for ever.*

Cha mheallar am fear glic ach aon uair.—*The wise man is deceived but once.*

> Twice bitten, shy.—*Eng.*

Cha mhillear math ri olc dhiubh.—*The good of them won't be thrown away on the bad.*

Not much to choose between them.

Cha mhinig a bha moll aig sabhal pìobaire.—*Seldom is there chaff at a piper's barn.*

Pipers and poets are generally not very good husbandmen.

Cha mhisd' a' ghealach na coin a bhith comhartaich rithe.—*The moon is none the worse of the dogs' barking at her.*

Al.—Cha dean e coire don ghealaich na coin a bhith deileann rithe. The moon heeds not the barking of dogs.—*Eng.* La luna non cura l'abbaiar de' cani.—*Ital.* Was kümmert 's den Mond wenn ihn die Hunde anbellen?—*Germ.*

Cha mhisde cùil ghlan a rannsachadh.—*A clean corner is not the worse of being searched.*

Cha mhisde gnìomh math a dhèanamh dà uair.—*A good deed is not the worse of being done again.*

Δὶς καὶ τρὶς τὸ κάλον.—*Gr.*

Cha mhisde sgeul math aithris dà uair.—*A good tale is none the worse for being twice told.—Eng.*

Cha mhò air e 's air seann each athair.—*He cares no more for him than an old horse for his sire.*

Cha mhol duin' a sheud 's e aige.—*A man doesn't praise his jewel while he has it.*

Probably not till he loses it.

Cha mhurtar an luchag fon chruaich-fheòir.—*The mouse is not crushed under the haystack.*

A wee mous will creep under a muckle cornstack.—*Scot.*

Chan abair mi mo bhràthair ach ris a' mhac a rug mo mhàthair.—*I will not say brother but to my mother's son.*

> *Al.*—Cha phiuthar is cha bhràthair ach neach a bheireas a' mhà-thair.—*None is sister or brother whom the mother bore not.*
>
> This looks like a relic of a time when birthrights and blood-ties were calculated from the maternal rather than the paternal side, of which Mr Skene has found traces in the early history of our country.—*Celtic Scotland*, Vol. I, p. 252. See also MacLennan's *Primitive Marriage*, 2nd ed., p. 129.

Chan aithne dhut dol air d'each gun dol thairis air.—*You cannot mount your horse without going over.*

Chan aithnich am fuachd tighead na lùirich.—*The thickest coat of mail won't keep out the cold.*

Chan aithnicheadh e bhròg seach an t-osan.—*He couldn't tell his shoe from his stocking.*

> Very incapable, even beyond pronunciation of 'Bri'sh const-t-'sh'n'.

Chan aithnichinn e ged thachradh e 'nam bhrochan orm.—*I shouldn't know him if I met him in my gruel.*

Chan àm cadail an cogadh.—*War is no time for sleep.*

Chan ann a h-uile latha bhios mòd aig Mac an Tòisich.—*It is not every day that Macintosh holds a court.*

> "Toschach or Macintosh of Monyvaird, chamberlain to the Earl of Perth, held a regality court at Monyvaird: it is commonly reported that he caused one to be hanged each court day, in order to make himself famous, and to strike terror into the thieves, which severity occasioned the above saying."—Note by Macintosh on this proverb, 1st ed., p. 13.
>
> The word *mòd*, the same as the Saxon and Scottish *mote*, signifies a meeting, assembly, court of justice. The Celtic courts of justice were held on hills or mounds made for the purpose, of which several, called *moats*, or *mutes*, are still to be seen in Kirkcudbrightshire, and elsewhere. Skene, *De verb. signif.*, 1681, p. 93, says, "Quhen King Malcolme the Second gave all his landes to the barrones of this realme; he reteined to himself 'montem placiti de Scona,' the mute hill of Scone, quhair he might hald his courtes, and do justice to his subjects, in deciding their pleyes and controversies."—See Jamieson's *Dict. s.v. mote.*

Chan ann a h-uile latha thèid MacNèill air each.—*It is not every day that MacNeil mounts his horse.*

> This refers to MacNeil of Barra, whose rocky island territory was more suited for boating than for riding.

Chan ann ag èigheach às do dheaghaidh, ach—Càit a bheil thu dol?—*Not calling after you, but—Where are you going?*

Chan ann air chnothan falamh a fhuaradh siud uile.—*It was not for empty nuts all that was got.*

Chan ann am Bòid uile tha 'n t-olc—tha cuid deth sa Chumradh bheag làimh ris.—*The mischief is not all in Bute—there's some in the little Cumbrae near it.*

> The use of *uile* here as an adverb is peculiar.

Chan ann às an adhar a tha e toirt a chodach.—*It's not out of the air he gets his living.*

Chan ann de mo chuideachd *thu*, chan ann de mo chuideachd *thu*, ars an calman.—*You are not of my flock, not of my flock, said the dove.*

> This is a pretty imitation of the cooing of a dove.

Chan ann den ghuin an gàire.—*Smiles do not suit with pain.*

> *Al.*—Gàire mu adhbhar a' ghuin.

Chan ann de shìolachadh a' phoca-shalainn thu.—*You are not of the seed of the salt-pock.*

> Sometimes said to boys sent out in the rain = You won't melt.

Chan ann gun fhios carson a bheireas a' chearc ugh.—*It's not for nothing the hen lays an egg.*

> The husband knows this to his cost, but the wife also knows the value of an egg.

Chan ann gun fhios carson a nì an clamhan fead.—*It's no for nought that the gled whustles.—Scot.*

Chan ann leis a' chiad bhuille thuiteas a' chraobh.—*The tree faas na at the first strake.—Scot.*

> One stroke fells not an oak.—*Eng.* Es fällt keine Eiche vom ersten Streiche.—*Germ.* Al primo colpo non cade l'albero.—*Ital.* Au premier coup ne chet pas l'arbre.—*Fr.* Τὸ δένδρον μὲ μίαν πελεκειὰν δὲν κόφτεται.—*Mod. Gr.*

Chan atharraich caraid gnùis caraid.—*A friend won't change a friend's countenance.*

Chan aotruim' òr na chudthrom.—*Gold is no lighter than its weight.*

Chan e 'm beagan an gràn-lagain, ma ghabhas e togail.—*The grain that falls is not trifling if it can be lifted.*

> The *gràn-lagain* is the grain that falls through the straw when it is put on the kiln.

Chan e 'm bòrd a theirig dhut ach am beagan fearainn.—*Not your mould-board was done, but your little land.*

> The mould-board of the old plough was made of wood, like all the rest of it except the share. But the failing of the plough was a small matter, compared with want of land to plough.

Chan e an ro-chabhag as fheàrr.—*Great haste is not best.*

> The more haste, the worse speed.—*Eng., Scot.* Hoe meerder haast, hoe minder spoed.—*Dutch.* Qui nimis propere minus prospere.—*Lat.* Plus on se hâte, moins on avance.—*Fr.* Chi va piano, va sano, e va lontano.—*Ital.* Quien mas corre, menos vuela.—*Span.*

Chan e ciad sgeul an t-sagairt bu chòir a chreidsinn.—*It is not the priest's first story that should be believed.*

> This is probably a very old saying, and it quite accords with the strain of the Ossianic ballads narrating St Patrick's attempts to convert Ossian. The Celt is not easily convinced of anything new or opposed to his old beliefs, but once he believes, he believes intensely.

Chan e cruadhachadh na h-àtha sealltainn foidhpe.—*Looking under the kiln won't dry the grain.*

Chan e dubh a dh'fhuathaicheas, 's chan e geal a ghràdhaicheas.—*Hate comes not of black, nor love of white.*

Chan e faighinn na feudalach as miosa, ach a cumail an deaghaidh a faotainn.—*The getting of the cattle is not so hard as the keeping after getting.*

Chan e gogadh nan ceann a nì an t-iomradh.—*It is not the nodding of heads that does the rowing.*

Chan e mheud a bhòidhicheas no ghil' a ghràdhaicheas.—*Bulk makes not beauty, nor white loveliness.*

Chan e mo charaid a nì m'aimhleas.—*He is not my friend that hurts me.*

> 'Candid' friends are sometimes the worst of enemies.

Chan e 'n latha math nach tigeadh ach an duine dona nach fanadh.—*It is not that the good day came not, but that the unlucky man would not wait.*

Chan e na chosnar a nì saidhbhir ach na chaomhnar.—*Not what's gained but what's saved makes rich.*

> A penny hained 's a penny gained.—*Scot.* Magnum est vectigal parcimonia.—*Cic.*

Chan e na dh'ithear a nì làidir ach na chnàmhar.—*Not what's eaten but what's chewed makes strong.*

Chan e na leughar a nì foghlaimte ach na chuimhnichear.—*Not what's read but what's remembered makes learned.*

Chan e rogha nam muc a gheibh fear na faighe.—*It is not the pick of the swine that the beggar gets.*

> This saying suggests an Irish origin, pigs having never been very common in the Highlands. The practice of going 'air faighe' (or *faoighe,* Ir. *foighe*) was, however, common to parts of Ireland and of the Highlands, and was known also in the Lowlands of Scotland. See Jamieson's *Dict., s.v. thig.* In the 'good old times', when dearth was as common as a bad season, it was not considered degrading for respectable people to go foraging among their friends for grain, wool &c. See 'Bidh rud uime'. This kind of begging was also practised by or for young couples about to marry, or newly married, to help them in setting up house. The Highl. Soc. *Dict.* (1828) says this custom 'is still practised in many parts of the Highlands and Islands.' MacLeod and Dewar's *Dict.* (1830) also says that it is 'still partially practised.'

I think it may now (1880) be said to be obsolete. The practice, however, of giving useful presents to young couples is encouraged in the very highest ranks of modern society.

Chan e sealbh na faodalach a faotainn.—*The finding of a thing is not the owning of it.*

This is good law as well as good sense.

Chan e 'n tochradh mòr a nì an tiomnadh beairteach.—*'Tis not the big dowry that makes the wealthy will.*

The greatest tochers mak not the greatest testaments.—*Scot.* He that's needy when he's married shall be rich when he's buried.—*Eng.*

Chan eil ach a leth-taobh ris.—*He has but a half-side to it.*

Chan eil ach rabhadh gun fhuasgladh ann am bruadar na h-oidhche.—*The dream of the night is but a warning unsolved.*

Al.—Cha taisbeanadh bruadar cadail—*A dream is no revelation.*

In the multitude of dreams and many words there are also diverse vanities.—*Eccl.* v, 7.

Chan eil ach mòran eadar a' bhò 's a' mheanbh-chuileag.—*The cow is only a good deal bigger than the midge.*

The midge is as big as a mountain—amaist.—*Scot.*

Chan eil adharc cho cruaidh 's a tha langan àrd.—*His horn is not so hard as his roar is loud.*

His bark is waur nor his bite.—*Scot.*

Chan eil agad ach am bogadh, gun bhuidheachas dheth.—*You have got but the ducking, and no thanks.*

Chan eil agams' ach osain gheàrr dheth, ach tha triubhas fad' agadsa dheth.—*I have but short hose of it, and you have long trews of it.*

Chan eil air a' bhiadh ach teannadh ris.—*Eating needs but a beginning.*

Taste, you will eat.—*Arab.* Mangiando viene l'appetito.—*Ital.* En mangeant l'appetit vient.—*Fr.* Eten is een goed begin.—*Dutch.*

Chan eil air duine gun nàire ach duine gun nàire thachairt ris.—*There's nothing for a shameless man but his match to meet him.*

Chan eil airc ann gu airc na h-ainnis.—*There is no distress like that of the destitute.*

> See 'Eadar an t-euradh is aimbeairt'.

Chan eil àit' am bi meall nach bi fasgadh mu bhonn.—*Wherever a height is, there is shelter below.*

Chan eil am bonnach beag bruich fhathast.—*The little bannock is not toasted yet.*

> This is a phrase used at hide-and-seek, or blind-man's-buff, to announce that the players are not ready yet.

Chan eil am maoidheadh daonnan an cois a' chroin.—*Threatening does not always follow mischief.*

> It depends on who does it!

Chan eil an cuid 's an onair aca.—*They haven't kept their goods and honour.*

> Chan eil an cùil no 'n cuilidh
> Nach fhaic sùil a' Mhuilich,
> 'S chan eil an àird no 'n ìosal
> Nach làimhsich làmh an Ilich;
> Na dh'fhàgadh am Muileach,
> Ghrad sgrìobadh an Collach uaith' e,
> Ach 's mairg a dh'earbadh a chuid no anam
> Ris a' chealgaire Bharrach.

> *—There's not in nook or corner*
> *What the Mull man's eye won't see;*
> *There's not in height or hollow*
> *What the Islay man won't handle;*
> *What the Mull man would leave*
> *The Coll man soon would grasp;*
> *But woe to him, his goods or life,*
> *Who trusts to treacherous Barra man.*

These very calumnious estimates are, of course, to be taken *cum grano*. Other similar sayings are—

> Muileach is Ileach is deamhan—
> An triùir as miosa air an domhain:
> 'S miosa am Muileach na 'n t-Ileach,
> 'S miosa an t-Ileach na 'n deamhan.

> —*A Mull man, an Islay man and a devil*—
> *The three worst in creation:*
> *The Mull man is worse than the Islay man,*
> *The Islay man worse than the devil.*

Chan fhaic am Muileach nach sanntaich am Muileach; na shanntaicheas am Muileach, goididh an Collach; 's na ghoideas an Collach, cuiridh an Tirisdeach am folach.—*What the Mull man sees he covets; what the Mull man covets, the Coll man steals; and what the Coll man steals, the Tiree man hides.*

> Sliob am Muileach, is sgròbaidh e thu; sgròb am Muileach, is sliobaidh e thu.—*Stroke the Mull man, and he'll scratch you; scratch him, and he'll stroke you.*
> Ged a bhiodh tu cho carach ris a' Mhuileach, gheibhear a-mach thu.—*Were you as tricky as the Mull man, you'll be found out.*
> All these dreadful imputations remind one of an Eastern saying: 'The Koords are worse than the Arabs, the Arabs are worse than the Yezidees, and the Yezidees are worse than Eblis.'

Chan eil ann ach an t-uan nas duibhe na mhàthair.—*It's merely the lamb blacker than its dam.*

Chan eil ann ach an dara duine bhreith, 's an duine eile bhreith is àrach.—*One man needs but to be born, another to be born and bred.*

> This is an acute observation on the advantages of hereditary aristocracy and primogeniture.

Chan eil ann ach fear ri caomhnadh 's fear ri caitheamh.—*One man saves and another spends.*

> Cuid an taisgeoir ag an chaithteoir.—*Ir.* Narrow gathered, widely spent.—*Eng., Scot.*

Chan eil ann ach Iain is Dòmhnall—Dòmhnall cho math ri Iain, 's Iain cho math ri Dòmhnall.—*It is plain John and Donald—Donald as good as John, and John as good as Donald.*

Chan eil ann ach leth-phlaide gun fhuaigheal.—*He is but an un-hemmed half-blanket.*

Chan eil ann ach mogan gun cheann.—*He is a stocking without foot.*

[MacInnes has 'without head or foot'.]

Chan eil ann don t-seann amadan.—*No fool to the old fool.*—*Eng.*

Chan fhuil amadan ar bith is measa ná sean-amadán.—*Ir.* Nae fules like the auld fules.—*Scot.* The head grey, and no brains yet?—*Eng.* Je älter der Geck, je schlimmer.—*Germ.*

Chan eil beart an aghaidh na h-èiginn.—*There is no contrivance against necessity.*

'Ανάγκη ουδὲ θεοί μάχονται.—*Gr.* Ingens telum necessitas.—*Cic.*

Chan eil bradan gun a lethbhreac.—*There's no salmon without peer.*

Anglers sometimes need to be reminded of this.

Chan eil carraig air nach caochail sruth.—*There is no rock that the stream won't change.*

See 'Chan eil sruth'. [MacInnes adds 'Gutta cavat lapidem'.—*Ovid.*]

Chan eil Clann MhicNeacail dioghaltach.—*The Nicolsons (or Mac-Nicols) are not revengeful.*

Chan eil cleith air an olc ach gun a dhèanamh.—*There's no hiding of evil but not to do it.*

Chan eil cù eadar e 's a' chroich.—*There is not a dog between him and the gallows.*

Chan eil de dh'uaill air an aodach ach am fear a dh'fhaodas a cheannach.—*There's nothing in dress to be proud of but the power of buying it.*

Chan eil de mhath air fuighleach a' chait ach a thoirt da fhèin.—*The cat's leavings are fit only for himself.*

> Applied to men who would palm the dregs on others after they have drunk the cream.

Chan eil dearbhadh gun deuchainn.—*There is no proof without trial.*

> Experto crede.—*Virgil.* The proof of the pudding is in the eating.—*Eng.*

Chan eil deathach an taigh na h-uiseige.—*There is no smoke in the lark's house.*

> This is a pretty saying. The bird of most aspiring and happy song has untainted air in its lowly home.

Chan eil deireadh ann as miosa na 'n sìolman-coirce.—*There is no refuse worse than that of oats.*

> 'Said of mean gentry'—Note by Macintosh. 'Corruptio optimi,' oats being the staff of life, and men the 'crown of things'.

Chan eil dìochuimhne ann as bòidhche na 'n dìochuimhne ghlèidh-teach.—*The finest forgetfulness, forgetting what was kept.*

Chan eil do dhuine sona ach a bhreith, 's bidh duine dona 'na lom-ruith.—*The lucky man needs but to be born, the unlucky runs ever bare.*

> Nid rhaid i ddedwydd namyn ei eni.—*Welsh.* Char chaill duine dona a chuid a riamh.—*The unlucky man never lost his means* (because he had none!)—*Ir.* The happy man canna be harried.—*Scot.* Give a man luck, and throw him into the sea.—*Eng.*

Chan eil doras gun làib, 's tha cuid aig a bheil a dhà.—*There's a dub at every door, some hae twa.—Scot.*

Chan eil duine creachta 's a long aige.—*A man is not ruined while he has his ship.*

Chan eil e pisearlach.—*He is no conjurer.*

Chan eil eadar an duine glic 's an t-amadan ach gun ceil an duine glic a rùn, agus gun innis an t-amadan e.—*'Twixt the wise man and the fool, all the difference is this, that the wise man keeps his counsel and the fool revealeth his.*

> The fool's heart is in his mouth, the wise man's tongue is in his heart.—*Arab.*

Chan eil eadar an t-amadan 's an duine glic ach tairgse mhath a ghabhail nuair a gheibh e i.—*All the difference between the fool and the wise man is in taking a good offer.*

> Eptir koma ósvinnum ráð í hug.—*After all is done, the unwise thinks of a plan.—Icel.* Quando el necio es acordado, el mercado es ya pasado.—*Span.* O que faz o doudo á derradeira, faz o sesudo á primeira.—*Port.*

Chan eil eadar duine 's tuille fhaighinn ach na th' aige chaitheamh.—*Nothing keeps from getting more but the spending of your store.*

Chan eil earbsa sam bith ri chur anns na h-Eileanaich.—*There is no trust to be put in the Islanders.*

> A Lorn saying, originating probably in the difficulty of Islanders, who had to depend on the weather, in keeping their engagements.

Chan eil euslainte gun ìocshlaint, ach chan eil tilleadh air an Aog.—*There's no sickness without salve, but for Death no check.*

> Contra vim mortis non est medicamen in hortis.—*Med. Lat.* Para todo hay remedio sino para la muerte.—*Span.*

Chan eil fèill aig na h-inean ach Dihaoine 's Didòmhnaich.—*There's no holiday for nails but Friday and Sunday.*

> Paring the nails on these particular days was held unlucky.—see Sir T. Browne's *Vulgar Errors*, v. 10, and Chambers's *Book of Days*, I, 526; II, 322.

Chan eil fèill no faidhir air nach faighear Maol Ruainidh.—*There's no holiday nor fair but Mulrony will be there.*

> M.—a nickname for a foolish woman who frequents fairs and other diversions too much.—Note by Macintosh.

Chan eil fhios cò às a thàinig na h-eich bhàna 's na droch mhna-than.—*Nobody knows where the white horses and the bad wives come from.*

> *Al.*—Tha h-uile nighean gu math, ach cò às tha na droch mhnathan a' tighinn!
> All are good maids, but whence come the bad wives?—*Eng.* Aa are guid lasses, but where do aa the ill wives come frae?—*Scot.*

Chan eil fhios cò as glice—fear a chaomhnas no fear a chaitheas.—*None can say which is wiser, he that saves or he that spends.*

Chan eil fhios cò dhiubh 's fheàrr luathas no maille, 's b'e 'n gille-mirein am pòsadh.—*None can tell which is better, haste or tardiness, and marriage is a very whirligig.*

> See 'Am fear a dh'imich'.

Chan eil fhios air an uair seach a' mhionaid.—*The hour (of Death) is as unknown as the minute.*

Chan eil gach iuchair san tìr an crochadh ri aon chrios.—*All the keys in the land do not hang from one girdle.*

> Aa the keys o the country hang na on ae belt.—*Scot.* Tutte le chiavi non pendono a una cintura.—*Ital.* Toutes les clefs ne pendent pas à une ceinture.—*Fr.* Die Schlüssel hängen nicht alle an einem Gürtel.—*Germ.*

Chan eil i beag, bòidheach no mòr, grànda.—*She is neither small and bonnie nor big and ugly.*

> Chan fhuil sí beag, deas nó mór, grána.—*Ir.*

Chan eil eun sa choille nach bi greis 'na bhantraich.—*There is no bird in the wood but is at times in widowhood.*

Chan eil maide cam no dìreach nach fhaigh feum an Ròdhag.—*There is no stick, straight or crooked, but will find use in Roag.*

> Trees are still comparatively scarce in the Hebrides, and this saying reminds one of Dr. Johnson's reply to Boswell, on being consoled with the hope that his oak stick, which he had lost, would be recovered. 'No, no, my friend,' said the Doctor, 'it is not to be expected that any man in Mull who has got it will part with it. Consider, sir, the value of such a piece of timber here!'

Chan eil math gun mhilleadh.—*There is no good but may be marred.*

Chan eil math nach teirig ach math Dhè.—*All good has an end but the goodness of God.*

> Alle dingen hebben ein ende behalve God.—*Dutch.*

Chan eil fealladh ann as mò na gealladh gun cho-ghealladh.—*There is no greater fraud than the promise unfulfilled.*

> Cas a addawo bob peth ac ni chywiro ddin.—*Hateful is he that promises everything and performs nothing.*—*Welsh.*

Chan eil mi am sgoilear, 's chan àill leam a bhith, mun duirt am madadh-ruadh ris a' mhadadh-allaidh.—*I'm not a scholar, and don't wish to be, as the fox said to the wolf.*

> The fox and the wolf, walking together, came upon an ass quietly grazing. The fox pointed out an inscription on one of his hind hooves, and said to his companion, 'Go you and read that; you are a scholar, and I am not.' The wolf, flattered by the request, went proudly forward, and coming too close to the ass, got knocked on the head, leaving the fox to enjoy their common spoil!
>
> A different version of this fable is given in Campbell's *W.H.T.*, I, 278.

Chan eil m'earball fo chois.—*My tail is not under his foot.*

Chan eil mo theanga fo d'chrios—bu mhiosa dhòmhsa nam bith-eadh.—*My tongue is not under your belt—worse for me if it were.*

> My tongue is na under yir belt.—*Scot.*

Chan eil port an asgaidh ann; tha Port na Bàn-righ'nn fhèin tasd-an.—*There is no tune for nothing; Queensferry itself costs a shilling.*

> This is a mild attempt at a pun. *Port* means both 'tune' and 'harbour'.

Chan eil port a sheinneas an smeòrach san Fhaoilleach nach caoin i mun ruith an t-Earrach.—*For every song the mavis sings in February, she'll lament ere the Spring be over.*

> As lang as the bird sings before Candlemas, he greets after it.—*Scot.*
> Choud as hig y scell greinney stiagh Laa'l Breeshey, hig y sniaghtey my jig laa Boayldyn.—*As far as the sun shines on St Bride's Day, the snow will come before Beltane.*—*Manx.*

Chan eil ri dhèanamh air an dàn ach an còmhradh a chàradh gu caoin.—*The one thing in making of verse is sweetly to order the words.*

Chan eil rud sam bith gun dà latha, 's tha trì latha aig na h-Oisgean.—*Everything has two days, and the Ewes have three.*

> Three days in the third week of April, Old Style.—See App. IV.

Chan eil saoi air nach laigh leòn.—*No hero is proof against wound.*

Chan eil thu eòlach air a' ghiullachd each.—*You are not skilled in looking after horses.*

> Chan eil tom no tulach,
> No cnocan buidhe fiarach,
> Nach bi seal gu subhach
> Is seal gu dubhach deurach.
>
> *—There is no knoll nor mound,*
> *Nor hillock dight with flowers,*
> *That sometimes is not bright*
> *And sometimes dark with showers.*

Chan eil treun ris nach cuirear.—*The brave will be tried.*

Chan eil tuil air nach tig traoghadh.—*Every flood will have an ebb.*

> Every tide (flood) hath its ebb.—*Eng., Scot.* Alle vloed heeft zijne ebbe.—*Dutch.*

Chan fhac' thu bò de d'chrodh fhèin an-diugh.—*You saw no cow of your own today.*

> Said of one who seems in deshabille and out of humour.—Note by Macintosh.

Chan fhaic thu 'm feasd bàrr na coille còmhla.—*The tree-tops are never seen on a level.*

Chan fhaca mi leithid on a chaidh slat am chòta.—*I haven't seen the like since a yard made my coat.*

Chan fhacas a' mhuc riamh gun chabhaig oirre.—*The sow was never seen but in a hurry.*

Chan fhacas fear-faoighe riamh gun tombaca.—*A beggar was never seen without tobacco.*

Chan fhada bhuat a chuir thu 'n athais.—*You haven't removed the reproach very far from you.*

Chan fhaigh cù gortach cnàimh.—*A starving dog gets no bone.*

Chan fhaigh fear mabach modh.—*A stammerer won't get respect.*

So much for the wickedness of human nature.

Chan fhaigheadh tu e nas mò na 'n t-iarann a ghearr d'imleag.—*You should as soon get the knife that cut your navel as that.*

Chan fhaigheadh tu seo ged a b'e 'n rìgh bràthair do mhàthar.—*You should not get this were the king your mother's brother.*

Chan fhaighear an-dè air ais an-diugh.—*You can't today recall yester-day.*

Chan fhaighear math gun dragh.—*Good is not got without trouble.*

Strait is the gate and narrow is the way which leadeth unto life.— *Matth.* vii, 14. Χαλεπὰ τὰ καλά.—*Gr.* (Solon).

Chan fhaod duine fàs beairteach mur leig a bhean leis.—*A man can't get rich unless his wife allow him.*

A man that would thrive must ask his wife's leave.—*Scot.*

Chan fhaodar a' bhò a reic 's a bainne òl.—*Ye canna sell the cou and sup the milk.—Scot.*

I cannot eat my cake and have my cake.—*Eng.*

Chan fheàrr an seud na luach.—*The jewel is no better than its worth.*

The value, sure, of anything
Is as much money as 'twill bring.—*Hudibras.*

Chan fheàrr an t-urras na 'n t-earras.—*The security is no better than the principal.*

Chan fhearr Siorram na Sarram.—*Sheriff is no better than Shariff.*

This is one of the jingling sayings of which the Gael were rather fond, caring sometimes more for sound than for sense. Here, indeed, there is an obvious meaning, if I have rightly rendered it, indicating that aversion to the Saxon office of Sheriff which Chalmers, in his *Caledonia*, several times refers to.

Similar jingling sayings are 'Chan fheàrr singeas na sangas' and 'Chan fheàrr an gille siar na 'n gille sear'. They are not wholly meaningless, however, being much of the same import as Pope's now classic comparison "twixt Tweedledum and Tweedledee'.

Chan fheòil sgamhan, 's cha bhainne blàthach.—*Lights are not meat, nor buttermilk milk.*

Chan fheòil grùthan, 's cha shùghan làgan.—*Liver is not meat, nor bran-juice sowens.*

Chan fhèum an tì a shealbhaicheas an toradh am blàth a mhill-eadh.—*He that would enjoy the fruit must not spoil the blossom.*

Chan fhiach bròn a ghnàth, 's chan fhiach ceòl a ghnàth.—*Sorrow always is not good, nor is mirth always.*

> To everything there is a season . . . a time to weep, and a time to laugh, a time to mourn, and a time to dance.—*Eccl.* iii, 1, 4.

Chan fhiach cuirm gun a còmhradh.—*A feast is worth nothing without its conversation.*

> It is creditable to our Celtic ancestors that in their view eating and drinking were not the chief charms of a dinner.

Chan fhiach duine gun neart gun innleachd.—*A man with neither strength nor art is worth nothing.*

Chan fhiach e bhith dèanamh dà latha dheth.—*It's not worth making two days of it.*

Chan fhiach fear furachail Foghar.—*A man that's very watchful doesn't deserve a harvest.*

> This does not seem good doctrine, but it is meant that he should be too busy to have time for spying about anxiously.

Chan fhiach òrdagh oidhche.—*Night orders are not good.*

> This is of the same sense as 'Day will bring counsel'. There are old legends of hunters and others who wished for their loves at night and were visited by fairy women or vampires, and killed.

Chan fhiach sagart gun chlèireach.—*A priest is nothing without a clerk*.

> Cha dual sagart gan chléireach, is cha dual Domhnach gan aifreann (*Sunday without mass*).—*Ir*.

Chan fhiach sgeul gun urrainn.—*A tale unvouched is worth nothing*.

> Ní fiú scéal gan údar éisteacht.—*Ir*.

Chan fhiach taigh mòr gun straighlich.—*A great house without noise is worth nothing*.

> The Celtic idea of a Chief's house of the right sort is thus expressed by Mary MacLeod in *An Talla bu Ghnàth le MacLeòid*:
>
> > Taigh mòr macnasach, meaghrach
> > Nam macan 's nam maighdean,
> > Far 'm bu tartarach gleadhraich nan còrn.
> >
> > *Great house gay and cheery*
> > *With young men and maidens,*
> > *Where loud was the clatter of horns.*

Chan fhiosrach mur feòraich.—*Nothing ask, nothing learn*.

> Fróðr er hverr fregnvíss.—*Who asks will become learned.*—*Icel*.

Chan fhuiling am broc 'na shloc ach e fhèin.—*The badger in his hole no company can thole*.

Chan fhuiling an onair clubhd.—*Honour can't bear patching*.

Chan fhuiling ceann carrach fuachd no teas.—*A scabby head can't bear cold or heat*.

> Een schurft hoofd ontziet de kam (*fears the comb*).—*Dutch*.

Chan fhuirich muir ri uallach.—*The sea won't wait for a load*.

> See 'Cha stad'.

Chan i bhò 's àirde geum as mò bainne.—*The loudest lowing cow is not the best milker*.

Chan iad na ro-chlèirich as fheàrr.—*The very learned are not the best.*

Merus grammaticus, merus asinus.—*Med. Lat.* A mere scholar is a mere ass.—*Eng.* The greatest clerks be not the wisest men.—*Chaucer.* Les grands clercs ne sont pas le plus fins.—*Fr.* De geleerdsten zijn de wijsten niet.—*Dutch.*

Chan iochd leam cnead mo leas-mhàthar.—*I pity not my stepmother's sigh.*

Chan ioghnadh an clamhan a dh'fhalbh le aon isean circe doille.— *No wonder if the kite take a blind hen's only chicken.*

Chan ioghnadh boladh an sgadain a bhith den t-soitheach sam bi e.—*It's no wonder that the herring vessel smells of herring.*

It's but kindly (i.e., natural) that the pock savour of the herring.—*Scot.* La caque sent toujours le hareng.—*Fr.*

Soon after Henry of Navarre had joined the Church of Rome, he was one day out hunting, and, leaving his attendants behind, came to an inn, and sat down to dinner with a company of merchants, to whom he was unknown. Their talk naturally turned on the king's conversion. 'Ne parlons pas de cela,' said one, a dealer in pigs, 'la caque sent toujours le hareng.' The king said nothing till his retinue came in, when the unfortunate merchant discovered his *bêtise.* 'Bon homme,' said the king, clapping him on the shoulder, 'la caque sent toujours le hareng, mais c'est en votre endroit, et non pas au mien. Je suis, Dieu merci, bon Catholique, mais vous gardez encore du vieux levain de la Ligue.' Méry's *Hist. des Proverbes,* II, 322.

The translation of the above in the 2nd ed. of Macintosh is 'No wonder that the cask smells of the herring in which they are.'

> Chan ioghnadh duine dall
> A dhol le allt no le creig,
> Ach thusa don lèir a' chòir,
> 'S nach dèan le d'dheòin dith ach beag.

> —*No wonder is when blind men fall*
> *Over rock or into river;*
> *But strange art thou who see'st the good,*
> *And willingly hast done it never.*

Chan ionann a fhreagras dà latha margadh.—*Two days don't suit equally for market.*

Chan ionann do fhear na neasgaid agus do fhear ga fàsgadh.—*It's different with the man of the boil and the man that squeezes it.*

Chan ionann fear air mhisg 's fear air uisge.—*The drunk man and the water-drinker differ.*

The only merit of this truism is the clink of the words.

Chan ionann iùl do dhithis no slighe do thriùir.—*Two men will take diverse roads, and three will go different ways.*

Raad ta jees ta reih (*roghainn*), as raad ta troor ta teiy (*taghadh*).— *Where two go there is choice, where three go there is picking.*—Manx.

Chan ionann sgeul a' dol don bhaile mhòr 's a' tighinn dachaigh.— *It's a different story, going to town and coming back.*

See 'Cha duine glic' and 'Am fear a thèid don taigh-mhòr'.

Chan ionann a bhios air a' chreich 's air an tòir.—*The foray and the pursuit have different tales to tell.*

This and the next but one are purely Highland.

Chan ionann togradh do dhuine, a' dol a dh'iarraidh mnatha 's ga cur dhachaigh.—*Very different is a man's desire, going for his wife and sending her home.*

Chan olc a' chreach às an gleidhear a leth.—*It's not a bad foray where the half is kept.*

Chan òr a h-uile rud buidhe, 's chan uighean a h-uile rud bàn.—*All that's yellow is not gold, and all white things are not eggs.*

The second half of this proverb is tacked on for the sake of assonance and alliteration. The first half is nearly in the same words in all European languages. The only difference in the Gaelic version is the use of the phrase 'the yellow' instead of 'what glitters' or 'shines,' which occurs in all the rest. The Gaelic phrase seems the more descriptive.

Chan òrdagh bat' aig bàillidh.—*A bailiff's staff is not an order.*

This is an expression of the Celtic aversion to mere display of authority without the recognised right.

Chan uaisle duine na chèaird.—*No man is above his trade.*

> He that thinks his business below him will always be above it.—*Eng.*
> Schäme dich deines Handwerks nicht.—*Germ.*

Chan uaisle mac rìgh na chuideachd.—*A king's son is no nobler than his company.*

> Chan uaisle mac rí ná 'chuid (his food)—*Ir.*
> An Ulster chief of the O'Neills was found by a bard in the act of toasting a cake. He looked rather ashamed, on which the bard addressed him:

> Is tusa an tighearna Ó Néill,
> Is mise mac 'n t-séin Mhic Cuirc;
> Tiontamaois an t-súdóg ar aon—
> Chan uaisle mac rí ná a chuid.

> *Thou art the chief O'Neill,*
> *And I son of old MacCork;*
> *In turning the cake we are one,*
> *No king's son's above his food.*
>
> > *Ulster Journal of Arch.*, Vol. VI, p. 260.

Chan uisge ach à tuath, 's cha turadh buan ach à deas.—*No rain but from the north, no long dry weather but from the south.*

> This saying, which comes from Tiree, is contrary to the experience of most other places.

Chan urrainn domh a' mhin ithe 's an teine shèideadh.—*I cannot eat the meal and blow the fire.*

> *Al.*—Cha dean mi ithe na mine is sèideadh an teine. Cha dtig le duine a bheith ag ithe mine, is ag feadalaigh ar a bhall (*whistling at the same time*).—*Ir.* He canna haud meal in his mouth and blaw.—*Scot.* Niemand kann zugleich blasen und schlucken.—*Germ.* Met vollen mond is 't kwaad blazen.—*Dutch.* Soplar y sorber no puede junto ser.—*Span.*

Chan urrainn domh h-èigheach agus a h-iomradh.—*I cannot raise the boat-song and row her.*

> The *iorram*, or boat-song, was generally raised by the man at the helm, if able, and chanted or shouted with great vigour, the rowers joining in the chorus. 'Suidheam air stiùir, 's èigheam *Creagag*'—'*Let me sit at the helm, and shout* Creagag.' *Creagag Mhic Iain 'Ic Sheumais* was a favourite *iorram*.

Cha nàr do dhuine bean ga dhiùltadh, bàta ga fhàgail no làir ga thilgeadh.—*It is no shame to a man to be refused by a woman, left by a boat or thrown by a mare.*

Cha nigh na tha dh'uisge sa mhuir ar càirdeas.—*All the water in the sea won't wash out our kinship.*

> This is intensely Highland, as is the use of the same word, *càirdeas*, for 'friendship' and 'kinship'.

Cha phàigheadh a' chàin a bh' aig Pàdraig air Eirinn e.—*St Patrick's tribute from Ireland would not pay it.*

> 'Dh'itheadh (or 'dh'òladh') e chàin a bh' aig Pàdraig air Eirinn'—'*He would eat (or drink) Patrick's tribute from Ireland*'—is another saying in reference to this tax, applied to a great eater or drinker. According to Keating (O'Connor's tr., p. 333), Aengus of Ulster obliged himself and his successors to deliver 500 cows, 500 bars of iron, 500 shirts, 500 mantles and 500 sheep to the convents and religious houses founded by St Patrick in Ulster, instead of three pennies per head for every person baptized. This, probably, was the *càin* referred to in the above sayings.

Cha rachadh tu cho deas air mo ghnothach-sa.—*You wouldn't go so fast on my business.*

Cha reic e chearc ris an latha fhliuch.—*He'll no sell his hen on a rainy day.*—Scot.

> Cha ndíolaidh sí a cearc a riamh sa lá fhliuch.—*Ir.*

Cha riaraich briathrachas bàs.—*Words will not satisfy death.*

Cha robh air dheireadh nach robh air thoiseach ach fear na droch mhnatha; 's bhiodh am fear sin fhèin ann a' dol don mhuileann.— *None was ever last that was not first except the ill-mated man; and he too would be first going to the mill.*

Because his house would be ill-kept.

Cha robh balg falamh riamh sàthach.—*Empty bag was never satisfied.*

Macintosh translates this in the sense of *Prov.* xxx, 16.

Cha robh balach riamh de Chloinn Ghriogair, no caile de Chloinn an Aba.—*There never was a clown of the Macgregors, nor a hussy of the Macnabs.*

The Macgregors trace their descent from King Alpin, and their motto is ''S rìoghail mo dhream'—*My line is royal.*' The Macnabs are a branch of that great clan. The above saying, unlike most of those referring to clans, was not invented by an enemy.

Cha robh bàs fir gun ghràs fir.—*One man's death is grace to another.*

See 'An nì nì subhach'.
Ni ddaw drwg i un, na ddaw da i arall—*Ill comes not to one without good to another.*—*Welsh.* Baase y derrey voddey, grayse y voddey elley—*One dog's death, another dog's grace.*—*Manx.*

Cha robh breugach nach robh bradach.—*None lied that would not steal.*

Very shrewd Ethics. He that can confound Yea and Nay cannot be trusted to respect Meum and Tuum. Truthfulness has, in fact, been laid down by some writers as the basis of all Virtue, and its opposite of all Vice.

Cha robh brù mhòr riamh 'na seise mhath.—*Big belly was never good mate.*

Al.—Cha robh làmh mhòr riamh aig caolan gionach.—*Greedy gut never had large hand.* Cha raibh bolg mór fial a riamh.—*Big belly was never bountiful.*—*Ir.*

Cha robh call mòr gun bhuinnig bhig.—*There was never great loss without a little gain.*

Cha robh cam nach robh crosda.—*The one-eyed was ever cross.*

Cha robh caraid riamh aig duine bochd.—*The poor are ever friendless.*

>The poor is hated even of his own neighbour.—*Prov.* xiv, 20.
>In contradiction to this, those who have had any experience among
>our poor know that their kindness to one another is often very great,
>and much beyond that of the rich.

Cha robh coille riamh gun chrìonaich, no linn gun ugh-gluig.—
Never was wood without dry brushwood, nor brood without addle-egg.

>*Al.*—Cha robh gur gun ghoirean. Chan fhuil coill ar bith gan a losgadh
>féin de chrìonlach innti—(*as much dry wood as would burn it*).—*Ir.*

Cha robh coimheart mòr gun choimheart beag.—*Great was never
without small comparison.*

Cha robh coirce math riamh gun shìolman.—*No good oats ever were
without refuse.*

Cha robh cron air ach an cron a bh' air Fionn.—*He had no fault but
that of Fingal.*

>Fingal's one fault was that he was only eight feet high, while all the
>rest of his comrades were taller.

Cha robh cùil an amharais riamh glan.—*The suspicious corner was
never clean.*

Cha robh dithis riamh a' fadadh teine nach do las eatarra.—*Two were
never making a fire that didn't light between them.*

>See 'Cha do chòrd'.
>There is a neat double meaning here, the suggestion being that the
>two would quarrel about it. Two seldom agree as to the best way of
>making a fire.

Cha robh do chuid riamh air chall.—*Your portion was never a-missing.*

Cha robh duine riamh gun dà latha ach am fear gun lath' idir.—*No
man was ever without two days but the man who had none at all.*

>No man ever lived without some vicissitude.

Cha robh duine riamh gun lochd.—*Man was never without fault.*

> *Al.*—Tha chron fhèin aig a h-uile fear.—*Every man has his own fault.*
> Odid ddyn teg dianaf.—*Scarcely a comely man faultless.*—*Welsh.* Man
> is the son of imperfection.—*Arab.* Humanum est errare.—*Lat.* Fàr er
> vamma vaur.—*Icel.*

Cha robh gaoth mhòr riamh gun bheagan uisge.—*There never was a
high wind without some rain.*

Cha robh math no olc riamh gun mhnathan uime.—*There was never
good or ill but women had to do with.*

> Few of the proverbs in other languages attribute any influence to
> women except for mischief. This is not only more chivalrous but more
> true.

Cha robh meadhail mhòr riamh gun dubh-bhròn 'na dèidh.—*There
never was a burst of joy that deep grief did not follow.*

> *Al.*—Chan fhacas riamh meadhar mòr nach robh 'na dhèidh dubh-
> bhròn.
> After joy comes annoy.—*Scot.* Sadness and gladness succeed each
> other.—*Eng.* These violent delights have violent ends.—*Rom. and
> Jul.*, II, 6. Extrema gaudii luctus occupat.—*Lat.* Æ koma mein eptir
> munuð.—*Icel.*

Cha robh molach nach robh sona.—*None was hairy but was happy.*

> See 'Cha bhi sonas air bus lom'.

Cha robh reithe leathann liath riamh reamhar.—*A broad gray ram
was never fat.*

Cha robh reothart riamh 'na h-àirde ach Dimàirt 's Dihaoine.—
Spring-tide never was at height save on Tuesday or on Friday.

> I can neither confirm nor contradict this.

Cha robh Samhradh riamh gun ghrian;
Cha robh Geamhradh riamh gun sneachd;
Cha robh Nollaig mhòr gun fheòil;
No bean òg le deòin gun fhear.

> *—Summer ne'er was without sun;*
> *Winter never without snow;*
> *Christmas never without flesh;*
> *Nor willing woman without man.*

Cha robh saoidh gun choimeas.—*Peerless hero never was.*

Cha robh 'Seo' riamh gun mhaoidheadh, ach 's fheàrr a mhaoidheadh na dhìobradh—*'Take it' was never without grudge; but better grudged than not at all.*

Cha robh slibist gun tubaist.—*Slips and slovens go together.*

> See 'Bidh na tubaistean' and 'Is trom na tubaistean'.

Cha robh sgeulach nach robh breugach.—*Tale-tellers will tell lies.*

> *Al.*—Cha robh cèileach nach robh breugach.—*Tattlers will be telling lies.* Cèileach, a person addicted to going 'air chèilidh,' making calls and gossiping.

Cha robh thu a-staigh an uair a chaidh an ciall a roinn.—*You were not in when sense was being shared.*

> Cha raibh sé ar fáil nuair a bhí an chiall dá roinn.—*Ir.*

Cha robh thu riamh air fèill eile.—*That was aye your traffic.*

> *Lit.* You were never at any other fair.

Cha robh thu riamh gun do bhiadh sa mhuileann.—*You were never without your food in the mill.*

Cha ruig am beagan fuilt air cùl a' chinn's air clàr an aodainn.—*The scanty hair won't cover the back and front.*

> Some men try it, notwithstanding!

Cha ruig fuachd air airgead-iomairt.—*Gaming-money won't get cold.*

> Gaming for money was never much practised in the Highlands, one reason being that money was scarce in days of old. One of our historians has even attributed the noble contempt shown for the price for Prince Charlie's head to simple ignorance of the value of cash, and

incapacity to understand the meaning of £30,000! But though among the class of people who produced most of our Gaelic proverbs coin of any kind was seldom seen, there is sufficient evidence that not only was gaming with dice and cards practised in the Highlands very long ago, but that so intellectual a game as chess was well known to the Scoto-Irish Celts so far back as the time of Fingal and Cuchullin, whensoever that may have been. Even that game was sometimes played for high stakes—not in money but in horses, mantles and armlets of silver. The Norsemen also were very much given to gaming.

Cha sgàin màthair leanaibh.—*Bairn's mother bursts never.—Scot.*

'Because,' says Kelly, 'she will keep meat out of her own mouth to put into theirs.'

Cha sgal cù ro chnàimh.—*A dog won't howl at a bone.*

A dog winna yowl if ye fell him wi a bane.—*Scot.* Non si offende mai cane gettandogli le ossa.—*Ital.*

Cha sgaoilear taigh an arain.—*Bread's house skailed never.—Scot.*

The identity of *sgaoil* and *skail* will be noted here. Kelly interprets this proverb as meaning that, while people have the staff of life, they need not give over housekeeping. Hislop, on the other hand, explains it as meaning that a hospitable house never wants visitors.

Cha sgeith bò feur.—*A cow won't vomit grass.*

Wise creatures won't quarrel with their bread and butter.

Cha sgeul-rùin e 's fios aig triùir air.—*It's no secret, if three know it.*

Al.—'S triùir ga chluinntinn—*If three hear it.* An rud bhios eadar triùir, chan fhiù e chleith—*What three know is not worth concealing.*
Ní scéal rúin é, o chluinneas triúir é.—*Ir.* Skeeal eddyr jees, skeeal dyn insh (*gun innseadh*); skeeal eddyr tree, te ersooyl (*tha e air siubhal*).—*Manx.* Nid cyfrinach ond rhwng—*No secret but 'twixt two.—Welsh.* Three may keep counsel, if twa be awa.—*Scot.* Tre lo sanno, tutti lo sanno.—*Ital.* Puridad de dos, puridad de Dios: puridad de tres, de todos es.—*Span.* Secret de deux, secret de Dieu: secret de trois, secret de tous.—*Fr.* þjóð veit ef þrír 'ro—*People know, if three are.—Icel.* Was drei wissen, erfahren bald dreiszig.—*Germ.*

Cha shaltair duin' air a phiseach.—*No man will trample on his luck.*

Cha shaothair bà-laoigh do shaothair, no deagh ghamhnaich.—*Your labour is not that of a calving cow, nor of a good farrow cow.*

Cha shean de m'shean 's chan òg de m'òige thu.—*You are not an old one of my old ones, nor a young one of my youth.*

Cha sheas a' bhreug ach air a leth-chois.—*A lie stands on but one leg.*

> *Al.*—Chan eil casan aig breugan, ach tha sgiathan aig tuaileas.—*A lie has no legs, but a scandal has wings.*—*Eng.* Truth stands aye without a prop.—*Scot.* Bugie hanno corte le gambe.—*Ital.* La mentira tiene cortas las piernas.—*Span.* Lügen haben kurze Beine.—*Germ.*—*Lies have short legs.*
>
> These sayings are true enough, in the sense that lies have no stability, and are easily overtaken. But not less true is the Welsh saying: Goreu cerddedydd gau—*The best traveller is a lie.*

Cha sheas càirdeas air a leth-chois.—*Friendship won't stand on one leg.*

Cha sheas poca falamh.—*An empty bag cannot stand upright.*—*Eng.*

> Cha seasann sac falamh.—*Ir.* Sacco vuoto non sta ritto.—*Ital.* Ein leerer Sack steht nicht aufrecht.—*Germ.*

Cha shìn duin' a chas ach mar a ruigeas aodach.—*A man will stretch his foot no farther than his clothes allow.*

> Κατὰ τὸ πάπλωμα, καὶ των ποδων τὸ ξάπλωμα.—*According to the blanket must the feet stretch.*—*Mod. Gr.*

Cha shoirbh triubhas a chur air cat.—*It is not easy to put trews on a cat.*

Cha shuaicheantas còrr air cladach.—*A heron on the shore is not peculiar.*

> *Lit.* not an ensign, or escutcheon.

Cha stad na tràithean, 's chan eil bàidh aig seòl-mara.—*Time won't wait, nor tide show mercy.*

> Time and tide tarry for no man.—*Eng.* Time and tide for nae man bide.—*Scot.* Zeit Ebbe und Fluth warten auf Niemand.—*Germ.* Tiempo ni hora no se ata con soga.—*Span.*

Cha teich ach cladhaire, 's chan fhuirich ach sèapaire.—*None but a craven will fly, and none but a sneak will stay.*

Cha teich an earba gus am faic.—*The roe won't fly till she sees you.*

Cha tèid a' bhreug nas fhaide na 'n craiceann.—*A lie won't pierce beyond the skin.*

Cha tèid an sionnach nas fhaide na bheir a chasan e.—*The fox will go no farther than his feet will carry him.*

Cha tèid anam à mac bodaich le mùiseig.—*Threats won't drive the life out of a churl's son.*

> Ni lladd gogyfaddaw—*Threats won't kill.*—*Welsh.* Threatened folks live long.—*Eng., Scot.*

Cha tèid àrdan nam ban fon ùir.—*The pride of women will never be laid in the dust.*

Cha tèid bòidhchead nas doimhne na 'n craiceann.—*Beauty is but skin deep.*—*Eng.*

Cha tèid dad san dòrn dùinte: 'Mur tèid, cha tig às,' arsa moisean.—*Nothing gets into the closed fist: 'Nor out of it,' said the scrub.*

Cha tèid e timcheall a' phris leis.—*He won't go about the bush with it.*

> Cha deachaidh sé ar scáth an tuir leis.—*He didn't go behind the bush with it.*—*Ir.*

Cha tèid fiach air beul dùinte, 's cha tog balbhan fianais.—*Shut mouth incurs no debt, and dumb men give no evidence.*

> *Al.*—Cha toirear balbh gu mòd.—*The dumb don't get into Court.* Repentance for silence is better than repentance for speech.—*Arab.* Nulli tacuisse nocet, nocet esse locutum.—*Dion. Cato.* Be checked for silence, but never taxed for speech.—*All's Well that Ends Well,* I, 1.

Cha tèid plàsd air bagairt.—*A threat needs no plaster.*

Cha tèid pòsadh thar muir.—*Marriage goes not beyond sea.*

> I understand this saying is meant to be jocular, in allusion probably to the fact that sailors have been known to have wives in more than one port.

Cha tèid stad ort nas mò na air eas na h-aibhne.—*You no more pause than the waterfall.*

Cha tig a-nuas an nì nach eil shuas.—*Nothing can come down that is not up.*

Cha tig à soitheach le goc ach an deoch a bhios ann.—*A vessel with a cock lets out no liquor but what's in.*

Cha tig air a' cholainn nach fhaodar fhulang.—*Nothing comes on the body that can't be borne.*

Cha tig am bàs gun leisgeul.—*Death comes not without excuse.*

> *Al.*—gun fhios carson—*without knowing why.*
> Cha daink rieau yn baase gyn lestal.—*Manx.* Cha dtig an bás gan adhbhar.—*Ir.* Addfed angeu i hen.—*Death is ripe for the old.—Welsh.*

Cha tig am bàs gus an tig an t-àm.—*Death comes not till the time comes.*

> Death's day is doom's day.—*Eng.* Ekki kemr ófeigum í he!—*You can't kill an 'unfey' man.—Icel.* De dood kent geen' almanak—*Death keeps no almanack.—Dutch, Eng.*

Cha tig an caitheamh crìonnta ach do shìol nam bodach.—*The penurious spending suits only the mean sort.*

> This saying must have been uttered by a person of the 'superior' sort.

Cha tig an còta glas cho math don a h-uile fear.—*The gray coat becomes not every man alike.*

> Macintosh says, 'King James the V's wearing a gray coat when in disguise might probably give rise to this saying.'
> *Al.*—an còta fad'—*the long coat.*
> Luthers Schuhe sind nicht jedem Dorfpfarrer gerecht—*Luther's shoes don't fit every country parson.—Germ.*

Cha tig an crodh uile cho math don bhuaile.—*All the cows don't come equally well to the fold.*

Cha tig an Fhèill Anndrais gu ceann bliadhna tuilleadh oirnn.—*St Andrew's Day won't come to us for another year.*

> Christmas comes but once a year.—*Eng.*
> St Andrew's Day, 30th Nov., is the festival of the patron saint of Scotland, and as such holds its proper place in the esteem of Scotchmen and in the ecclesiastical calendar. It regulates, in fact, the beginning and end of the ecclesiastical year. See Chambers's *Book of Days*, II, 636.

Cha tig an latha 's cha chiar an tràth a chì thu sin.—*The day will never come, nor the evening darken, when you'll see that.*

Cha tig an t-anabarr.—*Too much never comes.*

Cha tig às a' phoit ach an toit a bhios innte.—*Nothing comes out of the pot but the smoke that's in it.*

Cha tig air crannaibh gu 'n tig Càisg.—*Till Easter come no tree will bloom.*

Cha tig den àtha ach am bàrr a th' oirre.—*You can't take off the kiln but the grain that's on it.*

Cha tig fiacail dhut ach na thàinig.—*You'll get no more teeth than you have.*

> Cha tig fuachd gu Earrach,
> Cruaidh-chàs, no droch cheannach.
>
> —*Cold comes not until Spring,*
> *Hardship and bad marketing.*
>
> *Al.* Cha tig fuachd gu 'n tig Earrach,
> Le gaoith tuath 's le cruaidh-ghailleann.
>
> —*Cold comes not until Spring*
> *North wind and tempest bring.*

Cha tig Geamhradh gu cùl Callainn, no Earrach gu cùl Fhèill Pàraig.—*Winter comes not till after New Year, nor Spring till after St Patrick's Day.*

> St Patrick's day is 17th March.
> As the day lengthens, the cold strengthens.—*Eng., Scot.*
>   Wenn die Tage beginnen zu langen,
>   Dann kommt erst der Winter gegangen.—*Germ.*
> Jours croissants, froids cuisants.—*Fr.*

Cha tig muir mhòr tron chaolas chumhann.—*A great sea comes not through a narrow strait.*

Cha tig olc à teine ach ugh glas na feannaig.—*Nothing evil will come out of the fire but the crow's gray egg.*

> *Al.*—ach feòil na glas-fheannaig—*the gray crow's flesh.*
> There is a strange story in Rannoch about the great Michael Scott to account for this saying. It is that fearing his wife, to whom he had taught the Black Art, would excel him in it, he killed her by means of crows' eggs heated in the fire and put into her arm-pits, as the only thing against which no counter-enchantment could prevail!

Cha tig on mhuic ach uircean.—*From the sow comes but a little pig.*

Cha tig piseach air duine a bheir cat thar allt.—*He will have no luck who takes a cat across a stream.*

Cha tig rath à ràiteachas, no math à milleadh.—*No luck comes of idle talk, nor good of spoiling.*

Cha tig smaointean glan à cridhe salach.—*Clean thoughts come not from a foul heart.*

> How can ye, being evil, speak good things?—*Matth.* xii, 34.

Cha tig snàth mo mhnà-sa air snàth do mhnà-sa.—*My wife's thread won't match your wife's.*

Cha tigear bhon ghàbhadh tric.—*Jeopardy is not often escaped from.*

Cha toill iarrtas achmhasan.—*Asking merits not reproof.*

Cha toir a' bhò don laogh ach na th' aice.—*The cow can give her calf only what she has.*

Cha toir a' bhòidhchead goil air a' phoit.—*Beauty won't boil the pot.*

> *Al.*—Cha ghoil an uaisl' a' phoit.—*Gentility won't boil the pot.*
> Beauty will buy no beef.—*Eng.* Send yir gentle bluid to the market, and see what it will bring.—*Scot.*

Cha toir am fitheach an t-sùil dha isean fhèin.—*The raven won't give the eye to his own chicken.*

Cha toir a' ghaoth dhìot, ge teann leat a shèideas.—*The wind won't strip you, though it blow hard.*

> This seems to be founded on the old story of the traveller and his cloak.

Cha toir duin' a chall da charaid.—*No man gives his friend his loss.*

Cha toir duine rath air èiginn, 's gheibhear e gun èiginn idir.—*A man cannot force his lot, and without stress it may be got.*

> See 'Bheir duine beath' air èiginn' and 'Thig ri latha'.

Cha toir muir no monadh a chuid o dhuine sona; 's cha ghlèidh duine dona 'n t-allt.—*Neither main nor moor can make the lucky poor; but the unlucky man can't keep to the burn.*

> See 'Chan eil air an duine shona'.

Cha toir thu 'n aire gus an tèid am bior san t-sùil.—*You won't take heed till the prick is in the eye.*

Cha toirear on chat ach a chraiceann.—*You can take nothing from the cat but its skin.*

> Cre yiow jeh 'n chayt agh y chrackan.—*Manx.* Man faaer ei meer af Ræven end Bælgen—*One can't take more off the fox than his skin.*—*Dan.*

Cha treabh gach bliadhna da chèile.—*Each year's ploughing is for itself.*

Cha truagh leam cnead mo mhàthar-cèile.—*I don't pity my mother-in-law's sigh.*

> The sayings of all nations about mothers-in-law are of the same wicked kind. See 'Is math a' mhàthair-chèil' an fhòid' and 'Mar dhòbhran'. One of the liveliest is an Ulster rhyme quoted by Mr Kelly (Walter K.) in his admirable little book, *Proverbs of All Nations* (London, 1859):

> Of all the ould women that ever I saw,
> Sweet bad luck to my mother-in-law!

Cha truagh leam cù 's marag mu amhaich.—*I don't pity a dog with a pudding round his neck.*

Cha tugadh an donas an car às.—*The devil couldn't cheat him.*

Cha tugadh an Cille Mo Cheallaig breith bu chlaoine.—*No worse judgment was given in Kilmacheallag.*

> The parish of Kilmacheallag is as difficult to find out as the town of Weissnichtwo. The story is that a man was tried there by a jury of women for stealing a horse, and was acquitted, while the horse was condemned to be hanged! The man had been tried before for stealing the same horse, and got off, and the poor horse liked him so well that he ran away from his proper master and came back to the thief.
> This story is referred to by the bard Iain Lom, as an illustration of his own iniquitous treatment by the murderer of young Keppoch. In his *Oran do Shìol Dùghaill* he says:

> Cleas na linne nach maireann
> Bha 'n sgìr' Chill Mo Cheallaig,
> Nuair a dhìt iad an gearran sa mhòd.

> Lagh cho ceàrr 's a bha 'm Breatann
> Rinn am meàirleach a sheasamh,
> Bhith ga theàrnadh o leadairt nan còrd.

> —*Like the people of old, in the parish of Kilmacheallag, who sentenced the horse at the court; as bad law as ever was in Britain, which upheld the thief, and saved him from the mangling of ropes.*

> See MacKenzie's *Sàr Obair nam Bàrd Gaelach*, p. 38, and Campbell's *W.H.T.*, II, 372, 381.

Cha tugadh cù geàrr earball às uat.—*A tail-less dog wouldn't take his tail from you.*

> Said of very sharp people.

Cha tugadh i dèirc don dall air muin a' chrùbaich.—*She wouldn't give alms to the blind on the cripple's back.*

Cha tugadh na h-eich an casan às.—*The horses couldn't take their feet out of it.*

> Said of very thick porridge &c.

Cha tuig an sàthach an seang: 's mairg a bhiodh 'na thràill da bhroinn.—*The full man understands not the empty: ill for him who is the slave of his belly.*

> *Al.*—Chan fhidir—*considers not.*
> Ní thuigeann an sáthach an seang.—*Ir.* Cha dennee rieau yn soogh y shang.—*Manx.* It's ill speaking 'twixt a fu man and a fastin.—*Scot.* Corpo satollo non crede al digiuno.—*It.* Ὁ χορτασμένος τὸν νηστικὸν δὲν τὸν πιστεύει.—*Mod. Gr.*

Cha tuig an t-òg aimbeart, 's cha tuig amadan aimhleas.—*Youth foresees not poverty, nor the fool his mischief.*

Cha tuit a h-uile rud air an tig crathadh.—*Everything falls not that is shaken.*

> Every wind bloweth not down the corn.—*Eng.* Ogni vento non scuote il noce.—*Ital.*

Cha tuit caoran à cliabh falamh.—*Peats don't fall from empty creels.*

Cha tuit guidhe air cloich no air crann.—*Curse won't fall on stock or stone.*

> The curse causeless shall not come.—*Prov.* xxvi, 2.
> Le bestemmie fanno come le processioni; ritornano donde partirono—*Curses, like processions, return whence they came.*—*Ital.*

Chaidh a phronnadh 'na shùgh fhèin.—*He was pounded in his own juice.*

Chaidh an ceòl air feadh na fìdhle.—*The music went through the fiddle.*

> All went into confusion.

Chaidh an taoim os ceann nan tobhtaichean.—*The bilge-water was over the thwarts.*

Chaidh an tonn gun dìreadh air.—*The wave went over him without climbing.*

Chaidh e don choille 'ghearradh bata gu gabhail air fhèin.—*He went to the wood for a stick to beat himself.*

Chaidh mi thar lus.—*I went over a plant.*

> In Macintosh the translation is 'I stepped over a weed,' with this note
> in the 2nd ed.:'Said when a person is seized suddenly with sickness.'
> I have not been able to find any trace of the idea that stepping over a
> plant causes sickness; but it is suggested that it refers to women in an
> interesting condition, when they have curious fancies. *Lus* might be a
> misreading of *lùths*, 'pith', in which case the proper rendering would
> be 'I went beyond my pith'. 'She gaed by hersel and fell ower'
> expresses the same thing.

Chaidh tu gu Dùn Bheagain orm.—*You went to the extreme with me.*

> *Lit. to Dunvegan.* A Lochaber saying.

Chaill e 'm baile thall, 's cha do bhuinnig e 'm baile bhos.—*He lost
yonder farm, and didn't get this one.*

> *Al.*—Chaill e Dall a bha thall, 's cha do bhuinnig e Dall a tha bhos—in
> reference to two farms in the parish of Barvas, Lewis.

Chaill e 'n seòl-mara.—*He lost the tide.*

Chaill Eòghann a Dhia, ach chaill an t-Iarl' a chuid airgid.—*Ewen
lost his God, but the Earl his money.*

> This singular saying is founded on the transaction thus mentioned in
> an old MS:
> 'Sir E. Cameron was bound by alliance, money, and solemn oath to
> the MacLeans, but renounced all on Argyll's quitting to him a debt
> of 40,000 merks.'—McFarlane's *Genealog. Coll.*, MSS Adv. Lib. II,
> 191.

Chailleadh tu do chluasan mur biodh iad an ceangal riut.—*You
would lose your ears were they not fastened to you.*

Chì an duin' acrach fada uaithe.—*The hungry man sees far.*—*Scot.*

Chì dithis barrachd air aon fhear.—*Two see more than one.*

> *Al.*—Chì ceithir sùilean nas mò na dhà. Four eyes see more than
> two.—*Eng.* Deux yeux voyent plus clair qu'un.—*Fr.* Vedon più
> quattr' occhi che due.—*Ital.* Mas ven quatro ojos que dos.—*Span.*
> Vier Augen sehen mehr als zwei.—*Germ.*

Chì mi sin, 's fuaighidh mi seo.—*That I see, but this I sew.*

A brave tailor in the little town of Beauly wagered that he would sew a pair of hose at midnight in the old church of Kilchrist, which was known to be haunted by a very dreadful ghost. He was duly escorted to the place and left in a seat near the door, with his cloth and thread and candles, about eleven o'clock. He set manfully to work, and sewed away undisturbed for about an hour. At length the clock struck the witching hour of twelve, and as the last stroke vibrated through the dead silence, the tailor with a beating heart became aware of a fearful head bending towards him, and a hoarse voice addressed him: 'Fhaic thu 'n ceann mòr liath 's e gun bhiadh, a thàilleir?'—*'See'st thou the big gray head without food, O tailor?'* 'That I see,' said the tailor, 'but this I sew', and went bravely on. Then the horrid thing drew nearer, and again the voice was heard: 'Fhaic thu 'n sgòrnan fada riabhach?' &c.—*'See'st thou the long grizzled throat?'* &c. The tailor answered as before, sewing with all his might. Still the thing drew nearer, and the voice said, 'Fhaic thu cholann fhada riabhach?' &c.—*'See'st thou the long grizzled trunk?'* &c. The tailor answered as before. Still nearer and nearer it came, and asked, 'Fhaic thu 'n t-sliasaid fhada riabhach?'—*'See'st thou the long grizzled thigh?'* and again, 'Fhaic thu 'n gàirdean fada riabhach?'—*'See'st thou the long grizzled arm?'*, and as it spoke, the horrid bony hand was stretched towards him. Still the tailor sewed away, having now but two or three stitches to do. The spectre was now close to him, its eyeless sockets glaring, its fleshless mouth grinning, the long brown arm and fingers menacing him, and for the last time the voice was heard: 'Fhaic thu chròg mhòr fhada riabhach 's i gun bhiadh, a thàilleir?'—*'See'st thou the great grizzled paw without food, O tailor?'* At that moment the tailor had finished his last stitch; he caught up the hose hastily and made for the door. Behind him clattered the skeleton, and just as he got out at the door he felt the bony fingers like hot pincers grazing his buttock. They left their mark there, but the tailor escaped alive and heard the bony hand rattling against the cheek of the church door, knocking a dint there in the stone which may be seen to this day, to testify to the truth of the brave tailor's story!

Chì sinn dè 'n taobh a thig a' mhaodal às a' mhart.—*We'll see on which side the paunch comes out of the cow.*

> This is suggestive of something like the Roman divination from intestines; but it really means nothing more than a joke sometimes played on young people present on the great occasion of killing a winter cow. They would be asked to guess on which side of the animal the paunch would appear, which was of course a matter of mere accident.

Chì sinn, mar a thuirt an dall.—*We'll see, as the blind man said.*

> Nous verrons, dit l'aveugle.—*Fr.*

Chì thu thugad e, 's chan fheàirrd' thu agad e.—*You'll see it coming to you, and you'll be none the better.*

Chlisg am brochan nach d'òl e.—*The gruel he drank not trembled.*

> Intended to indicate great trepidation.

Chluicheadh e h-uile bun rùdain deth.—*He would play his very knuckles off.*

> A desperate gamester.

Chual' luchan an àrd-dorais e.—*The mice of the lintel heard it.*

> A supposed secret.

Chluinneadh e 'm feur a' fàs.—*He would hear the grass growing.*

Cho àlainn ri Aghaidh-shneachda.—*As lovely as Snow-face.*

> This is the 'Agandecca' of Macpherson, known in Highland story long before his time.

Cho an-iochdmhor ris an Turcach.—*As merciless as the Turk.*

> The fame of Turkish corsairs found its way to the remotest Hebrides.

Cho binn ri smeòraich air gèig.—*As tuneful as a mavis on a bough.*

Cho bìth ris an luch fo ladhar a' chait.—*As quiet as a mouse under the cat's paw.*

> *Al.*—Cho umhail ri luch fo spòg a' chait.
> As quiet as a mouse.—*Eng.*

Cho bochd ris a' chirc.—*As poor as a hen.*

Cho bodhar ri cloich.—*As deaf as a stone.*

Cho bodhar ri gèadh as t-Fhoghar.—*As deaf as a goose in Autumn.*

Cho breugach 's a tha 'n cù cho bradach.—*As lying as the dog is thievish.*

Cho bròdail ris a' mhac-mhallachd.—*As proud as the son of perdition.*
> As proud as Lucifer.

Cho cam ri imir an amadain.—*As crooked as the fool's furrow.*

Cho carach ri MacChrùislig.—*As tricky as MacCruslick.*
> See 'Cha b' ann mar a fhuair'.

Cho carach ris a' mhadadh-ruadh.—*As wily as a fox.—Eng.*

Cho ciallach ri cnoc.—*As wise as a hill.*
> The alliteration is the chief thing here. The sense, such as it is, is better than the English 'As wise as a wisp'.

Cho corrach ri ugh air droll.—*As unsteady as an egg on a stick.*
> Mal wy ar trosol.—*Welsh.*

Cho crosda ris an dris.—*As cross as a bramble.*

Cho cruaidh ri seiche Ruairidh—nì i fuaim, 's nuair a thèid a bualadh nì i srann.—*As hard as Rory's hide—it sounds, and when it's struck, it resounds.*

Cho cuimseach làmh ri Connlaoch.—*As unerring of hand as Connlaoch.*

> Connlaoch was one of the Ossianic heroes, son of Cuchullin, and brought up at Dùn Sgàthaich in Skye, of which the ruins still remain. There are several ballads on the tragic story of Connlaoch to be found in Campbell's *Leabhar na Féinne*, pp 9–15. It forms the subject also of one of the finest pieces in Macpherson's Ossian.

> The name Connlaoch cannot, unfortunately, be represented as pronounced by any English letters, the diphthong *ao* in particular (something like the French *oeu* and the German *ö*) having no place in the English language.

Cho dall ri bonn do chois.—*As blind as the sole of your foot.*

Cho dall ri dallaig.—*As blind as a dog-fish.*

Cho dall ri damh ann an ceò.—*As blind as an ox in mist.*

Cho daor ris an t-salann.—*As dear as salt.*

> See 'Cha b'e sin an salann saor'.

Cho disgir ri cat.—*As nimble as a cat.*

Cho dona dheth ri làir a' ghobha.—*As ill off as the blacksmith's mare.*

> The smith's mear and the soutar's wife are aye the warst shod.—*Scot.*

Cho dudach ri circ.—*As thin-skinned as a hen.*

Cho eòlach 's a tha 'm brìdean 's an tràigh.—*As well acquainted as the oyster-catcher is with the shore.*

Cho eòlach 's a tha 'n ladar air a' phoit.—*As intimate as the ladle and the pot.*

Cho fad' 's a bhios bainne geal aig boin dhuibh.—*As long as a black cow gives white milk.*

> This is said to have been once the term of lease of a farm in Uist.

Cho fad 's a bhios craobh sa choill, bidh foill anns a' Chuimeanach.—*As long as trees are in the wood, the Cumming will be treacherous.*

> This is one out of several similar sayings which, it is hoped, will give no offence now to any members of the clans so characterized. The Cumming one is selected as a leading specimen because it is perhaps the oldest, having probably originated in the time of King Robert the Bruce, who punished the treachery of his cousin the Red Cumyn in such a memorable way at Dumfries.

> 'Cho fad' 's a bhios slat an coill, bidh foill ann an Caimbeulach' bestows the same character on the great Campbell clan, a saying probably dating from the massacre of Glencoe.

> > Cho fad' 's a bhios maid' 'an coill,
> > Cha bhi Mathanach gun fhoill

> euphoniously proclaims the same of the respectable tribe of Mathesons. The Munros are similarly libelled.

More stiffly, and with as little known reason, it is said of the Mac-Phails:

> Fhad 's a bhios fuachd ann an stoc càil,
> (*or* uisge am bun càil)
> Bidh an fhoill ann an Clann Phàil.
>
> —*While there's cold in stock of kail,*
> *Will be guile in a MacPhail.*

Lastly, and worst of all, it has been said, probably by some Mainland or Long Island victim of Skye treachery, 'Fhad 's a bhios fiodh an coill, bidh an fhoill san Sgitheanach.'

Cho fad 's a bhios monadh an Cinn t-Sàil', cha bhi MacCoinnich gun àl sa chrò.—*As long as there are moors in Kintail, Mackenzie won't want cattle in the pen.*

> This referred to the ancient lords of Kintail, the last of whom died in 1815. The word *crò* has a double meaning here, being the name of a part of Kintail, so called from the river Croe.

Cho fad 's a bhios muir a' bualadh ri lic.—*As long as sea beats on stone.*

Cho fada sa cheann 's a bha Fionn sna casan.—*As long in the head as Fingal was in the legs.*

> In some of the Ossianic legends, Fingal figures as a man of gigantic dimensions, and that is the general tradition about him and his followers.

Cho fallain ris a' bhreac.—*As healthy as a salmon.*

> It is a sad fact that the immunity from disease of this noble fish can be claimed for it no longer, after the evidence of 1879.

Cho fileanta ri uileann fìdhleir.—*As tuneful as a fiddler's elbow.*

Cho fuar ri màthair a' chlèirich.—*As cold as the beadle's mother.*

> The beadle's mother was in the habit, where this proverb originated (Tiree, apparently), of doing duty for her son occasionally, and in the collection of dues or taxes she was as coldly severe as any head of a Financial Department could desire.

Cho geal ri sneachd na h-aon oidhche.—*As white as the one night's snow.*

Cho glic ri sagart 's eallach leabhraichean air.—*As wise as a priest with a load of books.*

Cho gionach ris a' chù.—*As greedy as a dog.*

Cho gnù ri broc.—*As grippy as a badger.*

Cho gòrach ris na h-eòin.—*As thoughtless as the birds.*

Often said of children by nice old women.

Cho labhar ris a' ghaoith.—*As noisy as the wind.*

Cho làidir ri Cù Chulainn.—*As strong as Cuchullin.*

Cuchullin is one of the principal characters in Scoto-Irish legendary poetry and history, and is represented as not only a prodigy of strength but gifted with every manly grace—a Celtic Achilles, and something more. In the wonderful old Irish legend of the *Táin Bó Cuailgne*, he figures as the hero of the great struggle, in which he perished fighting against fearful odds, simply through his magnificent sense of honour and chivalry, knowing perfectly what he risked. This strange weird story is embodied by Mr O'Grady in his *History of Ireland*.

The description of Cuchullin in his chariot, in the 1st Book of Macpherson's *Fingal*, is one of the passages in that poem of which there can be no doubt that he at least was not the author, and that the original was Gaelic, and old. It contains one amusing example of Macpherson's inaccuracy, or imperfect knowledge of his native tongue. The two lines, describing one of the horses,

> Bu shoilleir a dhreach, 's bu luath
> Shiubhal: Sith-fada b'e ainm,

are well translated by Dr. Clerk:

> *Shining his coat, and speedy*
> *His pace—Si-fadda his name.*

Macpherson's translation is 'Bright are the sides of the steed! His name is Sulin-Sifadda!' The word *Sith-fada* means 'Long-pace,' an admirable name for a horse. Macpherson, misreading and mistranslating *shiubhal*, 'his going,' imagined that it was part of the horse's name, and tacked it on accordingly.

Cuchullin's name is still associated in Skye with the old vitrified fort of Dùn Sgàthaich at Ord (painted more than once by McCulloch), where his son Connlaoch was supposed to have been born and brought up by his mother, whom Cuchullin in *Fingal*, B. I., speaks of as

> Deò-ghrèine Dhùn Sgàthaich nan stuadh,
> Ainnir bhràigh-gheal nan rosg mall,
> Ise dh'fhàg mi 'n Innis an t-slòigh.

> —*The sunbeam of Dunscaaich of waves,*
> *White-bosomed fair of gentle eye*
> *Whom I left in the Isle of hosts.*

The fashion introduced by writers of guide-books and others of calling the Coolin Hills in Skye 'Cuchullin Hills' is without any local or historical warrant. They were never known in Skye by any other name than the *Cuilfhion*, pronounced 'Coolyun'. *Cuilfhinn*, 'fair', 'lovely', suggests a fit etymology, but I believe the name is derived from the fact that the Holly, *Cuileann*, was found in unusual abundance among the ravines of these mountains. It still flourishes on the rocky banks of several of the streams, and on the most conspicuous of the islets in Coiruisk.

The sweet-scented 'Queen of the Meadow' is named in Gaelic *Crios Chù Chulainn*—'Cuchullin's belt', of which Alexander MacDonald in his *Song of Summer* sweetly sings,

> 'S cùbhraidh fàileadh do mhuineil,
> A Chrios Chù Chulainn nan càrn.

> —*Sweet is the scent of thy neck,*
> *Thou belt of Cuchullin of cairns.*

Cho làidir ris a' Gharbh Mac Stàirn.—*As strong as Garv the son of Starn.*

'An Garbh' is simply 'The Strong', a Celtic name bestowed on a Scandinavian champion who figures largely in the old Gaelic ballads. In Macpherson's Ossian he is Swaran, son of Starno, and brother of Agandecca, whom Cuchullin overcame.

Cho làn 's tha 'n t-ugh den bhiadh.—*As full as an egg is of meat.*

Cho leisg ri seana chù.—*As lazy as an old dog.*

Cho lìonmhor ri muinntir Fhionnlaigh.—*As numerous as Finlay's people.*

> This is a Lewis name for the fairies, of unknown origin.

Cho lìonmhor ris na gathan dubha.—*As numerous as the black darts.*

> This is variously interpreted, and may be held descriptive of midges darting to and fro in myriads, or of the black spikes of small oats.

Cho luath ri aigne nam ban baoth.—*As swift as the fancy of foolish women.*

> A sharp, but not censorious, saying.

Cho luath ris na loin.—*As swift as the elks.*

> *Al.*—Cho luath ris na luinn—*As swift as the wavetops.*
>
> The primary rendering of this goes back to a prehistoric period. The other is very descriptive, and applies equally to the waving of corn or grass.

Cho marbh ri sgadan.—*As dead as a herring.*

> No other fish dies so quickly on being taken out of the water.

Cho math 's as fhiach am mèirleach a' chroich.—*As well as the thief deserves the gallows.*

> As well worth it as a thief is worth a rope.—*Eng.*

Cho mear ri ceann siamain ri latha gaoithe.—*As merry as the head of a straw-rope on a windy day.*

> Trivial, but graphic.

Cho mòr aig a chèile ri dà cheann eich.—*As thick as two horses' heads.*

> *Al.*—Cho rèidh ris na ceannaichean—*As well-agreed as merchants.*
> This version looks like a pun = *ceann-eich*. [May simply mean 'two horses'.]

Cho mosach ris na glasan.—*As mean as the locks.*

> Lock-fast places are still comparatively uncommon among the Highland peasantry. As for locking a main door at night, that is never thought of.

Cho nimheil ris an nathair.—*As venomous as a serpent.*

Cho reamhar ris an ròn.—*As fat as a seal.*

Cho sgìth dheth 's a bha 'n losgann den chlèith-chliata.—*As tired as the toad was of the harrow.*

> Many masters, quoth the toad to the harrow, when every tine (tooth) turned her over.—*Eng.* Mony maisters, quo the puddock, when ilka tynd o the harrow took him a toit.—*Scot.*

Cho sgìth ri cù.—*As tired as a dog.*

> No animal wearies himself so unsparingly as a dog; none is so ready, when most weary, to obey his master's call.

Cho sgìth 's a bha 'n gobha da mhàthair, nuair a thiodhlaic e seachd uairean i.—*As tired as the smith was of his mother, when he buried her seven times.*

> I don't know the origin of this ridiculous saying.

Cho sunndach ris an fhiadh.—*As hearty as the stag.*

Cho teòma ri Coibhi Druidh.—*As clever as Coivi the Druid.*

> Dr. John Smith, in his *Galic Antiquities* (p. 8, note), says that this was the Gaelic name for the Arch-Druid; and in Bede's interesting account of the conversion of King Aedwin of Northumbria (*Eccl. Hist.*, Lib. II, cap. 13), the high-priest is called Coifi. In Mr Moberly's note on this (ed. of Bede, 1869), he says: "This name has been derived from Coibhi, the Kymric for 'helpful,' and thus it has been argued that the Angle hierarchy was British. But see Kemble, *Archaeol. Soc. Proc.*, 1845, p. 83. Coifi is only an Anglo-Saxon nickname of easy translation. The word is equivalent to Coefig or Cêfig, just as Coinræd in the Northumbrian dialect represents Cênræd in West-Saxon. It is an adjective formed from *côf*, 'strenuous,' and merely denotes the 'bold or active one'."
>
> I cannot find the word *coibhi*, or anything like it, in any Cymric dictionary, but whatever its origin, the name has been handed down in Scottish Gaelic for an unknown length of time as that of an important Druid. The above saying might well be applied to King Aedwin's high-priest, who behaved with remarkable wisdom on the occasion above mentioned.

For another saying in reference to Coibhi, see 'Ge fagas clach'.

Cho teth ri gaol seòladair.—*As hot as a sailor's love.*

> *Al.*—'gaol tàilleir'—*a tailor's love.* Both sailors and tailors are accused of being apt to change their affections easily.

Cho tric 's a tha fiacail ad cheann.—*As often as there's a tooth in your head.*

> Chuala mi chuthag gun bhiadh am bhroinn,
> Chunnaic mi 'n searrach 's a chùlaibh rium,
> Chunnaic mi 'n t-seilcheag air an lic luim,
> 'S dh'aithnich mi nach rachadh a' bhliadhn' ud leam.

> *—I heard the cuckoo while fasting,*
> *I saw the foal with his back to me,*
> *I saw the snail on the flagstone bare,*
> *And I knew the year would be bad for me.*

Attributed to the *Cailleach Bheurra*, a distinguished Sybil.

Chuir am maor do thaigh an rùnair' e.—*The bailiff sent him to the secretary.*

> *Al.*—'an rìgh' *for* 'am maor'.
> The 'Circumlocution Office' on a small scale.

Chuir Brìghd' a làmh sa bhobhla.—*Bridget put her hand into the bowl.*

This seems to refer to St Bridget's miraculous power of turning water into ale. The following curious old rhyme is among the Gaelic MSS of the Advocates' Library (G. MS LXII).

> TUIREADH BRIGHID
> Gairim is guidhim tu, chlach,
> Na leig Brìghid a-mach.
> O 's i geurachadh an deoch,
> Is ioma saoidh gun lochd
> Dhan tug i bàs.
> Do thart a-nis o chaidh to thart,
> Tart sìorraidh ort, a Bhrighid.

Chuir e bhàt' air acair.—*He set his boat at anchor.*

Chuir e chliath-chaisg air.—*He put the harrow-check on him.*

> He put a stopper on him, or a spoke in his wheel.

Chuir e chrodh air àireachas.—*He sent his cattle to the hill pasture.*

This is an inland saying, as the one about the boat is maritime.

Chuir e 'n dubh-chapaill air.—*He quite outdid him.*

This is a Lochaber phrase of unknown origin. It used to be the practice at weddings to have a pleasant competition in singing between 'Dà thaobh an t-sabhail,' the two sides of the barn—often the bride's friends against the bridegroom's. The side that held out longest would then say to the others, 'An dubh-chapaill oirbh!'

Chuir e na buinn 's na breabanan air.—*He put the soles and half-soles on.*

He used all expedition, and finished the job.

Chuir iad am balgan-suain fo cheann.—*They put the sleeping-bag under his head.*

Applied, says Macintosh, to a person who sleeps too much, in allusion to the bag or cocoon in which the caterpillar sleeps.

Chuir thu ceann paib air mu dheireadh.—*You have put a tow-head on it at last.*

Al.—'ceann gràineil'—*a vile end.*
Said, says Macintosh, of those who destroy all the good they have done by an ill deed.
Desinit in piscem mulier formosa superne.—*Hor.*

Chuireadh e na h-eòin an crannaibh.—*He would make the birds go into trees.*

With the sweetness of his voice. Duncan MacIntyre, describing the Glen Etive women waulking cloth, says

Nuair a sheinneas iad na h-òrain,
Cuiridh iad na h-eòin an crannaibh.

Chuireadh e 'n òrrais air math-ghamhainn.—*It would sicken a bear.*

Chuireadh e na searraich bho dheoghal.—*It would put the foals from sucking.*

So bitter or disgusting.

Chuireadh iad na fèidh à fàsach.—*They would send the deer out of a wilderness.*

>   Said of very noisy people.

Chuireadh tu eagal air na Samhanaich.—*You would frighten the savages.*

>   This is an Islay saying.
>   *Al.*—Mharbhadh e na Samhanaich—*It would kill the savages*; said of something very overpowering or unwholesome.
>   See 'Aran'.

Chumadh e dha mun do chumadh triubhas dha.—*It was fitted for him before trews were made for him.*

>   It was predestined for him.

Chunnaic mise dà MhacCoinnich romhad!—*I have seen two Mackenzies before you!*

>   Two Mackenzie factors.
>   Factors have rarely been popular in the Highlands. The above was said by an indignant farmer to a disagreeable factor in Lewis when the Mackenzies of Seaforth were lords of that island. At the burial of a Lewis factor, amid dry eyes, the following verse was made:

>   >   Cuiribh air! Cuiribh air!
>   >   'S e chuireadh oirnne;
>   >   'S ma dh'èireas e rithist,
>   >   Cuiridh e 'n còrr oirnn!

>   >   *Heap on him! Heap on him!*
>   >   *It's he that would put on us;*
>   >   *And if he rise again,*
>   >   *He'll just put more on us!*

>   I have heard of even a stronger sentiment expressed in another island at the burial of a factor who had taken in a great number of confiding people, left lamenting, not for him, but for their hardly earned money. One of these victims, a sturdy old man, stood by the grave when all was over, and shaking his fist at it, said, 'Nam bu tig an là a dh'èireas tusa às a sin!'—'*May the day never come when you'll rise out of that!*'
>   The Celts of Scotland have never, in modern times, so far as I know, maltreated, much less killed, a factor, steward or magistrate. They

have often been treated unjustly; but they are neither so quick of tongue, nor so unsparing of hand, as their Irish brethren.

Ciall a dh'fhadaidheas teine;
Rian a chumas baile;
Cha mhair sliochd fir foille
No iochd ri chuid cloinne.

—*Sense builds up a fire;*
Order keeps a city;
False man's seed endures not,
Nor will they get pity.

Al.—Tùr a thogas teine; ciall a chuireas às e—*Wit to make a fire; sense to put it out.*

Cinnidh a' chrìontachd, 's thèid an ro-chrìontachd a dholaidh.—*Saving getteth store, over-saving mischief.*

Cinnidh Clann Fhearchair gus an deicheamh linn.—*The Farquharsons shall flourish to the tenth generation.*

The Farquharsons, says Macintosh, in a long note on this, are also called Clann Fhionnlaigh, i.e., the children of Finlay, "from Finlay More, one of their tall chieftains, who bore the royal standard at the battle of Pinkie; hence the surnames Finlay, MacKinlay and Finlayson. The Farquharsons," he adds, "are descended of Farchard Shaw, son of Shaw of Dalnavert; the present Farquharson of Invercauld, their chief, seems to deny this, and pretends that they are descended of Macduff, Thane, and afterwards Earl of Fife, for which assertion neither he nor any other can show vouchers."

Cinnidh mac o mhì-altram, ach cha chinn e on Aog.—*A child may survive bad nursing, but he can't escape Death.*

Cinnidh Scuit saor am fine,
Mur breug am fàisdine;
Far an faighear an Lia Fàil,
Dlighe flaitheas do ghabhàil.

—*The Scottish race shall flourish free,*
Unless false the prophecie;
Where the sacred stone is found,
There shall sovereignty have ground.

This saying is undoubtedly Irish, and not Scottish, in the modern sense of the latter word. As given by Keating (ed. 1811, p. 198) it is

> Cineadh Scuit saor an fine,
> Mun budh bréag an fhaisdine;
> Mar a fuighid an liagh-fháil,
> Dlighid flaitheas do ghabháil.

Keating gives this as his rendering of the Latin of Hector Boece, which must therefore be regarded as the first known version of this saying. Boece's couplet, which he says is engraved on the stone—'*Suprascriptio lapidi insculpta*' (ed. 1574, fol. 2)—is

> Ni fallat fatum, Scoti, quocunque locatum,
> Invenient lapidem, regnare tenentur ibidem,

thus translated into English:

> *The Scots shall brook that realm as native ground,*
> *If weirds fail not, where'er this chair is found.*

Keating, however, though indebted to Boece for this verse, quotes a still older one in reference to the *Lia Fáil*, from the poet Cinaeth O'Hartigan, who died, according to Tighernach, in 975:

> An cloch a tá fám dhá sháil,
> Uaithe ráidhtear Inis Fáil.

> —*The stone that is beneath my feet,*
> *From it is styled the Isle of Fáil.*

Keating's Hist., ed. 1811, p. 118.

The stone in question, so far as Scotland is concerned, was undoubtedly carried away from Scone by that prince of robbers, Edward I, and deposited in Westminster Abbey, in the coronation chair, where every British sovereign has been crowned ever since, down to our dearly beloved Queen Victoria. So much faith has the sturdy Saxon ever had, in spite of all his protests and prose, in Celtic sentiment and prophecy! Why, else, should he have made so much of a rough piece of what Professor Geikie has assured Mr Skene to be simply a bit of Perthshire sandstone? (See Skene's *Coronation Stone*). Archaeology and Geology combined to make sad havoc of traditional faith, for we are assured by Hector Boece that the precious stone in question was the royal chair of King Gathelus in Brigantia, and was carried from Spain to Ireland, and from Ireland to Scotland. Keating, on the other hand, tells us that it was brought by the Tuath Dé Dannan from Lochlann (Scandinavia) and sent over from Ireland to Scotland by Murtogh Mac Earc, that his brother, Fergus the Great, 'the first of our kings, I suppose', might be crowned on it (AD 503). Some imaginative Saxons, fired by Irish poetry, go a great deal further than this, and believe, or try to make believe, that this sufficiently venerable stone is *the very stone* on which Jacob pillowed his head on that memorable night when he slept and dreamed at Bethel; and that our possession of it in Westminster Abbey is one among a hundred clear proofs that we are the real Children of Israel—the remnant of the lost Ten Tribes!

Apart from all absurdity, that stone is very venerable, and ought, to every British person, English, Scottish, or Irish, to be really sacred. The above rhyme is interesting philologically and historically, whatever be thought of the legend. *Lia = Liag = Leac*, a flat stone, and *Fàl* = prerogative, privilege, privileged person, King, whence the old name of Ireland, *Innis Fáil*.

Another Irish name for the *Lia Fáil* is *Cloch na Cinneamhna*, the Stone of Destiny.

There is a Lochaber saying that possibly refers to the Irish origin of this sacred stone. It is said, when darning or patching a hole on a boy's jacket or trousers while on him, 'Fuaigheam seo mu chloich ghlais an t-sagairt—a' chlach ghlas a bha 'n Eirinn.'—'*Let me sew this round the priest's gray stone—the gray stone that was in Ireland.*'

Ciod a b'àill leat fhaighinn an nead an fhithich ach am fitheach fhèin?—*What would you expect in the raven's nest but the raven itself?*

Ciod a dh'iarradh tu air bò ach gnòsd?—*What would you expect from a cow but a groan?*

The word 'groan' does not quite represent the sound in question. Neither does 'moan' nor 'low'. It is that subdued noise which a cow utters as her ordinary expression of feeling.

Ciod as fheàrr a dh'innseas an cladh na 'n eaglais?—*What better guide to the churchyard than the church?*

Ciod as misde duin' a chreach, mur lughaid a phòr e?—*What is a man the worse of being plundered if it doesn't diminish his produce?*

A very philosophical view of the matter.

Cìrean a' choilich air a' chirc.—*The cock's comb on the hen.*

The woman wearing the breeks.

Clach an ionad càbaig, 's corc an ionad cuinnseir.—*A stone instead of a cheese, and a knife instead of a sword.*

> 'S MacEòghainn th' ann an dràsda,
> Mar chloich an ionad càbaig,
> An àite na bh' ann.
>
> Macintyre's *Cumha Choire Cheathaich.*

Clach air muin cloich MhicLèoid—*A stone on the top of MacLeod's stone.*

> A MacDonald saying, doubtless, these two clans having been always the great rivals for power in Skye.

Clachag 'nam bhròig, deargan 'nam mhuilchinn, càilean 'nam fhia-cail, 's mo leannan gam fhàgail—*A pebble in my shoe, a flea in my sleeve, a husk in my teeth, and my sweetheart leaving me.*

> A combination of annoyances.

Clachan an t-Srath, is mnathan Shlèibhte.—*The stones of Strath, and the women of Sleat.*

> Strath and Sleat are neighbouring parishes in Skye; the one possessing, among other distinctions, a vein of gray marble of which the road-side dykes are to a large extent built—the other noted, or claiming to be, for the beauty of its women.

Clachan beag a' dol an ìochdar, 's clachan mòr a' dol an uachdar.—*The little stones going down, and the big ones coming to the top.*

> A physical fact, and a human experience also.

Clachan dubha 'n aghaidh sruth.—*Black stones against the stream.*

Clachair Samhraidh, dìol-dèirc Geamhraidh.—*Summer mason, Winter beggar.*

> Sometimes the case still, but seldom compared with old times.

Claidheamh an làimh amadain, is slacan an làimh òinsich.—*A sword in a fool's hand, a beetle in an idiot's.*

> Ne'er put a sword in a wud man's hand.—*Scot.* Μὴ παιδὶ μάχαιραν—*Don't give a sword to a child.*—*Gr.* Ne puero gladium. Ne gladium tollas, mulier.—*Lat.*

Clann Diarmaid nam busa dubha, cuiribh riu is beiribh orra.—*The black-mouthed MacDiarmids, go at them and catch them.*

This probably refers to the MacDiarmids of Glen Lyon.

Clann Fhionghain nam faochag.—*The Mackinnons of wilks.*

A common nickname in Skye. This surname is usually written 'Mac Ionmhuinn,' founded on a pretty but fanciful etymology. A more probable derivation traces the clan to one called Fingan.

Clann MhicCodruim nan ròn.—*The seal MacCodrums.*

There is a legend about the MacCodrums having been metamorphosed into seals, too long to be given here. They retained, along with the amphibious shape, the human soul and, at times, human form. They were, in fact, seals by day but human creatures at night. No MacCodrum, for all the world, would, if in his proper senses, fire a gun at a seal.

Clann Mhuirich a' bhrochain.—*The gruelly MacPhersons.*

'Mac Neacail a' bhrochain 's an droch aran eòrna'—'*Nicolson of the gruel and bad barley bread*'—is a Skye saying. The same is sometimes said of the MacAskills. But it is apparently borrowed from a Badenoch song, in which an old woman says:

Tha 'n cnatan orm,
Tha 'n tùchan orm,
Tha 'm brochan an coinneamh mo lùths thoirt uam.
Am brochan dubh 'n còmhnaidh,
'S an droch aran-eòrna,
'S an t-annlann air bòrd 's a chùlaibh rium.

Clanna nan Gàidheal an guaillibh a chèile!—*The clans of the Gael shoulder to shoulder!*

This is one of the best known and oftenest quoted of all Gaelic sayings. Literally it is 'in each other's shoulders,' i.e., each with his arm around the shoulder of the other, as Highlanders would do in crossing a deep water together.

Claoidhidh foighidinn mhath na clachan.—*Patience will wear out stones.*

Clàr mòr fo bheagan.—*Big dish and little on it.*

> The *clàr* was a big wooden dish, and I suppose is not yet obsolete in the Highlands.

Cleamhnas am fagas, is goisteachd am fad.—*Affinity near, sponsorship far off.*

Cleas gille nan cual—cual bheag is tighinn tric.—*The porter's trick—a little load and frequent.*

> *Al.*—cuallach a' mhic leisg—*the lazy lad's herding.*
> *Al.*—tarraing chailleach—*old wives' drawing.*

Cloichearan spàgach, ogha na muile-màig.—*The waddling stonechat, the frog's grandchild.*

> A Lismore saying, suggestive of the development theory.

Cluich a' chas, a chompaich.—*Play the foot, my comrade.*

> Giving one's companion leg bail.

Cluich a' chuilein ris an t-seann chù.—*The play of the pup with the old dog.*

> *Al.*—Mir' a' chuilein ris a' mhial-chù.

Cluinnidh am bodhar fuaim an airgid.—*The deaf can hear the silver clink.*

Cluinnidh an dùthaich is cù Roib Cheàird e.—*The country will hear it, and Rob Tinker's dog too.*

Cluinnidh tu air a' chluais as buidhr' e.—*You'll hear it on your deafest ear.*

Cluinnear e far nach faicear e.—*He'll be heard where he is not seen.*

Cnàmhag na circe reamhair.—*The fat hen's refuse.*

Cnàimh mòr do dhuine gionach.—*A great bone to a greedy man.*—*Scot.*

Cnàimh mòr is feòil air, fuigheal clachair.—*A big bone and flesh on it, a mason's leavings.*

> See 'Fuighleach tàilleir'.

Cnàmhan a' chinn-adhairt.—*The pillow-head gnawing.*

A curtain lecture.

Cnatan Dhòmhnaill MhicMhàrtainn.—*Donald Martin's cold.*

A Lochaber saying. Donald was said to take a cold once a quarter which lasted three months. The MacMartins in that country are Camerons.

Cnò à uachdar a' mhogail.—*A nut from the upper side of the cluster.*

Supposed to be the best. See 'Bidh an ubhal as fheàrr'.

Cnoic is uisg' is Ailpeinich, ach cuin a thàinig Artaraich?—*Hills and water and MacAlpines, but when did the MacArthurs come?*

Al.—Cnoic is uillt—*Hills and streams.* Cnoic is uilc—*Hills and ills.* 'Meaning,' says Macintosh, 'that the MacGregors are as old as the hills.' As already noted, under 'Cha robh balach,' they trace their descent from Alpin, King of Scots in the first half of the 9th century, and Macintosh quotes an old verse in reference to their descent:

> Sliochd nan rìghribh dùthchasach
> Bha shìos an Dùn 's Dà Innis,
> Aig an robh crùn na h-Alb' o thùs
> 'S aig am beil dùthchas fhathast ris.

> *—Children of the native kings*
> *Who reigned down at Dunstaffnage,*
> *Who first the crown of Alba owned*
> *And still have native claim to it.*

The MacArthurs, as the above saying implies, claim a still older lineage, from a King Art, or Arthur, of prehistoric times. In Cormac's Glossary, the word 'art' has three meanings given—'*uasal*, unde dicitur *fine airt*, no *art fine*'—*noble*, whence *a noble tribe*.

Cnuasach uircein, buain is ithe.—*The pig's contemplation, pluck and eat.*

Cnuasachd na gràineig.—*The hedgehog's hoard.*

> This, says Armstrong, is 'expressive of the folly of worldly-minded
> people, who part with all at the grave, as the hedgehog is compelled
> to drop its burden of crab-apples at the narrow entrance of its hole'.
> Lightfoot says (*Flora Scotica*, 2nd ed., 1792, p. 13) the hedgehog is
> not 'found beyond the Tay, perhaps not beyond the Forth'. It is found
> at this day as far north as Lochaber.

Cò air a rinn thu siud?—Ort fhèin, a ghràidh.—*On whom did you do
that?—On yourself, my dear.*

Cò dha a b'fheàrr a b'aithne an cat a thoirt as a' mhuighe na don
fhear a chuir ann i?—*Who knows best to take the cat out of the churn
but he that put her in?*

> Ye served me as the wife did the cat—coost me in the kirn and syne
> harled me oot again.—*Scot.*

Cò dha bhios MacMhathain gu math, mur bi dha fhèin?—*To whom
will Matheson be good, if not to himself?*

Co-dhiù 's ann air srath no 'n gleann, 's ann às a ceann a bhlighear
a' bhò.—*Whether on strath or in glen, 'tis from her head the cow's milk
comes.*

> As a ceann a bhlichtear an bhó.—*Ir.* Godröid buwch oî phen.—*Welsh.*
> It's by the head that the cou gies milk.—*Scot.* As the cou feeds, so she
> bleeds.—*Do.* Die Kuh milcht durchs Maul.—*Germ.*

Co-dhiù 's fhusa bata dhèanamh den ghuairne mu ghuairn, no
cuaille den ghiùirne mu ghiùrn?—*Whether is it easier to make a stick
of the quill-pith, or a stake of the auger-dust?*

> This is another version of Tweedledum and Tweedledee, the phrases
> used having reference to the use of a turning-lathe.

Cò nì 'n t-olc ach na mnathan!—*Who can do ill but the women!*

> This is but another form of 'Corruptio optimi est pessima'. 'All
> wickedness,' says the son of Sirach (xxv, 19), 'is but little to the
> wickedness of a woman.'

Cò ris a thèid mi gam ghearan, 's gun Mac Mhic Ailein am Mùideart?—*To whom can I make my complaint, and no Clanranald in Moidart?*

> This natural gush of Celtic feeling refers to the Clanranald who was killed at Sheriffmuir, a chief who was the idol of his clan.

Cobhair nan geas.—*The succour from spells.*

> Said of a person to be relied on as an Oedipus, or Hercules, in cases of difficulty, to solve riddles, or break spells.

Coimeas a' gheòidh bhric 's a mhàthar.—*The comparison of the gray goose to his mother.*

Coimhearsnach bun an dorais.—*Next door neighbour.*

> *Al.*—C. na h-ursainn—*Door-post neighbour.*

Coin bhadhail is clann dhaoin' eile.—*Stray dogs and other people's children.*

Còinneach do thaigh, crìonach a chonnadh, blàth on bhoine, teth on teine.—*Moss to his house, brushwood for his fuel, warm milk from the cow, heat from the fire.*

> Attributed to the 'Ollamh Ileach' as an advice for old people.

Coinnichidh na daoine ged nach coinnich na cnuic.—*Men may meet, but mountains never.*—*Eng.*

> *Al.*—Tachraidh na daoine.
> Cynt y cwrdd dau ddyn na dau lan—*Sooner will two men meet than two banks.*—*Welsh.* Friends may meet, but mountains never greet.—*Eng.* We'll meet ere hills meet.—*Scot.* Deux hommes se rencontrent bien, mais jamais deux montagnes.—*Fr.* Βουνον με βουνὸ ν δὲν ἀνταμόνεται—*Mountain doesn't meet mountain.*—*Mod. Gr.*

Coltach ri casag Iain Ruaidh Bhuidhe, gun chumadh gun eireachdas.—*Like Yellow Red John's coat, without shape or elegance.*

Coltach ri earball an t-seana mhairt, daonnan air dheireadh.—*Like the old cow's tail, always last.*

Coltach ri mnathan MhicCarmaig, glè làidir san amhaich.—*Like MacCormack's wives, very strong in the neck.*

> Who MacCormack was, and where he lived, we know not; but it may be assumed that he was sadly henpecked.

Coltach ri m'sheana bhrògan, a' sìor dhol am miosad.—*Like my old shoes, ever getting worse.*

Comhairle caraid gun a h-iarraidh, cha d'fhuair i riamh am meas bu chòir dhi.—*A friend's advice unasked never got due esteem.*

> Ulster saying in same words.
> *Al.*—Comhairle gun iarraidh, cha robh meas riamh oirre.
> Ergyd yn llwyn cysul heb erchi—*Advice unasked is like a shot into the wood.—Welsh.*

Comhairle caraid gun a h-iarraidh,'s i 's fhiach a gleidheadh.—*A friend's advice unasked is well worth keeping.*

Comhairle do dhuine glic, slat do dhruim an amadain.—*Counsel for the wise man, for the fool's back a rod.*

> A wink to the wise, a kick to the fool.—*Arab.* A nod for a wise man, a rod for a fool.—*Eng.* A whip for the horse, a bridle for the ass, and a rod for the fool's back.—*Prov.* xxvi, 3.

> Comhairle Clag Sgàin:
> An rud nach buin dut, na buin da.
>
> —*Counsel of the Bell of Scone,*
> *Touch not what is not thine own.*
>
> The voice of the Bell of Scone, the ancient seat of Scottish royalty, was taken to represent the voice of Law and Justice, of which the fundamental maxim is 'Suum cuique'.

Co-dhaltas gu ceud, is càirdeas gu fichead.—*Fostership to a hundred, kindred to twenty.*

> See 'An co-dhalta'.

Cofhurtachd an duine dhona—duine eile cho dona ris fhèin.—*The bad man's consolation—that there's as bad as he.*

Comann mo ghaoil, comann nan ceàrd.—*The company I love—the tinkers.*

> One very distinguished literary man, Mr George Borrow, would not repudiate this sentiment.

Comann nam Maor.—*The bailiff's brotherhood.*

> See 'Mo chomain'.

Contrachd ort!—*Bad luck to you!*

Còrdadh a reubas reachd.—*Concord (or compromise) that bereaves the law.*

> Ammod a dyr ddefod.—*Welsh.* Law's costly; tak a pint and gree.—*Scot.* Meglio un magro accordo, che una grassa sentenza.—*Ital.* So *Fr., Span., Germ., Dutch, Dan.*

Cothrom a h-aon.—*Fair play—one to one.*

> Two to one is odds enough.—*Eng.* Ne Hercules quidem contra duos.—*Lat.*

Cothrom na Fèinne dhaibh.—*The Fingalian fair play to them.*

> The Fingalian idea of fair play was that of the previous saying, one to one, 'Gaisgeach air ghaisgeach, is laoch ri laoch'—*'Champion on champion, hero to hero'.*

Crann a rèir a' bhàta.—*A mast to suit the boat.*

Cridhe na circe an gob na h-airce.—*A hen's heart in the beak of want.*

Croiseam sgiorradh!—*The cross between me and mishap!*

Croiseam thu!—*The cross be between us!*

Cromaidh an coileach circ' a cheann an doras an taigh' mhòir.—*The cock bows his head at the great house door.*

> See 'Ged as iosal'.

Cruaidh mar am fraoch, buan mar an giuthas.—*Hard as the heather, lasting as the pine.*

> The heather is the badge of the MacDonalds, the pine of the Mac-Gregors.

Cruaidh mun pheighinn, 's bog mun mharg.—*Hard about the penny, soft about the merk.*

> Penny wise and pound foolish.—*Eng., Scot.*

Crùbaiche coin, leisgeul bhan 's mionnan marsanta—tha iad coltach ri chèile.—*A dog's limping, a woman's excuse, a merchant's oath—they are like each other.*

> No es de vero lagrimas en la muger, ni coxear en el perro—*Woman's tears and dog's limping are not real.—Span.*

Cruinneachadh cruaidh agus leigeadh farsaing.—*Hard gathering and free spending.*

> The father scraping and the son scattering.

Cruinnichidh na fithich far am bi a' chairbh.—*Where the carcase is the ravens will gather.*

> Wheresoever the carcase is, there will the eagles be gathered together.—*Matth.* xxiv, 28.

Cù an dà fhèidh, is minig a bha fhiadh air chall.—*The dog of two deer has often lost his deer.*

> *Al.*—Coltach ri cù an dà fhèidh, a' call romhad 's ad dhèidh.
> Rith na gcon i ndiaidh dhá fhiadh.—*Ir.* Ὁ δύο πτωκας διώκων οὐδέτερον καταλαμβάνει—He that chases two hares catches neither.—*Gr.* Duos insequens lepores neutrum capit.—*Lat.* Qui court deux lièvres, n' en prendra aucun.—*Fr.* Chi due lepri caccia, l' una non piglia, e l' altra lascia.—*Ital.* Wer zwei Hasen zugleich hetzt, fängt gar keinen.—*Germ.*

Cuid a' ghobha—an ceann.—*The smith's share—the head.*

> The smith's perquisite for killing a cow, which he was generally employed to do. That great event generally took place once a year, at Martinmas, whence possibly the word *mart*—'cow'.

Cuid an t-searraich den chlèith.—*The foal's share of the harrow.*

> Going beside his dam.

Cuidich leat fhèin, 's cuidichidh Dia leat.—*Help thyself, and God will help thee.*

> *Al.*—Dèan do dhìcheall, 's cuidichidh Dia leat.

Cuidigheann Dia leis an té a chuidigheas leis féin.—*Ir.* Hilf dir selbst, so hilft dir Gott.—*Germ.* Help u zelven, zoo helpt u God.—*Dutch.* Hielp dig selv, da hielper dig Gud.—*Dan.* Aide-toi, le ciel t-aidera.—*Fr.* Quien se guarda, Dios le guarda.—*Span.* Chi s' aiuta, Dio l'aiuta.—*Ital.* Σὺν 'Αθηνᾳ καὶ χειρα κίνει.—*Mod. Gr.*

Cuigeal don-snìomhaich.—*Bad spinning distaff.*

Said of an unthrifty or untidy woman.

Cuimhnich air na daoine bhon tàinig thu.—*Remember those you came from.*

A very Highland sentiment. Sometimes it is 'Cuimhnich air cruadal nan daoine' &c.—*Think of the fortitude of your forefathers;* a sentiment which has proved strong on many a battlefield.

Cuir a-mach an Sasannach, 's thoir a-staigh an cù.—*Put out the Englishman, and take in the dog.*

This is a Lochaber saying, supposed to date from the time of Cromwell, whose soldiers scourged that country severely.

Cuir an tuagh air an t-samhaich cheart.—*Put the axe on the right helve.*

Put the saddle on the right horse.

Cuir ceann na muice ri eàrr an uircein.—*Set the sow's head to the little pig's tail.*

Bring the head o the sow to the tail o the grice.—*Scot.*
This looks like a case of *hysteron proteron*, but Kelly interprets it 'Balance your loss with your gain'.

Cuir do làmh sa chliabh, 's thoir do rogha lèabaig às.—*Put your hand into the creel, and take your choice of flounders.*

If this be a version of the Scottish rhyme on matrimony, it is certainly improved—

Put yir hand in the creel
And draw an adder or an eel.

Cuir do mhuinghin san talamh—cha d'fhàg e falamh riamh thu.—*Put thy trust in the earth—it never left thee empty.*

A good motto for farmers.

Cuir innte, 's cuiridh an saoghal uimpe.—*Give her food, and the world will clothe her.*

> Macintosh's note on this is 'The back will trust, but the belly will still be craving'.

Cuir manadh math air do mhanadh, 's bidh tu sona.—*Interpret good from thy omen, and thou shalt be lucky.*

> As Caesar did, when he fell on the British shore.

Cuireadh cùl na coise.—*The back-leg invitation.*

> *Al.*—Fiathachadh cùl na h-iosgaid.
> That of a person who gives a faint invitation, and escorts one out of the house saying, 'I am sorry you couldn't stay'.

Cuireadh MhicPhilip—'Gabh no fàg'.—*MacKillop's invitation— 'Take or leave'.*

Cuiridh an teanga snaidhm nach fuasgail an fhiacail.—*The tongue will tie a knot which the tooth can't unloose.*

> Cuireann duine snaim lena theangaidh nach bhfuasglóidh a fhiacla.—*Ir.*

> The English and Scottish versions are nearly in the same words. Matrimony is referred to.

> > Cuiridh aon bheairt às gu lom
> > Do dhuine 's gun a chonn fo chèill;
> > Is cuiridh beairt eil' e ann,
> > Ach a gabhail 'na h-àm fhèin.

> > *—One deed may a man undo
> > When his reason ruleth not;
> > And a step may set him up,
> > If but taken in due time.*

Cuiridh aon tràth air ais laogh is leanabh.—*One meal if it lack, calf or child will go back.*

Cuiridh bean ghlic suas duine, ach bheir bean amaideach a-nuas e le dà làimh.—*A wise wife will set a man up, but a foolish one will bring him down with both hands.*

Cuiridh beul milis thu shireadh na dèirce.—*A sweet mouth will send you to beggary.*

Cuiridh e teine ris na tobraichean.—*He will set the wells on fire.*

This looks like setting the Thames on fire.

Cuiridh peirceall na caora 'n crann air an fharadh.—*The sheep's jaw will put the plough on the hen-roost.*

This prediction is attributed to a famous Highland seer of the 17th century, Coinneach Odhar, but it was made long before that by no less a person than Thomas the Rhymer. His saying, 'The teeth of the sheep shall lay the plough on the shelf,' is quoted by Dr. Chambers in his *Popular Rhymes of Scotland,* with special reference to the changes of tenantry in the Highlands, in some parts of which sheep-farming has entirely supplanted agriculture. Rushes and heather may be seen now in fields that once yielded fair crops, and sheep in place of the men that tilled them.

Cuiridh mi clach ad chàrn.—*I'll add a stone to your cairn.*

See 'Am fear nach meudaich'.

Cùl gaoith' is aghaidh grèine.—*Back of wind and face of sun.*

A phrase in the old stories, descriptive of a pleasant retreat.

Cùm an dò-dhuine air do thaobh; bidh an deagh dhuine agad daonnan.—*Keep the ill man on your side; the good man you'll always have.*

Cùm an fhèill air a latha.—*Keep the fair on its day.*

Keep the feast till the feast-day.—*Scot.*

Cùm an t-eathar bho chladach an fhasgaidh, 's fanaidh i fhèin bho chladach an fhuaraidh.—*Keep the boat from the lee-shore, and she'll keep herself from the wind-shore.*

Cùm do chù ri leigeadh.—*Hold your dog till the starting-time.*

Don't loose your hound where there is nothing to hunt.—*Arab.*

Cùm do theanga 'nad chuimse.—*Keep your tongue in hand.*

The mouth is the tongue's prison.-*Arab.* Ἀργυρὸ τὸ μέλημα, χρυσὸ τὸ σιώπα—Speech is silvern, silence golden.—*Mod. Gr.*

Cromadh gun ghainne sa chaol;
Aon eanga deug san osan;
Seachd eangan am beul a theach—
Is tearc an neach do nach foghain;
Air a chumadh gu dìreach;
Agus a trì sa ghobhal.

—A full finger-length to the small;
Eleven nails to the leg;
Seven nails to the band—
There are few whom that won't suffice;
Let it be shaped straight;
And three nails to the fork.

This quaint rhyme is called *Cumadh an Triubhais*—'The Shaping of Trews'. A 'nail' is 2¼ inches, and Macintosh says 'Perhaps some of these nails should be doubled'.

Cumaidh a' mhuc fhèin a fail fhèin glan.—*Even the sow will keep her own sty clean.*

The tod keeps aye his ain hole clean.—*Scot.*

Cumaidh an geàrr-phoca uiread ris a' chòrr-phoca.—*The little bag holds as much as the big bag.*

'Cumaidh mi ri m'leannan,' ars an nighean, 'beul sìoda 's cridhe cainbe.'—*'I will keep to my sweetheart,' said the girl, 'a mouth of silk and a heart of hemp.'*

Béal eidhneáin, is croidhe cuilinn—*A mouth of ivy, and a heart of holly.*—*Ir.*

Cumhachd do charaid, agus tràillealachd do nàmhaid a dhùthcha!—*Power to the friend, and thraldom to the enemy of his country!*

This is what used to be called a 'sentiment' for a toast.

Cunnradh math fada bho làimh.—*A good bargain far away.*

Cuspach, is gàg, is eill-bhuinn, 's mairg an spàg air am beireadh iad.—*Kibe and crack and burning heel, pity the foot they come on.*

> All these ailments are known only to people that go bare-footed. The second one gives rise to another saying: 'Ceum air gàig,' applied to persons who walk reluctantly, as if they had a sore foot, or delicately, like King Agag.

D

Dà bhuille dheug fodair, 's gun bhuill' idir airson sìl.—*Twelve strokes for straw, and no stroke for seed.*

> Great cry and little wool. See 'Buill' air gach craoibh'.

Dà cheann an taoid, is cead a tharraing.—*Both ends of the rope, and leave to pull it.*

Dà dhiù gun aon roghainn.—*Two evils and no choice.*

> At the battle of Inverlochy, 1645, Alexander MacDonell, son of Coll (Colkitto) having made prisoner of Campbell of Achnabreac, said he would honour him by giving him his choice, whether to be beheaded or hanged. Campbell answered in the above words, and MacDonell struck off his head with his own hand.—*Teachd. Gael.*, Vol. II, p. 135.

Dà thrian buidhinn barant.—*Assurance is two-thirds of success.*

Dàil gu là na sluasaid.—*Delay to the day of the shovel.*

> The day of burial.

Dail na Cille, 's Dail a' Ghlinne, 's Dail mhòr Chrònaig: nuair thèid sin a threabhadh, thèid a' ghort à Cinn a' Gheàrr-Loch.—*Dalnakill, Dalglen and great Dalchronaig: when these are ploughed, there will be no more dearth in Kingairloch.*

> Three sequestered and uncultivated spots in Kingairloch. The saying points to a state of things common in olden times but which now, happily, need not be feared.

Dàir na coille.—*The rutting of the wood.*

> Applied, according to Armstrong (*Dict.*), to the first night of the New Year, when the wind blows from the west.

Dàn' ath-bhuailte.—*Bold, twice beaten.*

Dallta aran-eòrna MhicPhilip, a' dol am feabhas 's am feabhas.— *Like MacKillop's barley bread, getting better and better.*

> I have been unable to ascertain anything about the MacKillop who gave rise to the various proverbs in which he is named.
> The word *dallta* is not common, and is not given in any of our dictionaries except Shaw's and MacAlpine's; and in O'Reilly's Ir. Dict. Shaw is given as authority for the word. It means 'like, likeness, in manner of'. It is not surprising that it was in the 2nd ed. of Macintosh confounded with *dalta*, 'foster-child', and translated accordingly in this and the next proverb.

Dallta 'chinn charraich, nach fuiling fuachd no teas.—*Like the scabby head that can't endure cold or heat.*

Dàrna bean a' chlàrsair—a' chlàrsach fhèin.—*The harper's second wife—the harp itself.*

> See 'Eud bean a' chruiteir'.
> Neil Gow's fiddle was said to be his second wife; and there is a tune so called.

Dè am fèum a tha sa phìob mur cluichear oirre?—*What's the good of the pipe if it's not played on?*

Dean àill den èiginn.—*Make a will of necessity.*

> Make a virtue of necessity.—*Eng.*

Dèan air d'athais, 's ann as luaithe.—*Take it easy, you'll speed better.*

See 'Chan i 'chabhag'.

Festina lente exactly expresses this.

Dèan an t-olc 's feith ri dheireadh.—*Do the ill and wait the end.*

The grave irony of this is very good.

Dèan àth no muileann deth.—*Mak a kirk or a mill o't*—Scot.

'Dean Eige no Arasaig dheth'—*Make Eigg or Arisaig of it*—is a Mull saying, used when a head wind and dirty weather come on, after the point of Ardnamurchan is passed, going northward.

> Dèan bonnach mòr mu Inid,
> Is fear eile mu Chàisg;
> 'S cho fad' 's a bhios rud agad,
> Cha bhi thu falamh gu bràth.

> —*Make a big cake at Shrove-tide, and another at Easter; and as long as you have anything, you'll never be wanting.*

Dèan cnuasachd san t-Samhradh a nì an Geamhradh a chur seach-ad.—*Gather in Summer what will serve for the Winter.*

Dèan do gharadh far an d'rinn thu d'fhuarachadh.—*Warm yourself where you got cold.*

Very cold advice, but not without point.

Dèan do ghearan ri fear gun iochd, 's their e ruit: 'Tha thu bochd.'—*Complain to a merciless man, and he'll say, 'You are poor.'*

Probably he will say, 'Depart in peace, be warmed and filled.'

Dèan do sheunadh bhon Diabhal 's bho chlann an tighearna.—*Sain thyself frae the Deil and the laird's bairns.*—Scot.

This was probably addressed first by a father to his daughters.

Dèan fanaid air do sheana bhrògan nuair a gheibh thu do bhrògan nodha.—*Make game of your old shoes when you get the new ones.*

Don't throw out the dirty water till you get in the clean.

Dèan maorach fhad 's a bhios an tràigh ann.—*Get bait while the tide is out.*

Dèan math an aghaidh an uilc.—*Do good against the ill.*

> Overcome evil with good.—*St Paul.*

> Dèan math do dheagh dhuine,
> 'S bidh an deagh dhuine do rèir;
> Dèan math do neo-dhuine,
> 'S bidh an neo-dhuine dha fhèin.

> —*Do good to a worthy man,*
> *And worthy will he be;*
> *Do good to a worthless man,*
> *And selfish still is he.*

> The Ulster version is nearly identical:

> Déan maith ar dheagh-dhuine,
> Is gheabhaidh tú dá réir;
> Ach ma ghnídhir maith air dhroch-dhuine,
> Beidh an droch-dhuine dó féin.

Dèan na thig dhut, 's chì thu na 's ait leat.—*Do what becomes you, and you'll see what pleases you.*

> A neat statement of the doctrine of the πρέπον.

Dèan suidhe, thàilleir; 's dèan suidhe, thuairneir; suidheadh càch mar as deise; suidhidh mise ri taobh an fhleisteir.—*Sit down, tailor; sit down, turner; let the rest sit as is best; I'll sit beside the arrow-maker.*

> In the Preface to Ronald Macdonald's collection of songs, a more imperfect version of this proverb is given, as an illustration of the fatherly hospitality of Highland lairds to their dependants.

Dèanadh do bhean fhèin brochan dhut.—*Let your own wife make gruel for you.*

Dèanamh gad den ghaineimh.—*Making a rope of sand.*

> Ex arena funiculum nectis.—*Lat.*
>
> According to tradition, this was a task imposed on his familiar spirit by Michael Scott, the result of which is still to be seen on the sands between Leith and Portobello. Another tradition is that it was imposed on the fairies by Sir Duncan Campbell of Glenorchy, Black Duncan of the Cowl.

Deireadh fèille fàg.—*Leave the fag-end of a fair.*

> An excellent advice.

> Deireadh gach luing a bàthadh,
> Deireadh gach àth a losgadh,
> Deireadh flaith a chàineadh,
> Deireadh slàinte osna.

> —*The end of each ship her drowning,*
> *The end of each kiln its burning,*
> *The end of a prince, reviling,*
> *The end of a health a sigh.*

> *Al.*—Deireadh gach comainn sgaoileadh,
> Deireadh gach bàta bristeadh,
> Deireadh gach àth a losgadh,
> Deireadh gach cogaidh sìth.

> —*The end of all meetings to part,*
> *The end of all boats to be broken,*
> *The end of all kilns to be burnt,*
> *The end of all wars peace.*

> The Ulster version is

> Deireadh gach luinge, báthadh,
> Deireadh gach áiche, loscadh,
> Deireadh gach cuirme, caitheamh,
> Is deireadh gach gáire osna.

Deireadh mo sgeòil mo sguidseadh, dol thugam air mo dhruim.—*The end of my story a switching on my back.*

> The identity of *sguidseadh* and 'switching' is obvious.

Deireadh nan seachd Satharn' ort!—*The end of the seven Saturdays to you!*

No satisfactory explanation can be got of this very familiar saying. It has been ingeniously interpreted as referring to the end of the seven weeks of Lent, when mutual congratulations are given in some Christian countries, in remembrance of the Resurrection day. But unfortunately for this explanation, the saying with us has always conveyed a bad wish instead of a good one. It is, in fact, an emphatic form of malediction. The word *seachd*, 'seven', is used, in Gaelic as in Hebrew, to express completeness; e.g., 'Tha mi seachd sgìth'—*I am utterly tired.* In this sense, 'The end of the seven Saturdays to you!' might be meant to express the wish that the mere fag-end of time might be all one would have to enjoy. But the more probable interpretation is that it refers to the Crucifixion and the end of Judas.

Deiseal air gach nì.—*The sunward course with everything.*

Deas—South, right-hand, ready, dexterous, proper, handsome. *Deiseil=deis-iùil*, south course, right direction.

The belief, and the customs associated with it, on this point are very natural, and common to all the principal races of the world.

Deoch air a' phathadh nach tàinig.—*Drink for the thirst that came not.*

Too common an indulgence.

Deoch an dorais.—*The door-drink.*

The door-drink, or stirrup-cup, is one of the oldest of institutions. The following pretty verses were composed by a very good man, Duncan Lothian:

> Slàn do d'mhnaoi ghil, slàn do d'mhacaibh,
> Slàn do d'theach om binne ceòl;
> Slàn do d'shràidibh geala gainmhich,
> Slàn do d'bheanntaibh om bi ceò.
> Bhon a thàrladh dhuinn bhith sona,
> Is beairt dhona nach tig rinn,
> Air ghaol sìth, 's air eagal conais,
> Thugar Deoch an Dorais dhuinn!

Deoch Chlann Donnchaidh.—*The Robertsons' stirrup-cup.*

Deoch mhòr do Bhrian, 's b'e sin a mhiann.—*A big drink to Brian, and that's his desire.*

> Brian's habits would not be considered so singular now as to become proverbial.

Dh'aithnich mi gur meann a bheireadh a' ghobhar.—*I knew it would be a kid the goat would bear.*

Dh'aithnichinn air do sheirc do thabhartas.—*I would know your gift by your graciousness.*

Dh'amais thu air do thapadh.—*You lighted on your luck.*

> Literally, *tapadh* means activity, cleverness, manliness; secondarily, the luck which follows. The only vernacular equivalent of 'Thank you' in the Gaelic language is 'Tapadh leat'.

'Dhèanadh e rudeigin do dh'aon duine, ach is beag a' chuid dithis e,' mar a thuirt Alasdair Uaibhreach mun t-saoghal.—*'It would be something to one man, but it's a small thing for two,' as Alexander the Proud said about the world.*

> Alexander the Great is always called *Uaibhreach* in Gaelic.

Dhèanadh e teadhair den ròinneig.—*He would make a tether of a hair.*

Dhèanadh Niall clàrsaichean, nan cuireadh càch ceòl annta.—*Neil would make harps, if others would put music into them.*

'Dhèanadh sin e,' mun dubhairt an cù mun chè.—*'That would do it,' as the dog said about the cream.*

> When the dog was desired to lick cream, he asked, 'Why?'
> 'Because it is spilt,' replied his mistress. 'That would do it,' said the dog.—Note by Macintosh.

Dhèanadh tu caonnag ri d'dhà lurgainn.—*You would quarrel with your own two shins.*

> *Al.*—Bheireadh tu conas à d'leth-lurga—*You would get a quarrel out of one of your legs.*

Dh'fhalbh 'B'fheàrr leam,' 's cha b'fheàrr beò e.—*'Would that' is gone, and it's no loss.*

Dh'fhalbh e 'na phrìneachan 's 'na shnàthadan.—*It went away in pins and needles.*

Dh'fhalbh Peairt, thuit an drochaid!—*Perth is gone, the bridge is down!*

> This is said on the occasion of some great catastrophe. The fall of the bridge of Perth in 1621 probably originated the saying. The old bridge, described by Cant as 'a stately building and a great ornament of the town,' was carried away by successive inundations in 1573, 1582 and 1589. On 14th Oct. 1621, says Calderwood (cited by Cant in *Muse's Threnodie*, 1774, pp 80–82), 'the stately bridge of Perth, newly completed consisting of 10 arches, was destroyed by the high swelling of the river Tay'. The destruction and alarm caused on this occasion appear to have been very great. Another saying in reference to that calamity is 'An uair a thuiteas drochaid Pheairt, nì i glag'— *When the bridge of Perth falls, it will make a noise.*

Dh'fhan do mhàthair ri d' bhreith.—*Your mother waited for your birth.*

> Said ironically to one in an excessive hurry.

Dh'fhaodadh dà chailleach a chur an dàrna taobh, gun dol o thaobh an teine.—*Two old women could dispose of it, without leaving the fireside.*

Dh'iarr a' mhuir a bhith ga tadhal.—*The sea wished to be resorted to.*

> A poetical idea, suggested by the daily return of the tide, which seems to invite acquaintance.

Dh'ith e chuid den bhonnach-shodail.—*He ate his share of the flattery-bannock.*

> Said of sycophantic people.

Dh'ith e 'm biadh mun d'rinn e 'n t-altachadh.—*He ate the food before saying grace.*

Dh'itheadh daoine na cruachan, ach thigeadh iad suas air na tud-anan.—*People could eat the big stacks, but they could do with the little ones.*

Dh'itheadh e chàin a bh' aig Pàdraig air Eirinn.—*He would eat St Patrick's tribute from Ireland.*

> See note to 'Cha phàigheadh'.
> In a story about Ossian, given in Campbell's *W. H. T.*, II, 105 (also in Smith's *A Summer in Skye*), it is said of him, 'Bha e dall, bodhar, bacach, 's bha naoi dealgan daraich 'na bhroinn; 's e 'g itheadh na càin a bh' aig Pàdraig air Eirinn'—'*He was blind, deaf, lame, and had nine oaken skewers in his belly; and was eating the tribute Patrick had over Ireland*'. This story was found in Barra and in Skye.

Dh'itheadh na caoraich an cuid throimhe.—*The sheep might eat through it.*

> Said of thinly woven cloth.

Dh'òladh e Loch Slaopain.—*He would drink Loch Slapin.*

> A Skye loch between Strath and Sleat.

Dh'oladh e 'n sgillinn nach fhac' e.—*He would drink the penny he hadn't seen.*

Dh'òladh e pheighinn-phisich.—*He would drink his luck-penny.*

> Even if he had the 'penny of Pases,' he would drink it.

Dhùraichdeadh tu mo luath le uisge.—*You would wish my ashes borne off on the waters.*

Dian-fhàs fuilt, crìon-fhàs cuirp.—*Great growth of hair, small growth of body.*

> Didòmhnaich Shlat-Phailm,
> 'S ann ris tha mo stoirm;
> Didòmhnaich Crum Dubh,
> Plaoisgidh mi 'n t-ugh.

—*On Palm Sunday is my stir; on crooked black Sunday I'll peel the egg.*

> This saying is obscure. *Crum Dubh*, apparently for *Crom Dubh*, is known in Ireland as the title of the first Sunday of August, but in Lochaber it is applied to Easter.

Diluain a' bhreabain.—*Shoe-sole Monday.*

> Monday of chastisement, the terror of boys.—H. Soc. *Dict.*

Diluain an deaghaidh na fèille.—*Monday after the fair.*

> A day after the fair.—*Eng.*

Dìochuimhneachadh a' phòsaidh, leis cho suarach 's a bha bhan-ais.—*Forgetting the marriage, from the wretchedness of the wedding.*

> I had nae mind I was married, my bridal was sae feckless.—*Scot.*

Dìoghailt fear na dàlach.—*The tardy man's revenge.*

Dìolaidh saothair ainfhiach.—*Industry pays debt.*

Diombuil buaile, bò gun laogh.—*A fold's reproach, a yeld cow.*

Diongam fear ma dh'fhuiricheas mi, agus fuilingeam teicheadh.—*I'll match a man if I stay, and I can suffer a retreat.*

Diardaoin' a' bhrochain mhòir.—*Great gruel Thursday.*

> It was at one time a custom in the Long Island, if the usual drift of seaweed were behind time, to go on Maunday Thursday and pour an oblation of gruel on a promontory, accompanying the ceremony with the repetition of a certain rhyme.

> > Diardaoin Là Chaluim Chille chaoimh,
> > Là bu chòir a bhith deilbh,
> > Là chur chaorach air seilbh.

—*When Thursday is dear Columba's day, the warp should be prepared, and sheep sent to pasture.*

> St Columba's day is 9th June. The epithet applied to the Saint is interesting.

Dìreachadh na cailliche air a lurga.—*The old woman's straightening of her leg* (breaking it).

Dithis a chur cuideachd agus am bualadh ri chèile.—*To put two together, and knock them against each other.*

Dithis a gheibh fois a-nochd, mise 's an t-each bàn, mun dubhairt a' bhean nuair a chual' i mu bhàs a fir.—*Two that will have peace tonight, myself and the white horse, as the woman said when she heard of her husband's death.*

> Dithis leis nach toigh a chèile—
> Bean a' mhic 's a màthair-chèile.
>
> —*Two that love not one another,*
> *The son's wife and his mother.*

Diù na comhairle, a toirt far nach gabhar i.—*The worst advice, given and not taken.*

Diù rath an domhain, is diù dath an domhain ann—buidhe, dubh is riabhach.—*Worst lot in the world, and worst colours on earth are there—yellow, black and brindled.*

> A punning satire on Jura, by a discontented poetess—Campbell's *W. H. T.*, II, 353.

Diùthaidh nam beathaichean fireann.—*The refuse of male creatures.*

> Said of a very contemptible man.

Dleasaidh airm urram.—*Arms merit honour.*

Dlùthas nan càirdean ri chèile.—*The nearness of kindred to each other.*

Do rogha leannain, 's do theann-shàth sprèidh ort!—*Thy choice of sweetheart, and full store of cattle to thee!*

Do spuir fhèin an each fir eile.—*Your own spurs in another man's horse.*

> *Al.*—Mo shlat fhèin—*My own switch.*
> See 'Cha bhi each'.

Dona uime, dona aige.—*Ill with it, ill with him.*

> This means that a curmudgeon gets little good of that which he so grudges to part with.

Dòmhnall da fhèin.—*Donald for himself.*

Dorcha, doireannta, dubh,
Chiad trì làithean den Gheamhradh;
Ge b'e bheir gèill don sprèidh,
Cha tugainn fhèin gu Samhradh.

—Dark, sullen and black,
The three first days of Winter;
Whoever depends on the cattle,
I would not till Summer.

It was considered a good sign to have Winter beginning with dark weather; but the reference to the cattle seems to imply that one ought not to be sanguine about them, notwithstanding.

Droch bhàs ort!—*A bad death to you!*

Al.—Droch dhiol—*Bad usage*; Droch sgiorram—*Bad stumbling.*

Droch còmhdhail ort!—*Bad meeting to you!*

The wish conveyed is that one may meet a person or animal whom it was considered unlucky to meet.

Druidear beul nam breug.—*The lying mouth will be shut.*

Druididh gach eun ri ealtainn.—*Each bird draws to his flock.*

Eunlaith an aon eite in éinfheacht ag eiteallaigh.—*Ir.* The birds will resort unto their like.—*Son of Sirach.* Ὅμοιον ὁμοίῳ φίλον.—*Gr.* Simile appetit simile.—*Lat.* Pares cum paribus facillime congregantur.—*Cic.* Birds of a feather flock together.—*Eng., Scot.* Vögel von gleichen Federn fliegen gern beisammen.—*Germ.* Elk zijns gelijk, 't zij arm of rijk.—*Dutch.* Qui se ressemble s'assemble.—*Fr.* Simili con simili vanno.—*Ital.* Cada oveja con su pareja.—*Span.*

Druim an sgadain, tàrr a' bhradain, 's cùl-cinn a' bhric-dhuibh.—*The herring's back, the salmon's belly, and back of head of black trout.*

The choice parts.

Duais fir dhathaidh a' chinn.—*The reward of the man that singes the head.*

Duin' a sheasadh an gràpa 'na dhùnan.—*A man in whose dunghill the fork would stand.*

A man of substance.

Duine còir an rathaid mhòir 's bèist mhòr a-staigh.—*A fine man abroad, and a great beast at home.*

> Angel pennford, a diawl pentan.—*Welsh.* A causey saint, and a house deil.—*Scot.*
> See 'Euchdach' and 'Olc mun'.

Duine dùr, duine gun tùr.—*A stubborn man, a senseless man.*

Duine gun rath gun seòl, 's còir a chrochadh; 's fear aig am bi tuille 's a chòir, 's còir a chrochadh.—*A man with no luck or shift should be hanged; and so should a man with too much.*

> Hang him that has nae shift, and hang him that has ower mony.—*Scot.*

Dùnan math innearach, màthair na ciste-mine.—*The muck-midden is the mither o the meal-kist.—Scot.*

Dùthaich nan cluaran, nam fuaran, nan cuaran, 's nam fuar-bheann!—*The land of thistles, and fountains, of brogues, and of mountains!*

> This is a toast.

E

Eadar a' bhadhbh 's a' bhuarach.—*'Twixt the vixen and the cow-fetter.*

'Betwixt the Devil and the deep sea.'
It was a superstitious fancy that if a man got struck by the *buarach* he would thenceforth be childless!

Eadar a' chlach 's an sgrath.—*'Twixt the stone and the turf.*

Eadar a' chraobh 's a rùsg.—*Between the tree and its bark.*

Eadar am bogha 's an t-sreang.—*Between the bow and the string.*

Eadar am feur 's am fodar.—*Between the hay and the straw.*

Eadar an long nodha 's an seann rubha.—*Between the new ship and the old headland.*

Nodha is a less common form of *nuadh*.

Eadar an sùgh 's an t-slat.—*Between the sap and the sapling.*

Eadar an t-euradh is aimbeairt.—*Between denial and want.*

This was said by Fingal to be the worst plight he ever was in.—See 'An uaisle'.

Eadar an tughadh 's an raineach.—*Between the thatch and the bracken.*

Eadar dhà chathair, tuitear gu làr.—*Between two seats one comes down.*

Tháinig a tóin chun talamh eadar a dhá stól.—*Ir.* Eddyr daa stoyl ta toyn er laare.—*Manx.* Between two stools the tail goeth to ground.—*Eng.* Tusschen twee stoelen valt de aars op de aarde.—*Dutch.* Entre deux selles, le cul à terre.—*Fr.*

Eadar dhà lionn.—*'Twixt sinking and swimming.*

> *Lit.* 'Between two liquids,' i.e., the upper and lower water.

Eadar dhà sgeul.—*By the way.*

> *Lit.* 'Between two stories.'
> *Al.*—dhà naidheachd.

Eadar dhà theine.—*Betwixt two fires.*

Eadar long is laimhrig.—*Betwixt ship and landing-place.*

Eadar fhealla-dhà 's a rìreadh.—*Betwixt fun and earnest.*

Eadar làmh is taobh.—*Betwixt hand and side.*

Eadar leòr is eatarras.—*Betwixt plenty and mediocrity.*

Eadar na sruthaibh.—*Betwixt the currents.*

Eadraiginn nan ceàrd.—*Going between tinkers.*

> Those who in quarrels interpose
> Must often wipe a bloody nose.—*Gay.*
> See 'Bidh dòrn'.

Eallach mhòr an duine leisg.—*The lazy man's great burden.*

> Who more busy than they that have least to do?—*Eng., Scot.* Uomo
> lento non ha mai tempo.—*Ital.*

Earbsa à claidheamh briste.—*Trusting to a broken sword.*

Earrach fad' an dèidh Càsga, fàgaidh e na saibhlean fàs.—*Long
Spring after Easter makes empty barns.*

Earrag-chèilidh.—*A visiting stroke.*

> Said of one hurt when on a visit.

Easgaidh mun rathad mhòr seach a dhoras fhèin.—*More quick to
show the high road than his own door.*

> See 'Am fear nach eil math'.

Eibheall air gruaidh—mnathan-luaidh is tàillearan.—*Live-coal on cheek—waulking-women and tailors.*

> The good-wife who had to provide for a company of vigorous women coming to assist her in waulking cloth, or tailors coming to work in the house for days, and expecting of course, to be well treated, might be supposed to have no sinecure.

Eireachdas mnathan Loch Obha, am brèid odhar a thionndadh.—*The elegance of the Loch Awe women, turning the dun clout inside out.*

> A Lorn saying.

Eiridh tonn air uisge balbh.—*Wave will rise on silent water.*

> And calm people when stirred may astonish.

Eisd ri gaoth nam beann gus an traoigh na h-uisgeachan.—*Listen to the mountain wind, till the streams abate.*

> Eisd le goith na mbeann, go dtraoghaidh na h-uisgibh.—*Ir.*

Eòin a chur don choille.—*Sending birds to the wood.*

> Sending owls to Athens &c.

Euchdach a-muigh, is brèineach a-staigh.—*Distinguished abroad, disgusting at home.*

> See 'Olc mun'.

Eud bean a'chruiteir.—*The harper's wife's jealousy.*

> See 'Dàrna bean' and 'Cha dèan sinn'.

Eudail de dh'fhearaibh an achaidh!—*Treasure of all men of the field!*

> *Al.*—de dh'fhearaibh na dìle.

Eudail de mhnathan an domhain!—*Treasure of all women of the world!*

> These emphatic phrases are sometimes used jocosely, sometimes in real earnest.

Eug is imrich a chlaoidheas taigheadas.—*Death and flitting are hard on housekeeping.*

> Éag is imirce a chlaoidheas tigheachas.—*Ir.*

F

Facal ann, a Mhaighstir Iain, 's am Brugh a' lionadh.—*Get on, Mr John, the channel is filling.*

> The Rev. John MacLean was minister of Kilninian (see p. 213) in Mull, including Ulva and Gometra. These islands are separated by a narrow channel called the *Brugh*, which is passable on foot except at high water. Mr M. was preaching at Gometra, and the beadle reminded him in the above words, proverbial in Mull, that it was time to be winding up.

Fad a choise don laogh, 's fad an taoid don chuilean-choin.—*The length of his foot to the calf, the length of the leash to the whelp.*

Fad fìn foinneach an là.—*The live-long day.*

> *Al.*—Fad fionna-fuaireanach.

Fada bhon t-sùil, fada bhon chridhe.—*Far from the eye, far from the heart.*

> *Al.*—As an t-sealladh, às a' chuimhne.
> I bhfad as amharc, i gcian as intinn.—*Ir.* Ass shilley, ass smooinagtyn.—*Manx.* Allan o olwg, allan o feddwl.—*Welsh.* Qui procul ab oculis, procul a limite cordis.—*Lat.* Far from eye, far from heart—Out of sight, out of mind.—*Eng.* Aus den Augen, aus dem Sinn.—*Germ.* Langt fra Öine, snart af Sinde.—*Dan.* Uit het oog, uit het hart.—*Dutch.* Loin des yeux, loin de coeur.—*Fr.*

Fada bhuaithe, mar a chunnaic Ailean a sheanmhair.—*Far off, as Allan saw his grandmother.*

> At a distance, as Paddy saw the moon.

Fadal Chlann an Tòisich.—*The delay of the Macintoshes.*

Fàg cuid dithis a' feitheamh an fhir a bhios a-muigh.—*Leave the share of two for him that is away.*

'Fàg, fàg!' thuirt an fheannag, ''s i mo nighean a' gharrag dhonn.'—'*Go, go!' said the crow, 'that brown chick is my child.'*

> This is an imitation of the cry of the bird. Of the same kind are the following expressive nursery rhymes:
> *The Gull*—'Gliag, gliag,' ars an fhaoileag, ''s e mo mhac-s' an daobh-gheal donn.'
> *The Crow*—'Gòrach, gòrach,' ars an fheannag, ''s e mo mhac-s' an garrach gorm.'
> *The Raven*—'Gròc, gròc,' ars am fitheach, ''s e mo mhac-s' a chreim-eas na h-uain.'
> *The Eagle*—'Glig, glig,' ars an iolair, ''s e mo mhac-s' as tighearn' oirbh.'

> Fàgaidh sìoda, sròl is sgàrlaid
> Gun teine gun tuar an fhàrdach.

> —*Silk and satin and scarlet leave the hearth cold and colourless.*

> Silks and satins put out the fire in the kitchen.—*Eng.* Sammt und Seide löschen das Feuer in der Küche aus.—*Germ.*

Fàgaidh tu e mar gum fàgadh bò a buachar.—*You leave it as a cow her dung.*

Fàgar an t-inneach gu deireadh.—*The woof is left to the last.*

Faicill a' chuain mhòir air a' chaol chumhang.—*The wide ocean's watch o'er the narrow strait.*

Faicill gach duine dha fhèin, an sabhal, no 'n ceàrdaich air là an Fhoghair.—*Every man for himself in barn or smithy on a harvest day.*

Fàilte na circe mun àrd-doras.—*The hen's salute at the lintel.*

Fàinne mun mheur, 's gun snàithne mun mhàs.—*Ringed finger and bare buttock.*

> Fál fán mhéar, 's gan ribe fán tóin.—*Ir.* Of empty stomach, yet he chews incense.—*Arab.*

Falach a' chait air a shalchar.—*The cat's hiding of the nasty.*

> Trying to hush up an offence after it has been exposed.

> 'Falbhaidh mis' a-màireach,' ars an rìgh.
> 'Fanaidh tu riumsa,' ars a' ghaoth.

> *'I shall go tomorrow,' said the king.*
> *'You shall wait for me,' said the wind.*

> 'Sail,' quoth the king; 'Hold,' quoth the wind.—*Eng., Scot.*

Fanaidh duine sona ri sìth, is bheir duine dona duibh-leum.—*The fortunate man waits for peace, and the unlucky man takes a leap in the dark.*

> Fanann duine sona le séan (*for luck*) agus bheir duine dona dubh-léam.—*Ir.*

> Once upon a time a great man was getting a sword made. The smith's advice for the perfect tempering of the blade was that it should be thrust red hot through the body of a living man. A messenger was to be sent for the sword, on whom it was agreed that this experiment should be performed. The lad sent was overtaken by a thunderstorm, and took refuge till it had passed. Meantime the chief sent another messenger for the sword, who duly went and asked for it, and was served as had been arranged. Presently the first messenger came in, got the sword from the smith and took it to his master. The great man was not a little astonished to see him, and asked where he had been. He told him how he had done, on which the great man uttered the above saying.

> For another version, see Campbell's *W. H. T.*, III, 110, 394, where the story is connected with the making of Fingal's famous sword, *Mac an Luinn.*

Fanaidh Moisean ri latha.—*The Devil waits his day.*

> *Moisean* or *Muisean* means literally 'the mean fellow,' and it is very commonly applied to the Devil by old Highlanders.

Fannan de ghaoith 'n ear, leannan an t-sealgair.—*A gentle easterly breeze, the hunter's delight.*

Faodaidh a' chaora dol bàs a' feitheamh ris an fheur ùr.—*The sheep may die, waiting for the new grass.*

> Faghann na heich bàs, fhad is bheas an féar ag fás.—*Ir.* Live, ass, till the clover sprout.—*Arab.* Ζησε, μαυρέ μου, νὰ φᾳς τριΦύλλι—*Live, my donkey, till you eat trefoil.—Mod. Gr.* Mentre l'erba cresce, muore il cavallo.—*Ital.* Indessen das Gras wächst, werhungert der Gaul.—*Germ.* Ne meurs, cheval, herbe te vient.—*Fr.* While the grass groweth, the seely horse starveth.—*Eng.* The cou may dee ere the grass grow.—*Scot.*

Faodaidh cat sealltainn air rìgh.—*A cat may look on a king.—Eng.*

> *Al.*—Faodaidh luach sgillinn de chat sealltainn am bathais an rìgh—*A twalpenny cat may look at a king.—Scot.*
> Sieht doch wohl die Katze den Kaiser an.—*Germ.* Een kat kijkt wel een' keizer an.—*Dutch.*

Faodaidh duine dol air muin eich gun dol thairis air.—*A man may mount a horse without tumbling over.*

Faodaidh duin' a chuid itheadh gun a chluasan a shalachadh.—*A man may take his food without daubing his ears.*

Faodaidh duine sam bith gàir' a dhèanamh air cnoc.—*Any man may laugh on a hillside.*

Faodaidh e bhith gur duine math thu, ach chan eil gnùis deagh dhuin' agad, mun duirt Niall nam beann ris a' chat.—*You may be a good man, but you haven't the face of one, as Neil of the mountains said to the cat.*

Faodaidh fear 'na ruith leum.—*He that runs may leap.*

Faodaidh fearg sealltainn a-steach an cridh' an duine ghlic, ach còmhnaichidh i 'n cridh' an amadain.—*Anger may look in on a wise man's heart, but it abides in the heart of a fool.*

> Anger resteth in the bosom of fools.—*Eccl.* vii. 9.

Faodaidh freumhan cam a bhith aig faillean dìreach.—*A straight sapling may have a crooked root.*

Faodaidh gnothach an rìgh tighinn an rathad cailleach nan cearc.—
The king's business may come in the way of the henwife.

> The king may come in the cadger's gait.—*Scot.*

> Faodaidh luingeas mòr dol air taisdeal fada,
> Ach feumaidh sgothan beaga seòladh dlùth don chladach.
>
> *Big ships may sail to distant strand,*
> *But little boats must hug the land.*

Faodaidh seann each sitir a dhèanamh.—*An old horse may neigh.*

Faodaidh sinn eag a chur san ursainn.—*We may cut a notch in the
doorpost.*

> Said on the occasion of a long expected or unexpected visit—marking
> the day with a white stone. Macintosh's version is 'Feudaidh sinn crois
> a choir san tuire. Crois an tuire, crois an sguirre,' translated 'We may
> strike a hack in the post. "Nay, 'tis unlucky," replies the guest.'
> 'Eag' or 'crois sa chlobha,' a notch, or cross in the tongs, or 'sa
> ghobhal,' in the supporting-beam, are variations.

Faodar an t-òr fhèin a cheannach tuille is daor.—*Gold itself may be
bought too dear.*

> Féadaím ór do cheannach go daor.—*Ir.* Gowd may be dear cost.—
> *Scot.* Aurum irrepertum, et sic melius situm.—*Hor.*

Faoigh' a' ghliocais.—*The prudent begging.*

> Begging for assistance in setting up house.
> See note to 'Chan e rogha'.

Faoighe fir gun chaoraich.—*The contribution of a man without sheep.*

> *Al.*—fir falaimh.
> A contribution of wool from a man without sheep would be suspi-
> cious.

Faoileag an droch chladaich.—*The seagull of a bad shore.*

> Applied to poor creatures still preferring their wretched home.

Faoileag na h-aon chloiche.—*The seagull of one stone.*

> Faoilleach, Faoilleach, làmh an crios—
> Faoilte mhòr bu chòir bhith ris;
> Crodh is caoraich ruith air theas—
> Gal is caoin bu chòir bhith ris.

> —*February cold and keen,*
> *Welcome hath it ever been;*
> *Sheep and cattle running hot—*
> *Sorrow that will bring, I wot.*

> *Al.*—Faoilleach, Faoilleach, crodh air theas—
> Gal is gaoir nìtear ris;
> Faoilleach, Faoilleach, crodh am preas—
> Fàilt' is faoilte nìtear ris.

> —*February, cows in heat,*
> *Sorrow will the season greet;*
> *February, cows in wood,*
> *Welcome is the weather good.*

Faothachadh gill' a' ghobha: bho na h-ùird gus na builg.—*The relief of the smith's lad: from the hammer to the bellows.*

> Scíste ghiolla an ghabha, ó na builg chum na h-inneoin.—*Ir.*

Far am bi a' mhuc, bidh fail.—*Where the sow is, a sty will be.*

Far am bi an deagh dhuine, is duin' e 'n cuideachd 's 'na aonar.—*Where a good man is, he is a man, whether in company or alone.*

Far am bi an t-iasg, 's ann a bhios na h-eòin.—*Where the fish is, the birds will be.*

Far am bi bò bidh bean, 's far am bi bean bidh buaireadh.—*Where a cow is, a woman will be, and where a woman is will be temptation.*

> *Al.*—For 'buaireadh,' 'mallachd,' 'dragh,' 'aimhreit'—*mischief, trouble, strife.*
> This saying is attributed to St Columba, who for the time must have forgotten that he and his brethren needed mothers.

Far am bi cairbhean, cruinnichidh coin.—*Where carcases are, dogs will gather.*

Far am bi cearcan, bidh gràcan.—*Where hens are will be cackling.*

Far am bi cnocan, bidh fasgadh.—*Where a hillock is will be shelter.*

Far am bi do chràdh, bidh do làmh; far am bi do ghràdh, bidh do thathaich.—*Where your pain is, your hand will be; where your love is, your haunting will be.*

> *Al.*—Far am bi mo ghaol, bidh mo thathaich.

Far am bi geòidh, bidh iseanan.—*Where geese are will goslings be.*

Far am bi mi fhèin, bidh mo thuagh.—*Where I am myself, my axe will be.*

> Said by a smith who always carried an axe, on being asked to leave it behind him. He added, 'Gach nì riamh ge 'n d'fhuair, 's ann air mo thuaigh a bhuidheachas'—'*Whatever I have got, thanks to my axe for it.*' The axe looks very Icelandic.

> Far am bi saoir, bidh sliseagan;
> Far am bi mnài, bidh giseagan.

> —*Where carpenters are will be shavings;*
> *Where women are will be spells.*

> *Al.*—Far am bi cailleachan—*Where old wives are.*

Far am bi toil, bidh gnìomh.—*Come will, come deed.*

> Where there's a will there's a way.—*Eng.*

Far an caill duin' a sporan, is ann as còir dha iarraidh.—*Where a man loses his purse, he should look for it.*

> Donde perdiste la capa (*cape*), ay la cata.—*Span.*

Far am faic thu toll, cuir do chorrag ann.—*Where you see a hole, put your finger in.*

Far an laigh na fir, 's ann a dh'èireas iad.—*Where men lie down they will get up.*

> *Al.*—Far an suidh—*Where they sit.*

Far an sàmhaich' an t-uisge, 's ann as doimhn' e.—*Where water is stillest, it is deepest.*

> Is ciúin agus sostach sruth na linnte lána,
> Ní h-é sin don tsruth éadtrom, sí bhagras go dána.—*Ir.*
> Altissima quæque flumina minimo sono labuntur.—*Curtius.* Dove il fiume ha più fondo, fa minor strepito.—*Ital.* Do va mas hondo el rio, hace menos ruido.—*Span.* Stille Wasser sind tief.—*Germ.* Stille waters hebben diepe gronden.—*Dutch.* Det stille Vand har den dybe Grund.—*Dan.* Deepest waters stillest go.—*Eng.* Smooth waters rin deep.—*Scot.*

Far an taine 'n abhainn, 's ann as mò a fuaim.—*Where the stream is shallowest, greatest is its noise.*

> Sé an-tuisge is éadomhuine is mó tormán.—*Ir.* Basaf yw'r dwfr yn yd lefair.—*Welsh.*

Far nach bi am beag, cha bhi am mòr.—*Where no little is, no big will be.*

Far nach bi na coin, cha leigear iad.—*Where dogs are not, they can't be started.*

Far nach bi na fèidh, cha rèidh an toirt às.—*From the place where deer are not, they're not easy to be got.*

Far nach bi na fireanaich, cha bhi na fir mhòra.—*Where there are no mannikins, there will be no big men.*

Far nach bi na mic-uchd, cha bhi na fir-fheachd.—*Where there are no boys in arms, there will be no armed men.*

> So long as Britain keeps an army, this saying ought not to be forgotten, especially in the Highlands.

Far nach bi na failleanan, cha bhi na cnothan.—*Where no suckers are, there will be no nuts.*

Far nach bi nì, caillidh an rìgh a chòir.—*Where no cattle are, the king will lose his due.*

> Where there is naething, the king tines his right.—*Scot.*

Far nach cinnich an spàrr, cha chinnich nas fheàrr.—*Where the hen-roost thrives not, neither will what's better.*

Far nach ionmhainn duine, is ann as fhasa èigneachadh.—*Where a man is not beloved, it is easiest to overcome him.*

Faram 's na toiream, fasan Chlann Dòmhnaill.—*Give me, but let me not give—the MacDonald fashion.*

> *Al.*—'S ann de shliochd 'Faram's cha toirinn' thu.
> Ye come o the MacTaks, and no o the MacGies.—*Scot.*

Farraid air fios, farraid as miosa a th' ann.—*Asking what one knows, the worst kind of asking.*

> *Al.*—Faighneachd air fios, faighneachd as mios' air bith.
> See 'An rud a chuir na Maoir'.

Farraid de dhuin' a ghalar.—*Ask a man what his ailment is.*

Farraididh a h-uile fear, 'Cò a rinn e?' ach chan fharraid iad, 'Cia fhad a bha iad ris?'—*Everyone will ask, 'Who made it?' but they won't ask, 'How long was it in making?'*

Fàs a' ghruinnd a rèir an uachdarain.—*The yield of the ground is according to the landlord.*

> This is an important truth in Political Economy.

Fàsaidh an fheòil fhad 's is beò an smior.—*The flesh will grow while the marrow lives.*

> See 'Gleidhidh cnàimh'.

Fead air fuar-luirg.—*Whistling on cold track.*

> A wild goose chase—no scent.

Feadag, Feadag, màthair Faoillich fhuair.—*Plover, Plover, mother of cold Month of Storms.*

> This was the name of certain days in February. See App. IV.

Feadaireachd bhan is gairm chearc, dà nì toirmisgt'.—*Whistling of women and crowing of hens, two forbidden things.*

> *Al.*—Nigheanan a' feadaireachd, is cearcan a' glaodhaich.
> *Al.*—Gairm circe, is fead maighdne.
> A whistling wife, and a crowing hen,
> Will call the old gentleman out of his den.—*Eng.*
> Une poule qui chante le coq, et une fille qui siffle, porte malheur dans la maison.—*Fr.*
> See 'B' e sin a' chearc'.

Feadaireachd mun bhuail' fhàis, is gàrradh mun chnàmhaig.—*Whistling round the empty fold, and wall round the refuse corn.*

Feannadh na frìde airson a geire.—*Flaying the tetter for its tallow.*

Fear a' chinn duibh 's na feusaige ruaidhe, na teirg eadar e 's a' chreag.—*Black head, red beard—don't go between him and the rock.*

Fear a chuirear a dh'aindeoin don allt, bristidh e na soithichean.—*He that goes unwillingly for water will break the pitcher.*

Fear a' ghearain-ghnàth, chan fhaigh e truas 'na chàs.—*He that always complains is never pitied.*—*Eng.*

Fear am baile 's aire às, 's fhèarr às na ann e.—*A man in a farm and his thoughts away is better out of it than in it.*

Fear an àite fir, 's e dh'fhàgas am fearann daor.—*Tenant after tenant makes the land dear.*

Fear an ime mhòir, 's e 's binne glòir.—*The man of great wealth has the sweetest voice.*

> *Lit.* 'of great butter'.

Fear an t-saoghail fhada, cha bhi baoghal thuige.—*The man of long life will escape danger.*

> He can't die before his time. See 'Cha tig am bàs'.

Fear clèite gun bhogsa, is bleidire gun amharas.—*A quill-driver without a box, and a beggar without suspicion.*

Extraordinary things.

> Fear dubh dàna; fear bàn bleideil;
> Fear donn dualach; 's fear ruadh sgeigeil.
>
> —*Black man bold; fair man officious;*
> *Brown man curly; red man scornful.*
>
>> Fear dubh dana; fear fionn glídiúil (*timid*);
>> Fear donn dualach; fear ruadh scigiúil.—*Ir.*
>>
>> Fair and foolish; black and proud;
>> Long and lazy; little and loud.—*Eng., Scot.*

Fear eil' airson Eachainn!—*Another for Hector!*

> Said at the battle of Inverkeithing, 1652, in reference to the chief of the MacLeans, Hector Roy of Duart, who was killed there, with hundreds of his clan.—*Cuairtear*, 1842, pp 96–7. Sir Walter uses this saying in his description of the clan fight in *The Fair Maid of Perth*.

Fear faramach, 's e cothromach; ceann is casan math aige; is gun a mhàthair beò.—*A man of energy, and well-to-do; with good head and good legs; and his mother not alive.*

> The Lochaber 'beau-ideal' of an 'eligible' man.
> *Faramach* expresses the cheerful stir made by a man whose foot will have 'music in't as he gaes up the stair'.

Fear-faire na h-aon sùla.—*The one-eyed watcher.*

> This is a legendary character—Argus, but one-eyed.

Fear gealtach san aoir.—*A timid man at the main-sheet.*

> The wrong man for the place.

Fear gu aois, is bean gu bàs.—*A man to full age, a woman till death.*

> A son must be maintained till of age, a daughter, if unmarried, for life.
>
> My son is my son till he's got him a wife,
> My daughter's my daughter all the days of her life.—*Eng., Scot.*

Fear na bà fhèin sa pholl an toiseach.—*Let the cow's owner go first into the mire.*

> He that ows the cou gaes nearest her tail.—*Scot.*

Fear na foill' an ìochdar!—*Let the knave be kept under!*

Fear nach cuir cùl ri charaid no ri nàmhaid.—*A man that won't turn his back on friend or foe.*

Fear nach reic 's nach ceannaich a' chòir.—*A man who will neither sell nor buy the right.*

Fear nach trèig a chaileag no chompanach.—*A man that won't forsake his lass nor his comrade.*

Fear sam bith a dh'òlas bainne capaill le spàin chrithinn, cha ghabh e 'n triuthach ach aotrom.—*He that drinks mare's milk with an aspen spoon will take whooping-cough lightly.*

> The first part of this prescription is rational; the virtue of the spoon was supposed to be derived from the sacred character of the aspen tree.

Fear sam bith a loisgeas a mhàs, 's e fhèin a dh'fheumas suidhe air.—*Whoever burns his bottom must himself sit on it.*

Fear uiread fuighill rium ag iarraidh fuighill orm.—*A man with leavings as big as mine asking leavings of me.*

Fèath Faoillich is gaoth Iuchair, cha mhair iad fada.—*February calm and Dog-days' wind won't last long.*

> *Al.*—F. F. is trod chàirdean, chan fhada mhaireas—*F. calm and friends' quarrels.*
> *Al.*—F. F. is gaol seòladair—*F. calm and sailor's love.*
> *Al.*—F. F. is gaol guanaig, dà nì air bheagan buanais—*F. calm and flirt's love, two things of short endurance.*

Feith ri dheireadh.—*Await the end.*

> Respice finem.—*Lat.*
> This is the Kennedy motto: Avisez la fin—*Consider the end.*

Feitheamh an t-sionnaich ri sitheann an tairbh.—*The fox's waiting for the bull's flesh.*

Feitheamh fada ri eòrna na gainmhich.—*Long waiting for the sandy barley.*

> Barley sown in sand comes to nothing.

Feuch an laogh blàr-buidhe dhomh, 's na feuch a chuid domh.— *Show me the white-faced yellow calf, and not what he is fed on.*

> Taispéan an laogh biadhta, ach ná taispéan an ní a bhiathaigh é.—*Ir.* Dangos y llo, ac na ddangos y llaeth—*Show the calf and not the milk—Welsh.* Ne'er shaw me the meat but the man.—Scot.

Feuch gu bheil do theallach fhèin sguabte mun tog thu luath do choimhearsnaich.—*See that your own hearth is swept before you lift your neighbour's ashes.*

> Sweep before your own door.—*Eng.* Veeg eerst voor uwe eigene deur, en dan voor die uws buurmans.—*Dutch.*

Feuch nach gabh do shùil air.—*See that your eye doesn't rest on it.*

> Alluding to the dreaded gift of the Evil Eye.

Feumaidh am fear a bhios 'na èiginn beairt-èididh a dhèanamh.—*He that's in straits must make a shift to clothe himself.*

Feumaidh an talamh a chuid fhèin.—*The earth must have its portion.*

> This means the Grave = all must die.

Feumaidh fear-caithimh fhaoilidh sprèidh no bunachar.—*A liberal spender needs cattle or substance.*

Feumaidh fear na h-aona bhà car dha h-earball mu dhòrn.—*The man of one cow must twist her tail round his fist.*

> He must look well after her. This is a Uist saying.

Feumaidh fear nan cuaran èirigh uair ro fhear nam bròg.—*The man of the sock must rise an hour before the wearer of shoes.*

> The lacing on of the *cuaran* was a tedious affair.

Feumaidh gach beò a bheathachadh.—*Every living thing must have a living.*

Feumaidh na fithich fhèin a bhith beò.—*The ravens themselves must live.*

Fhad 's a bhios a shùil an cèilidh an t-saoghail seo.—*As long as he has an eye to sojourning in this world.*

Fhad 's a bhios cù cam, no duine dìreach.—*As long as a dog is bent, or a man straight.*

Fhuair e car tron deathaich.—*He got a turn through the smoke.*

> It was the custom to put a newly christened child into a basket and hand it across the fire, in order to counteract the power of evil spirits.—Note in 2nd ed. of Macintosh.

Fhuair thu fios an eagail.—*You have learned what fear is.*

> Said when one has had a narrow escape.

Fialachd don fhògarrach, 's cnàimhean briste don eucorach!—*Hospitality to the exile, and broken bones to the oppressor!*

> A generous and good sentiment.

Fìor no breug, millear bean leis.—*True or false, it will injure a woman.*

> Alas! for the rarity
> Of Christian charity
> Under the sun!—*Hood.*

Fios fithich gu ròic.—*The raven's boding of a feast.*

Fir a' chladaich is bodaich Nis; daoin'-uaisle Uige.—*The shore men and bodies of Ness; the gentlemen of Uig.*

> Ness is a district in the north of Lewis; Uig a parish in the west of the island. The above saying must have originated in the latter, the Ness men being generally regarded as fine specimens of mixed Scandinavian and Celtic blood.

Fitheach dubh air an taigh, fios gu nighean an dathadair.—*A black raven on the roof, warning to the dyer's daughter.*

> Probably a death omen.

Fliuch do shùil mun gabh i air.—*Wet your eyes lest it light on him.*

> *Al.*—mun cronaich thu e—*lest you hurt him.*
> This again alludes to the Evil Eye, against which wetting the eye acted like a counter-spell.

Fo mhaide na poite.—*Under the pot-stick.*

> Said of a henpecked man.

Foghar an àigh—ial is fras.—*Finest autumn, sun and shower.*

Foghar fada 's beagan buana.—*Long harvest and little reaping.*

> Foghar gu Nollaig,
> Is Geamhradh gu Fèill Pàdraig;
> Earrach gu Fèill Peadair;
> Samhradh gu Fèill Màrtainn.
>
> —*Autumn to Christmas; Winter to St Patrick's Day;*
> *Spring to St Peter's Day; Summer to Martinmas.*
> St Patrick's Day, 17th March; St Peter's Day, 29th June.

Foghar nam ban brèid-gheal.—*The harvest of young widows.*

> A prophecy of a time when all the men would be slain in battle.

Fòghnadh is fuidheall.—*Enough and to spare.*

Fòghnaidh feur nach d'fhàs don laogh nach d'rugadh.—*Grass that hasn't grown will suit the unborn calf.*

Fòghnaidh salann salach air ìm ròinneagach.—*Dirty salt will do for hairy butter.*

Foighidinn nam ban—a trì.—*Women's patience—till you count three.*

Fois luchaig am balg, 's fois deargainn an osan.—*A mouse's rest in a bag, and a flea's in a stocking.*

Fois radain an connlaich.—*A rat's rest among straw.*

Freagraidh a' bhriogais don mhàs.—*The trousers will suit the seat.*

> *Al.*—'Is coltach an triubhas ris' &c.
> This is a Cowal saying.

Fuachd caraid 's fuachd anairt, cha do mhair e fada riamh.—*The coldness of a friend and of linen never lasted long.*

Fuaim mòr air bheagan leòin.—*Great noise and little hurt.*

> This might apply to platoons of musketry, before arms of precision were known.

Fuath giullain, a chiad leannan.—*A boy's hate, his first love.*

Fuidhleach an tàilleir shàthaich, làn spàin' a chabhraich.—*The leavings of the full tailor, a spoonful of sowens.*

    Al.—Fuighleach tàilleir, dà bhuntàta—*A tailor's leavings, two potatoes.*

Fuil bhàn, is craiceann slàn.—*White blood, and whole skin.*

    Said to children who fancy they have been hurt.

Fuilingidh gach beathach a bhith gu math ach mac an duine.—*Every creature but the son of man can bear well-being.*

Fuine bean a' mhuilleir, làidir, tiugh.—*The miller's wife's kneading, strong and thick.*

Fuirich thus' an sin gus an tig feum ort, mar a thuirt am fear a thìodhlaic a bhean.—*Stay you there till you are wanted, as the man said who buried his wife.*

Furain an t-aoigh a thig, greas an t-aoigh tha falbh.—*Welcome the coming, speed the parting guest.*

    Foster the guest that stays, further him that maun gang.—*Scot.*

G

Gabh an dileag leis a' chriomaig.—*Take the drop with the sop.*

Gabh an latha math às a thoiseach.—*Take the good day early.*

Gabh an latha math fhad 's a gheibh thu e.—*Take the good day while you may.*

Gabh an toil an àit' a' ghnìomh.—*Take the will for the deed.*

Gabh eòlas Rubh' a' Bhàird air.—*Take it like the Bard's Point.*

> Avoid it. This is a Lewis saying.

Gabhadh iad air mo chrodh sa chladach; an uair a bhios mo bhreacan air mo ghualainn, bidh mo bhuaile-chruidh ann.—*Let them pelt my cattle on the beach; when my plaid is over my shoulder, it's in my cattle-fold.*

> Said by one who has nothing to lose = Omnia mea mecum porto.

Gabhaidh biadh na cnò roinn.—*The kernel of a nut can be divided.*

> *Al.*—Gabhaidh dà leth dèanamh air an eitean.
> *Al.*—Ge beag eitean na cnò, gabhaidh e roinn.

Gabhaidh an connadh fliuch, ach cha ghabh a' chlach.—*Wet fuel will burn, but stones won't.*

Gabhaidh connadh ùr le bhith ga shèideadh.—*Fresh fuel will burn if blown.*

> *Al.*—Gabhaidh fraoch nodha—*New heather will burn.*

Gabhaidh fear na sròine mòire a h-uile rud ga ionnsaigh fhèin.—*The big-nosed man takes everything to himself.*

He that has a muckle nose thinks ilka ane speaks o't.—*Scot.*

Gabhaidh gach sruth a dh'ionnsaigh na h-aibhne, 's gach abhainn don chuan.—*Every stream runs into the river, and every river into the sea.*

All the rivers run into the sea.—*Eccl.* i, 7.

Gabhaidh lothag fhiadhta sìol à bonaid.—*A shy filly will take corn out of a bonnet.*

> Gabhaidh sinn an rathad mòr,
> Olc no math le càch e!
>
> —*We will take the high road,*
> *Let them take it ill or well!*

This is the chorus of a song set to one of the most popular of Highland 'quick-steps'. It was composed on the occasion of a body of Mac-Gregors, MacNabs and Stewarts, commanded by Major Patrick MacGregor of Glengyle, marching boldly through hostile territory to join Montrose at the battle of Inverlochy. See *Gael*, Vol. I, p. 288, where the words are given, with a translation by the Rev. Mr Stewart of Nether Lochaber.

Gach cailleach gu cùil fhèin.—*Every old woman to her own corner.*

> Gach dàn gu Dàn an Deirg;
> Gach laoidh gu Laoidh an Amadain Mhòir;
> Gach sgeul gu Sgeul Chonaill;
> Gach cliù gu Cliù Eòghainn;
> Gach moladh gu moladh Loch Cè.
>
> —*All songs up to the Song of the Red One;*
> *All lays up to the Lay of the Great Fool;*
> *All tales up to the Tale of Connal;*
> *All fame up to the Fame of Ewen;*
> *All praise up to the praise of Loch Key.*

Each of these was regarded as a masterpiece or *ne plus ultra* in its own kind.—See App. V.

Gach dìleas gu deireadh.—*The best loved last.*

> Lit. 'the faithful,' but the above is the sense in which the phrase is generally used.
>
> *Al.*—Gach roghainn air thoiseach, 's gach dileas gu deireadh.—*The choice to the front, the faithful to the last.*

Gach olc an tòin a' choimhich.—*Let the blame of every ill be on the stranger.*

> This is clannishness in its worst aspect.

Gach diù gu deireadh.—*The worst to the last.*

Gach fear 'na ghrèim.—*Every man in his place.*

> Lit. 'his hold'—'All hands upon deck!'

Gach fiodh às a bhàrr, ach am feàrn' às a bhun.—*All wood from the top, but alder from the root.*

> This is a maxim as to the splitting of wood.

Gach eun gu nead, 's a shràbh 'na ghob.—*Each bird to its nest, with its straw in its beak.*

Gach eun mar a dh'oileanar.—*Bird is as his bringing up.*

> Gach éan mar oiltear é.—*Ir.*

Gad riabhach Samhraidh, gad geal Geamhraidh.—*Summer withe brindled, Winter withe white.*

> The bark would be left on the twigs cut in Summer.

Gàdag 's a dà cheann sgaoilte.—*A straw-rope with both ends loose.*

> Applied to a slovenly woman.

Gàire mu adhbhar a' ghuil.—*Laughing at the cause of weeping.*

> *Al.*—Gal is gàire, craos gun nàire—*Weeping, laughing, shameless mouth.*

Gàire Mhàrtainn ris an lite.—*Martin's smile at his porridge.*

Gàire na caillich sa chùil dhìonaich.—*The old woman's smile in the snug corner.*

Gàire ri do mhì-chiatadh.—*Laughing at your shame.*

Gairm Mhic Mhannain air na gobhair: 'Ma thig, thig; 's mur tig, fan.'—*The Manxman's call to the goats: 'If you are coming, come; if not, stay.'*

Galar as truime na 'n luaidhe, galar as buaine na 'n darach.—*Disease more heavy than lead, more lasting than oak.*

> This is a *dubh-fhacal*, or dark saying.

Galar fada 's eug 'na bhun.—*A long disease and death at its root.*

> Tinneas fada, is éag in a bhun.—*Ir.* Bod yn hir yn glaf, a marw eisys—*To be long sick, and die besides.*—*Welsh.*

Gall glas.—*A sallow Lowlander.*

> This epithet was formerly applied to the Gael, as is seen in Mr MacLean of Kilninian's verses to Lhuyd of the *Archaeologia* (1707), where 'Sliochd an Ghaoidhil ghlais' is contrasted with the 'Dubhghall' or 'Black Lowlander'. The term *glas* is never applied to the 'Sassenach' or Englishman.

Gaol an fhithich air a' chnàimh.—*The raven's love for the bone.*

> *Al.*—Suirghe airson a bhronna—*Pot-wooing.*

Gaol nam fear dìolain
Mar shruth-lìonaidh na mara;
Gaol nam fear-fuadain
Mar ghaoith tuath thig on charraig;
Gaol nam fear-pòsda
Mar luing a' seòladh gu cala.

*—Paramour's love, like the sea's flowing tide;
Wayfarers' love, like north wind from rock;
Married men's love, like ship sailing to harbour.*

Gaoth Deas, teas is toradh;
Gaoth 'n Iar, iasg is bainne;
Gaoth Tuath, fuachd is gailleann;
Gaoth 'n Ear, meas air chrannaibh.

—South wind, heat and plenty;
West wind, fish and milk;
North wind, cold and tempest;
East wind, fruit on branches.

Al.—Gaoth à Deas, teas is toradh; gaoth à Tuath, fuachd is feannadh (*skinning*); gaoth à 'n Iar, iasg is bainne; gaoth à 'n Ear, mil (*honey*) air crannaibh, *or* tart is crannadh (*drought and parching*).

This weather prophecy is said to have specially referred to the direction of the wind on the last night of the year.

Gaoth on rionnaig Earraich;
Teas on rionnaig Shamhraidh;
Uisg' on rionnaig Fhoghair;
Reothadh on rionnaig Gheamhraidh.

—Wind from the Spring Star;
Heat from the Summer Star;
Water from the Autumn Star;
Frost from the Winter Star.

Gaoth gun dìreadh ort!—*Wind without direction to you!*

Al.—Gun dìreadh ort!—*Want of guidance to you!*

Gaoth 'n Iar an dèidh uisge reamhair.—*West wind after heavy rain.*

Gaoth 'n Iar gun fhrois, bidh i 'g iarraidh Deas.—*West wind without shower will be seeking south.*

Gaoth ron aiteamh, 's gaoth tro tholl, is gaoth nan long a' dol fo sheòl—na tri gaothan a b'fhuaire dh'fhairich Fionn riamh.—*Wind before thaw, wind through hole, wind of ship when hoisting sail—the three coldest Fingal ever felt.*

Al.—Gaoth ath-thionndaidh—*An eddy wind.* Gaoth tro shabhal—
Wind through barn. Gaoth nan tonn a' tighinn fon t-seòl—*Wind of
waves coming under sail.*
Ny three geayghyn a' feayrey dennee Fion M'Cooil; gey hennew, as
gey huill, as gey fo ny shiauill.—*Manx.*

Gaoth fo sheòl agus sròn coin, dà rud cho fuar 's a th' ann.—*Wind
under a sail, and a dog's nose, are two of the coldest things.*

Garbh-innse nan uirsgeulan.—*The big telling of stories.*

Ge b'e air bith tha thu 'g ithe no 'g òl, 's lèir a bhlàth air d'aghaidh
gu bheil aghaidh do chrobhan ri d' chraos.—*Whatever your meat and
drink be, it's very clear on your face that your hands and your mouth are
good friends.*

> This was said by a master to a servant who protested that she ate
> nothing but bread and milk.

Ge b'e bhios gu math rium, bidh mi gu tric aige.—*Whoever is good
to me, I'll be often with him.*

Ge b'e bhios 'na fhear-muinntir aig an t-sionnach, feumaidh e
earball a ghiùlan.—*Whoever is servant to the fox must bear up his tail.*

> This may possibly have been suggested by the curious spectacle of a
> dignitary going in procession with his train upheld by pages.

Ge b'e bhios saor, cha dèan gaoth torrach.—*Whoever be innocent or
not, wind won't make pregnant.*

Ge b'e chaillear no nach caillear, caillear an deagh shnàmhaiche.—
Whoever is lost or not, the good swimmer will be drowned.

Ge b'e chaomhnas an t-slat, is beag air a mhac.—*He that spareth his
rod hateth his son.—Prov.* xiii, 24.

Ge b'e chì no chluinneas tu, cùm an cat mun cuairt.—*Whatever you see or hear, keep the cat turning.*

This was said on the last occasion that a horrid species of sorcery, called the *Taghairm*, was performed by two men in Mull. It was said to be one of the most effectual means of raising the Devil, and getting unlawful wishes gratified. The performance consisted in roasting cats alive, one after another, for four days, without tasting food; which if duly persisted in, summoned a legion of devils, in the guise of black cats, with their master at their head, all screeching in a way terrifying to any person of ordinary nerves. On the occasion in question the chief performer was Allan MacLean, a man of boundless daring, who adopted this means of securing additional power and wealth. His companion, Lachlan MacLean, was equally greedy, and not less brave, but as the house began to get filled with yelling demons, he cried out to Allan, who made the above answer to him. The performance, as the story goes, was successfully accomplished, and the result was that both men got a great accession of all worldly goods. See L. MacLean's *History of the Celtic Language*, p. 264.

Ge b'e don tug thu mhin, thoir dha a' chàth.—*Give the bran to him to whom you gave the meal.*

> Ge b'e fear as luaithe làmh,
> 'S leis an gadhar bàn 's am fiadh.
> —*He that is of quickest hand will get the white hound and the deer.*
> *Al.*—Am fear as treasa làmh, gheibh e &c.
> An té is luaithe lámh, bíodh aige an gadhar bán 's an fiadh.—*Ir.*
> This occurs in *Laoidh an Amadain Mhòir.*—See Campbell's *W.H.T.*, Vol. III, 163.

Ge b'e gheibheadh a roghainn, 's mairg a thaghadh an diù.—*Pity him who has his choice, and chooses the worse.*

Ge b'e ghleidheas a long, gheibh e latha.—*He that keeps his ship will get a day.*

> *Al.*—gheibh e fàth—*he will get a chance.*

Ge b'e ghoideadh an t-ugh, ghoideadh e chearc nam faodadh e.—*Who would steal the egg would steal the hen.*

Ge b'e mar a bhios an t-sian, cuir do shìol anns a' Mhàrt.—*Whate'er the weather be, sow your seed in March.*

> See 'An ciad Mhàrt'.

Ge b'e 'n coireach, 's mis' an creanach.—*Whoever is to blame, I am the sufferer.*

Ge b'e nach beathaich na coin, cha bhi iad aige latha na seilge.—*He that does not feed the dogs won't have them on the hunting-day.*

> See 'Am fear nach biath'.

Ge b'e nach dèan a ghnothach cho luath ri sheise, nì e uair as aimh-dheis' e.—*He that doesn't do his work as quickly as his mate must do it at a less convenient time.*

Ge b'e nach fuiling docair, chan fhaigh e socair.—*He gets no ease who suffers not.*

> This is substantially the Platonic doctrine of Pleasure and Pain.

Ge b'e nach stiùir coir' a' bhrochain, cha stiùir Coire Bhreacain.—*He that can't steer the porridge-pot won't steer Corryvreckan.*

> The moral seems to be the same as 'reason in roasting eggs,' with a play on the words. In a well-known comic song, describing a sea-voyage of two land-lubbers, this verse occurs:

> > 'Ciamar a stiùreadh tu poit?'
> >   Arsa Calum Figheadair;
> > 'Ladar a sparradh 'na corp,'
> >   Ars Alasdair Tàillear.

Ge b'e 's miosa, mas e 's treasa, bidh e 'n uachdar.—*The worst, if strongest, will be uppermost.*

> *Al.*—Thèid neart thar ceart.

Ge b'e thig an tùs, 's e' gheibh rogha coisrich.—*Whoso comes first gets the best of the banquet.*

> First come, first served.—*Eng., Scot.*

Ge beag an t-ugh, thig eun às.—*Though the egg be small, a bird will come out of it.*

Ge b'oil leis a' mhnaoi, tha 'n còta saidhbhir.—*In spite of the wife, the coat is unstinted.*

> A Lochaber saying. The goodwife, who made the cloth, wished to scrimp the measure, in the spirit of 'Tak yir auld cloak aboot ye'.

Ge bu don' an saor, bu mhath a shliseag, mun duirt bean an t-saoir nuair a chaochail e.—*Though bad was the carpenter, good was his chip, as his wife said when he died.*

Ge bu leat earras an domhain, na cuir e 'n coimheart ri d'nàire.— *Were the wealth of the world yours, weigh it not against your shame.*

Ge cruaidh reachd a' Bhàillidh, chan fhearr reachd a' Mhinisteir.— *Hard as is the Factor's rule, no better is the Minister's.*

> See 'Glèidh do mhaor'.
> The factor and the minister are naturally the most influential persons in rural parishes, and the most popular, or unpopular, as the case may be. The above saying is given by Dr. MacLeod in one of his delightful Gaelic dialogues. A somewhat profane saying, attributed to a satirical person in one of the Western Islands, described the three chief powers as 'Fear a'—, Nì Math agus Maighstir—'.—*The Chamberlain, Providence and the Rev.—*.

Ge cruaidh sgarachdainn, cha robh dithis gun dealachadh.—*Though separation be hard, two never met but had to part.*

Ge dàil do dh'fhear an uilc, cha dearmad.—*Though there be delay, the evil-doer is not forgotten.*

> *Al.*—Ge fada rè fear an uilc, cha teid e gun dìoghailt bho Dhia— *Though the time of the wicked be long, he won't go unpunished of God.* Though hand join in hand, the wicked shall not be unpunished—*Prov.* xi. 21. Ὀψὲ θεων ἀλέουσι μύλοι, αλέουσι δὲ λεπτά—*The mills of the gods grind late, but grind fine.*—*Gr.*

Ge dlùth do dhuin' a chòta, is dlùithe dha a lèine.—*Though near be a man's coat, nearer is his shirt.*

> Más fogas domh mo chóta, is foisce ná sin mo léine.—*Ir.* Near's my sark, but nearer's my skin.—*Scot.* Near is my kirtle, but nearer is my smock.—*Eng.* Het hemd is nader dan de rok.—*Dutch.* Più mi tocca la camicia che la gonnella.—*Ital.*

Ge don' an t-eun, 's mios' an t-isean.—*Though bad the bird, the chicken is worse.*

> *Al.*—Ge dona mise, 's miosa Iain òg—*Bad though I be, young John is worse.*

Ge dubh a cheann, 's geal a chridhe.—*Though black his head, his heart is fair.*

Ge dubh am fitheach, is geal leis isean.—*Black as is the raven, he thinks his chicken fair.*

> Every craw thinks his ain bird whitest.—*Scot.*

Ge dubh an dearcag, 's milis i; ge dubh mo chaileag, 's bòidheach i.—*Black is the berry but sweet; black is my lassie but bonnie.*

> *Al.*—Ge geal an sneachd, is fuar e—*Though white the snow, 'tis cold.*

Ge dubh an saor, is geal a shliseag.—*Though black the carpenter, white are his chips.*

> *Al.*—Ge h-olc an saor, is math a shliseag.
> Más olc an saor, is maith a scealpóg.—*Ir.*

Ge fad' an duan, ruigear a cheann.—*The longest chant has an end.*

Ge fagas clach don làr, is faisge na sin cobhair Choibhi.—*Though near the stone be to the ground, closer is the help of Coivi.*

> This saying is a very old one. See 'Cho teòma ri Coibhi'.

Ge fagas 'dhuinn,' 's faisge 'oirnn.'—*Though 'to us' be near, 'upon us' is nearer.*

Ge fuar an tràigh, is blàth an coire.—*Though cold be the shore, the corrie is warm.*

Ge glas am feur, fàsaidh e.—*Though gray the grass, it will grow.*

Ge h-olc am bothan bochd, 's e tha olc a bhith gun olc gun mhath.—*Bad as is the poor bothie, worst is without bad or good.*

> An Ulster rhyme on this subject given by Mr MacAdam in *Ulst. Journ. of Arch.* is very characteristic:
>
> > Cúradh mo chroidhe ort, a bhothain!
> > 'S tú nach mbíonn a choidh ach i gcothan;
> > Ach cáil bheag bhídeach de do shochair,
> > Moch nó mall a thiginn,
> > Gur b'ionat is fusa domh mo chosa 'shíneadh!

> *—Plague of my heart on thee, bothie!*
> *'Tis thou that art always in confusion;*
> *But one nice little virtue there's in thee,*
> *Late or early that I come,*
> *It's in thee I can easiest stretch my legs!*

Ge h-olc gill' a' ghille, 's miosa gill' an ath-ghille.—*Though bad be the servant's servant, worse is the substitute's servant.*

Ge h-olc 'siud', chan e 'siad' as fheàrr.—

> This appears to be a protest against certain modes of speech common in some parts of the Highlands, but regarded in other parts as affected. *Siud*, 'that,' is pronounced *sid* in Inverness-shire. *Siad*, instead of *iad*, 'they,' is never used in that county.

Ge math a' chobhair an t-sealg, cha mhath an saoghal an t-sealg.—*Hunting is a good help, but a bad living.*

Ge math an ceòl feadaireachd, fòghnaidh dhuinn beagan deth.—*Whistling may be good music, but a little of it will do for us.*

> *Al.*—fidilearachd—*fiddling.* See 'Mas ceòl'.

Ge math an gille cam, cha fhritheil e thall 's a-bhos.—*Good though the one-eyed servant be, he cannot attend here and there.*

> *Al.*—'Ge beadaidh,' 'ge èasgaidh'—'cha fhreagair e.' 'Ge math an cù cam'.

Ge milis a' mhil, cò a dh'imlicheadh bhàrr na dris' i?—*Sweet as is the honey, who would lick it off the brier?*

> Más milis an mhil, ná ligh-sa den dreasóig í.—*Ir.* Dear bought is the honey that's licked from the thorn.—*Eng.* Trop achète le miel qui le lèche sur les épines.—*Fr.* Theurer Honig den man auf Dornen muss lecken.—*Germ.* Hij koopt den honig wel duur, die ze van de doornen moet lekken.—*Dutch.*

Ge milis am fìon, tha e searbh ri dhìol.—*Though sweet the wine, 'tis bitter to pay.*

> *Al.*—Ge milis ri òl, is goirt ri phàigheadh e.
> Is milis fìon, is searbh a íoc.—*Ir.* Millish dy ghoaill, ach sharroo dy eeck.—*Manx.*

Ge mòr àrdan na h-easaich, cha tig i seach an luath.—*Great as is the gruel's rage, it won't go beyond the ashes.*

> *Al.*—Ge mòr aintheas na poite bige, cha tig e &c.

Ge teann dòrn, 's faisge uileann.—*Though fist be near, elbow is nearer.*

> Sniessey yn uillin na yn doarn.—*Manx.* Nesoc'h eo ilin evit dorn.—*Breton.* Nes penelin nag arddwrn.—*Welsh.* Γόνυ κνήμης ἔγγιον—*Knee is nearer than leg.*—*Gr.*

Ge ùrag, cha 'n ùrag mun bhiadh.—*Though bland she be, she is not so about food.*

> The word *ùrag* = a nice, bland, young woman is not in any of the dictionaries, but is used in various districts. The above saying is from Lewis.

Gealach bhuidhe na Fèill Mhìcheil.—*The yellow moon of Michaelmas.*

> The Harvest Moon.
> *Al.*—Gealach an abachaidh—*The ripening moon.*

Gealladh bog socharach nì duine air sgàth nàire; gealladh gun a cho-ghealladh, 's miosa siud na diùltadh.—*The soft yielding promise, made for shame's sake; promise unfulfilled, worse than refusal.*

Gealladh math is droch phàigheadh.—*Good promise and bad payment.*

Geallaidh am fear feumach an nì breugach nach faigh; saoilidh am fear sanntach gach nì a gheall gum faigh.—*The needy man will promise what he cannot give; the greedy man will hope to get everything that's promised.*

Geallar faoigh do cheann-cinnidh, 's leigear da fhèin tighinn ga shireadh.—*A gift will be promised to the chief, and it will be left to him to come for it.*

> *Al.*—Geallar faoigh do MhacGriogair, 's biodh eadar e fhèin 's a togail.—*A gift will be promised to MacGregor, and the lifting will be left to him.*
> The old practice of taking presents of corn, cattle &c. was not confined to the poor. Chiefs expected them on certain occasions as well as humbler people: they were, in fact, not so much gifts as taxes. See 'Cha bhi rogha'.

Geamhradh reòthtanach, Earrach ceòthanach, Samhradh breac-riabhach is Foghar geal grianach, cha d'fhàg gorta riamh an Alba.—*Frosty Winter, misty Spring, chequered Summer and sunny Autumn never left dearth in Scotland.*

> Arragh chayeeagh, Sourey onyragh (*cloudy*),
> Fouyr ghrianagh, as Geurey rioeeagh.—*Manx.*

Gean a' bhodaich, às a bhroinn.—*The churl's suavity, from off the stomach.*

Ged a bhiodh bean an taghe lachdann—nam biodh i maiseach mun bhiadh!—*Were the housewife ever so plain—if she were only fair with the food!*

Ged a bhiodh do phoca làn, bu mhiann leat màm chur air a mhuin.—*Were your bag full, you would wish to heap it over.*

Ged a chual' iad an ceòl, cha do thuig iad am port.—*They heard the music, but understood not the tune.*

Ged a gheibhte duin' air chòir, cha bu chòir a shàrachadh.—*A good man should not be overtaxed.*

> If thy friend be honey, do not eat him all.—*Arab.*

Ged bheir thu 'n t-anam às, cha toir thu an aghaidh dhuineil às.—*You may take the life from him, but not the manly look from him.*

Ged bhiodh na tri gill san aon mhaide.—*If I had engagements three, I would fly to succour thee.*

> *Lit.* 'Were there three wagers on one stick,' an allusion to the old style of keeping a score by those who couldn't write.

Ged bhrist thu 'n cnàimh, cha d'dheoghail thu 'n smior.—*Though you broke the bone, you didn't suck the marrow.*

Ged chaochail e innis, cha do chaochail e àbhaist.—*He changed his haunt, but not his habit.*

> Cœlum non animum mutant qui trans mare currunt.—*Hor.*

Ged chitheadh tu do mhàthair a' dol ceàrr, dh'innseadh tu e.—*If you saw your mother going wrong, you would tell it.*

> He was scant of news who told that his father was hanged.—*Eng., Scot.*

Ged chluinn thu sgeul gun dreach, na h-aithris e.—*If you hear a hueless tale, don't repeat it.*

Ged chuirinn falt mo chinn fo chasan.—*Though I should lay the hair of my head under his feet.*

Ged dh'èignichear an seanfhacal, cha bhreugaichear e.—*Though the old saying be strained, it cannot be belied.*

> *Al.*—Ged shàraichear. See 'An seanfhacal'.
> Plant gwirionedd yw hen diarhebion—*Old proverbs are children of truth.—Welsh.*

Ged dh'imicheadh tu 'n cruinne, chan fhaigh thu duine gun choire.—*You may go round the world, but you'll not meet a man without fault.*

Ged is ann on bhior, chan ann on choire.—*Escaped from the spit, but not from the cauldron.*

Ged is don' an Donas, thoir a chothrom fhèin da.—*Give the Devil his due.*

> *Al.*—Thoir a dhlighe fhèin don Donas, ged is don' a chòir air.

Ged is e 'n duine an tuathanach, 's e 'n t-each an saothraiche.—*The man is the farmer, but the horse is the labourer.*

Ged is e 'n taigh, chan e mhuinntir.—*Though it be the house, these are not its people.*

> Said when an old house is tenanted by new people, a common thing in the Highlands.

Ged is fhad' a-mach Barraigh, ruigear e.—*Though Barra be far out, it can be reached.*

> Said by Mac Iain Gheàrr, one of the Mac Ians of Ardnamurchan, to MacNeil of Barra, who had been very hard on him at a Court of Justice.

Ged is feàirrd' a' chailleach a garadh, chan fheàirrd' i a losgadh.—*The old woman is the better of being warmed, but not of being burned.*

> Is fearrde don chailleach a goradh, ach is miste i a loscadh.—*Ir.*
> This has been supposed to refer to the atrocious practice of burning women for witchcraft, which was the statutory punishment in this country from 1563 to 1736.

Ged is ìosal an coileach, cromaidh e cheann.—*Though the cock be humble, he bends his head.*

Ged leagas tu mise, chan eil duin' an Nis nach leag thu fhèin.—*Though you knock me down, there's not a man in Ness but can knock you down.*

> Said by one of two pigmies, belonging to the parish of Ness in Lewis, to the other.

Ged nach beirteadh bò an Eirinn.—*Should never a cow be calved in Ireland.*

Ged nach bi mi bruidhneach, bidh mi coimheach, cuimhneach.—*Though I won't be talking, I'll be shy and mindful.*

> See 'Bi 'd thosd'.

Ged nach biodh ach dà leth-pheighinn san sporan, taobhaidh iad ri chèile.—*Were there but two half-pence in the purse, they'll come together.*

> *Al.*—dà thùrn-odhar—*two mites. Tùrn-odhar* is uncommon, but is found in MacAlpine's *Dictionary.*
> Pfennig ist Pfennigs Bruder.—*Germ.*

Ged nach biodh agad ach an t-ugh, 's e 'm plaosg a gheibhinn-sa.—*If you had but an egg, I should get but the shell.*

Ged nach biodh ann ach an rìgh 's fhear-muinntir, dh'fhaodadh duin' a chuid ionndrain.—*Were nobody by but a king and his man, one might miss his own.*

Ged nach duin' an t-aodach, cha duin' a bhios às aogais.—*The clothes are not the man, but he's no man without them.*

> Man tager meere Hatten af for Klederne end for Personen—*More hats are taken off for clothes than for persons.*—*Dan.* De kleederen maken den man.—*Dutch.* For the apparel oft proclaims the man.—*Hamlet* I, iii.
>
> Worth makes the man, and want of it the fellow,
> The rest is nought but leather and prunella.—*Pope.*
>
> A man's a man for aa that.—*Burns.* Society is founded upon Cloth.—*Sartor Resartus.* Lives the man that can figure a naked Duke of Windlestraw, addressing a naked House of Lords?—*Id.*

Ged nach eil e sìos 's a-suas, tha e null 's a-nall.—*Though it be not up and down, it is back and forward.*

Ged nach eil geir ann, tha fuil ann.—*Though there be no fat, there is blood.*

Ged a rachadh Cromba leis a' mhuir.—*Though Cromarty should go with the tide.*

Ged robh e gun mhòine, cha bhi e gun teine.—*Though without peats, he won't want fire.*

Ged tha mi bochd, chan eil mi bleideil.—*Though poor, I'm not a parasite.*

Ged tha mi 'n-diugh am chù-baile, bha mi roimh' am chù-mòintich.—*Though today a farm-dog, I was once a moor-dog.*

Ged tha mise òg, tha seana chluasan agam.—*Though I be young, I have old ears.*

> Little pitchers have wide ears.—*Eng.*

Ged theirteadh riut an cù, cha bu tu ach smior a' mhadaidh.—*Though you were called a dog, you would be the very marrow of a hound.*

Ged threabhadh tu dùthaich, chaitheadh tu dùthaich.—*If you tilled a countryside, you would spend its produce.*

> *Al.*—dh'itheadh tu i—*you would eat it.*

Ged thug thu beum dha, cha tug thu mìr dha.—*You gave him a taunt, but never a morsel.*

Geòlach ort!—*The death bandage on thee!*

Geinn dheth fhèin a sgoilteas an darach.—*A wedge of itself splits the oak.*

Geum bà air a h-eòlas.—*A cow's low on known ground.*

Geurad an leanna-chaoil.—*The sourness of small beer.*

Ghabhadh Mac-a-Phì 'na rabhadh e.—*MacPhie would take it for warning.*

> A Mull saying. MacPhie, chief of Colonsay, went to a feast at Duart Castle, Mull, where his hospitable friend MacLean intended to kill him. The door-keeper, being of friendly mind, asked him if he had come down Glen Connal. He said he had. "S am faca tu m'eich-sa, 's d'eich fhèin?—'*Did you see my horses and your own there?*' MacPhie took the hint, and escaped with all speed.

Ghabhamaid na cruachan mòra, 's dh'fhòghnadh na cruachan beaga.—*We would take the big stacks, and the little ones would do.*

> Contented wi little, and canty wi mair.—*Burns.*

Gheibh airc eirbheirt.—*Need will find means of moving.*

> Need makes the naked man run.—*Eng., Scot.* Need gars the auld wife trot.—*Scot.* Besoin fait vieille trotter.—*Fr.* La necesidad hace á la vieja trotar.—*Span.* De nood doet een oud wijf draven.—*Dutch.*

Gheibh badhbh a guidhe, ged nach fhaigh a h-anam tròcair.—*A wicked woman will get her wish, though her soul get no mercy.*

Gheibh bean bhaoth dlùth gun cheannach, 's chan fhaigh i inn-each.—*A silly woman will get the warp without paying, but won't get the woof.*

Gheibh bronnair mar a bhronnas e, 's gheibh loman an lom-dhonas.—*The liberal will get as he spends, but the niggard will get mere wretchedness.*

> The word *bronn* or *pronn*—'give', 'distribute'—is now obsolete in vernacular Gaelic, but occurs in Ossianic ballads.

Gheibh burraidh barrachd coire na 's urrainn duine glic a leas-achadh.—*A blockhead can find more fault than a wise man can mend.*

> Un matto sa più domandare, che sette savi respondere.—*Ital.* Ein Narr kann mehr fragen, als sieben Weise antworten.—*Germ.* A fool may ask more questions in an hour than a wise man can answer in seven years.—*Eng.*

Gheibh cearc an sgrìobain rudeigin, 's chan fhaigh cearc a' chrùbain dad idir.—*The scraping hen will get something, but the crouching hen will get nothing.*

Gheibh cobhartach spionnadh-iasaid.—*Helper will get loan of strength.*

> A very fine sentiment.

Gheibh Gàidheal fhèin a lethbhreac.—*Even a Gael will find his fellow.*

> The Gael, with all his self-esteem, has sense enough to know that there are as good in the world as he.

Gheibh foighidinn furtachd, 's gheibh trusdar bean.—*Patience will get help, and filthy fellows get wives.*

> Patience and perséverance
> Got a wife for his Reverence.—*Ir.*

Gheibh rìgh feachd, 's gheibh domhan daoine.—*Kings will find armies, and the world men.*

Gheibh sìth sìth, ach gheibh caise cothachadh.—*Peace will get peace, but heat will get contention.*

Gheibh thu air òran e.—*You'll get it for a song.*

Gheibh thu e far am fàg thu e.—*You'll find him where you leave him.*

> Said of a man to be relied on.

Gheibh thu e nuair a gheibh thu nead na cuthaig.—*You'll get it when you find the cuckoo's nest.*

Gheibheadh tu na feannagan-firich.—*You would find the forest-crows.*

> Said to persons who boast of doing impracticable things.

Gheibhear bean-chagair, ach 's ainneamh bean-ghaoil.—*A dear wife may be got, but a love-wife is rare.*

> This is a nice distinction. 'Mo ghaol' is a warmer expression than 'mo chagar'.

Gheibhear deireadh gach sgeòil an asgaidh.—*The end of a tale is got for nothing.*

Gheibhear laogh breac ballach an taigh gach àirich, Là Fhèill Pàdraig Earraich.—*A spotted calf will be found in every cowherd's house on St Patrick's day in Spring.*

Gheibht' iomramh san ràmh gun a bhristeadh.—*Rowing could be got from the oar without breaking it.*

Ghlacadh e 'na lìon fhèin.—*He was caught in his own net.*

Ghoid am mèirleach air braidean e.—*The thief stole it from the pilferer.*

Gille cas-fliuch.—*Wet-foot lad.*

> *Al.*—Gille uisge 's aibhne—*Water and river lad.*
> A servant that carried his master across streams, fetched water and made himself generally useful.

Gille fireann 's e ri fàs, ithidh e mar bhleitheas brà.—*A growing boy will eat as fast as a quern can grind.*

> *Al.*—Seana ghiullan 's e ri fàs, dh'itheadh e mar mheileadh brà.

Gille gun bhiadh gun tuarasdal, cha bhi e uair gun mhaighstir.—*A servant without food or wages won't be long without a master.*

> A boy-servant of all work without food or wages.—*Arab.*

Glac am mèirleach mun glac am mèirleach thu.—*Catch the thief before the thief catch you.*

> Take the thief before he take thee.—*Arab.*

Glac thusa foighidinn, 's glacaidh tu iasg.—*Get you patience, and you'll get fish.*

Glanadh mosaig air a màthair-chèile.—*The slattern's cleaning of her mother-in-law.*

Glas air an taigh an dèidh na gadachd.—*Locking the house after the theft.*

> Locking the stable door when the steed is stolen.—*Eng.*

Glas-labhraidh air nighinn, gun fhios, teang' an abhra dh'iom-raicheas.—*When a maid is tongue-tied, her eyelids tell a tale.*

> A thief sae pawkie is my Jean
> To steal a blink, by aa unseen;
> But gleg as light are lover's een
> When kind love is in the ee.—*Burns.*

Gleac nam fear fanna.—*The wrestling of faint men.*

Glèidh do mhaor 's do mhinistear, 's chan eagal dut.—*Keep your bailiff and your minister, and there's no fear of you.*

Gleidheadh a' chlamhain air na cearcan.—*The kite's guarding of the hens.*

> See 'B'e sin faire'.

Gleidheadh an t-sionnaich air na caoraich.—*The fox's keeping of the sheep.*

Gleidhear cuirm an dèidh Càisge.—*A feast will be kept after Easter.*

Gleidhidh airc innleachd, ged nach glèidh i oighreachd.—*Need will make a shift, though it keep not an inheritance.*

Gleidhidh cnàimh feòil, fhad 's as beò smior.—*Bone will keep flesh, while marrow lives.*

> *Al.*—Gheibh feòil cnàimh, 's gheibh cnàimh feòil—*Flesh will get bone, and bone flesh.*

Gleidhidh sùil seilbh.—*Eye keeps property.*

> The eye of the master does more than both his hands.—*Eng.*

Gleus ùr air seana mhaide.—*A new lock to an old stock.*

Glòir fhuar bhàrr uachdar goile.—*Cold talk from stomach surface.*

Glòir mhòr an colainn bhig.—*Great talk in small body.*

> *Al.*—Glaodh mòr à colainn bhig.

Glòir nan càirdean as mìlse na mhil.—*The praise of friends is sweeter than honey.*

Glòir mhilis a mheallas an t-amadan.—*Sweet words beguile fools.*

> Fair words make fools fain.—*Eng.* Fair hechts (promises) will mak fulis fain.—*The Cherrie and the Slae.* Fagre Ord fryde en Daare.—*Dan.*

Gnè fireann falbh.—*The male's nature is to move.*

> The man to go abroad, the woman to stay at home.

Gnothach duine gun chèill, dol gu fèill gun airgead.—*A fool's errand, going to market without money.*

Gnothaichean mòra fo thuinn.—*Great things under the waves.*

> Said of those who boast of things they neither have nor can have.

Gob a' chalmain-chàthaidh, bidh tu slàn mum pòs thu.—*Beak of the moulting dove, you'll be well before you marry.*

> The word *calman-càthaidh* is not in any of the dictionaries, except A. MacDonald's *Vocabulary*, where it is rendered 'Hoop'. The saying is applied to sick children.

Goirteas a chinn fhèin a dh'fhairicheas a h-uile fear.—*Every man feels his own headache.*

> Sí a chneadh féin is luaithe mhothaíos gach duine.—*A man feels his own hurt soonest.—Ir.*

Greadan feasgair, 's cead dol dachaigh.—*Evening spurt, and leave to go home.*

Grèim cruaidh aig curaidh.—*A champion's hard grip.*

Grèim cùbair.—*A cooper's grip.*

> A firm hold.

Grèim fad' an tàilleir leisg.—*The lazy tailor's long stitch.*

> *Al.*—Grèim fada, 's grad bhith ullamh—*Long stitch, and soon done.* Snaithe fada an taillear fhallsa.—*Ir.* Costurera mala, la hebra de a braza—*Bad seamstress's thread, a fathom long.—Span.*

Greimeachadh bàrr òrdaig.—*Holding by a thumb-top.*

Greis mu seach, an t-each air muin a' mharcaiche.—*Time about, the horse on the back of the rider.*

Gu dùmhail doimh, mar a bhios màthair fhir an taighe, an solas na cloinne, no 'n rathad nan eun.—*Crowding, cumbersome, like the goodman's mother, in the children's light, or in the way of the fowls.*

Gu dona dubh, mar a bha cas Aoidh.—*Bad and black, as Hugh's foot was.*

> Hugh was on a visit to the laird of Coll, and got his foot accidentally wounded. He was so well taken care of that he was in no hurry to get out of hospital, and continued to describe the state of his foot as 'bad and black'.

Gu h-olc innte, 's gu h-olc uimpe.—*Bad within, and badly clad.*

Gum biodh e 'n ceann-uidhe dha fhathast.—*That he would yet be the end of him.*

> This was one of the sayings attributed to James Stewart of Acharn, 'Seumas a' Ghlinne,' on the strength of which, chiefly, he was most iniquitously executed in 1752 for the murder of Colin Campbell of Glenure. Stewart's brother had forfeited his lands of Ardsheil for taking part in the Rebellion of 1745, and Campbell, judicial factor on the estate, was proceeding to eject a number of tenants when he was shot dead. Stewart was not accused of having committed the deed, but of having instigated Allan Breac, a kinsman of his. The presiding judge was the Duke of Argyll, Lord Justice-General, and eleven of the jury were Campbells.

Gum bu droch drùighleach dhut!—*Bad dregs to you!*

Gum ann a ghonar am fiosaiche, mun tig an fhiosachd fìor!—*Perish the prophet, ere the prophecy come true!*

Gum beir an riabhach mòr ort!—*The great grizzled one catch thee!*

> One of the epithets applied to the Devil.

Gum meal thu do naidheachd!—*May you enjoy your news!*

> Said to a person who is to be congratulated.

Guma fada bhios tu beò, agus ceò bhàrr do thaighe!—*Long may you live, and smoke rise from your roof!*

> *Al.*—Guma fada beò thu, is ceò às do thaigh.
> This is a very favourite and kindly saying.

Guma h-anmoch dhut!—*May it be late to thee!*

Guma h-olc dhut!—*Ill befall thee!*

Gual fuar ga shèideadh.—*Blowing cold coals.*

'Gùg, gùg,' ars a' chuthag, Latha Buidhe Bealltainn.—*'Coo, coo,' says the cuckoo, on yellow May Day.*

> The cuckoo is seldom heard so early now.

Gun aon tàmh air beul na brathann, 's gun aon ghràinn' air chionn an latha.—*Without ceasing of the quern, and not a grain at the end of the day.*

> Labour like that of the Danaids—the *toradh* or fruit of the grinding being carried away by a fairy as fast as it was made.

Gun gabh a' bhochdainn thu!—*Poverty take thee!*

Gun mheas gun mhiadh, mar Mhànus.—*Without esteem or honour, like Magnus.*

> This refers to a Scandinavian king, whom Fingal overcame and slew.—See Dr. Smith's *Sean Dàna*, p. 113, and Campbell's *Leabhar na Féinne*, p. 71 &c.

Gunnaiche mòr gun srad fhùdair.—*A great gunner without a grain of powder.*

Gus am bi Mac Cailein 'na rìgh, bidh I mar bha.—*Till Argyll be a King, Iona will be as she was.*

> This saying was familiar in Kingairloch more than 60 years ago to the person from whom it was got. The repair of the ruins of Iona by the Duke of Argyll, soon after the marriage of the Marquis of Lorne to the Princess Louise, was noted by some old people in connection with this saying.

An older saying, attributed to St Columba, is:

> An I mo chridhe, I mo ghràidh,
> An àite guth mhanach bidh geum bà;
> Ach mun tig an saoghal gu crìch,
> Bithidh I mar a bha.

> *—In dearest Iona, the isle of my love,*
> *In place of monks' voices shall cows' lowing be;*
> *But ere ever the world shall come to an end,*
> *As once was Iona, Iona shall be.*

Gus am faigh thu deoch as fhearr na 'm fìon, chan fhaigh thu biadh as fheàrr na 'n fheòil.—*Till you find better drink than wine, you'll find no better food than flesh.*

The Binny fish said, 'If you can find a better fish, don't eat me.'— *Arab.*

Gus an gabh a' mhuir teine, chan fhaigh duine clann duine eile.—*Till the sea takes fire, you can't be the sire of another man's children.*

Gus an tràighear a' mhuir le cliabh, cha bhi fear fial falamh.—*Till the sea is drained with a creel, the generous man won't want.*

A good sentiment, but unfortunately not a fact.

Guth na cuthaig am beul na cathaig, 's guth na faoileig am beul na sgaireig.—*The cuckoo's voice in the jackdaw's mouth, and the seagull's in the young scart's.*

I

I nam ban bòidheach.—*Iona of pretty women.*

Iallan fad' à leathar chàich.—*Long thongs of other men's leather.*

> De alieno corio liberalis.—*Lat.* Del cuoio d' altri si fanno le correggie larghe.—*Ital.* De cuero ageno correas largas.—*Span.* Du cuir d' autrui large courroie.—*Fr.* Het is goed snijden riemen uit eens andermans leer.—*Dutch.* A large thong of another man's hide.—*Eng.* Lang whangs aff ither folk's leather.—*Scot.*

Iarr gach nì air Camshronach, ach na iarr ìm air.—*Ask anything of a Cameron but butter.*

> See 'Camshronaich'.

Iarraidh MhicChrùislig air na h-eich.—*MacCruslick's search for the horses.*

> M.'s master sent him to search for his horses. 'Where shall I look for them?' said M. 'Look for them wherever they are or are not likely to be,' said his master. Presently M. was seen on the roof of the house scraping away with a sickle. On being asked what he was about, he replied that he was searching for the horses where they were not likely to be.—Campbell's *W. H. T.*, II, 309.

Iasad a' chaibe gun a chur san talamh.—*The loan of the spade without using it.*

Iasad caillich gun diasan, iasad as fhas' fhaotainn.—*An old wife's loan without ears of corn, the easiest loan to get.*

> I.e., loan from one who has nothing to give.

Iasgach muinntir Bharbhais.—*The Barvas folk's fishing.*

> Barvas is a parish in Lewis. It was alleged of the natives that they delayed going to fish till they heard of their neighbours' having got fish. The coast of Barvas strictly so called is peculiarly unsuited for boating, which might well excuse the natives for being slow to go to sea. Ness, on the other hand, which is part of the 'civil' parish of B., has a port, and is inhabited by a very dauntless fishing population.

Iasg no sitheann, àth no muileann.—*Fish or venison, kiln or mill.*

Iasgach amadain, corr bheathach mòr.—*A fool's fishing, an occasional big fish.*

> The meaning is that only fools despise littles.

Iasgach na curra.—*The crane's fishing.*

> A model of patience.

Im ri im, cha bhiadh 's chan annlann e.—*Butter to butter is neither food nor kitchen.*

> Imrich Shatharna mu thuath,
> Imrich Luain mu dheas;
> Ged nach biodh agam ach an t-uan,
> 'S ann Diluain a dh'fhalbhainn leis.

—*Saturday's flitting by north, Monday's flitting by south; had I but a lamb to move, 'tis on Monday I would go.*

> In other words, Saturday is an unlucky day for removing, Monday a lucky day. See 'Deiseal'.

Imridh breug gobhal.—*A lie needs a prop.*

> See 'Cha sheas a' bhreug'.

Imridh fear nam breug cuimhne mhath a bhith aige.—*Liars should have good memories.*—*Eng., Scot.*

> Be of good memory, if you become a liar.—*Arab.* Mendacem memorem esse oportet.—*Quintil.* Il bugiardo deve aver buona memoria.—*Ital.* Lügner muss ein gut Gedächtniss haben.—*Germ.* Een leugenaar moet een goede memorie hebben.—*Dutch.*

Innleachd Shasann agus neart Alba.—*England's art and Scotland's force.*

> The truth of this saying still holds good.

Innsidh a' chruinneag cò dh'ith a' chriomag.—*The tidy lass will tell who ate the tid-bit.*

Innsidh na geòidh as t-Fhoghar e.—*The geese will tell it in Autumn.*

Innsidh ùine h-uile rud.—*Time tells everything.*

> Foillsítear gach ní le h-aimsir.—*Ir.* Tempus omnia revelat. Veritas temporis filia.—*Lat.* Time trieth truth.—*Eng.* Zeit gebiert Wahrheit.—*Germ.*

Iomairt 'Coma leam'.—*The 'I don't care' play.*

Iongantas muinntir Mhuc-Càirn.—*The queerness of the Muckairn people.*

> M. is a parish in Argyllshire, the inhabitants of which somehow have the reputation of being uncommonly shy, unwilling to partake even of the simplest hospitality from strangers.

Ionnlaididh bùrn salach làmhan.—*Foul water will wash hands.*

Ionnsaich do d'sheanmhair brochan a dhèanamh.—*Teach your granny to make gruel.*

> *Al.*—lit' òl—*to sup porridge.*
> Seol do sheanmháthair lachanaí a bhleaghan (*to milk ducks*).—*Ir.*
> Teach your grandam to suck eggs—to spin—to grope her duck—to sup sour milk.—*Eng.* Learn your gudewife to mak milk kail.—*Scot.*
> Dysgu gradd i hen farch—*To teach a pace to an old horse.*—*Welsh.*
> *Gradd* is possibly a 'family' edition of what in a similar Gaelic saying is *bram.*

Is athaiseach cuid an fhir nach toir an doras air.—*His share is slow who doesn't take to the door.*

> The best interpretation of this is that he who doesn't go out for his living will be ill off.
> N.B.—In most of the sayings commencing here with 'Is,' the 'I' is in pronunciation entirely omitted. '*S ann*, '*S e* and '*S fheàrr* are the vernacular phrases, and not *Is ann, Is e* &c.

Is aimhleasach gach nochd.—*Nakedness is hurtful.*

> This is a very Celtic sentiment. The chief idea conveyed is that the destitute are liable to injury.

Is àirde 'n geum na 'm bleoghan.—*The low is greater than the milking.*

> See 'A' bhò'.

Is àirde ceann na gualainn.—*Head is higher than shoulder.*

> Uwch pen na dwy ysgwydd.—*Welsh.*

Is àirde tuathanach air a chasan na duin'-uasal air a ghlùinean.—*A farmer on his feet is taller than a gentleman on his knees.*

> *Al.*—Is fheàrr—*Is better.*
> This is a very suggestive saying.—See 'Is treasa tuath'.

Is aithne don chù a choire fhèin.—*A dog knows his own fault.*

> *Al.*—Tuigidh cù a chionta.

Is amaideach a bhith cur a-mach airgid a cheannach aithreachais.—*'Tis folly to spend money in buying repentance.*

Is anfhann a thig, 's làidir a thèid.—*Weak they come, and strong depart.*

> *Al.*—Is lag na thig. This refers to infants.

Is ann a bhios a' chòir mar a chumar i.—*The right will be as it's kept.*

> *Al*—Bidh a' chòir mar a chumar i, 's bidh an t-suirghe mar a nìtear i—*The right &c., and the wooing will be according as it's done.*
> Possession is nine points of the law.—*Eng.*
> See 'Am fear aig am beil'.

Is ann a cheart-èiginn 's a dh'aindeoin a dh'aithnicheas bean a ciad leanabh—mar a thuirt Iain Mac Mhurchaidh Mhic Ailein.—*It's barely and in spite of everything that a woman knows her first child, as John, son of Murdoch, son of Allan, said.*

Is ann a dh'fhàsas an sìol mar a chuirear e.—*The seed grows as it's sown.*

Is ann a tha 'n càirdeas mar a chumar e.—*Friendship is as it's kept.*

> A very true and good sentiment.

Is ann a tha 'n sgoileam air an sgoilear.—*It's the scholar that's the talker.*

Is ann agad tha bhathais!—*What a front you have!*

    Said to impudent people.

Is ann aig duine fhèin as fheàrr a tha fios càit am beil a bhròg ga ghoirteachadh.—*Every man knows best where his shoe hurts him.*

    The wearer best knows where the shoe wrings him.—*Eng.* Every man kens best where his ain shoe binds him.—*Scot.* Chacun sent le mieux où le soulier le blesse.—*Fr.* Ognuno sa dove la scarpa lo stringe.—*Ital.* Cada uno sabe donde le aprieta el zapato.—*Span.* Jeder weiss es am Besten, wo ihn der Schuh drückt.—*Germ.*

    The first use of this saying is attributed by Plutarch to Aemilius Paulus, who, being remonstrated with for divorcing his wife, an honourable and irreproachable matron, pointed to one of his shoes and asked his friends what they thought of it. They all thought it a handsome, well-fitting shoe. 'But none of you knows,' he said, 'where it pinches me.' This is now called 'incompatibility'.

Is ann aigesan as mò their as lugha tha ri ràdh.—*He that says most has least to tell.*

    Words are like leaves, and where they most abound,
    Much fruit of sense beneath is rarely found.

Is ann air a' bheagan a dh'aithnichear am mòran.—*From the little the much is known.*

Is ann air a dh'èirich a' ghrian!—*It is on him that the sun hath risen!*

Is ann air a' mhuic reamhair a thèid an t-ìm.—*It's on the fat pig the butter goes.*

    This applies metaphorically to some living animals.
    See 'Am fear aig am bi ìm'.
    Sin tóin na muice méithe do ghréisigheadh.—*Ir.* Al puerco gordo untarle el rabo.—*Span.*

Is ann air an tràghadh a rugadh e.—*He was born when the tide was ebbing.*

> Unlucky man, or born out of date.

Is ann air a shon fhèin a nì 'n cat an crònan.—*It's for itself the cat croons.*

> Is mar gheall ar féin a níos an cat crónán.—*Ir.* E ŵyr y gath pa farf a lyf—*Cat knows what beard he licks.—Welsh.*
> The cat is a thoroughly selfish animal, and there are human beings, aimed at in this proverb, of the same nice, soft, selfish sort.

Is ann air gnùis a bheirear breith.—*It is by the face we judge.*

> Vultus est index animi.—*Lat.*

> In the forehead and the eye
> The lecture of the mind doth lie.—*Eng.*

Is ann air deireadh an latha 's fheàrr na Dòmhnallaich.—*The Mac-Donalds are best at the end of the day.*

> This is a very complimentary saying. See 'Is ann feasgar'.

Is ann an àm a' chruadail a dh'aithnichear na càirdean.—*When fortune frowns, then friends are known.*

Is ann an casan coin a bhios earal.—*A dog's caution is in his legs.*

Is ann an ceann bliadhna a dh'innseas iasgair a thuiteamas.—*It's at the year's end the fisher can tell his luck.*

> *Al.*—amhaltas—*his trouble.*
> Is i gcionn na bliana insíos iascaire a thábhacht.—*Ir.*

Is ann an sin a thathas ga chaitheamh, eadar an t-srathair 's am plàta.—*So is it worn, 'twixt the pack-saddle and the straw-cloth.*

> Said of people assuming airs beyond their position.

Is ann an uair as gainn' am biadh as còir a roinn.—*'Tis when food is scarcest it should be divided.*

Is ann às a' bheagan a thig am mòran.—*From the little comes the much.*

> Many littles mak a muckle.—*Scot.* The proverbe saith that many a smale makith a grete.—*Chaucer.*

Is ann bòidheach 's chan ann dàicheil.—*Bonnie rather than graceful.*

Is ann da fhèin a dh'innsear e.—*It's to himself it will be told.*
> It's his own affair.

Is ann dà latha ro bhàs bu chòir do dhuin' a shàr-fhacal a ràdh.—*Till two days before he die, man should not speak his weightiest word.*
> There is much wisdom in this saying.

Is ann den aon chlòth an cathdath.—*The tartan is all of one stuff.*
> *Cath-dath*—battle-colour.—*Armstrong.*

Is ann den chèaird a' chungaidh.—*The tools are part of the trade.*
> *Al.*—Is i chèaird.
> Is i leath na céirde an uirléis.—*The tools are half the trade.*—*Ir.*

Is ann den tuaigh an t-samhach.—*The haft belongs to the axe.*
> See 'Cuir an tuagh'.

Is ann le làimh ghlain bu chòir altachadh.—*One should salute (or say grace) with a clean hand.*
> See *Psalm* xxiv, 3, 4.

Is ann feasgar a dh'aithnichear na fir.—*It's at evening the men are known.*

Is ann fhad 's a bhios an t-slat maoth as fhas' a lùbadh.—*When the twig is tender it is easiest bent.*

> > Am meangan nach snìomh thu,
> > Cha spìon thu 'na chraoibh e.—*Dug. Buchanan.*
>
> > Best to bend while it is a twig.—*Eng.* Piega l'albero quando è giovane.—*Ital.* Den Baum muss man biegen, weil er jung ist.—*Germ.*

Is ann goirid o d'bheul a mholadh tu e.—*It is near your mouth you would praise it.*

Is ann goirid ro bhàs a mholadh tu e.—*It is near his end you would praise him.*

Is ann mu seach a shèidear na builg.—*By turns the bellows are blown.*

Is ann mu seach a thogar an dùn.—*It is by degrees the fort is built.*
   Al.—'S ann uidh air uidh a thogar na caisteil.
   Rome was not built in a day.—*Ital., Fr., Germ., Eng.*

Is ann mar a bhios neach e fhèin a dh'fhidireas e choimhearsnach.—
As a man is himself he thinks of his neighbour.

Is ann oidhche ro a bhàs bu chòir do dhuine athais a thilgeadh.—*A
man should not vent his reproach till the night before his death.*
   Macintosh's gloss on this is 'Make a satire or proverb'.

Is ann Oidhche Shamhna chnagadh tu cnò.—*On Halloween you
would crack a nut.*
   One of the favourite Halloween pastimes was burning of nuts.

Is ann ort a chaidh uisge nan uighean.—*You had the egg-water spilt
on you.*
   Macintosh says, 'Water in which eggs are boiled is reckoned destruc-
   tive to the constitution' and that 'this proverb is applied to those that
   are seized with a fit of illness'.

Is ann ort a thàinig an ceal.—*What a stupor has come over thee.*

Is ann romhad a dh'èirich an naosg.—*It's before you the snipe rose.*
   This was reckoned a good omen.

Is aobhach duine an taice ri chuid.—*A man is cheerful near his own.*

Is aotrom air do dhruim an t-iomradh.—*The rowing is light on your
back.*

Is aotrom gach saoghalach sona.—*Light is the lucky long-liver.*

Is àrd ceann an fhèidh sa chreachann.—*High is the stag's head on the
mountain crags.*

Is bàidheil duine ris an anam.—*A man is tender of his life*.

> All that a man hath will he give for his life.—*Job*. ii, 4.
>
> Life is sweet.—*Eng*.
>
> In one of the West Highland Tales (Campbell, II, 355), Brian, son of the King of Greece, is asked by a giant whether he would rather lose his head or go to steal the White Sword of Light in the realm of Big Women. "S bàidheil duine ri bheatha'—'*Kind is a man to his life*,' said Brian, and chose the latter alternative.

Is balbh gach sian ach a' ghaoth.—*Dumb is all weather but the wind*.

> See 'An uair a laigheas'.

Is beadarrach an nì an onair.—*Honour is a tender thing*.

> This is very Celtic. 'Take my honour, take my life.'

Is beag a dhèanadh gròt don fhear a dh'òladh crùn.—*Little would a groat do for him who drinks a crown*.

> This probably refers to a soldier's pay, which was 4d a day at no very ancient date.

Is beag a ghearaineas sinn, ge mòr a dh'fhuilingeas sinn.—*Little we complain, though we suffer much*.

> This saying is given by Macintosh without any note. Whenever it may have originated, it expressed with native gentleness a very sad truth in reference to a considerable part of our Highland population. It was true a century ago, and it is true still.

Is beag a th' eadar do ghal 's do ghàire.—*Your crying and laughing are not far removed*.

Is beag an dèirc nach fheàrr na 'n t-euradh.—*Small is the alms that is not better than a refusal*.

> Is beag an rud nach fhearr ná diúltadh.—*Ir*.

Is beag am fathann nach cluinn dithis.—*It's a faint rumour that two won't hear*.

Is beag an leisgeul a bheir a' chailleach don chill.—*It's a little excuse that brings the old woman to the churchyard*.

> Excuse—cause, and churchyard—death.
>
> *Al*.—Is faoin an gnothach—*It's a slight thing*.

Is beag an rud a bheir duine don chill nuair a bhios a leannan innte.—*It's a small thing that brings a man to the churchyard when his sweetheart is there.*

Is beag an t-iongnadh amadan a bhith leannanachd ri òinsich.—*It's no wonder to see a fool courting an idiot.*

Is beag cuid an latha fhlich dheth.—*The rainy day's share of it is small.*

Meaning that little has been saved.

Is beag an nì nach deireadh as t-Fhoghar.—*It's a little thing that doesn't hinder in Autumn.*

Is beag fios aig fear an tàimh air ànradh fear na mara.—*The household man knows little of the seaman's hardship.*

Is beag 's is mòr a th' eadar a' chòir 's an eucoir.—*There is little and much betwixt right and wrong.*

Is beag atá eadar an chóir is an éagóir.—*Ir.* 'S mooar ta eddyr y chair as yn aggair.—*Manx.*

Ge mòr an diùbhras beusan
Eadar eucoir agus còir,
Chan eòl domh àite seasaimh
Gun a chos air aon diubh dhò.—*Rob Donn.*

Is beag orm an rud nach binn leam.—*I like not what I find not sweet.*

Is beag orm troigh air ais an t-seann duine.—*I like not the old man's backward step.*

Al.—Is coma leam fhèin an rud a bhiodh ann, ceum air ais an t-seann duine.

Said by young Ronald MacDonell of Strontian, at the battle of Kin-Loch-Lochy, 'Blàr nan Lèine' (1544), on seeing his father give way after receiving a wound on the head from 'Raghnall Gallta'. The remark was suggested by that of his father, on seeing his son for the first time for several years, after having been deserted by him in the hour of need, "S coma leam fhèin an rud a bhiodh ann, armachd a ghill' òig, 's e teicheadh'—*I don't care for the arming of the youth who runs away.'* Young Ronald is said to have added to the above remark 'Seo mar bu chòir a bhith—am mac a dhol an ionad an athar'—*'This is as it ought to be—the son in the place of the father'*; and rushed upon the enemy, whom he overcame. There is something wildly noble, though unpleasant, in this. See *Cuairtear*, Dec. 1841, pp 282-3.

Is beag orm nam biodh ann sruth-bheannachadh a' chreachadair.—*I should dislike to hear the fluent blessing of the plunderer.*

> This is still true, even though highway robbery be no more in fashion. Some grave and reverend Bank Directors have illustrated this shockingly in modern times.

Is bean-taighe an luchag 'na taigh fhèin.—*The little mouse is mistress in her own house.*

> Is maighistreás an luchóg air a tigh féin.—*Ir.*

Is beò duine an dèidh a shàrachadh, ach cha bheò e an dèidh a nàrachadh.—*A man may survive distress, but not disgrace.*

> *Al.*—an dèidh a dhaoine—*after his people*; an dèidh a nàire—*after his shame.*
> The Ulster version is identical with the latter. The sentiment is very Celtic and honourable, but common to all the higher races. 'Death before dishonour' has been the motto of all heroes and martyrs of every nation.
> El hombre sin honra peor es que un muerto.—*Span.*

Is beò duine air bheagan, ach cha bheò e gun dad idir.—*One can live on little, but not on nothing.*

> A good motto for Parochial Boards.

Is beò na h-eòin, ged nach seabhagan uil' iad.—*The birds live though not all hawks.*

> A fine quiet suggestion for statesmen and conquerors.

Is beò duine ged nach sàthach.—*A man may live though not full.*

> This is nowhere more illustrated than in the Highlands; what phrenologists call 'Alimentiveness' is at a very low figure there.

Is bitheanta na tràithean.—*The meals are frequent.*

> This saying must have originated with a very abstemious and probably miserly person.

'Is bigid e siud, is bigid e siud,' mar a thuirt an dreathan, an uair a thug e làn a ghuib às a' mhuir.—*"Tis the less for that, the less for that,' as the wren said, when he sipped a bill-full out of the sea.*

Is binn gach eun 'na dhoire fhèin.—*Sweet sings each bird in his own grove.*

> *Al.*—'S binn guth an eòin far am beirear e.—*Sweet is a bird's voice where he was born.*

> Is binn gach glòir bhon duine bheairteach,
> Is mil bho bheul a' ghobaireachd;
> Is searbh a' chòir bhon aimbeairteach,
> Is cian a ghlòir bho ghliocas.

> —*Sweet is the talk of the wealthy man,*
> *Like honey is his prattling;*
> *Harsh is the right from the poor man's mouth,*
> *Far is his talk from wisdom.*

> Milis glór gach fir
> I mbí cuid agus spré;
> Searbh glór an té bhíos lom,
> Bun-ós-cionn do labhrann sé.—*Ir.*

Is bior gach sràbh san oidhche.—*Every straw is a thorn at night.*

> This must have been said by a Celtic sybarite.

Is blàth an fhuil, ged as ann an craiceann nan con i.—*Blood is warm, though it be but in a dog's skin.*

> *Al.*—an sròn muice—*in a pig's nose.*
> *Al.*—Is blath fuil nan cat 'nan craiceann fhèin—*Cat's blood is warm in their own skin.*

Is blàth anail na màthar.—*Warm is the mother's breath.*

> The mither's breath is aye sweet.—*Scot.*
> A beautiful saying.

Is blàth lodan na bròige.—*Warm is the pool in the shoe.*

> Said to youngsters complaining of leaky shoes.

Is bochd am fear nach fhaigh a leòr as t-Fhoghar.—*He's a poor man who won't get his fill in Autumn.*

Is bochd am pòsadh nach fheàrr na 'n dubh-chosnadh.—*It's a poor marriage that is not better than hard service.*

> This seems a foolish sentiment, but the *dubh-chosnadh*, literally 'black-service', refers to outdoor work, seldom desirable for women.

Is bochd an ainnis lomanach.—*Truly poor is the naked needy.*

Is bochd an rud nach fhiach iarraidh.—*It's a poor thing that's not worth asking.*

Is bòidheach an luchag sa mhìr arbhair.—*Pretty is the mouse in the corn-plot.*

> This sentiment is worthy of Robert Burns.

Is bòidheach leis an fheannaig a gorm-gharrach fhèin.—*The crow thinks her own ghastly chick a beauty.*

> See 'Ge dubh am fitheach'.

Is bràthair don amadan an t-amhlair.—*The rude jester is brother to the fool.*

Is bràthair don chadal ceann ri làr.—*Head laid down is brother to sleep.*

Is bràthair don chuthach an òige.—*Youth is the brother of madness.*

> Foolishness is bound in the heart of a child.—*Prov.* xxii, 15.

Is bràthair don diosg an tuairnear.—*The turner is brother to the dish.*

Is bràthair don mhadadh am mèirleach.—*The thief is brother to the hound.*

> A very respectable sentiment.

Is bràthair do Niall Gille-Calum.—*Malcolm is brother to Neil.*

> 'Par nobile fratrum,' no doubt.

Is brèagh' cuid ceàird dhith.—*The tinker's part of her is fine.*

> Said of a woman more adorned without than within. [MacInnes has 'jeweller's'.]

Is buaine aon diùltadh na dà thabhartas dheug.—*One refusal is longer remembered than a dozen offers.*

> *Al.*—Millidh aon diùltadh &c.—*One refusal spoils &c.*

Is buaine 'm meangan a ghèilleas na 'n crann mòr a lùbas.—*The twig that yields will outlive the great tree that bends.*

> Is buaine an buinneán maoth (*tender twig*) ná an crann bromanta (*stubborn tree*).—*Ir.*

Is buaine bladh na saoghal.—*Renown is more lasting than life.*

> Is buaine cliú ná saoghal.—*Ir.*
> See 'Is beò duine'.

Is buaine bliadhna na Nollaig.—*Year lasts longer than Christmas.*

Is buaine dùthchas na oilean.—*Blood is stronger than breeding.*

> Is treise an dúchas ná an oileamhuin.—*Ir.* Naturam expellas furca, tamen usque recurret.—*Hor.*

Is buaine cùl na aghaidh.—*Back lasts longer than front.*

> A cheese, a stack of hay, peats &c. would be more freely used at first than at last. The moral meaning may be that feuds last longer than friendships.

Is buaine na gach nì an nàire.—*Shame is more lasting than anything.*

> This is very Celtic.
> Schande duurt langer dan armoede—*Shame lasts longer than poverty.*—*Dutch.*

Is buaine seud na luach.—*A gem lasts longer than its value.*

Is buaireadh gach sìne a' ghaoth.—*All change of weather is due to the wind.*

Is buan meacan na falachd.—*Long lasts the rod whose root sprang from blood.*

> *Al.*—Is buan cuimhne &c.—*Long is the memory &c.*
> A proverb worthy of Iceland or Corsica.

Is buan gach olc.—*Evil lives long.*

> 'S beayn dagh olk.—*Manx.* Onde Urter voxe mest, og forgaae senest—*Ill weeds grow best and last longest.*—*Dan.*

Is buidhe le amadan imrich.—*Fules are aye fond o flittin.*—*Scot.*

> *Al.*—Is miann. Is toigh.
> Is mian le amadán imirce.—*Ir.*

Is buidhe le bochd beagan.—*A poor man is glad of a little.*

> Is buidhe le bocht a bhfaghann (*what he gets*).—*Ir.* 'S booiagh yn voght er yn veggan.—*Manx.*

Is buidhe le bochd eanraich, ged nach bi e làn-bhruich.—*The poor are glad of broth, though it be not well boiled.*

> Poor folks are glad of pottage.—*Eng.*

Is buidheach Dia den fhìrinn.—*Truth is pleasing to God.*

Is buileach a thilg thu clach oirnn.—*You have thoroughly thrown a stone at us.*

Is càirdeach an cù don bhanais.—*The dog is friendly to the wedding.*

Is call do chaillich a poca, 's gun tuille aice.—*The loss of the old wife's poke is heavy, when it is her all.*

Is cam 's is dìreach a thig an lagh.—*The law comes crooked and straight.*

> See 'Is beag 's is mòr'.

Is caol an teud às nach seinn e.—*It's a slender string he can't take a tune from.*

Is caomh le fear a charaid, ach 's e smior a chridhe a cho-dhalt.—*Dear is a kinsman, but the pith of the heart is a foster-brother.*

> This is the strongest of all the sayings on this subject.

Is càraid sin, mar a thuirt an fheannag ri casan.—*That's a pair, as the crow said to her feet.*

> *Al.*—Is dithis dhuinn sin.
> They're a bonnie pair, as the craw said o his legs.—*Scot.*

Is ceannach an t-omhan air a' bhainne theth.—*The froth is scarcely worth the hot milk.*

> *Omhan* is the switched-up froth of warmed milk or whey.

Is ceannach air a mhìreanan a bheumannan.—*The morsels are scarcely worth the cuts.*

Is cliùitich' an onair na 'n t-òr.—*Honour is nobler than gold.*

> Is uaisle onóir ná ór.—*Ir.* Beter arm met eere (*poor with honour*) dan rijk met schande (*rich with shame*).—*Dutch.*

Is cho domhainn an t-àth 's an linne.—*The ford is as deep as the pool.*

Is cho fad' oidhch' is latha, Là Fhèill Pàdraig.—*Night and day are equal on St Patrick's Day.*

> This is nearly correct.

Is cho lìonmhor osna aig an rìgh 's aig an duin' as ìsle staid.—*The king sighs as often as the meanest man.*

> This occurs verbatim in D. Buchanan's *Bruadar.*
> Uneasy lies the head that wears a crown.—*Henry IV*, P. II, iii, 1.

Is cho math dhomh mo chorrag a ghabhail don chloich.—*I might as well try my finger against a stone.*

> *Al.*—Bu cho math &c. a thumadh san luath—*As well dip my finger in the ashes.*

Is cho math na 's leòr is iomadaidh.—*Enough is as good as abundance.*

> *Al.*—Tha gu leòr cho math ri cuilm—*Enough is as good as a feast.*

Is cho math peighinn a chaomhnadh is peighinn a chosnadh.—*A penny hained is a penny gained.*—*Scot.*

Is coimheach an tom ùire.—*Strange is the earthy mound.*

> This seems to refer to the grave.

Is còir comhairle fhir an taighe a ghabhail.—*The goodman's advice should be taken.*

> A polite and sensible suggestion.

Is còir nì a thasgadh fa chomhair na coise goirte.—*It's well to lay something by for a sore foot.*

> Is cóir ní a thaisgidh le h-aghaidh na coise galair.—*Ir.* Keep something for a sair fit.—*Scot.* Lay by something for a rainy day.—*Eng.*

Is còir smaoineachadh air gach gnothach an toiseach.—*Every busi-ness ought first to be thought over.*

> An excellent advice.

Is coltach an gunna ris a' phìob.—*The gun is like the pipe.*

> Like it as a means of living, somewhat precarious.

Is coltach an gunna ris an urchair.—*The gun is like the shot.*

> This would apply to many speeches of persons in and out of Parlia-ment.

Is coltach an trù ris an troich.—*The fool and the dwarf are alike.*

> The word *trù* is not found in any dictionary, and is not now in use. But it is given by Macintosh, with the translation of the above proverb—*It is all alike, whether the great man's fool or his dwarf.* I have therefore retained this saying as Macintosh gave it. The word *tnù* means 'envy,' 'wrath' &c., and the Irish word *tru* means 'face,' 'gaunt' &c.

Is coma leam an rud nach toigh leam, eireagan a' dol 'nan coilich.—*I like not pullets becoming cocks.*

> This is wittier than most of the oratory against female medical education and other Women's Rights.

Is coma leam comann an òil.—*I care not for the drinking fellowship.*

> Is cuma liom cumann bean-leanna (*ale wife*).—*Ir.*
> This saying illustrates the fact that the Celts, in Scotland or elsewhere, are not prone to excess either in meat or drink.

Is coma leam comann gille na geire; ge math a thoiseach, bu ro olc a dheireadh.—*I like not the tallow lad's company; however good at first, very bad at last.*

> *Al.*—mur bi an toiseach searbh, gu dearbh bidh an deireadh ann.
> This is a Lewis and Long Island saying, of which no explanation has been given.

Is coma leam fear-fuadain 's e luath labhar.—*I don't like a stranger who talks loud and volubly.*

> This is a very Highland sentiment.

Is coma leis an rìgh Eòghann; 's coma le Eòghann co-dhiù.—*The King doesn't care for Ewen; and Ewen cares not whether or no.*

> Who Ewen was is not said, but he was perhaps the independent miller that lived on the banks of the Dee.

Is coma leis an t-saoghal càit an tuit e.—*Wealth cares not where it falls.*

> There is a rich truth in this observation.

Is corrach culaidh air aon lunn.—*A boat is unsteady on one roller.*

Is corrach gob an dubhain.—*Unsteady is the point of the hook.*

Is corrach ugh air aran.—*An egg on bread is slippery.*

Is crìon a' chùil às nach goirear.—*It's a small corner from which no cry can come.*

> The propagation of the Penny Press and Telegraph illustrates this beautifully.

Is cruaidh an cath às nach tig aon fhear.—*It's a hard fight from which one man doesn't come.*

> *Al.*—Is olc am blàr as nach tàrr cuideigin.
> It's a hard-fought field where no man escapes unkilled.—*Eng.* It's a sair field where aa 's slain.—*Scot.*

Is cruaidh an cnoc air nach criomadh e.—*It's a hard hill where he couldn't get picking.*

Is cruaidh a leònar an leanabh nach innis a ghearan.—*The child is sadly hurt that doesn't tell his illness.*

> *Al.*—Is olc a bhuailear an leanabh nach fhaod gearain—*The bairn is sair dung (beaten) that maunna complain.—Scot.*

Is cruaidh an leanabh a bhreugadh nach urrainn a ghearan a dhèanamh.—*'Tis hard to soothe the child that cannot tell his ailment.*

Is cruaidh an t-Earrach anns an cunntar na faochagan.—*It's a hard Spring when the whelks are counted.*

> *Al.*—Is lom an cladach air an cunntar &c.—*It's a bare shore &c.*
> This is a painfully graphic illustration of the extent to which dearth in the 'good old times' often prevailed in the Highlands, when whelks were resorted to as the last resource from starvation.

Is cruaidh na dh'fheumar.—*What's needed is hard.*

Is cuagach ceartas an eucoraich.—*The justice of the unjust is twisted.*

Is cumhann beul do sporain.—*Narrow is the mouth of your purse.*

Is cuinge brù na biadh.—*There is more food than room for it.*
> Said of a hospitable house.

Is dà thrian tionnsgnadh.—*Begun is two-thirds done.*
> *Al.*—Is trian oibre &c.
> Is trian den obair tús a chur.—*Ir.* Ἀρχὴ ἥμισυ παντός—*Beginning is
> half of the whole.*—*Hesiod.* Dimidium facti qui caepit habet.—*Hor.* So
> *Fr., Ital., Span., Port., Germ., Dutch, Dan.*

Is dall duine ann an cùil fir eile.—*A man is blind in another man's
corner.*
> *Al.*—far nach eòlach—*where he is not acquainted.*
> Is dall súil i gcúil duine eile.—*Ir.*

Is dall gach aineolach.—*Blind is the unacquainted.*
> Dall pob anghyfarwydd.—*Welsh.* Dall fyddar pob trwch—*Blind and
> deaf is the blockhead.*—*Do.*

Is damh thu, 's gum meal thu d'ainm.—*You are an ox, and may you
enjoy the name.*

Is dàna cù air a dhùnan fhèin.—*A dog is bold at his own dunghill.*
> *Al.*—aig a dhoras fhèin—*at his own door.*
> Is teann gach madadh air a charnán féin.—*Ir.* Every dog is valiant at
> his own door.—*Eng.* Chien sur son fumier est hardi.—*Fr.*
> *Al.*—Is ladarna coileach air òtrach fhèin—*A cock is bold &c.* Every
> cock is proud on his own dunghill.—*Eng.* Every cock craws crousest
> on his ain midden.—*Scot.* Gallus in suo sterquilinio plurimum po-
> test.—*Seneca.* Cada gallo canta en su muladar.—*Span.* Een haan is
> stout op zijn eigen erf.—*Dutch.*

Is dàna cuilean an uchd treòir.—*Bold is the puppy in the lap of strength.*
> *Al.*—Is làidir an lag—*Bold is the weak &c.*
> This is finely illustrated sometimes in cases of the *Civis Romanus*; at
> other times more amusingly, or offensively, by puppies 'dressed in a
> little brief authority' or representing a 'great party'.

Is dàna duine 'na chùil fhèin.—*A man is bold in his own corner.*

Diau cynnadl taiog o' i dŷ.—*Bold talks the boor at home—Welsh.*

Is dàna thèid duine air a chuid fhèin.—*A man is bold with what's his own.*

> *Al.*—Is leòmhann gach duine &c.—*Every man is a lion &c.* A man's aye crouse in his ain cause.—*Scot.*
> Men's belief in their right to do what they like with 'their own' sometimes makes them forget entirely that 'The earth is the Lord's, and the fulness thereof'.

Is deacair a' chaor' a ghoid làmh ri taigh a' mhèirlich.—*It's difficult to steal the sheep near the thief's house.*

Is dìblidh cìochran gun mhàthair.—*Helpless is the motherless suckling.*

Is dìcheallach duine air a shon fhèin.—*A man is diligent for himself.*

Is dìleas duine dha fhèin.—*A man is faithful to himself.*

Is diombuan an tom is teine ris.—*Soon burns the hillock on fire.*

> The allusion is to the burning of heather, called in the Lowlands 'muirburn'.—See Professor Veitch's *Hillside Rhymes*, p. 14.

Is diombuan gach cas air tìr gun eòlas.—*Fleeting is the foot in a strange land.*

> Very characteristic of Celts, in whom the love of home, however far they may wander, is quite indestructible.

Is diù a' chèaird nach foghlaimear.—*It's a poor trade that is not learned.*

> A very sensible saying. Men of half-learned trades or professions are among the most useless of people.

> Is diù teine feàrn ùr;
> Is diù duine mì-rùn;
> Is diù dìbhe fìon sean;
> Ach 's e diù an domhain droch bhean.

> —*Worst of fuel, alder green;*
> *Worst of human, malice keen;*
> *Worst of drink, wine without life;*
> *Worst of all things, a bad wife.*

The literal meaning of *fion sean* is 'old wine,' but I think the old Celts knew what was what in wine as well as in other things.

Is diù nach gabh comhairle, 's is diù ghabhas gach comhairle.—*Who won't take advice is worthless; who takes all advice is the same.*

> *Al.*—Is truagh—*is pitiful.*

Is diùid fear na h-eisimeil.—*The dependant is timid.*

Is dòbhaidh an companach an t-acras.—*Hunger is a violent companion.*

Is don' an fheòil air nach gabh salann; 's miosa na sin na daoine nach gabh comhairle.—*The flesh that won't take salt is bad; worse are they that won't take counsel.*

Is don' an fhèile chuireas duine fhèin air an iomairt.—*It's an unhappy generosity that drives a man to his shifts.*

> This is true of many a good Highland family.

Is don' an gnìomh a bhith luchdachadh na luinge air sgeir-mhara.—*It's a bad thing to load a ship on a tidal rock.*

Is don' an leisgeul a' mhisg.—*Drunkenness is a bad excuse.*

> This saying is worthy of the wisest of judges, before whom intoxication has often been pleaded in mitigation. Lord Hermand's saying is specially memorable—see Cockburn's *Memorials*.
> *Per con.* Is fheàrr a' mhisg na bhith gun leisgeul—*Drunkenness is better than no excuse.*

Is don' a' mharcachd nach fheàrr na sìor-choiseachd.—*It's a bad mount that's not better than constant walking.*

Is don' an t-suirghe lethcheannach.—*The sheepish wooing is contemptible.*

Is draghaile caraid amaideach na nàmhaid glic.—*A silly friend is more troublesome than a wise enemy.*

> Better a wise enemy than a foolish friend.—*Arab.* Save me from my friends!—*Eng.*

Is dùth do chù donnalaich.—*Howling is proper to a dog.*

Is dual don bhàrd athair aithris.—*It's natural for the bard to tell of his father.*

Is dubh dha fhèin sin.—*That is black (sad) for himself.*

Is duilich a cleachdadh a thoirt bho làimh.—*The hand hardly gives up its habit.*

> *Al.*—Is duilich toirt bhon làimh a chleachd.—*It's hard to beat the skilled hand.*
> *Al.*—Is ionmhainn leis an làimh na chleachd.—*The hand loves what it has practised.*

Is duilich am fear nach bi 'na chadal a dhùsgadh.—*It is hard to waken him who is not asleep.*

Is duilich an coileach-dubh a ghleidheadh bhon fhraoch.—*It is difficult to keep the black-cock from the heather.*

Is duilich an nàire thoirt as an àit' anns nach bi i.—*It's difficult to get shame where it is not.*

Is duilich bò a chur air laogh, is a gaol air gamhainn.—*A cow won't take to a calf when her darling is a stirk.*

Is duilich bùrn glan a thoirt à tobar salach.—*It's difficult to draw pure water from a dirty well.*

Is duilich camadh thoirt à daraig a dh'fhàs anns an fhaillean.—*It's hard to take the twist out of the oak that grew in the sapling.*

> See 'An car a bhios'.

Is duilich ciall a thoirt do dh'amadan.—*It's hard to give sense to a fool.*

> This is the same as Dr. Johnson's saying about giving understanding to his hearer.

Is duilich cupan làn a ghiùlan.—*A full cup is hard to carry.*

Is duilich duin' a lorgachadh tro abhainn.—*It is difficult to track a man through a river.*

> Our greatest Scottish king, Robert the Bruce, once proved the truth of this when followed by bloodhounds in Galloway, set on by less respectable creatures. See Barbour's *Bruce*, B.V., II, 300-50.

Is duilich rath a chur air duine dona.—*You can't put luck on a worthless man.*

> Ekki má feigum forða — The fey one cannot be saved.—*Icel.*

Is duilich roghainn a thoirt à diù.—*'Tis hard to choose the best of worst.*

Is duilich triubhas a thoirt de mhàs lom.—*It's ill to take the trews off a bare buttock.*

> Is deacair bríste a bhaint de thóin lom.—*Ir.* It's ill to tak the breeks aff a Hielandman.—*Scot.*

Is duine còir e, 's na iarr a chuid.—*He's a fine man, if you don't ask him.*

> There is a delicate Celtic irony in this.

> Is duine còir fear dà bhò;
> Is duine ro chòir fear a trì;
> 'S chan fhaigh fear a còig no sia
> Còir no ceart le fear nan naoi.

—*The two-cow man is a worthy man; very worthy is the man of three; and the man of five or six can do nothing against the man of nine.*

Is duine dona gun fheum a chuireadh cuireadh orm fhèin is caitheamh.—*He is a pitiful fellow who would invite me and leave me to pay.*

Is duine gach òirleach dheth.—*He's a man every inch.*

Is e am beul a dh'obas mu dheireadh.—*It's the mouth that gives in last.*

Is e am brag a nì an cruadhachadh.—*When the cracking begins the grain gets dried.*

Is e 'm broc as luaithe dh'fhairicheas fhàileadh fhèin.—*The badger is the first to smell himself.*

Is e am bròn as fhasa fhaotainn.—*Grief is easiest to get.*

Is e 'm bualadh cluigeanach a nì an crodh trotanach.—*The bad thrashing makes the brisk cows.*

> Careless thrashing leaves ears of corn on the straw, which makes the cows all the more lively.

Is e 'm fàth mum bitheadh tu ciod e gheibheadh tu.—*Your quest always is what you can get.*

Is e am Foghar gaothmhor a nì an corc càthmhor.—*The windy Autumn makes the chaffy oats.*

Is e 'n cadal fada nì 'n t-iomradh teth.—*Long sleep makes hot rowing.*

Is e an ceann gòrach a nì na casan luaineach.—*Giddy head makes gadding feet.*

Is e 'n ceò Geamhraidh a nì 'n cathadh Earraich.—*The Winter mist makes the Spring snow-drift.*

Is e 'n ciall-ceannaich as fhearr.—*Bought wit is best.*—*Eng.*

> *Al.*—Is fhearr aon ghliocas-ceannaich na dithis (or dhà dheug) an asgaidh—*Better one wisdom bought than two (or a dozen) got for nought.* Keeayl chionnit yn cheeayl share, mannagh vel ee kionnit ro gheyr—*Bought wit is best, if not bought too dear.*—*Manx.* Is í an chiall cheannaithe is fearr.—*Ir.* Παθήματα μαθήματα—*Herod.* Nocumenta documenta.—*Lat.* Wit bought makes wise folk.—*Scot.* An ounce of wit that's bought is worth a pound that's taught.—*Eng. Per con.* Is fhearr aon chiall-caisg na dà chiall deug ionnsaich—*Better one mother-wit than twelve taught.* An ounce o mither-wit is worth a pund o clergy.—*Scot.*

Is e an ciad thaom den taigeis as teotha dhith.—*The first squirt of the haggis is the hottest.*

> The first fuff o a fat haggis is aye the bauldest.—*Scot.*

Is e 'n cleachdadh a nì teòma.—*Practice makes expert.*

> Usus promptum facit.—*Lat.* Practice makes perfect.—*Eng.*

Is e an cunntas ceart a dh'fhàgas na càirdean buidheach.—*Correct counting keeps good friends.*

> Cuntas glan fhágas cáirde buíoch.—*Ir.* Be brothers, and keep between you the accounts of merchants.—*Arab.* Count like Jews, and 'gree like Christians.—*Scot.* Short reckonings make long friends.—*Eng.* Kurze rechnung, lange Freundschaft.—*Germ.* Effene rekeningen maken goede vrienden.—*Dutch.* Les bons comptes font les bons amis.—*Fr.* Conta de perto, amigo de longe.—*Port.*

Is e 'n dealachadh-beò a nì 'n leòn goirt.—*Parting with the living makes the sore wound.*

> There is much truth in this. Parting with the dead is irremediable, and therefore tolerable—separation from the living is all the sorer, when reunion is possible, yet hopeless.

Is e 'n duine dìomhain as fhaide mhaireas.—*The idle man lives longest.*

> See MacIntyre's *Oran don Mhusg*. This is generally true, though many of the hardest workers have attained great age.

Is e 'n Geamhradh luath an Geamhradh buan.—*Early winter lasts long.*

Is e 'n gille 'n t-aodach, ach 's e 'n laochan am biadh.—*The clothes are the boy, but the food beats all.*

Is e 'n saor gòbhlach nì 'n gogan dìonach.—*It's the squatting joiner that makes the tight cog.*

Is e 'n seasamh as mò, ach 's e 'n suidhe 's ciallaiche.—*Standing is bigger, but sitting is wiser.*

Is e 'n suidhe bochd a nì 'n gàrradh beairteach.—*The poor seat makes the rich warming.*

> *Al.*—For *bochd* 'ìosal,' and for *beairteach* 'uasal'.
> Ghuidh suidh ìseal goradh ard.—*Ir.*
> The lowest seat is nearest the fire.

Is e an suidhe docharach san taigh-òsd' as fheàrr.—*The uneasy seat in the alehouse is the best.*

> Another testimony to the sober habits of Highlanders.

Is e 'n duine 'n t-aodach, 's chan i cholainn bhreugach.—*The clothes are the man, not the lying body.*

Is e 'n t-àicheadh math dara puing as fheàrr san lagh.—*Good denial is the second best point in law.*

> 'Denied' and '*Quoad ultra* denied' are stereotyped forms of expression in our Scottish lawsuits.

Is e 'n t-ionnsachadh òg an t-ionnsachadh bòidheach.—*The early learning is the pretty learning.*

> *Al.*—a nì foghlam gun taing—*makes the sure learning.*
> *Al.*—a nì ealanta—*makes expert.*

Is e 'n t-uisge salach a nì 'n nighe ghlan.—*The dirty water makes the clean washing.*

Is e ath-thilleadh na ceathairn as miosa.—*The return of the rievers is worst.*

> Because they would carry off what they spared before.
> *Ceatharn*—troop, fighting band, banditti, whence 'cateran' and 'kern'. *Ceathairne*—peasantry, males fit to bear arms.

Is e bacadh duin' òig aimhleas.—*Thwarting a young man is his mischief.*

Is e deireadh gach cogaidh sìth.—*The end of each war is peace.*

Is e deireadh nan ceannaichean dol a shnìomh shìoman.—*The end of merchants is twisting straw-ropes.*

> A Lewis modern saying. The 'merchants' referred to are the small dealers in country places, who often come to grief through ignorance of business and bad debts.

Is e dh'itheas mòran am fear nach fhaigh ach beagan.—*He will eat much who gets little.*

Is e Diluain iuchair na seachdain.—*Monday is the key of the week.*

> A good, sensible maxim.

Is e do chab nach deach fhalach san làr an là a rugadh tu.—*Your 'gab' was not hidden under ground the day you were born.*

> Said to forward talkative young people.

Is e do chiad chliù d'alladh.—*Your first repute is your renown.*

> *Al.*—Is e cliù duin' a chiad iomradh.
> *Al.*—Is e ciad iarraidh duin' a chliù.

Is e do shùil do cheannaiche.—*Thine eye is thy merchant.*

> To thine eye, O merchant.—*Arab.* Caveat emptor.—*Lat.*

Is e duin' a nì, ach 's e cù a dh'innseas.—*He's a man who does; he's a dog who tells.*

> Manly men may do things which to go and speak of is not manly. To boast of things never done is worse still.

Is e farmad a nì treabhadh.—*Emulation makes ploughing.*

> In letters of gold, put up in the Logic Classroom of Edinburgh University by Sir William Hamilton, are these words of Hesiod, stirring to young minds:
>
> 'Αγαθὴ δ' ἒρις ἤδε βροτοῖσι.

Is e farmad a nì treabhadh; 's e còmh-stri a nì buain.—*Emulation ploughs and rivalry reaps.*

Is e fortan no mì-fhortan fir bean.—*A man's wife is his fortune or misfortune.*

Is e galar a bheireadh air na gobhair nach itheadh iad an eidheann.—*Sickness only would keep goats from eating ivy.*

> See 'An rud a chum'.

Is e innleachd seilge a sìor leanmhainn.—*The art of hunting is ever pursuing it.*

Is e iomadaidh nan làmh a nì an obair aotrom.—*Many hands make light work.—Eng., Scot.*

> *Al.*—Lìonmhorachd nan làmh.

Is e leanabh fhèin as luaithe bhaisteas an sagart.—*The priest christens his ain bairn first.—Scot.*

> Is e a leanbh féin a bhaisteas an sagart ar dtús.—*Ir.*
> This saying must be held, by all who respect priests, to have originated before marriage was forbidden to them.

Is e meathadh gach cùise dàil.—*Delay makes causes dwine.*

> *Al.*—a bhith ga sìneadh—*adjourning.*

Is e miann a' chait a chniadachadh.—*The cat desires to be caressed.*

Is e miann na lach an loch air nach bi i.—*The duck's desire is the water where she's not.*

Is e mo charaide caraid na cruaidhe.—*My friend is the friend in straits.*

Is e mo roghainn a tha 'n uachdar.—*My choice is uppermost.*

Is e moch-èirigh na Luaine nì an t-suain Mhàirt.—*The Monday early rising makes the Tuesday sleep.*

Is e 'n greusaiche math an duine 's breugaich' air thalamh.—*The good shoemaker is the greatest of liars.*

Is e na deuchainnean a nì na dearbhainnean.—*Trials make proof.*

Is e sgeul an àigh a b'àill le Pòl.—*It's a lucky story that would please Paul.*

> Who Paul was we can't say—doubtless a critic of the 'nil admirari' school.

Is e sgeul an duine bheadaidh na gheibh e 'n taigh a choimh-earsnaich.—*The mannerless man tells what he gets at his neighbour's.*

Is e sin an toll a mhill an t-seiche.—*That's the hole that spoiled the hide.*

Is e sin cnag an sgeòil.—*That's the peg of the story.*

Is e sin maide 'g an stad e.—*That's the stick where he'll stop.*

> *Al.*—mum beil e 'g iomairt—*which he's playing at*—He'll come to that. The reference is to a game played at sticks or pegs, fixed at certain distances.

Is e sùil a nì sealbh.—*The eye makes wealth.*

> Das Auge des Herrn schafft mehr als seine beiden Hände—*The master's eye does more than both his hands.—Germ.*

Is e thòn a bha trasda nuair a rinn e e.—*He sat very awry when he did it.*

Is èasgaidh an droch ghille air chuairt.—*The bad servant is brisk abroad.*

> *Al.*—an taigh a' choimhearsnaich—*in the neighbour's house.*
> Esgud drygfab yn nhŷ arall.—*Welsh.*

Is èasgaidhe nòin na madainn.—*Noon is more lively than morning.*

>Is éascaí nóin ná maidin.—*Ir.*
>
>*Nòin,* derived doubtless like 'noon' from *nona* (3 p.m.), means both 'noon' and 'afternoon' in our Gaelic. In Irish and Welsh it means the former; in Manx, *traa nonney* = evening.
>
>Most people are more lively in the evening than in the morning.

Is èibhinn an obair an t-sealg.—*Hunting is delightful work.*

>This saying occurs in our oldest hunting song, known as *A' Chomha-chag,* 'The Owl,' by Donald MacDonald.
>
>Nid difyrwch ond milgi—ond gwalch—*No diversion like a greyhound— like a hawk.*—*Welsh.* Every run in the desert exhilarates.—*Arab.*

Is èiginn dol far am bi 'n fhòid.—*One must go where his grave awaits him.*

>See 'Bheir fòid'.

Is èiginn don fheumach a bhith falbhanach.—*The needy must keep moving.*

>This is a recognised maxim of Metropolitan Policemen.

Is eudar do chàirdean dealachadh.—*Friends must part.*

Is eudar gabhail le each mall, o nach faighear nas fheàrr.—*The slow horse must be taken if no better can be got.*

Is fad' an abhainn air nach fhaighear ceann.—*It's a long river whose head can't be found.*

>*Al.*—an rathad—*the road.*

Is fad' an dàil on oidhirp.—*Long is the delay from the attempt.*

Is fad' an eubh o Loch Obha, is cobhair o Chlann Ó Duibhne.— *Far's the cry from Loch Awe, and help from the race of O'Duine.*

>The Campbells claim descent from Diarmad Ó Duibhne, Dermid, grandson of Duine, the Launcelot of the Fingalian tragedy. The above saying is supposed to have originated at the time of a great defeat of the Campbells under the Earl of Argyll by the Gordons under the Earl of Huntly, at Allt Chuailleachain in Glenlivet, in 1594, where Campbell of Lochnell proved signally treacherous to his chief.—See Gregory's *West. Highl.* &c., p. 256.

Is fad' an oidhche gu latha do dh'fhear na droch mhnatha.—*It's a long night till morning for the husband of the bad wife.*

> See *Mrs. Caudle's Lectures.*

Is fad' an oidhche gu latha, arsa casan loisgte.—*Long is night till day, said the burned feet.*

Is fad' an timcheall nach tachair.—*It's a long round that meets not.*

Is fada cobhair o mhnaoi 's a muinntir an Eirinn.—*Far is aid from her whose folk are in Ireland.*

Is fada làmh an fheumaich.—*Long is the arm of the needy.*

> *Al.*—Is fada làmh an airc, ach mas fhada, cha reamhar—*The hand of poverty is long and lean.*

Is fada slios na bliadhna.—*The year's length is long.*

> *Lit.* The year's 'slope' or 'side'.

Is faoilidhe duine a chuid a thairgse ged is fheàirrd' e aige fhèin e.—*He is the more generous who offers his own though he would be the better of keeping it.*

> The Moral Philosophy of this is excellent, and is just that of the Saviour about the widow's mite. The virtue of donations implying no sacrifice is very small indeed.

Is farsaing an rathad mòr, agus faodar fhalbh.—*The highway is wide, and may be trod.*

Is farsaing a sgaoileas an dreathan a chasan 'na thaigh fhèin.—*The wren spreads his feet wide in his own house.*

> *Al.*—Is farsaing taigh an dreathain—*The wren's house is wide.*
> There is something felicitious in the idea of a wren spreading his legs like a potentate at his own hearth.

Is farsaing beul a' bhothain.—*A wee house has a wide mouth.*—*Scot.*

> Ulster proverb in same words.

Is fàs a' choill às nach goirear.—*It's a desert wood whence no voice is heard.*

Is fhad' a bha thu; 's luath a thàinig thu.—*You are long of coming, and have come full soon.*

Is fhad' a chaidh an Lùnasdal annad.—*The Lammas went far into you.*

> I.e., you are far gone; Lammas being the time of year when things had reached the verge of dearth before harvest, in olden times.

Is fhad' a dh'fhalbhas cas bheò.—*A living foot will go far.*

Is fhada bhios duine triall far nach miann leis a dhol.—*A man goes slowly where he doesn't wish.*

Is fhada bhon dà latha sin, 's bho bhliadhna 'n Earraich dhuibh.—*It's long since these two days, and the year of the black Spring.*

> The 'two days' mean 'changed times'; the 'black Spring' a peculiarly bad year.

Is fhada bhon uair sin bhon a bha cluas air ròn.—*It's long since the time when the seal had ears.*

> The seal's ears are hardly visible. The common phrase on meeting an old acquaintance is ' 'S fhad on uair sin'—'*It's long since that time*'.

Is fhada Dùn Eideann bhon fhear tha 'g èirigh san Stòr.—*Edinburgh is far from the man who rises at Stoer.*

> Stoer is a parish in the west of Sutherland.

Is fhad' o thaigh a' mhodh a rugadh tu.—*You were born far from the house of good manners.*

Is fhada tha bàs do sheanmhar 'nad chuimhne.—*Your grandmother's death is long in your memory.*

> Said to over-sentimental people, or to those who keep up too long the remembrance of anything.

Is fhaid' an latha na 'm bruthach; bidh sinn uiread uaireigin.—*The day is longer than the brae; we'll be at the top yet.*

> A very cheery and plucky sentiment.

Is fhaide d'fhiacail na d'fheusag.—*Your teeth are longer than your beard.*

> Tak a piece; yir teeth's langer than yir beard.—*Scot.*

Is fhaide gu bràth na gu Bealltainn.—*It's longer to Doomsday than to Whit Sunday.*

> Ulster proverb in same words.

Is fhaide gu Nollaig na gu Fèill Màrtainn.—*It's longer to Christmas than to Martinmas.*

Is fhasa cumail na tarraing.—*Better to haud than draw.*—*Scot.*

> Possession is nine points of the law.—*Eng.*

Is fhasa deagh ainm a chall na chosnadh.—*A guid name is suner tint than won.*—*Scot.*

Is fhasa sgapadh na tional.—*It's easier to scatter than to gather.*

> Is fusa scapadh ná cruinniú.—*Ir.*

Is fheàirrd' an càl an cat a chur ann.—*The kail will be the better of putting the cat in.*

> Better a mouse i' the pat as nae flesh.—*Scot.*

Is fheàirrd' an luch sàmhchair, mar a thuirt luch a' mhonaidh ri luch a' bhaile.—*The mouse is the better of quietness, as the moor-mouse said to the town-mouse.*

> This seems to be taken from the well-known fable of the Town Mouse and Country Mouse.

Is fheàirrde breugadair fianais.—*A liar is the better of a voucher.*

> Is fearrde a dhearcas bréag fianaise.—*Ir.*
> See 'Imridh breug gobhal'.

Is fheàirrde brà a breacadh gun a bristeadh.—*A quern is the better of being picked without being broken.*

> Is fearrde don mbró a bhreacadh gan a bhriseadh.—*Ir.*
> Picking the quern consisted in refreshing the roughness of the stone, which required to be cautiously done. The use of hand-mills was prohibited by the Scottish Parliament as far back as 1284, but continued privately notwithstanding, and is probably not entirely obsolete yet. The above saying is supposed to refer to the orders given by the lairds to have all the querns broken.

Is fheàirrde cù cù a chrochadh.—*A dog is the better of another dog being hanged.*

Is fheàirrde cù sgaiteach cnàimh a chur 'na bheul.—*A biting dog is the better of a bone.*

> Gwell cariad y ci na'i gas—*A dog's friendship is better than his hate.*—*Welsh.*

Is fheàirrde cuideachd cùis-bhùird.—*A company is the better of a laughing-stock.*

> *Al.*—culaidh-ghàire.

Is fheàirrde gach cneadh a ceasnachadh.—*A wound is the better of being probed.*

Is fheàirrde gach math a mheudachadh.—*Every good is the better of being increased.*

Is fheàirrde h-uile cù a dhìon a chinn a dhranndan.—*A dog's snarl defends his head.*

Is fheàrr a bhith bochd na bhith breugach.—*Better be poor than a liar.*

Is fheàrr a bhith cinnteach na bhith caillteach.—*Better be sure than lose.*

Is fheàrr a bhith cuimhneachadh air a' mhath a bha na bhith smaoineachadh air a' mhath nach eil 's nach bi.—*Better thinking of the good that has been than of that which is not, and never will be.*

A thoroughly Celtic and respectable Conservative sentiment.

Is fheàrr a bhith dhìth a' chinn na bhith dhìth an fhasain.—*Better want the head than want the fashion.*

> *Al.*—Is fheàrr dol às an amhaich na dol às an fhasan—*Better out of neck than out of fashion.*

A very human and especially feminine sentiment.

Is fheàrr a bhith dubh na bhith bàn;
Is fheàrr a bhith bàn na bhith ruadh;
Is fheàrr a bhith ruadh na bhith carrach;
Is fheàrr a bhith carrach na bhith gun cheann.

—Better be black than fair;
Better be fair than red;
Better be red than scabby;
Better be scabby than no head.

Al.—Is fheàrr an dubh na 'n donn;
'S fheàrr an donn na 'm bàn;
'S fheàrr am bàn na 'n ruadh;
'S fheàrr an ruadh na chàrr.

—Better black than brown,
Better brown than fair,
Better fair than red,
Better red than scabby.

Is fheàrr a bhith gun chloinn na clann gun rath.—*Better no children than children without luck.*

Is fheàrr a bhith gun mhart na bhith gun mhac.—*Better have no cow than have no son.*

Is fheàrr a bhith leisg gu ceannach na righinn gu pàigheadh.—*Better be slow to buy than stiff to pay.*

Is fheàrr a bhith sona na bhith saothaireach.—*Better be happy (or lucky) than laborious.*

Is fheàrr a bhith sona na crìonna.—*Better be happy (or lucky) than wise.*

Both these sentiments are very Celtic; and yet the wise Englishman, the cautious Lowland Scot and the astute Italian say the very same thing in the same words—' 'Tis better to be happy than wise'; 'Better be sonsy than soon up'; 'E meglio esser fortunato che savio'. So much faith is there in luck, even among the wisest people.

Is fheàrr a bhiathadh na ionnsachadh.—*He's better fed than bred.*—
Scot.

> Feárr a oileamhuin ná a oideachas.—*Ir.* Mieux nourrit qu' instruit.—*Fr.*

Is fheàrr a' chlach gharbh air am faighear rudeigin na chlach mhìn
air nach faighear dad idir.—*Better the rough stone which yields something than the smooth stone that yields nothing.*

> This, of course, has a moral meaning, but the physical reference is to
> the species of lichen called respectively *corcar* and *crotal*, which grow
> on rocks and were used extensively for dyes in the Highlands, the one
> a shade of crimson, the other a reddish brown. See Lightfoot's *Flora
> Scotica*, 2nd ed., Vol. II, pp 812, 818.

Is fheàrr a' chlach na bhith gun mhathachadh.—*Better stones than no
manure.*

> Instances have been told of stones having been gathered off a field so
> carefully as to do the land more harm than good, and even to lead to
> their being replaced!

Is fheàrr a thomhas fo sheachd na mhilleadh uile a dh'aon
bheachd.—*Better measure short of seven than spoil all at once.*

> This seems to refer to the measure for a kilt, for which seven yards
> are required for a well-grown man.
> Measure twice, cut once.—*Scot.*

Is fheàrr àgh na ealain.—*Luck is better than skill.*

> *Al.*—Is fheàrr an t-àgh na mhoch-èirigh—*Luck is better than early
> rising.*
> See 'Is fheàrr a bhith sona' and 'Ealain gun rath'.

Is fheàrr aithreachas fuireach na aithreachas falbh.—*Better repent for
staying than for going.*

> *Al.*—suidhe na aithreachas ruithe—*for sitting than for running.*

Is fheàrr altram ràithe na altram bliadhna.—*A quarter's nursing is
better than a year's.*

Is fheàrr am fear foghainteach feargach na 'm mìn-chealgaire 's e ro
chiùin.—*Better the sturdy passionate man than the smooth-deceiving and
very mild.*

Is fheàrr an cù a nì miodal riut na 'n cù a ghearras tu.—*Better the dog that fawns than the dog that bites.*

> Better a dog fawn on you than bite you.—*Eng.*
> *Al.*—Is fheàrr an cù a bhogas earball na 'n cù a chuireas draing air—*Better the dog that wags his tail than the dog that grins.*

Is fheàrr an cù dh'fhalbhas na 'n cù dh'fhanas.—*Better the dog that goes than the dog that stays.*

Is fheàrr an cù a ruitheas na 'n cù a mheathas.—*Better is the dog that runs than he that gives in.*

Is fheàrr an cumadair na 'n cronadair.—*The maker is better than the critic.*

Is fheàrr an dìcheall lag na 'n neart leisg.—*Better the weak diligence than the lazy strength.*

Is fheàrr an fhìrinn na 'n t-òr.—*Truth is better than gold.*

Is fheàrr an giomach na bhith gun fhear-taighe.—*Better a lobster than no husband.*

> *Al.*—am portan tuathal—*the awkward crab.*
> Two women lived together, one of whom stole the other's meal out of her bag. The sufferer then put a live lobster into the bag, and the next time the thief put her hand in she was caught. She cried out, 'Tha 'n Donas 'na do phoca !'—'*The Devil's in your bag!*' 'Tha,' said the other, 'nuair tha thus' ann'—'*Yes, when you are there.*' Hence the origin of this proverb.
> Sease velado, y sease un palo—*Let it be a husband, though it be but a hedge-stick.*—*Span.*

Is fheàrr an rath seo far am beil e na 'n rath ud far an robh e.—*This luck is better where it is than that where it was.*

Is fheàrr an rathad fada glan na 'n rathad goirid salach.—*Better the long clean road than the short dirty one.*

Is fheàrr an saoghal ionnsachadh na sheachnadh.—*Better teach (or learn) the world than shun it.*

> A very wise saying.

Is fheàrr an sneachd na bhith gun sian, an dèidh an sìol a chur san talamh.—*Better snow than no rainstorm, when the seed is in the ground.*

> *Al.*—Is fheàrr an sneachd na bhith gun uisge sa Chèitean.—*Better snow than no rain in May.*

Is fheàrr an teine beag a gharas na 'n teine mòr a loisgeas.—*Better a little fire to warm us than a great one to burn us.*—*Eng., Scot.*

> Is fearr tine bheag a ghoras ná tine mhór a loisceas.—*Ir.*

Is fheàrr an toit na ghaoth tuath.—*The smoke is better than the north wind.*

Is fheàrr an t-olc a chluinntinn na fhaicinn.—*Better hear the evil than see it.*

> *Per con.* 'S fheàrr an t-olc fhaicinn na chluinntinn.

Is fheàrr an t-olc eòlach na 'n t-olc aineolach.—*The known evil is better than the unknown.*

> *Al.*—Ma tha aon chron san eòlach, bidh a dhà dheug san aineolach— *If the known have one fault, the unknown will have twelve.*

> Is fearr eolas an uilc ná an t-olc gan eolas.—*Ir.* Share yn olk shione dooin na yn olk nagh nhione dooin.—*Manx.* Gwel i ddyn y drwg a gŵyr na'r drwg nis gŵyr.—*Welsh.*

> > And makes us rather bear those ills we have
> > Than fly to others that we know not of.—*Hamlet*, III, 1.

> > Better the ill ken'd than the guid unken'd.—*Scot.*

Is fheàrr am bonnach beag leis a' bheannachd na 'm bonnach mòr leis a' mhallachd.—*The little bannock with a blessing is better than the big one with a curse.*

> This saying occurs in some of the old Gaelic tales, when a son is going from home and is asked by his mother which he prefers. See Dr. MacLeod's *Caraid nan Gàidheal*, p. 273.
> *Al.*—an t-ugh beag—*the little egg*; an leth beag—*the little half.*

Is fheàrr aon eun san làimh na dhà dheug air iteig.—*A bird in the hand is worth a dozen on wing.*

> Fearr dreoilin ann dorn na corr air cháirde (*free*)—*Ir.* Ta ushag ayns laue chammag (*cho math*) as jees (*dithis*) sy thammag (*bush*).—*Manx.* Gwell aderyn (*one bird*) yn y llaw na dau yn llwyn (*two in wood*).—*Welsh.* A bird in the hand is worth two in the wood.—*Eng.* A bird in the hand's worth twa fleein by.—*Scot.* A thousand cranes in the air are not worth a sparrow in the fist.—*Arab.* Mas vale pajaro (*sparrow*) en la mano que buitre (*vulture*) volando.—*Span.* Beter eene vogel in de hand dan tien in de lucht (*sky*).—*Dutch.* E meglio un ucello in gabbia che cento fuori.—*Ital.*

Is fheàrr aon laogh na dà chraiceann.—*One calf is better than two skins.*

Is fheàrr aon oidhche Mhàirt na trì latha Foghair.—*One night in March is worth three days in Autumn.*

> For growth.

Is fheàrr aon sine bheò na dà bhoin mharbh.—*One living teat is better than two dead cows.*

> *Al.*—na dà làmhaig—*than two axes.* The axe was the weapon with which the cow was killed.

Is fheàrr aon sine na ceathramh coirce.—*One teat (of a cow) is better than a quarter of oat.*

> *Al.*—Is fheàrr aon sine bà na bolla dhen mhin bhàn—*Better one teat of a cow than a boll of Lowland meal.*
> Would that all lairds and sheep-farmers considered this who have crofters on their lands, with children, but no cows to give them milk! Unhappily, there is less of milk, both of cows and of human kindness, in some places where once they were not wanting.

Is fheàrr aon taisgeach na seachd teagraidh.—*Better one secure than seven to be gathered.*

Is fheàrr aon taigh air a nighe na dhà dheug air an sguabadh.—*Better one house washed than twelve swept.*

Is fheàrr aon tòrradh na dà chomanachadh dheug.—*One funeral is worth twelve communions.*

> For drink, especially—a very suggestive saying.

Is fheàrr bàrr mòr, ach fòghnaidh bàrr beag.—*A big crop is best, but a little crop will do.*

Is fheàrr beagan stòrais na mòran chàirdean.—*Better a little of one's own than many friends.*

Is fheàrr bean ghlic na crann is fearann.—*Better is a wise wife than a plough and land.*

Is fheàrr bò na bà; is fheàrr duine na daoine.—*A cow is better than kine; a man is better than men.*

> I.e., a good cow and a good man.

Is fhearr brèid na toll, ach 's uaisle toll na tuthag.—*A patch is better than a hole, but a hole is more genteel.*

> Is fearr paiste ná poll, acht is onóraí poll na paiste.—*Ir.* Gwelloc'h pensel evit toull.—*Breton.*
>
> The sentiment of this is very Celtic, and the Spanish saying is similar, 'Hidalgo honrado antes roto que remendado'—*A true gentleman would prefer his clothes ragged than patched.*
>
> Better a clout than a hole out.—*Eng.* Besser ein Flick als ein Loch.—*Germ.*
>
> *Al.*—Pìseag air toll, 's e sin an tairbhe; ach pìseig air pìseig, 's e sin an lùireach—*Patch on hole is economy; patch on patch is tatters.*
>
> Patch by patch is good housewifery, but patch upon patch is plain beggary.—*Eng.* Clout upon a hole is guid gentry, clout upon a clout is guid yeomanry, but clout upon a clouted clout is downright beggary.—*Scot.*

Is fheàrr buille na iomradh.—*A blow is better than gossip.*

> The meaning is that corporal punishment is less painful than being made a subject of disagreeable remark.

Is fheàrr caitheamh na meirgeadh.—*Better wear than rust.*

> A fine saying.

> Perséverance, dear my lord,
> Keeps honour bright; to have done is to hang
> Quite out of fashion, like a rusty mail
> In monumental mockery.—*Troil. and Cress.*, III, 3.

Is fheàrr caraid sa chùirt na crùn san sporan.—*A friend in the court is better than a crown in the purse.*

Al.—'na bò am buailidh'—*than a cow in the fold.* Is fearr cara sa chúirt ná bonn sa sparán.—*Ir.* Gwell câr yn y llys nag aur ar fys.—*Welsh. A friend at (or in) court is worth a penny in purse.*—*Eng., Scot.*

One of the best illustrations of the want of judicial purity in olden times, which gave rise to this maxim, is Lord President Gilmour's remark on hearing Cromwell's judges praised for their impartiality—'Deil thank them! they had neither kith nor kin'. Even in 1737, the advice given in a lawsuit in regard to the management of the Bench was as follows: 'By Lord St. Clair's advice, Mrs Kinloch is to wait on Lady Cairnie tomorrow to cause her to ask the favour of Lady St. Clair to solicit Lady Betty Elphinston and Lady Dun'. The ladies last mentioned were the wives of two of the judges. Lord St. Clair's exquisite caution, in leaving the management of Lady St. Clair to other people, is interesting. See Chambers's *Dom. Ann.*, III, 291.

Is fheàrr coimhearsnach am fagas na bràthair fad' o làimh.—*Better a neighbour at hand than a brother far away.*

 Al.—Is fheàrr coimhearsnach math sa bhaile seo na caraid anns a' bhail' ud thall.—*Better a good neighbour in this town than a kinsman in yon town.*

  Eun amezek mad (*math*) a zo gwell,
  Evit na e kerent (*na caraid*) a-bell.—*Breton.*

 God Nabo er bedre end Broder i anden By.—*Dan.* E meglio un prossimo vicino che un lontano cugino.—*Ital.*

Is fheàrr crathadh na cainbe na crathadh na cirbe.—*The shaking of canvas is better than the shaking of a rag.*

 The meaning of this is not apparent.

Is fheàrr cù beò na leòmhann marbh.—*Better a living dog than a dead lion.*

 This is a translation of *Eccles.* ix, 4.

Is fheàrr cù luath na teanga labhar.—*Better a dog swift of foot than loud of tongue.*

Is fheàrr cuid na ciad oidhche na na h-oidhche mu dheireadh.—*The first night's fare is better than the last night's.*

 The first and last night of the winter beef.

Is fheàrr cùl caraide na aghaidh coimhich.—*Better back of friend than face of stranger.*

> Gwell gwegil câr na gwyneb estron.—*Welsh.*

Is fheàrr deagh chainnt na h-asail na droch fhacal fàidh.—*The good speech of an ass is better than the bad word of a prophet.*

> This of course refers to Balaam. It is the only Gaelic saying in which the ass is mentioned. The animal was unknown in the Highlands until modern times.

Is fheàrr deagh earbsa na droch fhoighidinn.—*Full trust is better than impatience.*

Is fheàrr deathach an fhraoich na gaoth an reothaidh.—*Better the smoke of heather than the wind of frost.*

Is fhearr deireadh cuirme na toiseach tuasaid.—*Better the end o a feast than the beginning o a fray—Scot.*

> *Al.*—Is fhearr teachd an deireadh—*Better come at the end &c.*
> Fearr deireadh fleidhe ná tús bruidhne.—*Ir.*

Is fheàrr deireadh math na droch thoiseach.—*Better a good end than a bad beginning.*

> Macintosh translates this 'The refuse of the good is preferable to the best of the ill.'

Is fheàrr dhut do chuid fhàgail aig do nàmhaid na dol an innibh do charaide.—*Better leave your goods with an enemy than go to extremes with your friend.*

> *Lit.* 'than go into the bowels of'.

Is fheàrr dìol-farmaid na dìol-truaighe.—*Better be envied than pitied.—Eng., Scot.*

> *Al.*—Is fheàrr 'Fire, faire !' na 'Mo thruaighe!'—*Better 'Hey day!' than 'Alas!'*
> There is more wit in this version.

> Is fearr díol tnúith nà díol truaighe.—*Ir.* φθονέεσθαι κρέσσον ἐστιν ἢ ὀικτειρεσθαι.—*Herod.* Κάλλια νà σὲ ξηλεύον, παρὰ νà σ' ελεουν—*Mod. Gr.* So *Fr., Ital., Germ., Dutch* &c.

Is fheàrr dol a laighe gun suipear na èirigh ann am fiachan.—*Better go to bed supperless than rise in debt.—Eng.*

> Share goll dy lhie fegooish (*as eugais*) shibber, na girree ayns lhiastynys (*debt*).—*Manx.*

Is fheàrr do dhuin' a bhreith an deagh uair na deagh athair.—*Better be born in good time than a good father.*

> One of the questionable sayings on the importance of luck.

Is fheàrr do dhuine bhith snaim nan sop na bhith 'na thàmh.—*Better knot straws than sit idle.*

> The Scotch saying is the opposite—'Better be idle than ill employed'.

Is fheàrr duine na daoine.—*One man is better than many men.*

> Gwell gwr nâ gwŷr—('*S fheàrr fear na fir).—Welsh.*

Is fheàrr e na choltas.—*He is better than he looks.*

> She's better than she's bonnie.—*Scot.*

Is fheàrr èirigh moch na suidhe anmoch.—*Better rise early than sit late.*

> Is fearr éirí moch ná suí mall.—*Ir.* Gae to bed wi the lamb, and rise wi the laverock.—*Scot.* One hour's sleep before midnight is worth three hours after.—*Eng.*

Is fheàrr eòlas math na droch chàirdeas.—*Good acquaintance is better than bad relationship.*

> See 'Thèid an t-eòlas'.

Is fheàrr fheuchainn na bhith san dùil.—*It's better to try than to hope.*

> Very good doctrine.

Is fheàrr freasdal na gàbhadh.—*Better caution than danger.*

> Guid watch hinders harm.—*Scot.*

Is fheàrr froiseachan am bliadhna na sguab air cheann an-uiridh.—*A shaken sheaf this year is better than the standing sheaf of last year.*

> *Al.*—Is fheàrr sguab am bliadhna na adag an-uiridh—*A sheaf of this year is better than a shock (twelve sheaves) of last year.*

Is fheàrr fuachd caraide na blàths nàmhaid.—*Better the coldness of a friend than the warmth of an enemy.*

> An excellent saying.

Is fheàrr fuidheall fanaid na fuidheall farmaid.—*The remains of ridicule are better than the dregs of envy.*

Is fheàrr fuidheall na braide na fuidheall na sgeige.—*The residue of theft is better than that of scorn.*

> Macintosh's translation is 'The thief may have some profit, but the scorner none.' The doctrine is dubious.

Is fheàrr fuidheall na uireasbhaidh.—*Better leavings than want.*

> Is fearr fuigheall ná bheith ar easbhuidh.—*Ir.*

Is fheàrr fuine thana na bhith uile falamh.—*Thin kneading is better than no bread.*

> Bannocks are better than nae bread.—*Scot.* Half a loaf is better than no bread.—*Eng.*

Is fheàrr grèim caillich na tarraing laoich.—*An old woman's grip is better than a hero's pull.*

> *Al.*—Is fheàrr cumail caillich na tarraing tighearna.
> Better to haud than draw.—*Scot.*

Is fheàrr guth na meidh.—*A word is better than a balance.*

> This is a *dubh-fhacal*. The meaning probably is that the voice of a powerful friend is of more value than strict impartiality. In his first edition, Macintosh gives the word *mèithe*, and his translation is 'Better speak than lose right'.

Is fheàrr iarann fhaotainn na airgead a chall.—*Better find iron than tine siller.*—*Scot.*

Is fheàrr iasg beag na bhith gun iasg idir.—*Sma fish is better than nane*—*Scot.*

Is fheàrr iomall a' phailteis na teis-meadhan na gainne.—*Better the border of plenty than the centre of want.*

> *Al.*—na h-airce.

Is fheàrr làn an dùirn de chèaird na làn an dùirn de dh'òr.—*A handful of trade is better than a handful of gold.*

> A handfu o trade is worth a gowpen o gowd.—*Scot.* A handful of trade is a handful of gold.—*Eng.*
> This is undoubtedly a borrowed proverb. The trade of the smith or armourer was the only one the Highlanders looked on with any respect.

Is fheàrr leisgeul salach na bhith gun leisgeul idir.—*Better a bad excuse than none.*—*Eng.*

Is fhèarr leum-iochd as t-Fhoghar na sguab a bharrachd.—*A balk in Autumn is better than a sheaf the more.*

> The *leum-iochd*, or *bailc* (Scotch 'bauk'), is a strip of a cornfield left fallow. The fear of being left with the last sheaf of the harvest, called the *cailleach*, or *gobhar bhacach*, always led to an exciting competition among the reapers in the last field. The reaper who came on a *leum-iochd* would of course be glad to have so much the less to cut.—See App. VI.

Is fheàrr lùbadh na bristeadh.—*Better bow than break.*—*Eng.*, *Scot.*

> So *Fr.*, *Ital.*, *Span.*, *Port.*, *Germ.*

Is fheàrr màthair phocanach na athair claidheach.—*A begging mother is better than a sworded father.*

> This saying is borrowed from the south. The sworded and riding father means a freebooter.
> Better a thigging mither than a riding faither.—*Scot.* Is fearr máthair phocáin ná athair seilstrigh (*ploughing*).—*Ir.*
> The sentiment of this is not so respectable.

Is fhèarr meomhair luchd an tagraidh na cuimhne luchd nam fiach.—*The memory of creditors is better than of debtors.*

Is fheàrr na 'n t-òr sgeul innse air chòir.—*Better than gold is a tale rightly told.*

> This applies to the telling of stories, but still more to the telling of truth.

Is fheàrr na toimhsean na na tuairmeis.—*Measures are better than guesses.*

> Measure twice, cut but aince.—*Scot.* Measure thrice what thou buyest, and cut but once.—*Eng.*

Is fheàrr òirleach de dh'each na troigh de chapall.—*An inch of a horse is better than a foot of a mare.*

Is fheàrr ònrachd na droch cuideachd.—*Better be alone than in bad company.*—*Eng.*

> Better alane than in ill company.—*Scot.* Besser allein als in schlechter Gesellschaft.—*Germ.* Mas vale solo que mal acompañado.—*Span.*

Is fheàrr peighinn an fhortain na 'n rosad is còig ceud.—*The lucky penny is better than misfortune and five hundred.*

> Hap and ha'penny is warld's gear eneuch.—*Scot.*

Is fheàrr piseach anmoch na bhith gun phiseach.—*Better late luck than no luck.*

Is fheàrr rogha coimhearsnaich na rogha fuine.—*Better choice of neighbour than choice of baking.*

Is fheàrr rud fhàgail aig nàmhaid na rud iarraidh air caraide.—*Better leave a thing with an enemy than ask of a friend.*

Is fheàrr seann fhiachan na seann fhalachd.—*Better old debts than old feuds.*

> *Al.*—na seann ghamhlas.

Is fheàrr seòladh na obair throm.—*Directing is better than heavy work.*

> Better direct well than work hard.—*Eng.* Better guide weel than wark fair.—*Scot.*

Is fheàrr sgìths chas na meamna.—*Better weary foot than weary spirit.*

Is fhearr sgur na sgàineadh.—*Better cease than burst.*

> A facetious addition to this is 'ach 's e sgàineadh as iomraitiche'—'*but bursting is more notable.*' The supposed reply, ''S fheàrr sgàineadh na 'm biadh math a mhilleadh,' is merely a translation of the Saxon saying, 'Better belly burst than good meat spoil.'

Is fheàrr sìol caol coirce fhaotainn à droch fhearann na bhith falamh.—*Better small oats than nothing, out of bad land.*

> This is a characteristic Hebridean saying. Small black oats are the chief corn crop.

Is fheàrr sìor-obair na sàr-obair.—*Better steady work than severe work.*

Is fheàrr sìor-ruith na dian-ruith.—*Better steady running than full speed.*

Is fheàrr sìth à preas na sìth à glais.—*Better peace from the wood than from under lock.*

> Bedre at tinge ved Busken end ved Boien—*Better make terms in the bush than in prison.—Dan.*
> The identity of these sayings is curious.

Is fheàrr sìth na circe na h-aimhreit.—*Better peace with a hen than strife.*

> This shows the hand of a henpecked philosopher.

Is fheàrr suidhe goirid na seasamh fada.—*Better short sitting than long standing.*

> Is fearr suidhe gearr ná seasamh fada.—*Ir.* Share soie son veg na roie (*ruith*) son veg.—*Manx.*

Is fheàrr tàmh na obair an asgaidh.—*Better rest than work for nothing.*

> A Miso-Celt might point to this as illustrative of Celtic laziness but for the Scottish saying, 'Better sit idle than work for nought', and the English one, 'As good to play for nought as work for nought.'
> Per con. Is fhearr saothair fhaoin na daoine dìomhain—*Better useless work than be idle.*

Is fheàrr teicheadh math na droch fhuireach.—*Better a good retreat than stay to suffer.*

> *He that fights and runs away*
> *May live to fight another day*

is the common form of what in Hudibras is

> *For those that fly may fight again,*
> *Which he can never do that's slain.*

Older still, however, is the Greek saying, quoted in self-defence by Demosthenes, when twitted for leaving his shield on the field of Cheronœa, Ανὴρ ὁ φεύγων, καὶ πάλιν μαχήσεται , thus translated by Udall (1542), from the *Adagia* of Erasmus,

> *That same man that runnith awaie*
> *Maie again fight another daie.*

Is fheàrr tilleadh am meadhan an àtha na bàthadh uile.—*Better turn mid-ford than be drowned.*

> Is fearr pilleadh as lár an átha ná báthadh sa tuile.—*Ir.*
> Better wade back mid-water than gang forrat and droun.—*Scot.*
> Beter ten halve gekeerd (*turn halfway*) dan ten heele gedwaald (*be wholly lost*).—*Dutch.*

Is fheàrr tabhairt caillich na geall rìgh.—*An old wife's gift is better than a king's promise.*

> There is a democratic sharpness in this very uncommon in Gaelic sayings.

Is fheàrr treabhadh anmoch na bhith gun treabhadh idir.—*Better late ploughing than none at all.*

Is fheàrr uair de bhean an taighe na obair latha banoglaich.—*Better an hour of the mistress than a day's work of the servant.*

Is fheàrr unnsa toinisg na punnd leòm.—*An ounce of sense is better than a pound of pride.*

> An ounce of wisdom is worth a pound of wit.—*Eng.*

Is fhiach each math breab a leigeadh leis.—*A good horse may be forgiven a kick.*

Is fhurasd' am bàth a mhealladh gun a làmh a lomadh.—*The simpleton may be deceived without being robbed.*

Is fhurasd' a chur a-mach, fear gun an teach aige fhèin.—*'Tis easy to put out a man whose own the house is not.*

> The ejecting of a troublesome visitor may sometimes be a commendable process, but that is not the whole meaning of this saying. It is interpreted, not unreasonably, in the note of A. Campbell, as referring to the ejection of poor tenants in the Highlands. The ease with which that process has generally been accomplished is remarkable, pleasing in one point of view, sad and shameful in another.

Is fhurasd' aicheamhail na buille nach buailear a thoirt a-mach.—*It's easy to avenge the blow that's not struck.*

Is fhurasda buill' an treun-fhir aithneachadh.—*The mighty man's stroke is easily known.*

> The fox found the wren one day threshing corn with his twelve sons, and, wishing to find out the father, made the above flattering remark. Whereupon the old wren turned round and, leaning on his flail, said, with a smile of gratification, 'Bha latha dha sin'—'*That day was,*' adding, with a nod, 'Cha tuig iadsan, na garraich, sin'—'*They little know that, these chickens*'. What the fox did thereupon is painful to contemplate.

Is fhurasda caisteal gun sèisdeadh a ghleidheadh.—*It's easy to keep a castle that's not besieged.*

> It is easy to keep a castle that was never assaulted.—*Eng.*

> This was probably first said to a censorious old maid.

Is fhurasda clach fhaotainn gu tilgeadh air cù.—*It's easy to find a stone to throw at a dog.*

> Facilmente si trova un bastone per dar ad un cane.—*Ital.*

> > The ancient proverb will be well effected:
> > 'A staff is quickly found to beat a dog.'—*Henry VI*, P. II, iii, 1.

Is fhurasd' coire fhaotainn do dh'obair leth-dhèanta.—*It's easy to find fault with half-finished work.*

Is fhurasda dol an cuid fir, ach 's e chùis fuireach ann.—*To usurp is easy, to keep is another thing.*

Is fhurasda duine gun nàir' a bheathachadh.—*A shameless man is easily fed.*

> He that has no modesty has all the town for his own.—*Eng.*

Is fhurasda fear fhaotainn do nighinn gun athair.—*It's easy to get a match for a fatherless maid.*

Is fhurasda fuil a thoirt à ceann carrach, is gal a thoirt à craos cam.—*It's easy to draw blood from a scabby head, and cry from a wry mouth.*

> A scald head is soon broken.—*Eng.*

Is fhurasda fuin' a dhèanamh làmh ri min.—*It's easy to bake near meal.*

> Is furasta fuineadh de chois mine.—*Ir.* It's guid baking beside the meal.—*Scot.* Anhawdd pobi heb flawd—*Hard to bake without flour.*—*Welsh.*

Is fhurasda tein' fhadadh an cois craoibhe.—*It's easy to kindle a fire at the foot of a tree.*

> Is furasta tine a lasadh de chois connaidh.—*Ir.*

Is fhusa car a chur san teanga na san luing mhòir.—*It's easier to turn the tongue than a big ship.*

> This seems meant for an emendation on *James* iii, 4, 5.

Is fhusa chiad togradh a stamhnadh na na thig 'na dhèidh a thoileachadh.—*It's easier to subdue the first desire than to satisfy its followers.*

> A good statement of one of the most important principles of Moral Philosophy.

Is fhusa comhairle thoirt na comhairle ghabhail.—*'Tis easier to give advice than take it.*

> Do as I say, and not as I do.—*Eng.*

Is fhusa dà theallach a thogail na teine chumail ri h-aon diubh.—*It's easier to build two hearths than to keep a fire on one.*

Is fhusa duine chumail a-muigh na chur a-mach nuair thig e staigh.—*It's easier to keep a man out than to put him out when in.*

> Better haud oot than pit oot.—*Scot.*

Is fhusa sgapadh na tional.—*It's easier to scatter than to gather.*

> Is fusa scapadh ná cruinniú.—*Ir.*

Is fhusa teàrnadh na dìreadh.—*It's easier to go down than to climb.*

> Haws dringo na disgyn—*Easier to climb than to descend.*—*Welsh.*
> The Gaelic saying is true both literally and metaphorically.
> The Welsh saying is true only of climbing in very steep or rocky places.

Is fiach air duine na gheallas e.—*A man's promise is a debt.*

> Dyled ar pob ei addaw.—*Welsh.*
> See 'Am fear a gheallas'.

Is fiamhach an t-sùil a lotar.—*The hurt eye is timorous.*

Is follaiseach fuil air cù bàn.—*Blood is noticeable on a white dog.*

Is fuar an coimpir' an fhòid.—*The turf is a cold companion.*

> There is some pathos in this; and yet the saying may have been invented by a bereaved person, on the look-out for a new companion.

Is fuar an innis an càrn.—*The cairn is a cold shelter.*

Is fuar an goile nach teòdh deoch.—*It's a cold stomach that drink won't warm.*

> It's a cauld stamach that naething hets on.—*Scot.*

Is fuar comann an ath-chleamhnais.—*Cold is the society of a second affinity.*

> Macintosh's translation gives the meaning, which is not obvious—
> 'Cold is the connection with a first alliance, when a second is formed.'

Is fuar don'-chleamhnas.—*Cold is ill-sorted affinity.*

Is fuar gaoth nan coimheach.—*Cold is the wind that brings strangers.*

> Possibly applied first to the wind that brought Norsemen, afterwards to the coming of Southrons.

Is fuar leaba gun choimhleapach.—*Cold is the bed without bedfellow.*

Is gann a' ghaoth nach seòladh tu.—*Light would the breeze be that you couldn't sail in.*

> *Al.*—Is fann a ghaoth ris nach &c.
> Applied to trimmers and time-servers.

Is geal an airidh air an aran sgalagan a' chliathaidh.—*Well worthy of the bread are the farm-servants of the harrow.*

Is geal an cunnradh a thig fad' às.—*Fair is the bargain that comes from afar.*

> Far sought and dear bought's guid for ladies.—*Scot.*

Is geal gach nodha, gu ruig snodhach an fheàrna.—*Everything new is white, even to the sap of the alder.*

> See 'Is odhar'.

Is geal-làmhach bean iasgair, 's is geal-fhiaclach bean sealgair.—*The fisher's wife has white hands, the hunter's wife white teeth.*

> This is a Hebridean saying. The meaning is ambiguous.

Is geàrr gach reachd ach riaghailt Dhè.—*Short-lived is all rule but the rule of God.*

Is giorraid an Gall an ceann a chur dheth.—*The Lowlander is the shorter of losing his head.*

> This, no doubt, has been said more than once, with the action suited to the word.

Is glic an duine bheir an aire dha fhèin.—*He is a wise man that takes care of himself.*

Is glice an saoghal a thuigsinn na dhìteadh.—*Better understand the world than condemn it.*

> A philosophical and Christian sentiment.

Is glic duine 'na earalas.—*Wise is he who keeps a look-out.*

Is glic nach meallar, ach cha ghlic a mheallar tric.—*He is wise who is never deceived, he is not wise who often is.*

> See 'Cha mheallar'.

Is gnìomh nàr an gurraban.—*Crouching is a shameful thing.*

> This would be rendered in Scotch 'Sitting on one's hunkers.' The practice of 'hunkering' at prayer in church, instead of standing, has been seriously denounced by some of our divines, as a shameful thing.

Is glainid am bail' an cartadh ud.—*The farm (or town) is the cleaner of that clearing out.*

> Said when any nuisance is got rid of.

Is goirid an Carghas leothasan dan eudar airgead a dhìol air a' Chàisg.—*Lent is short to them who have money to pay at Whit Sunday.*

Is gorm na cnuic tha fada uainn.—*Green are the hills that are far from us.*

> Is glas iad na cnoic i bhfad uainn.—*Ir.*
> See 'Bidh adhaircean'.
> The word *gorm* means both blue and green, and the former is really the more true description of distant hills. What the saying means, however, is that the distant is most admired, and green grass was considered the best thing that could be on a hill.

Is i 'n àilleantachd maise nam ban.—*Modesty is the beauty of women.*

> For this beautiful saying we are indebted to Armstrong (*Dict.*), who translated it 'Delicacy is the ornament of females.' The word *àilleantachd*, translated by him and MacLeod and Dewar 'personal beauty, delicacy, bashfulness, modest reserve,' is unaccountably omitted in the Highl. Soc. *Dict. Maise* means both beauty and ornament. The meaning here is not unlike that of St Peter, 'the ornament of a meek and quiet spirit'.

Is i 'n Aoine bhagarrach a nì an Satharna deurach.—*The threatening Friday makes the weeping Saturday.*

Is i bharail a mhill a' bhan-tighearna.—*It was supposing that destroyed the lady.*

> The wife of the Laird of Keppoch (1650–80) ventured to cross the river Roy when in full flood. 'Tha barail agam,' she said, 'nach bàth Ruaidh bhochd mise co-dhiù'—'*I think poor Roy won't drown me at any rate.*' But the merciless river did.
>
> There is another more amusing account given of the origin of this saying, with the variation of *dùil* for *barail*. The story is that the poor lady allowed some liberty to be taken with her, and on being taxed by her husband, replied, 'Bha mis' 'an dùil gur sibh fhèin a bh' ann'—'*I thought it was yourself.*'

Is i bhonaid bhiorach a nì 'n gille smiorail.—*The cocked bonnet makes the smart lad.*

> The truth of this saying has been practically recognised in the British Army, and even in some foreign navies, in the adoption of the Glengarry bonnet, for undress or dress uniform.

Is i chiad dubhailc dol am fiachan, 's an ath tè teannadh ris na breugan.—*The first vice is to get into debt; the next is to go telling lies.*

Is i chneadh fhèin a nì gach duine a ghearan an toiseach.—*It's his own hurt a man complains of first.*

> Is socair a chodlas duine ar chneadh dhuine eile.—*A man sleeps sound on another's wound.*—*Ir.*

Is i chuileag bhuidhe bhuachair as àirde srann.—*The yellow dung-fly makes the loudest hum.*

Is i 'n deathach a bhios a-staigh a thig a-mach.—*It is the smoke that's within that comes out.*

Is i an dias as truime as ìsle chromas a ceann.—*The heaviest ear of corn bends its head lowest.*

> Ulster saying in same words.
> The empty stalk holds its head up.—*Hungar.*

Is i 'n fhoighidinn mhath a chlaoidheas an anshocair.—*Patience overcomes trouble.*

> *Al.*—a bhristeas cridh' an anrath—*breaks the heart of distress.*
> Patience with poverty is all a poor man's remedy.—*Scot.*

Is i ghaoth tuath a ruaigeas an ceò.—*It's the north wind that drives away mist.*

Is i 'n làmh shalach a dh'fhàgas a' ghualainn glan.—*The dirty hand makes the clean shoulder.*

> *Al.*—a nì a' mhuilicheann ghlan—*makes the clean sleeve.*
> Ni buttra llaw dyn er gwneuthur da iddio ei hun—*No man's hand is dirtied with his own business.*—*Welsh.* Dirty hands make clean money.—*Eng.*

Is i mhàthair bhrisg a nì 'n nighean leisg.—*The active mother makes the lazy daughter.*

> *Al.*—Is minig a thàinig nighean leisg o mhàthair èasgaidh.
> Is olc an bhean tí iníon na caillighe éascaidh.—*Ir.* A light-heeled mother makes a heavy-heeled daughter.—*Eng.* An olight mither maks a sweir dochter.—*Scot.* Madre ardida hace hija tullida.—*Span.* Mãi aguçosa, filha perguiçosa.—*Port.*
> *Per con.* Is i nighean èasgaidh a nì mhàthair leisg.—*The active daughter makes the lazy mother.*
> *Al.*—Is minig a thàinig nighean èasgaidh o mhàthair leisg.

Is i mhuc shàmhach a dh'itheas an drabh.—*It's the silent sow that eats the draff.*

> Yr hwch a daw a fwyty'r soeg.—*Welsh.* Still swine eat all the draff.—*Eng.* De lumske Sviin æde Masken—*The cunning swine eat the mash.*—*Dan.*

Is i 'n Nollaig dhubh a dh'fhàgas an cladh mèath.—*A black Christmas makes a fat churchyard.*

> A green Yule maks a fat kirkyard.—*Scot.* En grön Juul giver en fed Kirkegaard.—*Dan.* A green winter makes a fat churchyard.—*Eng.*

Is i 'n oidhche 'n oidhche, nam b'iad na fir na fir!—*The night is the night, were the men the men!*

> A watchword in view of a foray.

Is i an taois bhog a nì am màs rag.—*The soft dough makes the stiff buttock.*

> Raw dads make fat lads.—*Scot.*

Is i bhò fhèin as luaithe a mhothaicheas da laogh.—*The cow is the first to notice her own calf.*

Is i nàmhaid duine a' chèaird nach cleachd e.—*The trade which he practises not is a man's enemy.*

> Is namhaid an cheird gan a foghlaim (*unless learned*).—*Ir.*

Is iad na h-eòin acrach as fheàrr a ghleacas.—*The hungry birds fight best.*

Is ioma bò fhada reamhar nach deachaidh riamh air theadhair.—*Many a long fat cow was never tethered.*

> Applied to women who never marry.—Macintosh.

Is ioma caochladh thig air an t-saoghal fo cheann bliadhna.—*Many changes come over the world in a year.*

Is ioma car a tha 'n saoghal a' cur dheth.—*Many a turn the world takes.*

> Gur mairg a bheir gèill
> Don t-saoghal gu lèir—
> 'S tric a chaochail e cheum gàbhaidh.—*Mary MacLeod.*

Is ioma car a thig air an oidhch' fhad' Fhoghair.—*Many a turn comes in the long Autumn night.*

> Is iomaí taod (*change*) a thig i lá Earraigh (*Spring*).—*Ir.*
> Hverb er Haust-grima—*Unstable is the Autumn night.*—*Icel.*

Is ioma mùthadh a thig air an oidhche fhada Gheamhraidh.—*Many a change comes in the long Winter night.*

> This is said to have been uttered as a warning to his host by one of the murderers of Glencoe.

Is ioma ceann a thèid an currac mun tachair sin.—*Many a head will go into a cap before that happens.*

> The cap meant is the *currac-bàis*, the death-cap.

Is ioma cron a bhios air duine bochd.—*The poor man will have many faults.*

> Is iomaí cron a chíthear ar an duine bhocht.—*Ir.*

Is ioma cron a bhios air leanabh gun mhàthair.—*The motherless child will have many faults.*

Is ioma deagh ghnìomh a dhèantadh mur b'e a dholaidh.—*Many a good deed would be done but for miscarriage.*

Is ioma dòigh a th' air cù a mharbhadh gun a thachdadh le ìm.—*There are many ways of killing a dog without choking him with butter.*

Is ioma dragh a thig air aois.—*Many troubles come on age.*

Is ioma fàth a th' aig an Earrach air a bhith fuar.—*Spring has many reasons for being cold.*

> Another version, with the merit of assonance, is ''S ioma leisgeul fada, salach th' aig an Earrach gu bhith fuar'.—*Many a weary, foul excuse Spring has &c.*
> Is anamh Earrach gan fuacht.—*Ir.*

Is ioma fear a chaidh a dholaidh le deagh chunnradh a cheannach.—*Many a one has been ruined by getting a good bargain.*

Is ioma fear a chaidh don choille airson bata dha dhruim fhèin.—*Many a man has gone to the wood for a stick to beat himself.*

Is ioma fear a chuir gàrradh mu lios nach tug a thoradh às.—*Many a man has walled a garden who never tasted of its fruit.*

Is ioma fear a ghoid caora nach deachaidh leatha air taod do Steòrnabhagh.—*Many a one has stolen a sheep that didn't lead her in to Stornoway.*

> It is hardly necessary to say that this is a Lewis proverb.

Is ioma fear a tha glè mhòr às a shlabhraidh, ged is e maide-crom a bh' aig a sheanair.—*Many a one is proud of his pot-hanger, though his grandfather had but a crook.*

> The *slabhraidh* is an iron chain suspended over the fireplace, with a hook at the end, on which pots are hung for cooking. The *maide-crom* (al. *cròcan*) was simply a wooden crook.

Is ioma leannan a th' aig an aois.—*Old age has many followers.*

> *Al.*—Is ioma nì tha leanmhainn na h-aois—*Many things follow age.* See 'Thig gach olc'.

Is ioma long cho briste thàinig gu tìr.—*Many a ship as broken has come to land.*

Is ioma mìr a thug thu don bheul a mhol thu.—*Many a morsel you have put in the mouth that praised you.*

Is ioma nì a chailleas fear na h-imrich.—*Many a thing is lost in flitting.*

> Three removes are as bad as a fire.—*Eng., Fr., Germ.*
> Cha bhíonn imirce gan chaill.—*Ir.*

Is ioma nì thig air an laogh nach do shaoil a mhàthair.—*More things befall the calf than his dam dreamed of.*

Is ioma rud a dh'fheumas an euslaint nach fheum an t-slàinte.—*Sickness needs many things which health requires not.*

Is ioma rud tha 'm bùth a' cheannaiche nach leis fhèin.—*Much is in the merchant's shop which is not his own.*

Is ioma rud a tha 'n cuan a' falach.—*The ocean hides much.*

> Wedges of gold, great anchors, heaps of pearl,
> Inestimable stones, unvalued jewels,
> All scattered in the bottom of the sea.—*Richard III*, I, 4.

> Earth shall reclaim her precious things from thee!
> Restore the dead, thou sea!—*Mrs Hemans.*

Is ioma rud a th' eadar creathall agus uaigh.—*Much lies between cradle and grave.*

Is ioma rud a tha e cur fo earball.—*Many are the things he puts under his tail.*

> Said of shifty people.

Is ioma rud a thachras ris an fhear a bhios a-muigh.—*Many things happen to him who goes abroad.*

Is ioma tè bhios cearbach aig a' bhaile thèid gu rìomhach thun na fèille.—*Many a home-dowdy goes gay to the fair.*

Is ioma tè chuir càl 'na dhiosg.—*Many a she has put kail into his dish.*

Is ioma teine beag a bheothaichear.—*Many a small fire is kindled.*

Is ioma teine mòr a chaidh às.—*Many a great fire has gone out.*

Is ioma tonn a th' eadar thu 's tìr.—*There is many a wave between thee and land.*

Is ioma tonn a thig air a' chladach mun tachair sin.—*Many a wave will come on the shore ere that happens.*

Is iomadh 'thuirt' is 'thairt' a bhios an taigh an tuathanaich.—*Many are the 'on dits' in the cottage of the farmer.*

Is iomadh urchair tha dol san fhraoch.—*Many a shot goes into the heather.*

Donald can tell many a tale of Messrs Briggs & Co.

Is ionann aithreachas-crìche 's a bhith cur sìl mu Fhèill Màrtainn.—*Death-bed repentance is sowing seed at Martinmas.*

Is ionann deoch nimhe 's balgam.—*A mouthful of poison is as good as a draught.*

Is ionann duine 'na èiginn is duine air a' chuthach.—*A needy man is even as a madman.*

See 'B'fheàrr suidhe'.

Is ionnan tosd is aideachadh.—*Silence is consent.*

Admhaíonn an tostach.—*Ir.* Silence is often an answer.—*Arab.* 'Αὐτὸ δὲ τὸ σιγᾶν ὁμολογοῦντος ἐστι σου.—*Eurip.* Qui tacet consentire videtur.—*Lat. Law Maxim.* Chi tace acconsente.—*Ital.* Quien calla otorga.—*Span.* Wer schweigt bejaht.—*Germ.* Silence gives consent.—*Eng.*

Is iongantach cho geàrr 's a tha thu, 's nach bu bhàrd a b'athair dhut.—*It's wonderful how curt you are, not being a poet's son.*

Is ionmhainn leis gach neach a choltas.—*Everyone likes his like.*

Adar o'r unlliw a hedant i'r unlle—*Birds of one colour fly together.* Pob byw wrth ei ryw yr aeth—*Every living joins its kind.*—*Welsh.*

See 'Druididh gach eun'.

Is labhar na builg fhàs.—*Noisy are the empty bags.*

Macintosh's translation is 'Loud is the bouncing of the blown-up bladder,' which is free but felicitous. The bag, to make a noise, must have been made of skin of some sort.

Is lag grèim fear an neo-shunnd.—*Weak is the grasp of the downcast.*

Is lag gualainn gun bhràthair, an àm do na fir teachd an làthair.—
Weak is shoulder without brother when men are meeting one another.

> Berr er hverr á baki, nema sér bróður eigi—*Bare is one's back, unless
> he have a brother.*—Icel. (*Saga of Burnt Njal*).
> See 'Clanna nan Gàidheal' and 'Is maol'.

Is làidir a thèid, is anfhann a thig.—*Strong they go, and weak return.*

> All that was left of them,
> Left of six hundred!—*Tennyson.*

Is làidir òglach deagh thighearna.—*A good master's servant is strong.*

> *Al.*—Is math gille deagh thighearna.
> Corn him weel, he'll work the better.—*Scot.*

Is làidir tathann coin 's a shàth 'na bhroinn.—*A dog barks loud with
his belly full.*

Is le duine an grèim a shluigeas e, ach cha leis an grèim a chagnas
e.—*What one swallows is his own, but not what he is chewing.*

> This is going further even than the ' 'Twixt cup and lip' saying.

Is leam fhèin an gleann, 's gach nì ta ann.—*The glen is mine and all
that's in it.*

> These words have given its name to one of our favourite pibrochs,
> certain to be heard at any Highland gathering. The saying seems to
> be a curious parody on the well-known verse
>
> *The earth belongs unto the Lord,*
> *And all that it contains.*

Is lèigh fear an ath-chneidh.—*A man is surgeon for his second wound.*

Is leigheas air gach tinn
Creamh is ìm a' Mhàigh;
Ol an fhochair siud
Bainne ghobhar bàn.

—Garlick with May butter
Cureth all disease;
Drink of goats' white milk
At same time with these.

The garlick here mentioned is the wild kind, commonly called 'ramsons' in England, which is found in most parts of Scotland. Its medicinal virtues are well known; but, like many other plants once valued and used by our Highland ancestors, it is now quite superseded by pills and doses prepared by licensed practitioners. May butter is always the finest, the pastures then being in their most delicate and fresh condition. Goats' milk also has always been supposed to have some special virtues. Goat-milk whey is now run after in some parts of Switzerland as a specific cure for certain affections of the chest.

Is leis a' Ghobha fuigheall èibhle;
Is leis an Lèigh salach a làmh;
Is leis a' Bhàrd a theanga fhèin;
Is leis an t-Saor a shliseag bhàn.

—To the Smith belong the embers;
To the Leech soiled hands;
To the Bard belongs his tongue;
To the Carpenter white chips.

Is leis a' mhèirleach mhath na cheileas e, ach cha leis na ghoideas e.—*What the clever thief conceals is his, but not all he steals.*

Is leis an fhitheach as moiche dh'èireas sùil a' bheathaich anns an fhèith.—*The raven that rises first will get the eye of the beast in the bog.*

See 'Am fitheach'. This version is more rhythmical. It is not so pleasant as the 'early bird' proverb, but it is more forcible.

Is leisg an làmh gun treabhadh.—*Lazy is the hand that ploughs not.*

Is leisg an nì 'Is eudar'.—*'Must' is a lazy thing.*

Muss ist ein harte Nuss—*Must is a hard nut.—Germ.*

Is leisg le leisgean dol a laighe, 's is seachd leisge leis èirigh.—*Loath is the lazy to go to bed, seven times loather to rise.*

> Leisce luí agus leisce ag éirí, sin mallacht Cholm Chille.—*Ir.* Litcher-agh goll dy lhie, litcheragh dy irree, as litcheragh dy gholl dys y cheeill Jedoonee.—*Manx.*

> Ever sick of the slothful guise,
> Loth to bed and loth to rise.—*Eng.*

Is leòr luathas na h-earba gun na coin a chur rithe.—*The roe is swift enough without setting the dogs at her.*

> See 'Cha deic'.

Is lèir don dall a bheul, ge cam a shùil.—*The blind can see his mouth, though blind his eye.*

Is lìonmhor bàirnich mnà gun òrd.—*The hammer-less woman sees many limpets.*

Is lìonmhor bean-bhleoghainn, ach is tearc banachaig.—*Milking-women are plentiful, but dairy-maids are rare.*

> The milking of cows is a small matter, compared with the making of butter and cheese and the whole management of a dairy, which requires brains as well as hands.

Is lom an cladach air an cunntar na faochagan.—*'Tis a bare beach where the whelks can be counted.*

> See 'Is cruaidh an t-Earrach'.

Is lom an leac air nach criom e.—*It's a bare stone from which he can pick nothing.*

> *Al.*—air nach buaineadh tu bàirneach—*on which you would not get a limpet.*
> In other words, he is a skinflint.

Is lom an t-sùil gun an rosg.—*Bare is the eye without eyelash.*

Is lom teanga na meidh.—*The tongue of the balance is bare.*

> Mjótt er mundangs hófit—*Narrow is the mean of the balance.*—*Icel.*

Is luaithe aon chù a' ruith na dhà dheug ga ruagadh.—*One dog fleeing is swifter than twelve pursuing.*

Is luaithe cù na chuideachd.—*A dog goes before his company*.

> *Al.*—Cuiridh cù e fhèin air thoiseach.
> Said of forward ill-mannered persons.

Is luaithe deoch na sgeul.—*Quicker is drink than story*.

> *Al.*—Is giorra deoch &c.—*Shorter is drink*.
> '*S girrey jough na skeeal*.—*Manx*. Is túisce deoch ná scéal—*Drink before story*.—*Ir*. A drink is shorter than a tale.—*Scot*.
> This saying appears to be of purely Gaelic origin, though it found its way into the Lowlands, and from thence was duly translated into English. The very word 'tale,' in the Scottish and English version, shows it to be a translation, and does not fully represent its meaning, which includes *news* and information of any kind. There is no saying more characteristic of Highland ideas of hospitality, of which one of the first laws is to offer a drink of some kind, the best in the house, whatever it be, to a visitor. Mr Hislop, with all his sagacity and knowledge of Proverbs, seems to have misunderstood this one. He calls it 'an excuse for drinking during the telling of a story'. I have heard the saying hundreds of times in the Highlands, but never once in that sense. The proverb first appeared in print, so far as I can trace, in Allan Ramsay's collection of *Scottish Proverbs*, 1736. That was long before Macintosh's collection of Gaelic ones, but it does not follow that it was not a translation from the Gaelic. It first appears, so far as I know, as an English proverb, in Mr Hazlitt's valuable compilation (1869), along with a large number not only of Scottish but even of Latin proverbs, which Mr H. thinks it proper to call "English Proverbs". Being of opinion, apparently, that no good thing can grow in Scotland, Mr H. ventures to say that 'the Scots appear to have as few proverbs of their own as they have ballads,' a statement which sufficiently shows that his knowledge is not quite equal to his pretensions.
>
> Canon Bourke says (*Ir. Gr.*, 289) this proverb is 'suggested by the ancient practice of giving story-tellers a drink before they began to rehearse their tales.'

Is luaithe feum na sìde; faodaidh a' chaora &c—*Need is quicker than weather: the sheep may die, &c*.

> See 'Faodaidh a' chaora'. A worthy Lochaber man had a flock of goats, which he went to look after one day in Spring, after a very severe Winter. He found them lying here and there dead or dying. 'Thig side mhath fhathast,' said he; 'U, thig! Ach an Diabhal mir dhibhse chì e!'—'*Good weather will come yet, Oh yes! But Devil a bit of you will see it!*'

Is luaithe gnìomh na tuarasdal.—*Work is before wages.*

> See 'Cha d' fhuair duine'.

Is luaithe ròn na rionnach, is luaithe giomach na ròn.—*Seal is swifter than mackerel, lobster swifter than seal.*

> *Al.*—Sitheadh giomaich, sitheadh rionnaich, sitheadh ròin—na tri sithean as luaithe sa chuan mhor—*Rush of lobster &c., the three swiftest in the great ocean.* The swiftness with which the lobster propels himself by his powerful tail is not generally known; as a Scottish proverb shows, 'Ye look like a rinner, quo the Deil to the lobster.'

Is luaithid a' chas a bristeadh, mar a thuirt am fear a chunnaic gas rainich a' falbh leis a' ghaoith.—*The leg that breaks is all the quicker, as the man said who saw a stalk of bracken going before the wind.*

> There is something comical in this, though trivial.

Is luath agus mall comhairle an duine.—*Swift and slow is man's counsel.*

> This way and that dividing the swift mind.—*Tennyson.*

Is luath an tòn san tèid an t-eagal.—*He is swift on whom fear comes.*

Is luath fear doimeig air fàire, latha fuar Earraich.—*Swift goes the slattern's husband over the brae, on a cold Spring day.*

> See 'Aithnichear fear doimeig'.

Is lugha na frìde màthair a' chonnsachaidh.—*The mother of dissension is smaller than a mite.*

> The mother of mischief is no bigger than a midge's wing.—*Eng.*

Is luibh-chridhe leam fhèin e.—*It is heart's-ease to myself.*

Is maireann gus an crìon.—*Lasting till it wither.*

Is mairg a bheireadh às a' chlachan thu!—*Pity him who would bring you back from the church!*

> Said of ineligible young women—a saying belonging to the time when Highland marriages were performed in church.

Is mairg a bhiodh a' biathadh nan each agus gun phrìs orra.—*Pity him who would keep up horses when there is no price for them.*

Is mairg a bhiodh a' breith dhaoine, 's na h-eich cho gann!—*Pity them who would bring forth men, when horses are so scarce !*

That is, useless men.

Is mairg a bhiodh 'na chrann air doras duin' eile.—*Pity him who is a bar on another's door.*

The *crann* is a wooden bar fastened across the door when the inmates go out—the ordinary way of closing a Highland cottage. A person who helps to keep other people's doors closed as well as his own is not to be envied.

Is mairg a chailleadh as t-Earrach e.—*Pity him who would lose him in Spring.*

Said of a good workman or horse.

Is mairg a chaillear san an-uair!—*Alas for him who is lost in the storm!*

Is mairg a chitheadh adhaircean fad' air a' chrodh ghuineideach.—*Pity him who would see long horns on the butting cow.*

Al.—Is math nach eil adhaircean fad' air na bà luinneanach.—*It's well that the frisky cows haven't long horns.*
The puttin cou should be aye a doddy (*hornless*)—*Song by Sir A. Boswell.*

Is mairg a chuireadh a làmh gun adhbhar am beul a' mhadaidh.—*Pity him who would put his hand without cause into a dog's mouth.*

Is mairg a chuireadh an toiseach na luing' thu.—*Pity him who would put you in the ship's bow.*

As pilot, or look-out man.

Is mairg a chuireadh an ùir air sùil a charaide.—*Pity him who would put the earth on the eye of his friend.*

Who would do him to death.

Is mairg a chuireadh uile dhòigh an aon duine chaidh 'n deò 'na chrè.—*Woe to him that puts all his trust in any mortal sprung from dust.*

Is mairg a chuireas a chuid far nach urrainn da a toirt às.—*Pity him who puts his means where he cannot get it out.*

Is mairg a chuireas air chùl a dhaoine fhèin.—*Pity him who turns his back on his own people.*

Is mairg a chuireas farran air fann.—*Woe to him who vexes the weak.*

Is mairg a dh'àraicheadh a laogh gu moilleach, 's an galar guineach 'na dhèidh.—*Pity him who would pamper his calf, and sharp disease following.*

> Applied to spoiled children.

Is mairg a dhèanadh bàthach dhe bhroinn.—*Pity him that makes a byre of his belly.*

Is mairg a dhèanadh subhachas ri dubhachas fir eile.—*Woe to him that would rejoice at another's grief.*

Is mairg a dh'earbadh an oidhche fhad' Fhoghair ris.—*Pity him that would trust the long Autumn night to him.*

> This was said, no doubt, of a notorious riever or thief.

Is mairg a ghuidheadh làrach lom.—*Woe to him who would wish a ruined home to any one.*

Is mairg a loisgeadh a thaigh ron chreich.—*Pity him who would burn his house before the sack.*

Is mairg a loisgeadh a thiompan dut!—*Pity him who would burn his harp for you!*

> This alludes to the story of a Hebridean harper who, having nothing else to make a fire with to warm his wife, broke his harp in pieces and burned it. His wife's heart, it seems, was colder than her body, as she ran away with another man before morning! This story forms the subject of one of Hector MacNeill's poems.
>
> The word *tiompan* (tympanum) is used in the Scottish and Irish Gaelic Bible as the translation of timbrel, but the dictionaries give it as a term for 'any musical instrument'.

Is mairg a nì den olc na dh'fhaodas e.—*Woe to him that does as much ill as he can.*

Is mairg a nì droch chleachdadh.—*Woe to him who makes a bad habit.*

Is mairg a nì tarcuis air a bhiadh.—*Pity him that despises his food.*

Is mairg a rachadh air a bhannaig, is a theann-shàth aige fhèin.— *'Twere pitiful to go begging bannocks, with plenty of one's own.*

> The bannock here referred to is the *Bannag Challainn* or New Year cake, called in Brittany *Calanna* or *Calannat*, in Wales *Calenig*, given as a New Year gift to those who came on New Year's night, chanting certain rhymes. The Highland and Breton customs in this matter are very similar.

Is mairg as màthair do mhicean maoth an uair as e Diardaoin a' Bhealltainn.—*Alas for tender infant's mother when Beltane falls on Thursday.*

> This is one of the superstitious fancies of which no explanation can be given.

Is mairg a shìneadh làmh na h-airce do chridhe na circe.—*Pity him that stretches the needy hand to the hen-hearted.*

Is mairg a thachair dhan tìr thalmhanta far nach snìomh cailbh' cuigeal.—*Pity the one who comes to the land where a partition won't spin a distaff.*

> This absurd saying was uttered by a half-witted young woman who had a good and too kind mother. The young woman was fond of going out *air chèilidh*, to make long calls, and she would leave her distaff with its wool on its resting against the partition-wall, that divided the 'but' and 'ben'. Her worthy mother would take it herself, spin the wool and leave the distaff where her daughter left it; and the foolish creature believed that the spinning was done for her by some supernatural means. At length her mother died, and the poor girl went for some time to friends at a distance, where she tried the old trick with her distaff and, to her disappointment, found it on her return just as she left it. Then she made the above remarkable observation. It is applied to lazy or silly people who expect to have their work done for them.

Is mairg a thèid don tràigh an uair a tha h-eòin fhèin ga trèigsinn.— *Pity him who goes to the shore when its own birds are forsaking it.*

> Who goes in search of shellfish.
> *Al.*—Is mairg a thadhladh a' chreag 's a h-eòin fhèin ga fàgail—*Pity him who visits the rock which its own birds are leaving.*

Is mairg a thrèigeadh a chaomh-charaid.—*Woe to him that would forsake his dear friend.*

Is mairg a thrèigeadh a leannan buan airson fear-fuadain na h-aon oidhche.—*Woe to her who would forsake her constant love for the stranger of one night.*

Is mairg a thrèigeadh an tuath 's nach buannaicheadh an tighearnas.—*Woe to him who would forsake the tenantry without winning the laird.*

Is mairg aig am bi iad; 's mairg aig nach bi iad.—*Pity those who have them; pity those who haven't them.*

> *Al.*—Is truagh aig am beil iad; 's truaighe aig nach eil iad—*Pity those who have them; pity more those who haven't.*
> This refers to children, and reminds of the advice about marriage, 'You'll repent if you marry, and you'll repent if you don't!' The Lowland Scottish saying, though kindly, is rather too frugal—
>
> > Waly, waly! bairns are bonnie;
> > Ane's eneuch, and twa's ower mony.
>
> Is mairg aig am bi 'n tighearna fann;
> Is mairg aig am bi clann gun rath;
> Is mairg aig am bi 'm bothan gann;
> Ach 's miosa bhith gun olc no mhath.
>
> > —*'Tis ill to have a pithless lord;*
> > *To have children without luck;*
> > *Ill to dwell in bothy poor;*
> > *But worst is neither ill nor good.*
>
> The Irish version of this (Bourke's *Ir. Gramm.*, 288) is almost identical, the only difference being in the last words of the first line, where, strange to say, the Scottish Celt is more outspoken about lairds—
>
> > Is mairg a mbíonn a chairde gann;
> > Is mairg a mbíonn 'chlann gun raith;
> > Is mairg a mbíonn bothán gann;
> > Is mairg a bhíos gan olc no maith.

Is mairg air an tig na dh'fhuilingeas.—*Pity him on whom comes all that he can suffer.*

Is mairg air nach bi eagal na brèige.—*Woe to him that fears not to lie.*

Is mairg dom beul-iochd sùil a' choimhich.—*Pity him who is an object of pity to the stranger.*

Is mairg don cuid cuid duin' eile.—*Pity him whose goods belong to another man.*

> *Al.*—Is mairg dom faodail &c. The meaning is that it is ill for him who has nothing but what he picks up of another man's property.

Is mairg don dual am poll itheadh.—*Pity him whose birthright is to eat dirt.*

> This is a forcible way of expressing the disadvantage of being born of bad blood.

Is mairg don dùthchas droch ghalar.—*Sad is the inheritance of a bad disease.*

Is mairg don sguaban-stòthaidh bò mhaol odhar MhicGhill-Eòinidh.—*Pity him whose resource is MacGillony's hornless dun cow.*

> Macintosh says that MacGillony was a famous hunter in the Grampians, and that several vestiges of his temporary huts are still to be seen (1785) in the mountains of Atholl. His dun cow was the wild mountain doe. The text of this proverb in Macintosh is puzzling and unintelligible. 'Is mairg g'a 'n scuab bun staghail bo mhaol odhar Mhicalonabhaidh,' translated 'Woe to him whose main support is the white cow of Macgilony'. The word *staghail* is unknown, and the assonance required a word in which 'o' is the first vowel, which *stòthaidh* supplies. *Stòthadh* means the cutting of corn short, as would be done for a hasty supply. The MacGillonies belonged to the Clan Cameron, but originally, as the name implies, were allied to the MacLeans. See Gregory's *Hist. of the W. Islands*, p. 77.

Is mairg 'g am bi càirdean fann.—*Pity him who has weak friends.*

Is mairg 'g am bi comhaltas gann, is clann gun rath.—*Pity him who has few foster-friends, and luckless children.*

Is mairg nach beathaich a thruaghan.—*Woe to him who won't maintain his own poor creature.*

> This good old sentiment sometimes receives sad illustration in our Courts, in Poor Law and Filiation cases.

Is mall a mharcaicheas am fear a bheachdaicheas.—*He rides slowly who observes.*

Is mall adhart na leisge.—*Slow is the progress of the lazy.*

Is mall ceum nan dall.—*Slow is the step of the blind.*

Is maol guala gun bhràthair; is lom an làrach gun phiuthair.—*Bare is shoulder without brother; bare is home without sister.*

  See 'Is lom'.

Is marbh fear na h-eisimeileachd.—*Dead is the dependant.*

Is math a' bhean-taighe bheir a-nuas an rud nach eil shuas.—*She's a clever housewife that can bring down what's not up.*

  Al.—à bràigh an taighe rud nach bi ann—*from the inner room what's not there.*

Is math a bhiodh na cait gus an tugadh na luchain na cluasan dhiubh.—*The cats would do well till the mice would take their ears off.*

  This saying must have been invented by a man of the world.

Is math a' chobhair e, ach 's bochd an sabhal e.—*It's a good assistance, but a bad barn.*

  Said of such occupations as fishing, hunting &c.

Is math a' chùirt sam faighear rud ri iarraidh.—*It's a good court where a thing can be got for the asking.*

Is math a dh'fhimireadh an dàn a dheanamh, 's a liuthad fear-millidh a th' aige.—*The poem would need to be well made, since it has so many spoilers.*

  Bad reciters and carping critics.

Is math a dh'fhòghnas fir odhar do mhnathan riabhach.—*Sallow lads suit swarthy lasses.*

  Fóiridh fear odhar do bhean riabhach.—*Ir.*

Is math a ghabh e tomhas mo choise.—*Well did he take the measure of my foot.*

  I have got the length of his foot.—*Eng.*

Is math am margadh a riaraicheas an ceannaiche.—*It's a good market that satisfies the merchant.*

Is math am bathar a chòrdas ris a' cheannaiche.—*The goods are good that please the merchant.*

Is math a' mhàthair-chèile am fòid.—*The sod is a good mother-in-law.*

> A green turf is a guid guid-mither.—*Scot.* Die beste Schwieger, auf der die Gänse weiden—*The best mother-in-law, on whom the geese pasture.*—*Germ.*

Is math am modh a bhith sàmhach.—*It's good manners to be silent.*

Is math am baile sam faighear biadh ri iarraidh.—*It's a good town (or farm) where food can be got for the asking.*

Is math am buachaill an oidhche; bheir i dhachaigh gach beathach is duine.—*Night is a good herdman; she brings all creatures home.*

> *Al.*—gleidhidh i crodh is caoraich is cearcan—*she keeps cattle and sheep and hens.* The e'ening brings aa hame.—*Scot.*

> This is a pretty and poetical saying; the Scottish version has perhaps a deeper meaning.

Is math an cearcall-màis deagh bhean-taighe.—*A good housewife is a good under-hoop.*

> The lowest hoop on a cask is the most important of any. So long as it holds, the vessel will hold something.

Is math an cluich a lìonas a' bhrù.—*It's good sport that fills the belly.*

> *Al.*—an fhealla-dhà—an spùirt.

Is math an còcair' an t-acras.—*Hunger is a good cook.*

> Maith an t-annlan an t-ocras.—*Ir.* Fames est optimus coquns.—*Lat.* Optimum cibi condimentum fames, sitis, potus.—*Cic.* Buon appetito non vuol salsa.—*It.* Il n'y a sauce que d' appétit—*Fr.* Hunger ist der beste Koch.—*Germ.* Hunger er det bedste Suul.—*Dan.* Honger is de beste saus.—*Dutch.* Hunger is the best sauce.—*Eng.* Hunger's guid kitchen.—*Scot.*

> Alexander Stewart, Earl of Mar, son of Robert III, after being defeated at Inverlochy (1431) by Donald Balloch, suffered great hardships, wandering through Lochaber. One day in Glen Roy he met a poor woman, and asked her for some food. 'I have nothing,' she said, 'but a handful of barley meal, to which you are welcome.' The Earl took it thankfully, and sitting down by the side of a burn, Allt Acha na Beithich, took off one of his shoes, and mixed the meal in it with water from the stream. Thereupon he is said to have made this verse:

> Is math an còcair' an t-acras,
> 'S mairg a nì tarcuis air biadh;
> Fuarag eòrn' an sàil mo bhròige—
> Biadh a b'fheàrr a fhuair mi riamh.

> *—Hunger is a cook right good,*
> *Woe to him who sneers at food;*
> *Barley crowdie in my shoe—*
> *The sweetest food I ever knew.*

Is math an ealag a' chlach gus an ruigear i.—*The stone is a good chopping-block till it's reached.*

Is math an fhiacail a bhith ron teanga.—*It is well that the teeth are before the tongue.*

> Da daint rhag tafod—*Good are teeth before tongue.*—*Welsh.* The mouth is the tongue's prison.—*Arab.*

Is math an gleus toil.—*Will is a good putter-in-trim.*

> See 'Far am bi toil'.

Is math an latha nì am madadh-ruadh searmon.—*It's a fine day when the fox turns preacher.*

> Quando la volpe predica, gaurdatevi, galline!—*Ital.*
> See *Reynard the Fox.*

Is math an naidheachd a bhith gun naidheachd.—*No news is good news.*

Is math an rud a thig ri mhithich.—*It's a good thing that comes in season.*

Is math an rud air an tig piseach.—*It's a good thing which luck follows.*

Is math an saoghal seo ma mhaireas e.—*This is a good life if it would last.*

> Is maith an saoghal é, má mhaireann sé i bhfad.—*Ir.* It's a guid eneuch warld, if it haud.—*Scot.*

Is math an sgàthan sùil caraide.—*A friend's eye is a good looking-glass.*

> Is maith an scathán sùil charad.—*Ir.* Drŷch i bawb ei gymmydog—
> One's neighbour is his mirror.—*Welsh.* The best mirror is an old
> friend.—*Eng.* The image of friendship is truth.—*Arab.* No ay mejor
> espejo que el amigo viejo.—*Span.*

Is math an t-aighear a bhith glic.—*To be wise is good cheer.*

> Understanding is a wellspring of life.—*Prov.* xvi, 22.

Is math an t-aoigh a thig sonas ri linn.—*He is a good guest who brings good luck.*

> *Al.*—Is olc an t-aoigh as misd' an taigh.

Is math an t-each a thoilicheas am marcaiche.—*He's a good horse that pleases his rider.*

> Is maith an t-each a shásaíos gach marcach.—*Ir.*

Is math an t-each nach tuislich ceum.—*He's a good horse that never stumbles.*

> Is maith an gearrán nach mbainneann tuisleadh uair éigin dó.—*Ir.*
> See 'Tuislichidh'.

Is math an tom air am bi sealbh.—*It's a good hillock on which cattle are.*

Is math an tràth a dh'fhòghnas da fhèin.—*It's a good season (or meal) that suffices for its time.*

> *Al.*—Is math an là a bheir e fhèin às.

Is math an t-uaireadair a' bhrù, an t-sùil 's an coileach.—*The belly, the eye and the cock are good timepieces.*

> Men of old could guess the time of day very nearly by the sun. Their
> sensations informed them when it was breakfast or supper-time. The
> crowing of the cock was their morning call.

Is math an urra fear mulain.—*A man with some corn is a good security.*

Is math bean an deagh fhir, ach is fheàrr dha a faotainn math.—*The good man's wife is good, but it is best if he find her good.*

> That is, *find* her good, instead of *making* her good.

Is math Breunan an dèidh na cloinne sèimh.—*The bad boy is good when the gentle ones go.*

> When the good children die, the worst child becomes more valued.

Is math cobhair nam bioran le chèile.—*The union of sticks is helpful.*

> This is the old Roman parable.

Is math conach.—*Wealth is good.*

> *Conach* is a word obsolete in our vernacular.

Is math cruinneachadh na pille farsaing.—*Good is the gathering of the wide winnowing-cloth.*

Is math cuid na ciad oidhche ron ath-oidhch'.—*The first night's stock is good for the second night.*

> It is good to have so much that the first night's provisions may be spared for next night.

Is math dhuts' an t-sùil nach fhaca.—*Good for you the eye that saw it not.*

> A curious form of expression, meaning 'It's well for you that So-and-so didn't see you'.

Is math do chù nan gobhar nach robh cù nan caorach ann.—*Good for the goat-dog that the sheep-dog was not there.*

> The sheep-dog would be the superior officer.

Is math esan a bhith ann gus a' chas a chur air.—*Good that he was there to get the foot set on him.*

> *Al.*—gus a' choire chur air—*to get the blame.*

Is math far an saoilear.—*It's well to be well thought of.*

> *Lit.*—'It's well where it's supposed.' The meaning is that there is an advantage in getting credit, however erroneously, for more than is possessed.

Is math gach fliuch air a' phathadh.—*Whatever is wet is good for thirst.*

> *Al.*—Lag no làidir, 's math gach fliuch &c.—*Weak or strong, what's wet &c.*

Is math gach meas air a bhlas fhèin.—*Every fruit is good of its own taste.*

Is math gach urchair tron chlàr.—*Every shot is good that hits the mark.*
> *Lit.*—'goes through the board.'

Is math gum foghain ìm odhar do chabhraich.—*Dun butter does for sowens.*
> Like to like.

Is math gum foghain nighean gobha do dh'ogha ceàird.—*A blacksmith's daughter is a good match for a tinker's grandson.*

Is math lìonmhorachd nan làmh, ach mun mhèis seo.—*The more hands the better, except round this dish.*
> *Al.*—Is math na fir ach mun mhèis.
> Said to have been a warning given by an attendant who brought in a poisoned dish.

Is math ma mhaireas.—*Well if it last.*

Is math na fir, ach na chì iad.—*The men are good, but for what they see.*
> This is a feminine saying, meaning that men who stick at home and pry too much into domestic matters are out of place.

Is math na h-eòin far an gintear iad.—*The birds are good in their native place.*
> A very Highland sentiment, deeply felt even in St Kilda.

Is math na seirbheisich, 's olc na maighistirean, Teine, Gaoth is Uisge.—*Fire, Wind and Water are good servants, but bad masters.*
> Fire and water are good servants &c.—*Eng., Scot., Germ., Dan.*

Is math nach eil iuchraichean an domhain fo chrios na h-aon mhnatha.—*It's well that all the keys of the world are not under one wife's girdle.*
> *Al.*—air do chrios—*on your girdle.* See 'Chan eil gach'.

Is meanmnach gach moch-thràthach.—*Lively is the early riser.*

Is miann le triubhas a bhith measg aodaich, is miann leam fhèin a bhith measg mo dhaoine.—*Trews like to be among clothes; I like to be among my people.*

Is miann leis a' chlèireach mias mhèith bhith aig an t-sagart.—*A fat dish to the priest is the clerk's wish.*

> Is mian leis an chléireach mias mhéith chomh maith leis an t-sagart (*as well as the priest*).—*Ir.*

Is miannaiche aon ghille breac-luirgneach na seachd mnathan torrach.—*One spotty-legged lad has more appetite than seven pregnant women.*

Is milis corrag theth—mas milis, cha mhath.—*Sweet is a hot finger, but not to be desired.*

Is mìne min na gràn, is mìne mnài na fir.—*Meal is finer than grain, women are finer than men.*

> Very Celtic, and polite to women.

Is minig a bha beul luath aig droch charaide.—*A bad friend has often had a glib tongue.*

Is minig a bha breith luath lonach.—*A quick judgment is often wordy.*

Is minig a bha claidheamh math an droch thruaill.—*Good sword has often been in poor scabbard.*

Is minig a bha craiceann an laoigh air an fhèill ro chraiceann a mhàthar.—*The calf's skin often goes to market before his mother's.*

> Aussi tôt meurt veau que vache.—*Fr.* Daar komer zo wel kalver huiden als ossen huiden te markt.—*Dutch.*
>
> *Al.*—Is tric a bha craiceann an uain air a' chlèith cho luath ri craiceann na seana chaora—*The skin of the lamb has often been hung up as soon as that of the old sheep.*
>
> As soon comes the lamb's skin to the market as the auld tup's.—*Scot.* So *Eng., Germ., Port.*

Is minig a bha dreach brèagh air maide mosgain.—*A rotten stick is often nice to look at.*

Is minig a bha droch bhròg air mnaoi greusaiche.—*Often has a shoemaker's wife had bad shoes.*

Is minig a bha droch laogh aig deagh mhart.—*Many a good cow hath an evil calf.*—*Eng.*

'Ανδρων ἡρώων τέκνα πήματα..—*Gr.* Heroum filii noxii.—*Lat.*

Is minig a bha laogh math aig boin sgàirdich.—*A skittering cow has often had a good calf.*

Is minig a bha ùth mhòr aig boin chaoil-chasaich.—*The slender-legged cow has oftenest a large udder.*

Al.—a bha boinne mhath—*a good drop.*

Is minig a thainig comhairle ghlic à ceann amadain.—*Often has wise counsel come from a fool's head.*

Al.—à beul an amadain—*the fool's mouth.*
Al.—'S minig a bha comhairle rìgh an ceann amadain.
Is minic a fuaireas comhairle ghlic ó amadán.—*Ir.*

Is minig a bha leigeadh fad' aig fear gun chù, is urchair aig fear gun ghunna.—*A man without a dog or gun has often got a chance at game.*

Is minig a bha 'Math-an-airidh' gun nì, agus nì aig 'Beag-an-toirt'.—*'Well-deserved' has often been empty-handed, and 'Little matter' well off.*

Is minig a bha muir mhòr an caolas cumhang.—*A great sea has often run in a narrow strait.*

Is minig a bha 'n Donas dàicheil.—*The Devil is often attractive.*

The Prince of Darkness is a gentleman.—*K. Lear*, III, 4.

Is minig a bha rath air leirist.—*A silly has often been lucky.*

Al.—air mall-thriallair—*a slow traveller.*

Is minig a bha sùil-chruthaich air lèana bhòidheach.—*A fair meadow has often had a quagmire.*

Is minig a chaidh am màs à soitheach dìonach.—*The bottom has often gone out of a tight vessel.*

Is minig a chaill bodach làir agus a rinn e treabhadh.—*An old man has often lost a mare and done his ploughing.*

Is minig a dh'èirich muir gharbh à plumanaich.—*Rough sea has often followed noise of surge.*

> A muffled roar from the sea at night in calm weather often precedes a storm. The word *plumanaich* is also applied to a chopping sea, which, when seen in a calm, is a sure sign of coming storm.

Is minig a dh'fhàg làmhan luath cluasan goirid.—*Quick hands have often made short ears.*

> Alluding to the old punishment of cropping the ears.

Is minig a dhiomoil an ceannaiche 'n rud bu mhath leis 'na mhàil-eid.—*The merchant has often dispraised what he would like to have in his pack.*

> *Al.*—Is minig a chàin am marsant' am bathar &c.
> It is naught, it is naught, saith the buyer.—*Prov.* xx, 14.
> The 'merchant' generally referred to in these proverbs was simply a packman or pedlar, an important person in the Highlands before shops were common; of whom Wordsworth chose one as the hero of *The Excursion.*

Is minig a fhuair fear na h-eadraiginn buille.—*The interposer has often got a blow.*

> See 'Bidh dòrn'.

Is minig a bha an fhìrinn searbh ri h-innse.—*Truth is often harsh to tell.*

> *Al.*—Tha 'n fhìrinn fhèin searbh air uairean.

Is minig a thàinig boganach à blàthaich.—*Buttermilk has often made a bumpkin.*

Is minig a thàinig air laogh mear galair nach do shaoil a mhàthair.—*A merry calf has often taken a disease which his dam never dreamed of.*

Is minig a thàinig fìor à fanaid.—*Mockery has often turned to earnest.*

> See 'Is tric a chaidh'.

Is minig a thàinig gnothach na baintighearna gu bothan cailleach nan cearc.—*The lady's affairs have often found their way to the hen-wife's bothy.*

> See 'Faodaidh gnothach'.

Is minig a thàinig meathadh o mhathadh.—*Forgiveness has often caused degeneracy.*

Is minig a thàinig tart air deagh mhuileann.—*A good mill has often wanted water.*

Is minig a thog fear-rogha diù.—*A chooser has often taken the worse.*

Is minig a thugadh seachad air an t-sràic an rud a fhuaradh air bhleid.—*What was got with importunity has often been given away with swagger.*

> Rhoi'r dorth a gofyn y dafell—*To give the loaf and ask for the slice.—Welsh.*

Is mios' amaideachd na h-aois na amaideachd na h-òige.—*The folly of age is worse than the folly of youth.*

> See 'Chan eil amadan'.

Is mios' an fhead na 'n eubh.—*The whistle is worse than the cry.*

> The whistle of a thief or cateran.

Is mios' an t-eagal na 'n cogadh.—*Fear is worse than fighting.*

> A wise and manly sentiment.

Is mios' an t-sochair na mhèirle.—*Shyness is worse than theft.*

> More loss is caused by the one than by the other.

Is miosa na 'n uireasbhaidh tuille 's a' chòir.—*Too much is worse than want.*

> *Per con.* 'S mios' an t-uireasbhaidh na tuille 's a' chòir.—*Want is worse than too much.*
> There is some truth in both these, combined in the prayer of Agur, 'Give me neither poverty nor riches.'

Is mios' an t-urras na 'n t-earras.—*The security is worse than the principal.*

Is miosa droch earbsa na bhith gun earbs' idir.—*Ill-placed trust is worse than none.*

Is miosa 'm fear a chleitheas am mèirleach na 'm mèirleach fhèin.— *He that cloaks the thief is worse than he.*

Is miosa 'm fear beag na Frangach.—*The wee man is worse than a Frenchman.*

> This is said to have been spoken of a little Strathspey man called John MacAndrew, a noted bowman, who shot down his enemies one after another as they appeared at the door of his house, which they had invaded. See *Cuairtear*, 1842, p. 131.

Is miosa seo na 'n t-alum!—*This is worse than the alum!*

> A Highland minister once ordered some 'sugar-candy' from Glasgow by a little 'merchant,' one of his parishioners. When the sugar was tried, it turned out to be alum. The minister was naturally displeased, and to soothe him, the shopkeeper, on the advice of a knowing brother of the minister, determined to bring a peace-offering to the manse, in the shape of a small 'pig' of Ferintosh. Not feeling sure of his reception, however, he hid the jar outside, while he went in to make his call. The worthy minister was easily appeased, and Donald hastened out for the great reconciler, and proceeded at once to fill out a glass. To his astonishment, the minister had no sooner tasted than he spat it out again, exclaiming, with a strong interjection, ' 'S miosa seo na 'n t-alum!' The parson's wicked brother had emptied the jar and filled it with salt water.

Is misde na bochdan a bhith lìonmhor.—*The poor are the worse of being numerous.*

Is mis' a bha thall 's a chunnaic e, 's a thàinig a-nall 's a dh'innis e.—*'Tis I that was over and saw it, and came back and told it.*

Is mithich a bhith bogadh nan gad.—*It's time to be steeping the withes.*

> This native Gaelic saying, meaning 'It's time to be going,' belongs to the time when withes of birch or osier were used for halters and all the fastenings of horse harness. (See note to 'An gad'.) These withes would become stiff and brittle if laid by for some time, and would therefore be steeped for a while before taking to horse. There is an Ulster saying in the same words.

Is mò am fuaim na bhuil.—*The noise is greater than the effect.*

> Nid cymmaint Bleddyn a'i drwst—*Bleddyn is not so great as his noise.*—*Welsh.* Plus sonat quam valet.—*Seneca.*
> See 'Fuaim mòr'.

Is mò an-t-sùil na bhrù.—*The eye is bigger than the belly.*

> *Al.*—Is mò làn do shùla na làn do bhroinn—*The fill of your eye is more &c.*
>
> His eye is bigger than his belly.—*Eng.* Die Augen sind weiter denn der Bauch.—*Germ.* De oogen zijn groter dan de buik.—*Dutch.* The eye is not satisfied with seeing.—*Eccl.* 1,8. The dust alone can fill man's eye.—*Arab.* He'll hae eneuch some day when his mouth's fu o mools.—*Scot.*

Is mò do mholl na do shìol.—*Your chaff is more than your grain.*

Is moch a dh'èireas am fear a bheir an car às.—*He will rise early that outwits him.*

Is moch a dh'èireas am fear nach laigh.—*He rises early who goes not to bed.*

Is mòid a' mhuir Lòchaidh.—*The sea is the bigger of Lochy.*

> The Lochy, a fine river flowing out of a lake of the same name, falls into the sea near the base of Ben Nevis.

Is mòid i siud, mun duirt an dreathan-donn nuair a rinn e dhileag sa mhuir mhòir.—*It's the bigger of that, as the wren said when he added a drop to the sea.*

> Scottish proverb to same effect.

Is mòid rud a roinn.—*A thing is the bigger of being shared.*

> A generous sentiment.

Is mòr a dh'fhaodar a dhèanamh fo làimh deagh dhuine.—*Much may be done under a good man's hand.*

Is mòr a dh'fhuilingeas cridhe glan mum brist e.—*A clean heart will suffer much ere it break.*

> Meikle maun a guid heart thole.—*Scot.* Were na my heart licht I wad dee.—*Burns.*

Is mòr am beathach nach tiochd a-muigh.—*It's a big beast that there isn't room for outside.*

> *Al.*—Is mòr am fear—*He's a big man.*
> The irony of this is delicate. It is applied to persons so mighty that no house or hall seems big enough for them.

Is mòr am facal nach tiochd sa bheul.—*It's a big word that the mouth can't hold.*

> There is a wise irony in this also. For the word *tiochd* or *teachd* the word *toill* is used in Skye.

Is mòr a rinn thu de dheireadh air cho beag de bhrod.—*You made much refuse to so little grain.*

> See 'Is mò do mholl'.

Is mòr a thèid thar ceann slàn.—*A sound head will come through much.*

Is mòr facal ga lughadh.—*A word is big when it is lessened.*

> Qui s' excuse s' accuse.—*Fr.*

> Is mòr fiach na foighidinn;
> Is lughaid fearg fuireach;
> Chan e 'n t-ànradh a th' ann
> Ach cion foighidinn gu fuireach.

> —*Of great price is patience;*
> *Wrath declines with waiting;*
> *Not the evil is so great*
> *As impatience to wait.*

Is mòr thugam, 's is beag agam.—*Great appearance and little value.*

Is mòr le doimeig a cuid abhrais; 's chan e mhòid ach a dhorrad.—*The slattern's spinning-stuff looks great to her; not the bulk, but the bother.*

> Defnyddfawr pob anghelfydd.—*Unskilful requires much stuff.*—*Welsh.*

Is mòr òirleach bhàrr sròin duine.—*An inch off a man's nose is a great deal.*

> Possibly this Celtic saying may have been known to M. About when he composed his 'Nez d'un avocat'.

Is mòr stàth na h-Airde do Mhac Shimidh.—*Great is the profit of the Aird to Lovat.*

 The Aird is a farm belonging to the Lovat family.

Is mòr toirm cuilce gun dol troimhpe.—*The storm of reeds is loud till you go through them.*

 More formidable in sound than in reality.

Is nì air leth cè dòirte.—*Spilt cream is a thing by itself.*

 An irremediable loss.

Is niarachd don gealladh tu chroich.—*Lucky for him to whom you would promise the gallows.*

 Said to people whose word does not go for much.

Is obair-latha duin' a thìodhlaiceadh.—*To bury a man is a day's work.*

 So it used to be, and not in the Highlands only. Lord Brougham's account of the funeral of his grandmother gives an amusing illustration of this.

Is obair-latha tòiseachadh.—*Beginning is a day's work.*

 Deuparth gwaith ei ddechreu—*Two parts of a work is beginning.*—*Welsh*. See 'Is dà thrian'.

Is odhar gach sean, 's is geal gach nodha, gu ruig snodhach an fheàrna.—*Every old thing is dun, every new thing white, even to the sap of the alder.*

 The alder when stripped of its bark is very white, but very soon the colour changes to reddish brown and dun.

Is òg an Nollaig a' chiad oidhche.—*Christmas is young the first night.*

Is olc a bhith slaodadh cait air earball.—*It's ill to drag a cat by the tail.*

Is olc a' bhò-laoigh a' chreag, oidhch' air mhòr is oidhch' air
bheag.—*The rock is a bad milch-cow—one night fertile, another night
barren.*

> *Al.*—Is corrach gob an dubhain,
> Is mairg dom bò-laoigh a' chreag—
> Oidhch' air bheagan 's oidhch' air mhòran,
> 'S oidhche gun a' mhòr no bheag.
>
> *—Uncertain is the point of the hook,*
> *Ill for him whose milch-cow is the rock—*
> *One night little, another plenty,*
> *Some nights neither much nor little.*

Is olc a' chliath fheàrna nach toir bliadhna san ursainn.—*It's a poor
alder hurdle that won't hang for a year to the post.*

> *Al.*—Is olc an cabar feàrna nach dean ràidhl' air taigh—*It's a bad stick
> of alder that won't make a rafter.*
> Alder is one of the poorest kinds of timber.

Is olc a' chreag a thrèigeas a h-eòin fhèin.—*It's a bad rock which its
own birds forsake.*

Is olc a fhreagradh tu 'n ìochdar Thròndairnis.—*You wouldn't suit
well in the lower end of Trotternish.*

> Trotternish (*Trodda-ness*) is a general name applied to the northern
> part of Skye. The climate and soil there are somewhat colder than in
> the rest of the island, so that a lazy or delicate person would not do
> well there.

Is olc a' ghaoth leis nach seòl cuideigin.—*It's an ill wind with which
no one can sail.*

> *Al.*—nach sèid ann an seòl fireigin—*that doesn't blow in some man's
> sail.*
> It is an ill wind that blows no man to good.—*Eng.* It's an ill wund that
> blaws naebody guid.—*Scot.*

Is olc am bathar nach mol an ceannaiche.—*It is bad ware which the
merchant praises not.*

Is olc am mèirleach a dh'itheas 's a dh'innseas.—*He's a sorry thief
who eats and tells.*

Is olc am muileann a chuireas a chuid a dh'aon taobh.—*It's a bad mill that sends all its meal one way*

Is olc an sgrìoban nach lìon an sgròban.—*It's poor scraping that won't fill the crop.*

Is olc an t-òlach nach gabh 's nach toir.—*He's a bad fellow that won't take or give.*

Is olc a thig muc-saille air sòbhraichean na coille.—*The fat sow is ill-fed on the primroses of the wood.*

Is olc a thig saor sàr-bhuilleach, gobha crith-làmhach agus lèigh tiom-chridheach.—*A heavy-handed joiner, a trembling-handed smith and a soft-hearted leech do not suit.*

> A good surgeon must have an eagle's eye, a lady's hand and a lion's heart.—*Eng.*
> The use of *thig*—'fit'—without a preposition is peculiar and not according to present usage.

Is olc am bodach nach fheàirrde cailleach eadar i 's an doras.—*He's a wretched old man that an old wife is not the better of having between her and the door.*

Is olc am pàisd' nach cuir sop air dòigh.—*It's a bad child that can't arrange a wisp.*

Is olc an còcair' nach imlich a mheur.—*He's a poor cook that doesn't lick his finger.*

> Sá er brytinn vestr er sjalfan sik tælir—It is the worst cook that stints himself.—*Icel.*

Is olc an comann dhem bi dithis diombach.—*It's bad company with which two are displeased.*

> *Al.*—an còmhradh—*the colloquy;* an cluich—*the game;* an gnothach—*the business.*

Is olc an dithis nach fhoghain do dh'aon duine.—*It's a poor pair that are no match for one.*

Is olc an fheòil nach gabh ri salann; is miosa a' cholainn nach gabh guth.—*It's bad meat that won't take salt; worse is the body that won't take warning.*

Is olc an goile nach teòdh a chuid.—*It's a bad stomach that its food won't warm.*

Is olc an nì a bhith falamh.—*It's a bad thing to have nothing.*

> Proverbs of this kind must have suggested 'Proverbial Philosophy'.

Is olc an obair-latha nach toir duine gu cala mu oidhche.—*It'a a bad day's work that won't bring a man to port for the night.*

Is olc an ràmh nach iomair rubha.—*It's a bad oar that won't row round a point.*

Is olc an t-ana-charaid an rìgh.—*The king is a bad un-friend.*

Is olc an t-aoigh as misd' an taigh.—*He is a bad guest whom the house is the worse of.*

> A kindly and hospitable sentiment.

Is olc an t-each nach fhiach a chrudhadh.—*He's a bad horse that's not worth shoeing.*

Is olc an t-each nach giùlain fhasair.—*It's a poor horse that can't carry his harness.*

> He's a weak baist that downa bear the saiddle.—*Scot.*
> *Al.*—Is don' an t-each nach giùlain a shìol—*He's a wretched horse that can't carry his corn.*
> Superbo è quel cavallo che non si vuol portar la biada—*He's a proud horse that won't carry his oats.—Ital.*

Is olc an teanga as luaithe na 'n teine.—*Bad is the tongue that's swifter than fire.*

Is olc don luing an uair a dh'èigheas an stiùireadair.—*It's ill for the ship when the steersman sings out.*

> To 'sing out' is the duty of the man at the bow; if he fail in his duty, then the ship is in great danger.

Is olc cuid a' cheatharnaich ri thasgadh.—*The riever's goods are ill to keep.*

Is olc maoin gun leasachadh.—*Bad is property that gets no addition.*

> The moral is that of the Parable of the Talents.

Is prìseil a' chas air tìr.—*Precious is the foot on shore*.

> Loda il mar, e tienti alla terra.—*Ital*. Now would I give a thousand furlongs of sea for an acre of barren ground!—*The Tempest* I, 1.

Is rìgh an cam am measg nan dall.—*The blind of an eye is king among the blind*.

> In the kingdom of blind men the one-eyed is king.—*Eng*. Au pays des aveugles les borgnes sons rois.—*Fr*. Unter den Blinden ist der Einäugige König.—*Germ*. In het land der blinden is een-oog koning.—*Dutch*. En tierra de ciegos el tuerto es rey.—*Span*. The one-eyed is a beauty in the country of the blind.—*Arab*. In terra di ciechi beato chi ha un occhio.—*Ital*.

Is rìgh duine 'na thaigh fhèin.—*A man is king in his own house*.

> Halr er heima hverr—*Every one is somebody at home*.—*Icel*.

> An Englishman's house is his castle. This saying, singularly enough, is not in Mr Hazlitt's collection.

Is rìoghachd do gach duine a thoil.—*A man's will is his kingdom*.

> My mind to me a kingdom is.—Byrd's *Psalms*. Lord of himself, though not of lands.—*Wotton*.

> Mens regnum bona possidet:
> Rex est qui metuit nihil;
> Rex est qui cupit nihil;
> Hoc regnum sibi quisque dat.—*Seneca*.

Is sàmhach an obair dol a dholaidh.—*Going to ruin is silent work*.

> *Al*.—Is fàs a bhith dol a dholaidh.

Is sealgair math a mharbhas gèadh, is corr', is guilbneach.—*He is a good sportsman who kills wild goose, and heron, and curlew*.

> Three particularly wary birds.

Is sean an duine a dh'fhaodas fhortan innse.—*He is an old man that can tell his fortune*.

Is searbh a' ghlòir nach fhaodar èisdeachd; is dubh na mnathan ris nach bitear.—*Harsh is the praise that cannot be listened to; dark are the dames that none can flirt with*.

Is searbh clàrsair an aon phuirt.—*Harsh is the harper of one tune.*

> *Al.*—pìobair' an aon phuirt—*the piper &c.*
>
> Still harping on my daughter.—*Hamlet,* II, 2.

Is seasgair sàmhach a' chearc air a h-iris fhèin.—*The hen is snug and quiet on her own roost.*

Is seile air do bhrat fhèin sin.—*That is spitting on your own mantle.*

> Wie tegen wind spuwt, maakt zijn baard vuil—*Who spits against the wind fyles his beard.—Dutch.* Quien al cielo escupe, en la cara le cae—*Who spits above him will get it on his face.—Span.*

Is sgeul eile sin.—*That's another story.*

Is sleamhainn an laogh a dh'imlicheas a mhàthair.—*Smooth is the calf that his mother licks.*

Is sleamhainn leac doras an taigh-mhòir.—*Slippery is the flagstone of the mansion-house door.*

> There's a sliddery stane at the haa door.—*Scot.* Haa binks (*benches*) are sliddery.—*Do.* Is sleamhain leac doras tí móir.—*Ir.*
>
> John Morrison of Bragar is said to have illustrated this saying once in a lively manner by taking some sand out of his pocket at the door of Brahan Castle, and carefully sprinkling it on the flagstones. Being asked what he meant, he quoted the above proverb.
>
> > Is soilleir cù dubh air lèana bhàin;
> > Is soilleir cù bàn air lèana dhuibh;
> > Nam bithinn ri fiadhach nam beann,
> > B'e 'n cù riabhach mo roghainn.
>
> > —*The bright field shows the sable hound;*
> > *The white is seen on dusky ground;*
> > *Were I chasing the deer in forest free,*
> > *The brindled hound my choice should be.*

Is soilleir mìr à bonnach slàn.—*Bit from a whole cake is soon seen.*

Is soimeach fear-fearainn, is sona fear-cèairde.—*Easy lives the man of land, happy is the tradesman.*

> This is modern.

Is sona a' chailleach a thig ri linn an fhaothachaidh.—*Lucky is the old wife that comes at the turn of the disease.*

> She would get credit for the cure.

Is sona am fear a thig an ceann a chodach.—*He is lucky who comes in time for his share.*

Is sona gach cuid an comaidh; is mairg a chromadh 'na aonar.—*Happy is that which is shared; pity him who fares alone.*

> *Lit.* 'who stoops', or 'bends'. A good social sentiment.

Is stuama duine làimh ri chuid.—*A man is moderate near what's his own.*

Is suarach an càirdeas a dh'fheumas a shìor cheannach.—*It's poor friendship that must be constantly bought.*

Is suarach uisge teth a shireadh fo chloich fhuair.—*It's silly to seek hot water under a cold stone.*

> To seik het water beneith cauld ice,
> Surely it is a greit folie;
> I have asked grace at a graceless face,
> But there is nane for my men and me!
> —*Ballad of Johnie Armstrang*

Is taom-boileach an t-sealg, is farmadach an t-iasgach.—*Hunting is distracting, fishing is envious.*

Is teann leam innear an eich air an arbhar.—*I think the horse's dung too near the corn.*

> Said to aggressive or presuming people.

Is tearc each a dhiùltas a mhuing.—*Seldom will a horse refuse his mane.*

Is tearc teanga mhìn gun ghath air a cùl.—*Seldom is smooth tongue without sting behind.*

> Is annamh bhíos teanga mhilis gan gath ina bun.—*Ir.*
> Belle parole, ma guarda la borsa.—*Ital.*

Is teotha fuil na bùrn.—*Blood is hotter than water.*

> *Al.*—Is tighe—*is thicker.*
>
> Is tibhe fuil ná uisce.—*Ir.* Ta fuill ny s chee na ushtey.—*Manx.* Blood is thicker than water.—*Eng.*, *Scot.* Blut ist dicker als Wasser.—*Germ.*

> The Gaelic version is the better. The Spanish 'La sangre sin fuego hierve'—*Blood boils without fire* is similar, but not so good.

Is tiughaid' am brat a dhùbladh.—*The mantle is the thicker of being doubled.*

> Is teóide (*warmer*) don mbrat a dhúbladh.—*Ir.*
>
> Applied to the marriage of relatives. Here the Irish version is better.

Is toigh le bò mhaol bò mhaol eile.—*A hornless cow likes another without horns.*

> *Al.*—bò sgàirdeach.

Is toigh leam aran a' bhodaich, ach cha toigh leam anail a' bhodaich.—*I like the old man's bread, but not his breath.*

> Most proverbs have been composed by men; this seems to be an exception, and not a pleasant one.

Is toigh leis an fheannaig a h-isean garrach gorm.—*The crow likes her greedy blue chick.*

Is treasa dà chailleach lag na aon chailleach làidir.—*Two weak old women are stronger than one strong one.*

Is treasa deagh àrach na mèath-ghalair.—*Good nurture overcomes disease.*

Is treasa Dia na Doideag; is treasa Doideag na MacIlleathain.—*God is stronger than Doideag; Doideag is stronger than MacLean.*

> Doideag was a witch at one time much feared in the island of Mull. She was peculiarly dreaded for her power in raising storms. MacLean of Duart, the Chief of that great clan, was of course paramount in Mull. See MacLeod's *Rem. of a Highl. Parish* (2nd ed.), p. 247.

Is treasa dithis san àtha gun bhith fada bho chèile.—*Two crossing the ford are best near each other.*

Is treasa slat na cuaille.—*A rod is stronger than a club.*

> This is perhaps a hyperbolical way of saying that due chastisement is more effectual than extreme measures.

Is treasa tuath na tighearna.—*Tenantry are stronger than laird.*

> Stroshey yn Theay na yn Chiarn.—*Manx.*

> This is a remarkable saying to have originated among a race distinguished by their subordination and fidelity to their natural chiefs and lords. It belongs to a time when the rights of the clan or tenantry were real, and believed in by themselves.

Is treun fear an eòlais.—*The man that knows is powerful.*

> Knowledge is power.—*Bacon.*

Is trian suirghe samhladh.—*To be 'evened' is a third of courtship.*

> The Scotch phrase 'even,' to couple a man and woman in conversation as a likely match, is the only word that expresses here the meaning of *samhladh.*

Is tric a bha am beag treubhach.—*The little are often brave.*

Is tric a bha beag beag an toirt.—*The little is often of little account.*

Is tric a bha bean saoir gun chuigeil, 's bean greusaiche gun bhròig.— *A carpenter's wife has often wanted a distaff, and a shoemaker's wife shoes.*

Is tric a bha brèagh' air an fhèill mosach 'na thaigh fhèin.—*Fine at the fair may be mean at the fireside.*

Is tric a bha claidheamh fada an làimh gealtair'.—*A long sword has often been in a coward's hand.*

Is tric a bha dìcheall air dheireadh.—*Diligence has often been behind.*

> And luck in front.
> *Per con.* Cha bhi dìcheall air dheireadh.

Is tric a bha fortan air luid, 's a fhuair trusdar bean.—*Slatterns have often had luck, and dirty fellows got wives.*

> See 'Gheibh foighidinn'.

Is tric a bha gaoid an ubhal bòidheach.—*Often has flaw been in a fair apple.*

Is tric a bha mòr mì-sheaghail.—*The big is often stupid.*

Giants are always so represented in the old stories.

Is tric a bha 'n galar a bh' air Aodh air an fhear a bha ri thaobh.—*Hugh's neighbour has often had the same disease as he.*

This is true both physically and morally.

Is tric a bha na h-aibhnichean a' dèabhadh is na h-uillt a' ruith.—*The rivers are often dry while the brooks are running.*

Before a flood.

Is tric a bha na luingis mhòr a' crìonadh 's na h-amair-mhùin a' seòladh.—*Often have large ships been rotting, while the little pots are floating.*

Al.—Na luingis mhòr a' dol fon chuan, 's na h-amair-fhuail a' seòladh.

Is tric a bha sliochd na seilge air seachran.—*The hunting tribe has often been at fault.*

Is tric a bha slaodaire beairteach, is caonnag air duine tapaidh.—*Many a lout is wealthy, and clever man hard put-to.*

Is tric a bha sonas air beul mòr.—*Large mouth is often lucky.*

Muckle-mou'd folk has aye hap to their meat.—*Scot.*

Is tric a bha suaib-chuthaich air leanabh bodaich.—*An old man's child has often had a touch of madness.*

Is tric a bha urrainn gun nì, agus nì gun urrainn.—*The worthy has often lacked means, and means been enjoyed without merit.*

Is tric a bheothaich srad bheag teine mòr.—*A small spark has often kindled a great fire.*

Behold how great a matter a little fire kindleth!—*St James.* Parvula scintilla saepe magnum suscitavit incendium.—*Lat.* A single spark can burn the whole quarter.—*Arab.* Piccola favilla accende gran fuoco.—*Ital.* Von einem Funken kommt ein grosses Feuer.—*Germ.* A small spark makes a great fire.—*Eng.* A wee spark maks muckle wark.—*Scot.*

Is tric a chaidh an fhealla-dhà gu fealla-riribh.—*Joke has often come to earnest.*

> Mows may come to earnest.—*Scot.*

Is tric a chaillear fear na mòr-mhisnich.—*Daring often leads to death.*

> 'S mie ve daaney, ach s'olk ve ro ghaaney—*It is good to be bold, but bad to be too bold.*—*Manx.* Be bold, but not too bold.—*Eng.*

Is tric a chinn an cneadach, 's a dh'fhalbh an sodarnach.—*The delicate often survive, while the vigorous go.*

Is tric a chinn fuidheall fochaid, 's a mheath fuidheall farmaid.—*The refuse of mockery has often waxed, and that of envy waned.*

> Macintosh's rendering is 'Oft has the object of scorn arrived at honour, and that of envy fallen into contempt.'

Is tric a fhuair 'olc an airidh' car.—*'Poor fellow' has often been crossed.*

> *Lit.* 'Ill-deserved' has often got a turn.

Is tric a fhuair fear na roghainn diù.—*The man with choice has often got the worse.*

Is tric a fhuair gunna urchair-iasaid.—*A gun has often got a loan-shot.*

> It was sometimes believed that an unloaded gun might go off notwithstanding, and kill, if incautiously handled—an exaggeration of the proper horror of a reckless handling of fire-arms.

Is tric a mheall e sheis, an neach a gheall a bhith tairis da.—*Often has one failed his fellow, who promised to be true to him.*

Is tric a thàinig trod mòr à adhbhar beag.—*Often has great quarrel sprung from little cause.*

Is tric a thug fear na ciad chèilidh fìor bharail.—*The man of first visit has often judged truly.*

> Glöggt es gestz augat—*Sharp (gleg) is the eye of a guest.*—*Icel.*

Is tric as daoir' a' chomain na 'n dubh-cheannach.—*A favour often costs more than what's hard-bought.*

> Spesso i doni sono danni—*Gifts are often losses.*—*Ital.*

Is tric leis an droch sgeul a bhith fìor.—*Bad news is often true.*

Is tric nach tig ath-sgeul air droch sgeul.—*Ill news is not often contradicted.*

Is tric nach robh ach beagan sneachd air taigh a' mhèirlich.—*There has often been but little snow on the roof of the thief.*

> He would probably be out at night, and have a fire kept on while honest people were in bed which would melt the snow in the thatch.

Is trom air taigh gun nàire.—*A shameless house has its burden.*

Is trom an cat ri shìor ghiùlan.—*The cat is heavy if carried constantly.*

> Children are fond of carrying cats; but even a grown-up person would tire in time of a light burden.

Is trom an eire an t-aineolas.—*Ignorance is a heavy burden.*

> *Al.*—Is cruaidh cuing an aineolaich—*Hard is the yoke of the ignorant.*
> Is trom an t-ualach aineolas.—*Ir.*

Is trom an iorram 's an t-iomradh.—*'Tis heavy to chant and row.*

> See 'Chan urrainn domh h-èigheach'.

Is trom an t-uallach an aois.—*Age is a heavy load.*

> Grave senectus est hominibus pondus.—*Lat.*

Is trom buill' an t-seann laoich.—*Heavy is the old hero's blow.*

> See 'Is fhurasda buill' '.

Is trom dithis air aon duine.—*Two to one are heavy odds.*

> See 'Cothrom'.

Is trom dithis air an aon mhèis, gun ac' ach an t-aon ghleus.—*Two are heavy on one dish, when there is but one ration.*

Is trom eallach gun iris.—*Heavy is the load without a rope to hold by.*

> None of the dictionaries gives this meaning of the word *iris*, which in the Hebrides is the common term for the rope with which a creel or a bundle of any kind is carried.

Is trom geum bò air a h-aineol.—*Heavy is the cow's low in a strange fold.*

> Is ard géim bó air a h-aineolas.—*Ir.*

Is trom na tubaistean air na slibistean.—*Mishaps many fall on slovens.*

Is trom snighe air taigh gun tughadh.—*Raindrops come heavy on a house unthatched.*

Is truagh a' bhantrach a' phìob.—*The bagpipe is a miserable widow.*

> Pipers have generally been very improvident.

Is truagh nach bu cheàird sinn gu lèir an-diugh.—*'Tis a pity we were not all tinkers today.*

> Said by Alexander MacDonell, son of Colla Ciotach (Colkitto), after having received great help in a fight from an Atholl tinker named Stewart.

Is truim' a' chnead na 'n eallach.—*The groan is heavier than the load.*

Is tu fhèin a thòisich an toiseach, mar thuirt an t-amadan ris an tarbh.—*You began it yourself, as the fool said to the bull.*

> The story is that a fool was passing through a field where a bull was pasturing and, hearing him growling, began to mimic him, which naturally excited the bull to give him chase, bellowing furiously. The fool was clever enough to get over a dyke just in time, and then, safe behind the wall, he addressed the bull as above. The Lowland version, which I have heard told in Galloway of a baronet, is 'Boo to yirsel! Who begoo'd it?'

Is tu thilg a' chlach air a' chaisteal!—*What a stone you threw at the castle!*

> Said ironically, when some small person hits his superior.

Is uaine feur na faiche as fàsaiche.—*Green is the grass of the least trodden field.*

Is uaisle toll na tuthag.—*Hole is genteeler than patch.*

> *Per con.* Is mios' an clùd na 'n toll—*The clout is worse than the hole.* See 'Is fheàrr brèid'.

Is uasal a bhith 'nad shuidhe, 'nad ruith.—*It's noble to be sitting and running.*

> Said of driving in a carriage.

Is uasal mac an an-uasail an tìr nam mèirleach; is an-uasal mac an uasail, mur bi e treubhach.—*The lowly-born is a gentleman among thieves; the gentleman's son is no gentleman, if he be not brave.*

> A very characteristic sentiment.

Is ùrachadh atharrachadh.—*Change is refreshing.*

> Caghlaa obbyr aash—*Change of work is ease.*—*Manx.*

Isean deiridh linne, cinnidh e no thèid e dholaidh.—*The last chicken of a brood comes to either grief or good.*

> In the case of the more prolific lower animals, the last of a brood or litter is generally the weakest. It is not so, however, with the youngest offspring of the higher animals, especially of human beings. But the youngest is sometimes spoiled by petting.

Ith do leòr, 's na pòc dad.—*Eat your fill, and pocket nothing.*

> Eat yir fill, but pouch nane, is gairdener's law.—*Scot.*

Ith nas lugha, 's ceannaich e.—*Eat less, and buy it.*

> Lay yir wame to yir winnin.—*Scot.*

Itheadh na goibhre air an nathair.—*The goat's eating of the serpent.*

> It is believed in some parts of the Highlands that goats eat serpents, and that they eat them tail foremost, first stamping on the head. It is said that while the goat is thus engaged, it utters a querulous noise, not liking the wriggling of the adder. A verse in reference to this is

> > Cleas na goibhre 'g ith' na nathrach:
> > Ga sìor itheadh, 's a' sìor thalach.

> > —*The goat's trick with the serpent:*
> > *Eating away, and still complaining.*

> Be this as it may, it is positively affirmed by persons of experience that serpents disappear where goats pasture.

Itheadh nan con air a' bhlianaich.—*The dogs' eating of the bad flesh.*

> For want of any better.

Itheam, òlam, caidileam.—*Let me eat, let me drink, let me sleep.*

> Quite a Carlylean saying, supposed to be uttered by one of the 'fruges consumere nati'.

Ithear cruach 'na breacagan.—*A stack can be eaten in cakes.*

Ithear na cruachan mòra, 's nìtear leis na cruachan beaga.—*The little stacks will do when the big ones are eaten.*

> By that time the new corn will be nearly ripe.

Ithidh a cheann a chasan dheth.—*His head will eat his feet off.*

> This is like the common saying about an idle horse eating his head off. It might refer also to human beings.

Ithidh na cait fuidheall nan caolan.—*Cats will eat the refuse of small guts.*

L

Là a' bhlàir, 's math na càirdean.—*Friends are good on the day of battle.*

Là air mhisg, 's là air uisge.—*Today drunk,* tomorrow on water.

Lạ er meshtey, as la er ushtey.—*Manx.*

Là buain an lìn.—*The day of lint-reaping.*

Nevermas, lint being never cut but plucked up.

Là Buidhe Bealltainn.—*Yellow May Day.*

Là Fhèill Brìghde bàine, bheir na cait an connadh dhachaigh.—*On fair St Bride's Day the cats will bring home the brushwood.*

Another saying, apparently better founded, associates this with St Patrick's Day, about which time (17th March) the weather is generally dry, compared with Candlemas.

The Manx 'Laa 'l Breeshy bane' corresponds with the above.

Là Fhèill Brìghde, thig an rìbhinn as an toll; cha bhean mise dhan rìbhinn, 's cha bhean an rìbhinn rium.—*On St Bride's day the nymph will come out of the hole; I won't touch the nymph, and she won't touch me.*

> *Al.*—Seachdain ro Fhèill Brìghde,
> Thig nighean Iomhair as an tom;
> Cha bhi mise ri nighean Iomhair,
> 'S cha mhò bhios nighean Iomhair rium.

> —*A week before St Bride's Day Ivor's daughter will come out of the knoll; I won't molest her, and she won't hurt me.*

The *rìbhinn* and *nighean Iomhair* are both euphemistic or deprecatory names for the adder, the one known in Skye, the other in Rannoch. A lady called 'Nighean Iomhair,' wife of John MacKenzie, constable of Eilean Donnain Castle, was suspected of having poisoned there (1550) John Glassich of Gairloch, who claimed the Kintail estates. This may possibly have given rise to the application of her name to the serpent. Another version is *an niomhair*, 'the venomous one'.

Là Fhèill Eòin as t-Samhradh, theid a' chuthag gu taigh Geamhraidh.—*On St John's day in Summer, the cuckoo goes to her Winter home.*

St John's day, 24th June.

Là Fhèill Eòin, their iad aighean ris na gamhna.—*On St John's Day they call the stirks heifers.*

St John's Day is ordinarily called *Fèill Eathain*, as the MacLeans are called *Clann 'IllEathain*, a mere phonetic spelling of *Eòin* or *Iain*, John or Ian.

Là Fhèill Math-Cheasaig, bidh gach easgann torrach.—*On St Kessock's day every eel is pregnant.*

St Kessock's day is 21st March. Fairs named after this saint are still held at Callander and at Cumbrae on or about that date. Kessock Ferry at Inverness is also named after him.

In the MS Collection of Ewen MacDiarmid, mentioned in the Preface, of which the present editor has had the benefit, the word *easan*, 'little waterfall,' is substituted for *easgann*. This is intelligible, though the use of the word *torrach* as applied to water is anomalous. The reference to eels is more singular, that fish being of ill-repute in the Highlands. The fresh-water eel, in particular, is never eaten in Scotland, though at one time it appears to have been largely used as an article of diet. See Innes's *Scotland in the Mid. Ages*, p. 124. I have been unable to get any scientific information as to the spawning time of eels.

Là Luain.—*The moon day.*

Another version of Nevermas, or the Greek Kalends.

Là sheachnaidh na bliadhna.—*The day of the year to be avoided.*

Armstrong (*Dict.*) says this term was applied to the 3rd of May; others say the 2nd, others the 5th. It was held unlucky to begin any important work, and unpardonable to commit any crime, on that day for the extraordinary reason that on that day the fallen angels were believed to have been expelled from Heaven.

Laideann aig na gabhraibh—tuigeam ged nach labhraim.—*Goat-Latin I can understand, but speak not.*

> *Al.*—aig na gadhraibh—*Dog-Latin.*
>
> Said of people who pretend to know and say more than the hearer understands. It may possibly have been first applied to priests.

Laighe fada air taobh taighe duin' eile.—*Lying long in another man's house.*

Laighe leis an t-sùil, is falbh an leis a' ghlùin.—*Lie still with a (sore) eye, and move about with a (sore) knee.*

Laighidh dubh air gach dath, ach cha laigh dath air dubh.—*Black will lie on any colour, but none other will lie on black.*

> See 'Cha chaochail'. It appears now that this old belief is not correct, and that black will take more than one other dye such as brown and green.

Làir chaol-chasach agus each bonn-chasach.—*A slender-legged mare and a stout-legged horse.*

Làmh ann an earball a' ghill.—*Holding the pledge by the tail.*

Làmh an ceann bò maoile.—*Holding a hornless cow by the head.*

Làmh d'athar 's do sheanar!—*By the hand of your father and grand-father!*

> Properly, 'Air làmh' &c. Martin in his *Western Islands* (2d ed., p. 120) says this form of adjuration was considered very insulting. It would be more correct to say that it was an insult to be thought capable of disregarding it.
>
> Another form, 'Làmh d'athar 's do sheanar ort!', is used as a threat; and a story is told of its application by a blacksmith, who strongly suspected that his wife's baby was a changeling and satisfactorily proved it. He came in one day exclaiming, 'An sithean ri theine!'— '*The fairy knoll is on fire*'!—on which the little imp, thrown off his guard, cried out, 'O, m'òrd 's m' innean!'—'*O my hammer and anvil!*' The smith now saw that the creature was not only a fairy but a fellow-craftsman; and taking him out to the smithy, placed him on the anvil, and swinging his big hammer, said, 'Gobha mi fhèin, gobha m'athair, gobha mo sheanair; 's làmh d'athar 's do sheanar ort! An t-òrd mòr!'—'*Smith am I, smith was my father, smith my grandfather; thy father's and grandfather's hand on thee! The big hammer!*' Before the

hammer could descend the little sprite vanished, and when the smith returned home, he found his own true and pretty child sitting cosily at the fireside!

Apparently another version of this saying is 'Làmh a thart, tart do sheanar dhut!'

Làmh fhad', agus cead a sineadh.—*A long arm, and leave to stretch it.*

Làmhan leanaibh, agus goile seann duine.—*The hands of a child, and an old man's stomach.*

Làn beòil de bhiadh, is làn baile de nàire.—*A mouthful of meat, and a town-(or farm-)ful of shame.*

> Lán duirn de shógh, agus lán baile de náire.—Ir. A mouthfu o meat may be a tounfu o shame.—*Scot.*
> Supposed to allude to a stolen egg.

Laogh buabhall an dorais.—*The calf of the door-stall.*

> Likely to be first attended to.

Lasair crèathaich is èigheach caillich.—*Brushwood flame, and the cry of an old woman.*

> Both easily excited, and soon over.

Le muineal na cuing a bhristeadh, bheir thu misneach do dh'fhear na h-airce.—*Breaking the neck of his yoke will encourage the man in distress.*

Leac is ùir eadar sinn!—*Stone and earth divide us!*

> Said of those whom one would wish to be separate from, even in the grave.

Leaghaidh a' chòir am beul an anfhainn.—*Justice melts in the mouth of the feeble.*

Leaghaidh am bròn an t-anam bochd.—*Sorrow melts the miserable.*

Lean gu dlùth ri cliù do shinnsre.—*Follow close the fame of your fathers.*

> This is supposed to be Ossianic—said by Fingal to Oscar.

Leanaidh blianach ris na sràbhain.—*Bad flesh sticks to straws.*

> Applied, says Macintosh, to mean or worthless people who cleave to
> each other.
> *Al.*—Leanaidh a' bhì ris a' bhòrd, 's an sop ris an sgait—*The sap will
> stick to the wood, and the straw to the skate.*

Leathaineach gun bhòsd; Dòmhnallach gun tapadh; Caimbeulach
gun mhòrchuis.—*A MacLean without boast; a MacDonald without
cleverness; a Campbell without pride.*

> Three rarities.

Leathann ri leathann, is caol ri caol.—*Broad to broad and small to
small.*

> Caol le caol, agus leathan le leathan.—*Ir.*
> This is an old rule of Gaelic orthography, devised by Irish gramma-
> rians, and in modern times upheld by some as of absolute authority,
> by others denounced as inconvenient and vicious. The broad vowels
> are *a*, *o*, *u*, the slender *e*, *i*, and the rule is that where a consonant
> intervenes, a broad or narrow vowel must be followed by one of the
> same kind; e.g., *leathann*, instead of 'leathinn,' which would better
> represent our pronunciation; while the comparative degree of the
> same word is written, not 'leathne' nor 'leithna,' but *leithne*. For an
> explanation and discussion of this rule, see Stewart's *Gaelic Grammar*,
> Part I, sect. 3; and for citation of the authorities on both sides, see
> Bourke's *Irish Grammar*, pp 16–20.

Leig an t-earball leis a' chraiceann.—*Let the tail go with the hide.*

> Shegin goaill ny eairkyn marish y shea (*seichge*)—*The horns must be
> taken with the hide.*—*Manx.* Let the tail follow the skin. Let the horns
> gang wi the hide.—*Scot.*

Leig do cheann far am faigh thu sa mhadainn e.—*Lay your head
where you'll find it in the morning.*

Leig fad na teadhrach leis.—*Let him have his tether's length. Give him
rope enough.*

Leig tro na meòir e.—*Let it through the fingers.*

Leigear cudthrom na slait air an sgòd.—*The weight of the yard will be
on the sheet.*

Leigheas air leth, losgadh.—*Burning is a singular cure.*

> Whether this refers to the actual cautery or to accidental burning may be left to conjecture.

Leigheas air sùilean goirt.—*A cure for sore eyes.*

Lèintean farsaing do na leanaban òga.—*Wide shirts to young bairns.*

> Barnið vex, en brókin ekki—*Bairns wax, but the breeks don't.*—*Icel.*
> The moral significance of this, in favour of freedom of thought to new generations, is remarkable.

Leisgeul arain gu ith' ime.—*The excuse of bread for eating butter.*

Leisgeul duine 's e air dram.—*The excuse of a tipsy man.*

Leth na Galltachd ort!—*Half the Lowlands be upon thee!*

> *Al.*—dhut—*to thee.*

Leum an gàrradh far an ìsl' e.—*Leap the dyke where it is lowest.*

> Every ane loups the dyke where it's laichest.—*Scot.* Where the hedge is lowest, men may soonest over.—*Eng.* Waar de hegge het laagste is, wil elk er over.—*Dutch.* Ou la haie est plus basse on saute dessus.—*Fr.*

Leum chasa tioram.—*A dry foot jump.*

Lìonar beàrn mhòr le clachan beaga.—*Great gaps may be filled with small stones.*

Lìonar long le sligean.—*A ship may be loaded with shells.*

Lionn-dubh air mo chridhe.—*Melancholy on my heart.*

> *Lit.*—'black humour'.

Loisgidh sinn na cruachan mòra, 's fòghnaidh na cruachan beaga.—*We shall burn the big stacks, and the little ones will suffice.*

> This refers to peat stacks.

Lòn tuathair is sguabach dheisear.—*Meadow facing north, corn facing south.*

> The best exposure for each crop.

Losgadh do chridhe ort!—*Heart-burning to thee!*

Losgadh sona is losgadh dona.—*Lucky burning and unlucky burning.*

Luath no mall gun tig am Màigh, thig a' chuthag.—*Late or early as May comes, so comes the cuckoo.*

Luathas as fhaisge air a' mhaille.—*Speed that's nearest to slowness.*

Raw haste, half-sister to delay.—*Tennyson.*

Lùb am faillean, 's chan fhairtlich a' chraobh ort.—*Bend the twig, and the tree won't defy you.*

Luchd a' chrùin dol thun a' cheapa,'s luchd a' cheapa thun a' chrùin.—*Crowned heads go to the sod, and tillers of the soil to crowns.*

See I. *Sam.*, ii, 7, 8; and *Luke*, i, 52.

Luchd nan casag.—*The long-coated folk.*

Lowlanders.

Ludh an spioraid, dol timcheall na drochaid.—*The way of the ghost, going round the bridge.*

Macintosh's translation of this saying, which Armstrong also gives, is 'Go about the bridge as the ghost did'. The superstition here referred to is illustrated in *Tam o Shanter*, where the infernal pursuers have no power to go beyond the keystone of the bridge. Another saying is 'Thàinig mi mun cuairt, cleas a' bhòcain'—*'I came round about, the ghost's trick'*—in reference to which the following story is told. A certain man was haunted by a ghost, which met him wherever he went, so that he became known in the countryside as 'Dòmhnall Mòr a' bhòcain'—*'Big Donald of the ghost'*. Weary of his life, he went away to America, hoping there to be rid of his tormentor—but in vain. The very night of his arrival, the first person he met in the streets was his old friend. He cried out in amazement, 'Ciamar a thàinig thus' an seo?'—*'How did you come here?'* 'Thàinig mi mun cuairt,' said the imperturbable ghost. Donald in disgust returned home.

Ludh an t-sneachda—tighinn gun sireadh, gun iarraidh.—*The way of the snow, coming unsought, unasked.*

Al.—Mar a thàinig a' ghailleann as t-Fhoghar—gun sireadh &c.—*As the storm came in Autumn, unsought &c.*
Thig sé gan iarraidh, mar thig an do-aimsir.—*Ir.*

Luibh Chaluim Chille, gun sireadh gun iarraidh, 's a dheòin Dia cha bhàsaich mi nochd.—*St Columba's wort, unsought, unasked, and please God, I won't die tonight.*

> Said by children on unexpectedly finding this flower, called in English St John's Wort.

Luideag is Doideag, is Corrag nighean Iain Bhàin; Cas a' Mhogain riabhach à Gleann Comhainn; is Gormshuil mhòr bhàrr na Mòighe.—*Raggie and Frizzle, and Fair John's daughter's Finger; brindled Hoggan-foot from Glencoe; and big Blue-eye from Moy.*

> The names of a gathering of witches. See Dr. MacLeod's *Rem. of a Highl. Par.*, p. 249.

Lus Phàra liath, cuiridh e ghiamh às a' chnàimh.—*Grey St Patrick's Wort (grundsel) will drive pain from the bone.*

M

Ma bheir thu Muile dhiom, cha toir thu muir is tìr dhiom.—*You may take Mull from me, but you can't take sea and land from me.*

Ma bheir thusa dhomhsa dealg fhraoich gun dhath dhubh, gun ghaoid, bheir mise dhutsa buaile de chrodh geal maol.—*If you give me a heather pin without luck or flaw in it, I'll give you a fold of white hornless cows.*

Ma bhios taod agad, gheibh thu each.—*If you have a halter, you'll get a horse.*

Ma bhristeas bun-feann, bidh fios aig do cheann cò dhorchaich an toll.—*If the tail breaks, your head will know who darkened the hole.*

> The story is that two men went to a wolf's den, when wolves still flourished in Scotland, for the purpose of carrying off the whelps. The den was in a cairn with a narrow entrance, through which one of the men crept in while the other stood on guard outside. Presently the yelping of the young ones called their mother to the rescue, and she bolted past the man outside, who was dexterous enough, however, to seize her by the tail while she was disappearing. So they stood, the she-wolf blocking the entrance and darkening the den, while the man outside held on like grim death. The man within, finding the light suddenly obscured, called out to his companion, 'What's that darkening the hole?' To which the reply was made as above. See Campbell's *W. H. T.*, Vol. 1, 273, for a Sutherland version of this story.

Ma bhuaileas tu cù no balach, buail gu math e.—*If you strike a dog or a clown, hit him well.*

> See 'Balach'.

Ma chaidh i don allt, cha b'ann le clùd nan soithichean.—*If she went to the burn, it was not with the dish-clout.*

> Má chuaidh sí chun an tstrotha, ní leis an discleád.—*Ir.*
>
> In a note on this in the 2nd ed. of Macintosh, it is said to be used as an apology for a woman's going astray with a gentleman. Mr MacAdam, in his note on the Ulster version, says it is applied to such women when they make a good marriage unexpectedly.

Ma cheannaicheas tu feòil, ceannaich feòil laoigh, 's ma cheannaicheas tu iasg, ceannaich iasg sgait.—*If you buy meat, buy veal, and if you buy fish, buy skate.*

> This is said to mean that you will get a good bargain in weight, as the bone in veal is soft, and that of skate is eatable.
>
> *Al.*—Ma tha iasg a dhìth orm, chan iasg leam sgat—*If I want fish, skate is no fish to me.*
>
> The Highland prejudices against certain meat and fish are sometimes very absurd. The skate is most unjustly undervalued by the natives of the western coasts of Scotland.

Ma cheannaicheas tu rud air nach eil feum agad, 's eudar dhut an ùine ghoirid do ghoireas a reic.—*If you buy what you don't need, you'll soon have to sell what you do need.*

Ma chuireas tu do làmh am beul a' mhadaidh, feumaidh tu toirt às mar a dh'fhaodas tu.—*If you put your hand in the hound's mouth, you must take it out as best you can.*

Ma chumas tu do dhubhan fliuch an còmhnaidh, gheibh thu iasg uaireigin.—*If you keep your hook always wet, you'll get a fish some time.*

> Ma dh'èireas dut a bhith air d'aineol,
> Na cuir earbs' an còmhradh banail—
> Mar as fhaide nì thu 'n leanail,
> 'S ann as mò a thèid do mhealladh.

> *—If you chance on foreign parts,*
> *Do not trust in female talk—*
> *The longer after them you follow,*
> *The more you'll be cheated hollow.*

Ma dh'fhadaidh thu 'n teine 'nad uchd, altraim e, ge duilich leat.—*If you kindled the fire in your breast, nurse it, though you like it not.*

Ma dh'fhalbh an t-eun, faodaidh an nead a dhol 'na theine.—*If the bird be flown, the nest may burn.*

Ma dh'innseas duine na 's lèir dha, innsidh e na 's nàr dha.—*If a man tell all he sees, he'll tell what will shame him.*

> Quien acecha por agujero, ve su duelo—*Who peeps through a hole will discover his dole.—Span.*

Ma dh'itheas tu cridh' an eòin, bidh do chridhe air chrith ri d'bheò.—*If you eat the bird's heart, your heart will palpitate for ever.*

> This and the next are meant for children.

Ma dh'itheas tu teanga na caora, bidh tu mèilich ri d'bheò.—*If you eat the sheep's tongue, you will bleat for ever.*

Ma gheibh duin' idir rud, 's e fireannach falbhaiteach.—*If anybody can get anything, it's the man that keeps moving.*

Ma mharbhas tu beathach Dihaoine, bidh ruith na h-Aoin' ort am feasda.—*If you kill a beast on Friday, the Friday fate will follow you forever.*

Ma nì thu pìobaireachd do Mhac 'Ille Chaluim, nì thu pìobaireachd dhòmhsa.—*If you pipe to MacLeod of Raasay, you will pipe to me.*

> This is apparently a Skye saying, but its origin has not been ascertained.

Ma ruitheas an sionnach am broilleach a' ghadhair, cò aig' tha choire?—*If the fox rush into the hound's embrace, who is to blame?*

Mas àill leat a bhith buan, gabh deoch gu luath an dèidh an uighe.—*If you wish to live long, drink quickly after an egg.*

> After an egg drink as much as after an ox.—*Eng.*

Mas beag leat e, crath sonas air.—*If you deem it little, shake luck on it.*

Mas beag mo chas, cha mhò mo chuaran.—*If small my foot, my sock is no bigger.*

Mas bonnach brist' e, is bonnach itht' e.—*A broken bannock is as good as eaten.*

> See 'Cha bhi bail'.

Mas breug bhuam e, is breug thugam e.—*If it be a lie from me, it's a lie to me.*

> This is a favourite expression when one has something to tell which is not well vouched.

Mas ceòl fidilearachd, tha gu leòr againn deth.—*If fiddling be music, we have enough of it.*

> This was said by the famous harper, Rory Morrison (see App. II), after having had to endure the performance of all his favourite airs by a fiddler, whose instrument he naturally looked on as a contemptible squeaking thing. 'Fidilearachd' expresses more contempt than the ordinary 'fìdhlearachd'.

Mas dubh, mas odhar, mas donn, is toigh leis a' ghobhair a meann.—*Be it black or dun or brown, the goat loves her kid.*

> Más dubh, más odhar, ná donn, is dá meannán féin bheir an gabhar a fonn.—*Ir.*

Mas duine tha 'n seo, 's aotrom e, mun duirt an t-each-uisge.—*If this be human, it's light, as the water-horse said.*

> The story is that the water-horse came in the shape of a young man (*riochd fleasgaich*) out of his native element, and sat down beside a girl who was herding cattle on the banks of the loch. After some pleasant conversation, he laid his head in her lap, in a fashion not unusual in old times, and fell asleep. She began to examine his head and, to her alarm, found that his hair was full of sand and mud. She at once knew that it was none other than the *Each-Uisge*, who would certainly conclude his attentions by carrying her on his back into the depths of the loch. She accordingly proceeded, as dexterously as she could, to get rid of her skirt, leaving it under the head of the monster. No sooner did he awaken than he jumped up and shook the skirt, crying out several times, 'Mas duine tha 'n seo' &c., then rushed down the brae, and plunged into the lake.

Mas fearail thu, na biodh gruaim ort.—*If you are manly, don't be gloomy.*

> A very good sentiment.

Mas fhiach an teachdaire, 's fhiach an gnothach.—*If the messenger be worthy, the business is.*

> *Al.*—Mas fiù an gille, 's fiù an gnothach.
> The embassy is judged of by the quality of the ambassador.

Mas lite dhut i, cha mhòr leat i.—*If it's porridge to you, it's not much to you.*

> This is one of the few specimens of Gaelic puns, and a fair one. A young man in Lochaber went to woo a young girl called Mòr, Marion. The father entertained him hospitably, and after dinner proposed a smoke, saying, 'Gabhaidh sinn a-nis am biadh a ghabhas os cionn gach bìdh'—'*We'll now have the food that goes above all food.*' 'An e sin an lite?' said the stupid young man—'*Do you mean porridge?*' The father, disgusted by his stupidity, made the above reply, indicating that Marion was not for him.

Mas math an t-each, 's math a dhreach.—*If the horse be good, his colour is good.*

> A bep liou marc'h mad.—*Breton.* A good horse cannot be of a bad colour.—*Eng.*

Mas math leat do mholadh, faigh bàs; mas math leat do chàineadh, pòs.—*If you wish to be praised, die; if you wish to be decried, marry.*

> This is a shrewd saying, neatly expressed.

Mas math leat sìth, càirdeas agus cluain, èisd, faic is fuirich sàmh-ach.—*If you wish peace, friendship and quietness, listen, look and be silent.*

> Más maith leat síocháin, cairdeas is moladh, éist, feic is fan balbh.—*Ir.* Audi, vide, tace, si vis vivere in pace.—*Lat.* Odi, vedi, e taci, se vuoi viver in pace.—*Ital.* Oy, voy, et te tais, si tu veux vivre en paix.—*Fr.* Ver, oir, y callar, si quieres vivir en paz.—*Span.* Ouve, ve, e calla, se queres viver em paz.—*Port.*
>
> He that would live in peace and rest
> Must hear, see and say the least.—*Eng.*

Mas olc a' phìobaireachd, chan fheàrr a duais.—*If the piping be bad, the pay is no better.*

Mas olc am fitheach, chan fhearr a chomann.—*If bad be the raven, his company is no better.*

> Myr 's doo yn feeagh, yiow eh sheshey.—*Manx.*

Mas olc an leanabh, chan fheàrr a luasgadh.—*If the child be bad, his rocking is no better.*

Ma sheallas bean air a glùn toisgeal, gheibh i leisgeul.—*If a woman but look on her left knee, she will find an excuse.*

> Is foisce do bhean leithscéal ná bráiscín—A woman's excuse is nearer than her apron.—*Ir.*

Ma stad iad mu Ghot, stad iad mu Ghot.—*If they stopped at Gott, they did stop there.*

> A Tiree saying, applied to people who stop halfway. Gott is a hamlet a little way from the port of Scarinish.

> Mac an Luin a bh' aig Mac Cumhail,
> Nach d'fhàg fuigheal de dh'fheòil dhaoine.
>
> —*The son of Lun, Fingal's sword,*
> *That left no remnant of men's flesh.*

> From the 'Ceardach,' Gillies, p. 236; Campbell's *Leabhar na Féinne*, p. 65. See 'Cha d'fhàg claidheamh Fhinn,' *ante*, p. 104.

Ma tha Dia ann, 's chan eil fhios a bheil, fàg eadar sinn fhèin 's na biodagan!—*If there be a God, and no one knows whether there be, leave it between ourselves and the dirks!*

> The fervent prayer for fair play of an old Highland heathen on the eve of a fight.

Ma tha mise truagh, 's e mo thruaighe MacAoidh!—*If I am miserable, woe's me for Mackay!*

Ma tha mo chuid airgid anns a' chapall, thig e dhachaigh uaireigin.—*If my money is in the mare, it will come home some day.*

Ma tha thu coma, dèan comaidh ris a' mhuic.—*If you don't care, go and share with the sow.*

> Every man to his taste, as the man said when he kissed his cow.—*Eng., Scot.*

Ma tha thusa 'nad fhear-ealaidh, cluinneamaid annas do làimhe.—*If you are a man of skill, let us hear your masterpiece.*

Ma thèid gus an tèid, thèid fear an t-sìor ghalair.—*Whoever goes or does not go, the man of long disease will.*

Ma tha 'n long briste, chan eil a' chreag slàn.—*If the ship be broken, the rock is not whole.*

Ma their mi fhèin, 'Mach thu!' ri m'chù, their a h-uile fear e.—*If I say, 'Get out!' to my dog, everybody will say it.*

Ma thuiteas clach leis a' ghleann, 's ann sa chàrn a stadas i.—*If a stone fall down the glen, it's in the cairn it will stop.*

> Ma thuiteann cloch le fánaidh (*slope*), is ins an gcarnán a stadaidh sí.—*Ir.*
> Another case of 'like to like'.

MacArtair Srath Churra o bhun an stoc fheàrna.—*MacArthur of Strachur, from the root of the alder.*

> Strachur, on Loch Fyne, is said to have been the original seat of the MacArthurs.

> Mac bantraich aig am bi crodh,
> Searrach seann làrach an greigh,
> Madadh muilleir aig am bi min—
> Triùir as meanmnaich' air bith.

> —*The son of a widow rich in cows,*
> *The foal of an old mare in a herd,*
> *The dog of a miller rich in meal—*
> *Three of the merriest things alive.*

MacCuaraig an lòin, chuir a' chuag air a bhròig.—*Kennedy of the meadow, who put his shoe out of shape.*

MacIllEathain Locha Buidhe, ceann-uidhe nam mèirleach.—*MacLaine of Loch Buie, the chieftain of thieves.*

> This epithet is shared with another great Highland chief— 'Camshronach bog an ime, ceann-cinnidh nam mèirleach'.

MacLeòid no 'n t-airgead—*MacLeod or the money.*

> MacLeod of MacLeod was once on a visit to Edinburgh, and was suddenly called away, leaving his servant behind him, without any money. The servant now found that nothing but MacLeod's note, or hard cash, would avail him anywhere.

Mac mar an t-athair.—*Like father, like son.*

> *Al.*—Mac an daidein—*Dad's son.*
> Mab diouc'h tad—*Mac an dèidh daidein.—Breton.* Sic faither, sic son.—*Scot.*

Mac màthaireil 's nighean athaireil.—*A son like the mother, and a daughter like the father.*

> *Al.*—Mac ri mhàthair, 's nighean ri h-athair.

Maighdeann Sàbaid, is capall Lùnasdail.—*A Sabbath maiden, and a Lammas mare.*

> *Al.*—Each Samhna, 's bean Dòmhnaich—*Hallow Fair horse, and a Sunday wife.*
> More showy at those times, and therefore not to be hastily chosen.
> Choose your wife on Saturday, rather than on Sunday.—*Scot., Eng.*
> Si quieres hembra, escogela el Sabado y no el Domingo.—*Span.*

Maise nam bonnach a bhith faisg air an teallaich.—*The beauty of bannocks is to be near the fire.*

Màm air an t-sac gun fheum.—*The handful heaped on the sack, where it is not needed.*

Manadh do chrochaidh ort!—*The omen of your hanging to you!*

Maor eòlach, maor as mios' a thèid an crò.—*A bailiff acquainted with the stock, the worst to send among the flock.*

Maorach caillich MhicArtair—partan is dà fhaochaig.—*Old Mrs MacArthur's shellfish, a crab and two wilks.*

Mar a bha chailleach air Eòghann, a dheòin no dh'aindeoin,—*Like the old woman upon Ewen, will he, nill he.*

> See 'Ceum air do cheum'.

Mar a bha gille mòr nam bram—chan fhuirich e thall no bhos.—*Like the great windy lad—he won't stay there or here.*

Mar a bha 'n t-each bàn an doras a' mhuilinn—a' smaoineachadh tuilleadh 's a bha e 'g ràdh.—*Like the white horse at the mill-door, thinking more than he said.*

> *Al.*—Mar a bha 'n gamhainn san doras, a' feitheamh 's ag èisdeachd—*Like the stirk at the door, waiting and listening.*

Mar a b'umhail, gum b'fhìor.—*As foreseen, so has been.*

Mar a chàireas duine a leabaidh, 's ann a laigheas e.—*As a man makes his bed, so he must lie.*

> As you make your bed, so you must lie on it.—*Eng., Scot.* Comme on fait son lit, on se couche.—*Fr.* Quien mala cama hace, en ella se yace.—*Span.* Som man reder til, saa ligger man.—*Dan.*

Mar a chaitheas duine a bheatha, bheir e breith air a choimhearsnach.—*As a man leads his life, so he judges his neighbour.*

Mar a' mhil air bhàrr nan cuiseag.—*Like honey on the top of the stalks.*

Mar as àirde thèid an calman, 's ann as dòch' an t-seabhag breith air.—*The higher the dove goes, the likelier is the hawk to catch it.*

Mar as fhaide bhios sinn gu math, 's ann as giorraid a bhios sinn gu h-olc.—*The longer we are well, the shorter will our illness be.*

Mar as fheàrr iad, chan ann as buain' iad.—*The better they are, they live not the longer.*

> God takes the good, too good on earth to stay,
> And leaves the bad, too bad to take away.

Mar as gainn' am biadh, 's ann as fial' a roinn.—*The scarcer the food, the more bounty to share it.*

Mar as luaithe a' ghailleann, 's ann as cruaidhe a' ghailleann.—*The swifter the storm, the stronger it is.*

Mar as lugha theirear, 's ann as fhusa leigheas.—*The least said, the soonest mended.—Eng.*

Mar as miann le broinn, bruichear bonnach.—*As the belly craves, bannock will be baked.*

Mar as mò gheibh an cù, 's ann as mò a dh'iarras e.—*The more the dog gets, the more he desires.*

Mar as sine 'm boc, 's ann as cruaidhe 'n adharc.—*The older the buck, the harder his horn.*

Mar as toigh leis na gobhair na coin.—*As goats like dogs.*

Mar as truime 'n uallach, 's ann as teinn' an crios-guailne; mar as teinn' an crios-guailne, 's ann as luaithe bhristeas.—*The heavier the load, the tighter the shoulder-strap; the tighter the shoulder-strap, the nearer to breaking.*

Mar a thèid an t-eun o dhuilleag gu duilleag, thèid am mèanan o dhuine gu duine.—*As the bird goes from leaf to leaf, the yawn goes from man to man.*

    Al.—Thèid am mèanan &c., mar thèid an t-eunan o dhoire gu doire.

Mar a thuiteas a' chraobh, 's ann a laigheas i.—*As the tree falls, so shall it lie.*

    In the place where the tree falleth, there it shall be.—*Eccl.* xi, 3.

Mar an crodh a' dol don bhuaile, cuid romham 's cuid am dhèidh.—*Like the cattle going to the fold, some before me, some behind me.*

> Mar astar doill an cabaraich,
> No imeachd air garbh-leacannan,
> Mar thathainn gadhair an gleann fàs,
> Tha teagasg dha na h-aineolaich.

> —*Like blind man going through a wood,*
> *Or walking on rough rocky slopes,*
> *Or bark of hound in desert glen,*
> *Is teaching to the ignorant.*

    Nil ach tafann gadhair i ngleann glas a bheith tagradh le ceann gan eolas.—*Ir.*

Mar chlach a' dol an aghaidh bruthaich, feasgar righinn Earraich; mar chlach a' ruith le gleann, feasgar fann Foghair.—*Like stone sent uphill is the long Spring evening; like stone running down glen is soft Autumn evening.*

Mar cho-shogan ris a' chuideachda, mar a chaidh an luid a dhann-sa.—*For mirth to the company, as the slattern went to dance.*

Mar dhòbhran am bun uisge,
Mar sheabhag gu eun slèibhe,
Mar chù gu cat, mar chat gu luch,
Tha bean mic gu màthair-chèile.

—Like otter at a river mouth,
Like hawk to mountain bird,
Like dog to cat, like cat to mouse,
The son's wife is to his mother.

Mar fhear air chàrn.—*Like a man on a cairn.*

An outlaw. See 'Am fear nach meudaich'.

Mar Fionn nam buadh, 'na fhasgadh do shluagh na Fèinne.—*Like peerless Fingal, a shelter to the Feinne.*

Mar gum biodh an teine air do chraiceann.—*As if the fire were on your skin.*

Dèan sin mar a bheadh tine air do chraiceann.—*Ir.*

Mar gum biodh cearc air tòir nid.—*Like a hen in search of a nest.*

Mar gum biodh e air a leaghadh, mar bha caman Neacail.—*As if it had been cast in a mould, like Nicol's club.*

Mar gun tigeadh saighead à bogha.—*Like an arrow from a bow.*

Mar itheadh na goibhre air an dris.—*Like the goat's eating of the brier.*

Mar lus an Dòmhnaich—gun mhath, gun dolaidh.—*Like the herb plucked on Sunday, it does neither good nor ill.*

Mar mhart caol a' tighinn gu baile, tha camhanach na maidne Earraich.—*Like a lean cow coming to a farm is the dawn of a Spring morning.*

Mar Oisean an dèidh na Fèinne.—*Like Ossian after the Feinne.*

The last of his race.

Mar thathann coin ris an rè.—*Like dog's barking at the moon.*

Mar madadh ag tafann an aghaidh na gealaí.—*Ir.*

Mar thig triubhas don mhuic.—*As trews become a sow.*

Like a sow playing on a trump.—*Scot.*

Marbhaidh droch ainm na coin.—*A bad name kills dogs.*

> Give a dog an ill name and hang him.—*Eng., Scot.*

Marbhphaisg ort!—*Death-wrapping be on thee!*

Mas tuath a ghoireas an cù càin, 's gearr gu bàs fear dhe mhuinn-tir.—*If the dear dog bark to the north, soon shall one of his household die.*

Mas tù th' ann, 's tu chaidh às.—*If it be you, you are so sadly changed.*

> Quantum mutatus ab illo Hectore!—*Virgil.* If thou beest he, but O, how fallen, how changed!—*Milton.*

Math air seann duine, math air feall-duine, 's math air leanabh beag—trì mathan caillte.—*Good done to an old man, good to a worthless man, good to a little child, three goods thrown away.*

> One of the few objectionable sentiments found in these proverbs; partly true, but unchristian.

Meal is caith e!—*Enjoy and wear it!*

Meallaidh am biadh am fitheach bhon chraoibh.—*Food will lure the raven from the tree.*

Mèanan bodaich air àirigh 's a shàth 'na bhroinn.—*An old man's yawn on a hill-pasture after meat.*

Mèananaich, iarraidh gun fhaighinn.—*Yawning, wishing and not getting.*

Measar an t-amadan glic ma chumas e theanga.—*The fool may pass for wise if he hold his tongue.*

Meath am facal mun leig thu mach e, 's cha chuir e dragh ort fhèin no air duin' eile.—*Weaken the word before you utter it, and it won't trouble yourself or any other.*

Mèinnearaich bhog a' bhruthaist'.—*The soft brose Menzieses.*

> *Bruthaist* is the original of the 'kale brose o auld Scotland'—oatmeal with boiling water poured on it, much used formerly in the Menzies district in Perthshire, 'Apann nam Mèinnearach'.

A childish Fortingall rhyme is

> Bruthaiste bog,
> Ga shuathadh le stob,
> Ga chur ann an gob
> Nam Mèinnearach.

Mhealladh e 'n t-ugh bhon chorra-ghlais, ged bhiodh a dà shùil a' coimhead air.—*He would cheat the heron of her egg, though her two eyes were fixed on him.*

> Ghoidfeadh sé an ubh on chorr, is a chorr féin fa dheireadh.—*Ir.*
> *Al.*—Bheireadh e à sùilean nam feannag e—*He would take it from the crows' eyes.*
> Said of a very greedy person.

Mhic an rath-dhorcha!—*Son of the moonless night!*

> *Rath-dorcha*, the dark or interlunar time.

Mhic na grèine!—*Son of the sun!*

Mhill e troich 's cha d'rinn e duine.—*He spoiled a dwarf and didn't make a man.*

Mi fhèin 's mo bhean air a' bhrathainn.—*My wife and I at the quern.*

Miann a' chait san tràigh, 's cha toir e fhèin aist' e.—*The cat's desire is on the shore, but she won't go for it.*

> E fynai y gath bysgod, ond no fynai wlychu ei throed.—*Welsh.* Catus amat pisces, sed non vult tingere plantas.—*Med. Lat.* The cat would eat fish, and would not wet her feet.—*Eng.* Letting 'I dare not' wait upon 'I would,' like the poor cat i' the adage.—*Macbeth*, I, 7. La gatta vorrebbe mangiar pesci, ma non pescare.—*Ital.* Le chat aime le poisson, mais il n'aime pas à mouiller la patte.—*Fr.*

Miann an duine lochdaich, càch uile a bhith contrachd.—*The wicked man's desire, mischief to all others.*

> Malus malum vult, ut sit sibi similis.—*Lat.*

Miann de mhianntan an iarrsalaich, cuibhreann mhòr den bheagan.—*The wish above wishes of the covetous, a great share of the little.*

> Miann mnà mac, miann fir feachd;
> Miann eich aonach, miann coin sneachd;
> Miann bà braon, miann caora teas;
> Miann goibhre gaoth, 's dol an aodann creig.

> —*A woman's desire a son, a man's desire a host;*
> *A horse's desire a heath, a dog's desire snow;*
> *A cow's desire a shower, a sheep's desire heat;*
> *A goat's desire wind, and climbing up a crag.*

Rhyme is more considered than reason in some of these.

Miann na maighdne aig a' chaillich.—*The maiden's desire in the old woman.*

See 'Nàire nam maighdeann'.

Mil fo thalamh, currain Earraich.—*Underground honey, Spring carrots.*

Exceptional luxuries. The Spring-carrot is the root of the silver-weed, *brisgean*, very palatable.

Milleadh dàna, bhith ga ràdh far nach tuigear.—*Waste of song, reciting where not understood.*

Millidh airc iasad.—*Poverty destroys lending.*

Millidh an ainnis an t-iasacht.—*Ir.* Wha canna gie will little get.—*Scot.* When ye are puir naebody kens ye; when ye are rich aabody lens ye.—*Do.*

Millidh an cleas thar fhichead am fichead cleas.—*The twenty-first game may spoil the twenty.*

Millidh an t-srathair an t-each.—*The pack-saddle will spoil the horse.*

Millidh aon leibid a' chuinneag.—*One little mishap will destroy the pail.*

Millidh aon othaisg chlaimheach an treud.—*One scabby ewe will spoil the flock.*

See 'Salaichidh'.

Millidh aon tarrang an t-each, 's millidh aon each an t-seisreach.—
One nail will spoil the horse, and one horse spoil the team.

> *Al.*—'Crann' for 'seisreach'.
> For want of a nail the shoe is lost; for want of a shoe the horse is lost;
> for want of a horse the rider is lost.—*Eng.* Por un punto se piedre un
> zapato.—*Span.*

Millidh bò buaile, 's buairidh bean baile.—*One cow will spoil a fold,
and one woman will lead astray a town.*

Millidh dànadas modh.—*Forwardness spoils manners.*

> *Al.*—Thig dànadas gu droch oilean.

Millidh droch chomhluadar deagh bheusan.—*Evil company corrupts
good manners.*

> This is a translation of Menander's φθείρουσιν ἤθη χρησθ' ὁμιλίαι
> κακαί, quoted by St Paul in I *Cor.*, xv, 33.
> 'Truaillidh' for 'millidh' is the word in the authorised Gaelic version.

Millidh smugaid cuideachd.—*A spittle will spoil a company.*

> This is an extreme but not extravagant illustration of the Celtic sense
> of propriety. Our Celts require to cross the Atlantic to get rid of this
> objection to careless spitting.

Min air iasad, itheadh na cruaiche fon t-sìoman.—*Lent meal, eating
the stack under the rope.*

> Consuming things before the time.

Ministear-maide.—*A wooden minister.*

Mionach a' bheathaich as maoile air adhaircean a' bheathaich as
bioraiche.—*The entrails of the blunter (hornless) beast on the horns of
the sharper one.*

Mìos bho aon dèis gu làn-dèis, is mìos bho làn-dèis gu crìon-dèis.—
*A month from the first ear to the full ear, and a month from the full ear
to the withered ear.*

Mìos chrochadh nan con.—*The dog-hanging month—July.*

> Mìos Faoillich; seachdain Feadaig;
> Ceithir là deug Gearrain; seachdain Caillich;
> Trì là Sguabaig—suas e, 'n t-Earrach!
>
> —*A month of the Stormy; a week of the Plover;*
> *A fortnight of the Gelding; a week of the Old Woman;*
> *Three days of the Brushlet—up with the Spring!*

For explanation of these terms see App. IV.

Mìos ro gach ràith a choltas.—*A month before each season, its appearance comes.*

> Apparently this is a correct observation.

Mìr am beul na bèiste.—*A bite for the monster's mouth.*

> Cast a bane i' the deil's teeth.—*Scot.*
> This saying is probably founded on the story of the traveller and the wolves, whom he temporarily stopped by throwing out one thing after another.

Mìr a chur am beul na h-èisge.—*A morsel for the lampooner's mouth.*

Mìr' a' chuilein ris an t-seana chu.—*The play of the pup with the old dog.*

> *Al.*—ris an aois—*with the aged.*
> Chwarae hen gi a chenaw.—*Welsh.*

Mire ri cuilean, cha sguir e gus an sgal e.—*Play with a puppy, it ends in a howl.*

Mire gach struidheir ris an t-struidhear mhòr.—*The sport of every spendthrift with the big spendthrift.*

Misg gun leann as miosa th' ann.—*Intoxication without ale is the worst of all.*

> *Al.*—Misg an leanna nach d'òl e—*The intoxication of the ale he drank not.*
> The meaning seems to be that stupid or disorderly conduct, without the excuse of drink, is much worse. Ale, and not whisky, was the common stimulant when this saying arose.

Mo chomain-sa 's comain a' mhaoir,
Do mo thaobh-sa bhiodh e gann;
Is math leis comain a-null,
Ach cha mhath leis comain a-null 's a-nall.

—*The bailiff's favours and mine would be all one one side; he likes to get,
but not to give and take.*

This is attributed to John Morrison of Bragar (see note to 'Balach'),
with great probability. Another version, with *comann* for *comain*, is

Chan ionann is comann nam maor
Air an taobh-san nach bi fann;
'S e 'n comann-san tarring a-null,
'S cha chomann ach a-null 's a-nall.

—*Very unlike the bailiff's fellowship,
On their own side never weak;
Draw all one way is their rule,
And 'giff-gaff' is the only fellowship.*

Still another version is given in Duncan Lothian's *Sean Fhocail*, q.v.,
p. 439.

Mo chuid fhèin, mo bhean fhèin is 'Tiugainn dachaigh,' trì faclan
as blaisde th' ann.—*My own property, my own wife and 'Come home,'
three of the sweetest of words.*

Al.—Na trì rudan as mìlse th' ann—mo chuid fhèin &c.
Al.—M' ulaidh, m' ulaidh! mo chuid fhèin.—*My treasure, my treasure!
my own goods.*

Mo chuideachda fhèin, coin Thròndairnis!—*My own friends, the dogs
of Trotternish!*

See 'Is olc a fhreagradh tu'.

Mo nàire 's mo leaghadh!—*My shame and my melting*!

Mo thruaighe fear gun fhear-cronachaidh!—*Alas for him that has no
reprover*!

Mo thuras dubh a thug mi dh'Eirinn.—*My sad journey that took me to Ireland.*

> Said in a story by a king's daughter, transformed into a swan.

Modh na circe, gabhail ealla rithe.—*Hen politeness, letting her alone.*

Mol an latha math mu oidhche.—*Praise the good day at night.*

> Moyle y laa mie fastyr (*mu fheasgar*).—*Manx.* Ruse the fair day at night.—*Scot.* Praise day at night, and life at the end.—*Eng.* La vita il fine e 'l dì loda la sera.—*Ital.* Schönen Tag soll man loben, wenn es Nacht ist.—*Germ.*

Mol am monadh, 's na ruig e; diomoil a' choille 's na fàg i.—*Praise the moor and avoid it; dispraise the wood and keep to it.*

> *Al.*—Mol a' mhachair, 's na treabh; diomoil a' choille 's na trèig.—*Praise the plain, and plough it not &c.*
> *Al.*—'Lombair' for 'monadh'.
> Praise the hill, but keep below.—*Eng.* Loda il mare e tienti alla terra.—*It.* Il faut louer la mer et se tenir en terre.—*Fr.*
> Different, but creditable, is the Welsh saying, 'Canmol dy fro, a thrig yno'—*Praise thy country and tarry there.*

Moladh gach fear an t-àth mar a gheibh.—*Let every one praise the ford as he finds it.*

> Moladh gach duine an t-áth mar gheobhaidh sé é.—*Ir.* Moyll y droghad myr hen harrish.—*Manx.* Canmoled pob y bont a'i dycs drawo—*Welsh.*—*Praise the bridge as you get over.* Ruse the ford as ye find it.—*Scot.*

Moladh na maraig a feuchainn.—*The praise of the pudding is tasting it.*

> Cruthú na putóige a h-ithe—*The proof of the pudding is eating it.*—*Ir.* The pruif o a puddin 's the preein o't.—*Scot.*

Moladh mairbh.—*The praise of the dead.*

> De mortuis nil nisi bonum.—*Lat.*

Moladh na daoidheachd.—*Praise from the worthless.*

Molaidh an t-each math e fhèin.—*The good horse commends himself.*

Mallachd an fhir a ghoid air an fhear a dh'ionndrain—'An làmh a rinn gun dèan a-rithis!'—*The curse of the thief against the man that missed his own—'The hand that did it will do it again!'*

Molt mnatha gun chaoraich, is saothrach a ghlacadh.—*The wedder of a woman without sheep is difficult to catch.*

> *Al.*—'s e 's saoire gheibhte—*would be cheapest got.*
> *Al.*—'s e 's faoilidhe th' ann—*is the most freely given.*

Mòr a-muigh, 's beag a-staigh.—*Great abroad, small at home.*

Mòr bhuam, is beag agam.—*Much thought of until got.*

Mòr orm, is beag agam.—*Mighty to me, but little esteemed.*

> Said of an offensively patronizing but not superior person.

Mòran gleogaireachd, is beagan gleidhidh.—*Much talk and little done.*

Mòran sgalan, 's beagan ollainn, mun dubhairt Muisean 's e lomairt na muice.—*Great cry and little wool, as the Devil said when he sheared the sow.*

> Great cry and little wool, quoth the Devil when he sheared his hogs.—*Eng.*

Mòran shligean 's beagan bhiadhan.—*Many shells and little meat.*

Mu thionndadh na boise bidh a' chrois a' tighinn.—*In the turning of the hand the mishap will come.*

Mun cailleadh e buileach an t-iteach, bheireadh an t-eun a bhiodh glic ris an t-snàmh.—*The wise bird would take to swimming before he lost the power of flying.*

Mullach do bhaistidh.—*The top of your baptism.*

> The forehead.

Mur b'e an reothadh, threabhte gach tìr.—*But for the frost, all lands might be tilled.*

Mur b'e eagal an dà mhàil, bheireadh Tiridhe an dà bhàrr.—*But for fear of double rent, Tiree would yield a double crop.*

> Very suggestive, and not confined to Tiree.

Mur bi thu ris an olc, na bi coltach ris.—*If you are not doing ill, don't look like it.*

>Abstain from all appearance of evil.—*St Paul.*

Mur biodh an dris san rathad, cha rachadh a' chaor' innte.—*If the brier were not in the way, the sheep would not go into it.*

Mur biodh mun phoit ach Mac Sheoc 's an liadh—.—*If there were none about the pot but Jock's son and the ladle——.*

Mur biodh 'Mur b'e,' cha bhiodh duine beò.—*But for 'Were it not,' no man would be alive.*

>An aposiopesis. The omitted conclusion is 'I should fare better then'.

>Si ce n'etait le 'Si' et 'Mais,' nous serions tous riches à jamais.—*Fr.* If 'Ifs' an 'Ans' were pots and pans, where wud be the tinklers?—*Scot.*

Mur biodh 'Mur bhith' marbh, 's fhada bhon a thàinig e.—*If 'Were it not' were not dead, he would have come long ago.*

Mur biodh na suidheachan, thuiteadh na taighean.—*But for the roof-supports, the houses would fall.*

>This is used as a retort when some stupid 'If it weren't' is mentioned.

Mur biodh tu 'm shèomar, chan fhaiceadh tu mo chuid.—*If you hadn't been in my chamber, you wouldn't have seen my goods.*

>This reminds one of Posthumus and Iachimo in *Cymbeline.*

Mur cluinneadh tu sin chan abradh tu e.—*If you hadn't heard that, you wouldn't have said it.*

Mur comas dut teumadh, na rùisg do dheudach.—*If you cannot bite, don't show your teeth.*

>Ná taispeán do fhiacal san áit nach dtig leat greim a bhaint amach.—*Ir.* Ne'er shaw yir teeth unless ye can bite.—*Scot.*

Mur dean e lionn, millidh e braich.—*If he can't make ale, he'll spoil malt.*

>Same as making a spoon or spoiling a horn.

Mur dean mi spàin, millidh mi adharc.—*I'll make a spoon, or spoil a horn.*

>He'll mak a spune, or spoil a horn.—*Scot.*

Mur eil e còrdadh riut, chan eil e pòsda riut.—*If he doesn't please you, he is not married to you.*

> *Al.*—Mur eil mi &c.

Mur eil thu airson goid mo chàil, na tig air sgàth mo lios.—*If you are not coming to steal my kail, don't come for the sake of my garden.*

> *Al.*—Mur bi thu goid a' chàil, na bi air sgàth an lios.
> Stealing kail-stocks out of a neighbour's garden was part of the recognised usages on old New Year's Night.

Mur faigh fear da dhùthaich, 's math leis a bhith mu coinneamh—*If a man can't get to his country, it's good to be in sight of it.*

Mur h-e Bran, 's e bhràthair.—*If it be not Bran, it's his brother.*

> Bran was said to be Fingal's favourite hound.

Mur tig ach Pàl, gabhar Pàl; ach ma thig nas fheàrr na Pàl, chan fhiach Pàl bonn-a-h-ochd.—*If none come but Paul, Paul will be taken; but if better come, Paul won't be worth a piece of eight.*

> A piece of eight was less than a halfpenny.

Mur tig an rìgh, nach fhuirich e.—*If the king won't come, let him stay.*

Mur toir thu chuid don duine bhochd, na bi dèanamh fochaid air.—*If you don't give the poor man his due, at any rate don't mock him.*

> This seems a truism, but needs to be kept in mind.

N

Na abair ach beag, 's abair gu math e.—*Say but little, and say it well.*

Na abair 'Diug' ris an eun gus an tig e às an ugh.—*Don't say 'Chuck' to the chick till it be out of the egg.*

> *Al.*—Na abair bìg.
> Count not your chickens before they be hatched.—*Eng.* Non far conto dell' uovo non ancor nato.—*Ital.*

Na abair do sheanfhacal gus an toir thu do long gu caladh.—*Don't quote your proverb till you bring your ship to port.*

Na àireamh a chaoidh an t-iasg gus an tig e às a' mhuir.—*Never count the fish till they come out of the sea.*

> Ná beannaigh an t-iasc go dtiocfaidh sé i dtír.—*Ir.*

Na bi bogadh do liop san lite nach òl thu.—*Don't be dipping your lip in the porridge you sup not.*

Na bi ga shireadh 's ga sheachnadh.—*Don't be seeking and shunning it.*

> An excellent advice to shilly-shallying people, of either sex.

Na bi teann orm, 's na bi fada bhuam.—*Don't be near me, and don't be far from me.*

> This was said by a Highland catechist, the prototype of *Lachann nan Ceistean* of Dr. MacLeod's Dialogues. On one occasion he went to Inverness, accompanied by his wife, whom he did not think sufficiently presentable in 'society'. The above was the characteristic direction given to her.

Na biodh do theanga ann ad sporan.—*Let not your tongue be in your purse.*

> The meaning of this is not obvious at first, but it is good advice.

Na buail ach mar a bhiathas tu.—*Don't strike but as you feed.*

> Strike as ye feed, and that's but soberly.—*Scot.*
> 'A reproof,' says Kelly, 'to them that correct those over whom they have no power.'

Na caill am magh air a' chluain.—*Lose not the field for the meadow.*

Na creid an droch sgeul gus an dearbhar i.—*Believe not the bad report till it be proved.*

Na creid gur h-aithne dhut duine gus an roinn sibh creach.—*Don't suppose that you know a man till you come to divide a spoil with him.*

> A very shrewd observation, applicable equally in the 19th century, whether to potentates or private persons.

Na cuir a-mach an t-uisge salach gus an toir thu staigh an t-uisge glan.—*Don't throw the dirty water out till you bring in the clean.*

> Ná cuir an t-uisge salach amach go dtiobhraidh tú an t-uisge glan isteach.—*Ir.* Cast na oot the dowed water till ye get the clean.—*Scot.* Cast not out thy foul water till thou hast clean.—*Eng.* Man muss unreines Wasser nich eber wegiessen bis man reines hat.—*Germ.*

Na cuir do chorran gun chead ann an gead fir eile.—*Put not your sickle without leave into another man's corn-patch.*

> *Al.*—gart fir eile—*another man's standing corn.*
> Ná cuir do chorrán i ngort gan iarraidh.—*Ir.*

Na cuir do làmh eadar a' chlach 's an sgrath.—*Don't put your hand 'twixt the stone and the turf.*

Na cuir do spàin an càl nach buin dut.—*Don't put your spoon in kail that's not yours.*

> *Al.*—Na loisg do theanga an càl fir eile.
> Dinna scaud yir mou wi ither folk's kail.—*Scot.*

Na cuir 'nam ruith le leathad mi,
Na greas a' direadh bruthaich mi,
'S na caomhain air a' chòmhnard mi.

—*Don't make me run down a decline,*
Don't urge me going up a hill,
But spare me not on level ground.

Up hill spare me;
Down hill bear me;
Plain way, spare me not;
Let me not drink when I'm hot.—*Scot.*

Excellent advice from a horse to his rider or driver.

Na cumain bheag a' seòladh, 's na luingeas mhòr a' sìoladh.—*The little cogs sailing and the big ships sinking.*

See 'Is tric a bha na loingis'.

Na dèan bailc air iomaire math treabhaidh.—*Make no balk in good plough-land.*

Make not balks of good ground.—*Eng.* Mak nae bauks in guid bear-land.—*Scot.*
See 'Is fheàrr leum-iochd'.

Na dèan tàir air na 's leat; an nì nach leat, chan e dh'fhòghnas dut.—*Despise not what is your own; nothing else will suffice you.*

Lit.—'What is not your own will not be sufficient for you.'

Na dèan uaill à cuid duine eile.—*Boast not of another's means.*

Na dèanadh duine tùrsa, an earalas nach faigh e cuimse.—*Let no man despond of hitting the mark.*

Na dìobair caraid sa charraid.—*Forsake not a friend in the fray.*

Na dòirt e; cha tog na cearcan e.—*Don't spill it; the hens won't pick it up.*

Said of the spilling of drink.

Na earb thu fhèin ri gràisg.—*Don't trust the rabble.*

> The 'many-headed beast'. The maker of this proverb may have read
> Plato, but it is not very likely.

> Na falbh Diluain
> 'S na gluais Dimàirt;
> Tha Diciadain craobhaidh
> 'S tha Diardaoin dàlach;
> Dihaoine, chan eil e buadhach,
> 'S cha dual dut falbh a-màireach.

> —*Go not upon Monday,*
> *Stir not upon Tuesday;*
> *Wednesday is nervous,*
> *Thursday is dilatory;*
> *Friday is not fortunate,*
> *And 'tis not right for thee to go tomorrow.*

> This is called 'Triall a' bhodaich às a thaigh,' a wife's reasons for not
> letting her husband go away. Another version of the first part is

> Siubhal Dòmhnaich na toir bhuat,
> Diluain na èirich moch,
> Iom-sgaradh Dimàirt—
> Leig seachad na trì làithean sin.

Na feann am fiadh gus am faigh thu e.—*Don't skin the deer till you
get it.*

> First catch your hare.—*Mrs Meg Dods.*

Na gabh tè air bith mar mhnaoi ach tè air am bi athais agad.—*Take
no woman for a wife in whom you cannot find a flaw.*

> Ná gabh bean gan locht—*Take no faultless wife.*—*Ir.*
> This is an admirable saying, which I have not found in any other
> language. The Irish version is more laconic.
> He is lifeless that is faultless.—*Eng.*

Na geàrr do sgòrnan le d'theanga fhèin.—*Cut not thy throat with thine
own tongue.*

> Take heed that thy tongue strike not thy neck.—*Arab.*

Na gèill do ghis—cha ghèill gis dhut.—*Don't give in to spells—they won't give in to you.*

Na innis do rùn do d'charaide gòrach, no do d'nàmhaid glic.—*Tell not thy mind to thy foolish friend, nor to thy wise enemy.*

Na innis d'uile inntinn do d'mhnaoi no do d'chompanach.—*Tell not all your mind to your wife or your companion.*

> *Al.*—Na dèan fear rùin dhe d'dhlùth-chompanach.
> Trust ye not in a friend; . . keep the doors of thy mouth from her that lieth in thy bosom.—*Micah* vii, **6**.
> He is master of himself who keeps his secret from his friend.—*Arab.*
> Open not thine heart to every man.—*Sirach*, viii, 19. Que ta chemise ne sache ta guise.—*Fr.* Di' all' amico il tuo segreto, e ti terrà il piè sul collo.—*Ital.* A quien dices tu puridad, á ese das tu libertad.—*Span.*

Na ith am bonnach tha briste, 's na brist am bonnach tha slàn.— *Don't eat the broken bannock, nor break the whole one.*

> A story is told of a hungry servant-maid to whom her mistress gave the above order, when the girl told her, in the harvest field, that she was fainting for hunger. The mistress said,
>
> > Theirg dhachaigh 's ith do shàth—
> > Na ith am bonnach tha briste &c.
> >
> > —*Go home and eat your fill—*
> > *Eat not the bannock that's broken &c.*
>
> The girl thought she was justified in evading this prohibition by taking enough to appease her hunger out of the centre of the whole bannock.

Na ith sùil, no ùth, no àra, 's cha bhi galar cìch gu bràth ort.—*Eat not eye, or udder, or liver, and thy breasts shall ail thee never.*

Na ith 's na ob cuid an leanaibh bhig.—*Neither eat nor refuse the child's bit.*

> Very good manners.

Nam b'e 'n-diugh an-dè!—*Had today been yesterday!*

> How often is this thought felt.

Nam b'Eileanach mi, gum b'Ileach mi; 's nam b'Ileach mi, bu Rannach mi.—*Were I an Islander I should be an Islay man; and were I an Islay man, I should be a Rinns man.*

> This should compensate for the ill opinion of Islay men expressed in 'Chan eil an cùil' &c. The Rinns of Islay, like the Rinns of Galloway, is a low-lying and fertile tract of land, compared with the upper country. The Gaelic is *Roinnean*, n. pl. of *roinn*, of which gen. is *ranna*, whence *Rannach*.

Nam beireadh tu ugh, dhèanadh tu gloc.—*If you laid an egg, you would cackle.*

Nam biodh a' chòir air a cumail, cha bhiodh Rìgh Deòrsa 'n Lunnainn.—*If the right had been maintained, King George had not in London reigned.*

> This is comparatively modern, but has the proper ring of a popular saying, now harmless.

Nam biodh an t-earball na bu rìghne, bhiodh an sgeulachd na b'fhaide.—*Had the tail been tougher, the tale would have been longer.*

> This is the abrupt wind-up of a story, of which there are various versions, where the whole depends on the strength of the animal's tail, which gave way at the critical moment. See Campbell's *West Highland Tales*, II, 477. The English admits of a play on words which is not in the Gaelic.

Nam biodh cugainn aig a' chat, 's tric a rachadh e ga feuchainn.—*If the cat had standing milk, she would often go to try it.*

> See 'Cha tig cè'.

Nam biodh mo chù cho olc ionnsachadh riut, b'e 'n ciad rud a dhèanainn a chrochadh.—*If my dog were as ill-bred as you, the first thing I should do would be to hang him.*

> If I had a dog as daft, I wud shoot him.—*Scot.*

Nam biodh na coin air do dhìot itheadh, 's air falbh le d'shuipear, cha bhiodh tu cho mear.—*If the dogs had eaten your dinner, and run off with your supper, you would not be so merry.*

Nam bu bheò, bu mhithich.—*If alive, 'twas high time.*

Said of one who appears, or does a thing, after long expectation and delay.

Nam bu bhuan, bu mhath.—*Good if it lasted.*

Nam bu chaomh leat mi, bu bhinn leat mi.—*If you liked me, you would like my voice.*

Nam bu duin' eile gun dèanadh, 's mise gun dìoladh!—*If another man had done it, it's I that would avenge it!*

Said by a giant, on being told by his son that *Myself* had hurt him, that being the name which the person gave him who inflicted the punishment on the innocent and (as usual) stupid young giant. For another version of the story, see Campbell's *W. H. T.*, II, 189.

Nam bu mhac, bu mhithich.—*If a son, 'twas high time.*

Applied to the birth of an heir long looked for.

Nam bu toigh leat mi fhèin, cha bhuaileadh tu mo chù.—*If you liked myself, you would not strike my dog.*

See 'Am fear a bhuaileadh'.
Love me, love my dog.—*Eng.* He that strikes my dog wud strike mysel, if he daur'd.—*Scot.* Qui aime Bertrand, aime son chien.—*Fr.* Chi ama me, ama il mio cano.—*Ital.*

Nam bu toigh leat mi, cha bu trom leat mi.—*If you liked me, you would not think me heavy.*

Nam bu tu Brian, b'àrd a ghoireadh tu.—*Were you Brian, you would cry out loudly.*

> Nam faigheamaid an t-im as t-Earrach
> Is uachdar a' bhainne as t-Samhradh,
> 'S ann an sin a bhiomaid fallain,
> 'S cha bhiomaid falamh de dh'annlann.

—*If we could get butter in Spring and cream in Summer, it's then we should be healthy, and well off for kitchen.*

A Highland housewife's sarcasm on unreasonable men.

Nam faighte ceud sagart gun bhith sanntach;
Ceud tàillear gun bhith sunndach;
Ceud greusaich' gun bhith breugach;
Ceud figheadair gun bhith bradach;
Ceud gobha gun bhith pàiteach;
Is ceud cailleach nach robh riamh air chèilidh—
Chuireadh iad an crùn air an rìgh gun aon bhuille.

—Were a hundred priests got, not greedy;
A hundred tailors, not cheery;
A hundred shoemakers, not lying;
A hundred weavers, not thievish;
A hundred blacksmiths, not thirsty;
And a hundred old women that never went gossiping—
They would crown the king without a blow.

Ceathrar sagart gan a bheith sanntach,
Ceathrar Frangach gan a bheith buidhe,
Ceathrar gréasaighe gan a bheith bréagach,
Sin dhá fhear dhéag nach bhfuil sa tír.—*Ir.*

A hundred tailors, a hundred weavers and a hundred millers make three hundred thieves.—*Eng.* Cien sastres, cien molineros y cien texederos son trecientos ladrones.—*Span.* Honderd bakkers, honderd molenaars, en honderd kleêrmakers, zijn drie honderd dieven.—*Dutch.*

Na mealam mo shlàinte!—*May I forfeit my health (or salvation)!*

A form of abjuration.

Nan dèanadh mo làmh mar a dh' iarradh mo shùil!—*If my hand could do as my eye would desire!*

This might be the utterance of grasping ambition, but a better interpretation makes the yearning of a true artist towards his ideal.

Nan ruigeadh an daingeann an ceart.—*If the strong could attain the just.*

> Which it seldom does.

Nan sealladh cù air comain.—*If a dog could but see his obligation.*

> *Al.*—Cha sheall cù air comain. Cha chuimhnich cù comain.
> *None of these sayings do justice to the dog, which is a grateful animal.*

Nan tugadh aithreachas air ais, cha dèanadh neach na b'aithreach leis.—*If repentance could restore, none would make his own heart sore.*

Na nì am bodach le chrògan, millidh e le sgòpan.—*What the carl does with his hands he spoils with his feet.*

> See 'An rud a nì'.

'Na phiuthair-màthar don t-sluagh.—*A mother's sister to the people.*

> A warm saying, applied to a very kind friend of the peasantry.

> Na pòs as t-Fhoghar
> 'S dèan foighidinn sa Gheamhradh;
> Bidh tu cabhagach as t-Earrach,
> 'S bidh gainn' air aran as t-Samhradh.

> —*Marry not in Autumn*
> *And have patience in Winter;*
> *In Spring thou wilt be busy,*
> *And in Summer bread will be scarce.*

> A bachelor's excuses for delaying marriage.

Na sia buadhan a bha cumail suas na Fèinne—àgh Fhinn, làmh Ghoill, bras-bhuillean Osgair, iomairt ealamh Oisein, ruith chruaidh Chaoilte agus suidheachadh Chonain air a' chath.—*The six virtues that kept up the Feinne—Fingal's fortune, Gaul's hand, Oscar's impetuous strokes, Ossian's deft play, Coilt's hard running and Conan's planning of the battle.*

Na sèid sop nach urrainn dut fhèin a chur às.—*Kindle not a fire which you can't put out.*

> *Lit.*—'a wisp'.

Na sìn do chasan nas fhaide na thèid d'aodach.—*Stretch not your feet further than the clothes will go.*

> See 'Cha shìn duine'.
> Stretch your legs according to your coverlet.—*Eng.* Man muss sich strecken nach den Decken.—*Germ.* Steek uw voeten niet verder dan uw bed reikt.—*Dutch.* Cada uno estiende la pierna como tiene la cubierta.—*Span.*

Na sir 's na seachain an cath.—*Nor seek nor shun the fight.*

> *Al.*—Na seachain an iorghaill 's na h-iarr i.—*Neither shun the strife nor seek it.*
> Ná seachain is na h-agair an cath.—*Ir.*
> This resembles, but expresses more pithily, the sentiment of 'Defence, not defiance'. It is an Ossianic line.
> Bellum nec timendum nec provocandum.—*Plin. Jun.*

Na spìon feusag fir nach aithne dhut.—*Don't pluck a man's beard whom you don't know.*

Na tagh Binneagag, no Grinneagag, no Gaogag;
No ruadh bheag, no ruadh mhòr, no ruadh mhàsach;
Ach ciarag bheag air dhath na luch, na sir 's na seachain i.

> This is supposed to be an old man's advice to his son about choosing a wife, 'Comhairle Charmaig do mhac'—*'Cormack's advice to his son'*; and there are several versions, all with words which it is impossible to translate, being mostly fanciful inventions, not to be found in any dictionary, but not meaningless.
> *Al.*—Na tagh Cinnebheag, 's na tagh Ainnebheag, 's na tagh pìobaire na tot'; 's na tagh meallaire-slugaid; 's ciarag bheag &c., &c.
> Na pòs Ginnebheag, 's na pòs Innebheag; na pòs maoltach thràghad; na pòs glag-air-gàrradh; 's na pòs maighdeann Shàbaid; ach pòs bean bheag odhar, 'na seasamh an doras a sabhail fhèin, fuath aic' air fir an domhain, 's gràdh aic' air a fear fhèin.
> The conclusion is in favour of a sallow little woman, with charms more substantial than birth or beauty. The son is supposed to reply:

> > Bean-uasal dom bi stòras,
> > Cha phòs i mis' am bliadhna;
> > 'S bean-uasal lom fhalamh,
> > Cha tèid mis' ga h-iarraidh.

Na tarraing mi gun adhbhar, 's na pill mi gun chliù.—*Draw me not without cause, nor return me without honour.*

An inscription for a sword.

Na tilg dhiot an seann aodach gus am faigh thu 'n t-aodach ùr.—*Cast not the old clothes till you get the new.*

Na tog mi gus an tuit mi.—*Don't lift me till I fall.*

Ná tóg mé go dtuitfidh mé.—*Ir.* Dinna lift me before I faa.—*Scot.*

Na tog trògbhail air an aineol.—*Don't quarrel with a stranger.*

Na toilich do mhiann gus am feuch thu do sporan.—*Try your purse before you please yourself.*

Ask yir purse what ye sud buy.—*Scot.*

Na toir bean à taigh-mòr no bò bho ghàrradair.—*Don't take a wife from a big house, nor a cow from a gardener.*

See 'Bean à taigh-mòr'.

Na toir bò à Paibil, 's na toir bean à Boighreigh.—*Don't take a cow from Paible, or a wife from Borerary.*

Paible is a farm and village in N. Uist, Boreray another island near it.

Na toir breith a rèir coltais: faodaidh cridhe beairteach bhith fo chòta bochd.—*Judge not by appearance: a rich heart may be under a poor coat.*

Na toir breith chabhagach air mac luideagach, no air loth pheall-agaich.—*Don't judge hastily of a ragged boy or a shaggy colt.*

A raggit cowte may prove a noble aiver.—*Scot.* A ragged colt may make a good horse.—*Eng.* Méchant poulain peut devenir bon cheval.—*Fr.* Cavallo formoso de potro sarnoso.—*Port.* Aus Klattrigen Fohlen werden die shönsten Hengste.—*Germ.*

Na toir iasad air an iasad.—*Don't lend the loan.*

Na trì rudan as daoire th' ann: uighean chearc, feòil mhuc, glòir chailleach.—*The three dearest of things: hen eggs, pork and old women's praise.*

Na triùir mharbh as bòidhche air bith: leanabh beag, breac geal is coileach-dubh.—*The three prettiest dead: a little child, a salmon and a black-cock.*

Nàdar circe 's nàdar muice 's nàdar mnatha—gabhaidh iad an rathad fhèin.—*The nature of a hen, of a sow and of a woman—they take their own way.*

> Swine, women and bees cannot be turned.—*Eng.* Donne, asini e noci, voglion le mani atroci—*Women, asses and nuts need strong hands.*—*Ital.*

Nàire nam maighdeann an luirgnean nan cailleachan.—*Maidens' modesty in old women's shanks.*

> Nead air Brìghde, ugh air Inid, eun air Chàisg—
> Mur bi sin aig an fhitheach, bithidh am bàs.
>
> —*Nest at Candlemas, egg at Shrove-tide, bird at Easter—*
> *If the raven have them not, death then is his lot.*

Neart teine, neart mara 's neart balaich air bàinidh.—*The strength of fire, the strength of sea and the strength of a mad fellow.*

> *Al.*—Neart mara, neart teine 's droch bhean, na trì as uabhasaiche th' ann—*The strength of sea and of fire, and a bad wife—the three most dreadful of things.*

Neo-ar-thaing do rìgh na Fraing—chan eil mi 'n taing a shiùcair.—*No thanks to the King of France—I don't need his sugar.*

> This is modern, and probably originated in the time of the Napoleonic war.

Nì amadain cuirmean, ach nì daoine glic an ithe.—*Fules mak feasts and wise men eat them.*—*Scot., Eng.*

> So *Ital., Fr., Span., Dutch.*
> This is undoubtedly an importation from the South, but worth giving, if only for the sake of the happy repartee made by the Duke of Lauderdale when, at a great entertainment given by him in London, he heard this proverb maliciously cited by one of his guests. 'Aye,' said he, 'and wise men mak proverbs and fules repeat them.'

Nì an imrich thric an àirneis lom.—*Frequent flitting bares the furnishing.*

> See 'Eug is imrich'.

Nì airc innleachd.—*Necessity devises.*

> Necessity is the mother of invention.—*Eng.* De armoede is de moeder van alle Kunsten.—*Dutch.* Necessité est mère d'invention.—*Fr.* Need maks a man o craft.—*Scot.* Noth lehrt Künste.—*Germ.*

Nì an sporan falamh ceannach tais.—*Empty purse makes slow purchase.*

> A tume purse maks a blate merchant.—*Scot.*

Nì càilean am fiacail inntinn loisneach.—*A husk between the teeth disturbs the mind.*

> See 'Càilean'.

Nì Carcair càise nuair thèid crodh chàich an dìosg.—*Carcar will make cheese when other people's cows run dry.*

> A Lewis version of this is 'Nuair a thèid crodh a' bhaile dìosg, 's ann a nì catalach càise.' The interpretation of this must be left to conjecture. 'Carcar' is an unknown name, and *catalach* a rare word, unless it be simply a corruption of *cadalach*.

Nì cridhe subhach gnùis shuilbhir.—*A glad heart makes a cheerful face.*

Nì droch dhuine dàn da fhèin.—*A bad man makes his own destiny.*

> An exceedingly wise saying, especially among people believing so firmly in Fate.

Nì droch thaisgeach mòran mhèirleach.—*Bad keeping makes many thieves.*

> Opportunity makes the thief.—*Eng.* L'occasion fait le larron.—*Fr.* La commodità fa l'uomo ladro.—*Ital.* La ocasion hace el ladron.—*Span.* Gelegenheit macht den Dieb.—*Germ.* Leilighed giör Tyve.—*Dan.* De gelegenheid maakt den dief.—*Dutch.*

Nì dubh-bhreac an loch suain; bidh sàr-bhreac srutha a' sìor leum.—*The loch trout sleeps; the prime stream salmon ever leaps.*

Nì e dhìotsa feumannach, 's nì e dhìomsa breugadair.—*He will make of you a tool, and of me a liar.*

Nì òigear leisg bodach brisg.—*A lazy youth will make a brisk old man.*

Nì robh còta dubh air cealgaire, no còta dearg air cladhaire!—*No black coat cover hypocrite, nor red coat a coward!*

    A toast for Clergy and Army.

Nì siud feum nuair a nì am poca dubh a chaidh leis an abhainn.—*That will be of use when the black bag is that went with the stream.*

Nì thu gàire nuair a gheibh thu min.—*You'll smile when you get meal.*

    This is said to be part of a verse composed by John Morrison of Bragar to his wife, who was somewhat shrewish:

> Nì thu gàire nuair gheibh thu min;
> Is misde do ghean a bhith gun bhiadh;
> Is b'fheàrr leam fhèin na 'n t-each dearg
> Nach tigeadh fearg ortsa riamh.

    See *Proc. of Scot. Soc. of Ant.*, Vol. XII, p. 530.

Nigh' a' mhadaidh air a mhàthair.—*The dog's washing of his dam.*

Nighean an droch mhairt, 's ogh' a' mhairt mhath.—*The daughter of the bad cow, the grandchild of the good one.*

    The meaning probably is that a good ancestry is more important than a good mother.

Nigheanan a' feadaireachd is cearcan a' glaodhaich.—*Girls whistling and hens crowing.*

    Two things considered unnatural. See 'Feadaireachd'.

Nimh gun neart, nimh na cuileig, a bheir fuil air a' chraiceann.—*Pithless poison, the fly's bite, that bleeds but the skin.*

    The Arabic saying is wiser: 'Despise not a weak man in his conversation, for the gnat pierces the lion's eye.'

Nìtear càrn mòr de chlachaibh beaga.—*A big cairn is made of little stones.*

Nollaig an-diugh 's Bealltainn a-màireach.—*Christmas today and May Day tomorrow.*

    This is the result of an ingenious calculation, showing, e.g., that if Christmas Day falls on Monday, May Day will be Tuesday. It is generally, but not absolutely, correct.

O

Obair an doill.—*The work of the blind.*

Obair gun bhuannachd, a' cur sìl ann an talamh gun todhar.—*Profitless work, sowing in unmanured ground.*

Obair gun iarraidh, cha dèanainn do chliamhainn no charaid i.—*Work unasked I would not do for son-in-law or relative.*

Obair gun iarraidh, is e fiach a lochd.—*Work unasked, the better the worse.*

> Obbyr dyn (*gun*) oardagh, obbyr dyn booise (*bhuidheachas*).—*Manx.*

Obair is ath-obair.—*Work and work again.*

> Work hastily or ill done.

> Oidhch' a-muigh, is oidhch' a-staigh—
> Math na caorach 's olc an eich.

> *—In tonight, out tomorrow—*
> *Good for sheep, but horse's sorrow.*

> Oiee mooie, as oiee elley sthie—
> Olk son cabbil, agh son kirree mie.—*Manx.*

> Oidhche Shamhna, theirear gamhna ris na laoigh;
> Oidhch' Fhèill Eòin, theirear aighean ris na gamhna.

> *—On Hallowe'en the calf is called a stirk;*
> *On St John's Eve the stirk is called a heifer.*

Oidhche Challainn, bu math cuileann is calltainn a bhith bualadh a chèile.—*On Hogmanay Night it were good that holly and hazel should be striking each other.*

A windy night was considered a good sign of the season,

Ol Mhurchaidh is Fhearchair—dithis aig Murchadh, 's aig Fearchar a h-aon.—*Murdoch and Farquhar's drinking—two to Murdoch, one to Farquhar.*

Olc mun fhàrdaich, is math mun rathad mhòr.—*Bad at home, good abroad.*

Olc na cùise gu deireadh.—*Leave the disagreeable part of the case to the last.*

Olc no math mo bhriogais fhèin, 's i 's fheàrr dhòmhsa.—*Be my breeches good or bad, my own are the best for me.*

Olc no mhath le fear ga h-iarraidh, thig i 'n iar an dèidh an uisge.—*Let it please a man or no, after rain from west 'twill blow.*

See 'Gaoth 'n iar'.

Onfhadh na poite bige.—*The raging of the little pot.*

When the pat's fu it will boil ower.—*Scot.*

Oran na bà maoile—'Tha mi ullamh dhiot.'—*The song of the hornless cow—'I am done with you.'*

Oran na circe beadaidh.—*The song of the pert hen.*

P

Pàighear e Diluain mall.—*It will be paid on tardy Monday.*

Same as Nevermas.

Pàighidh a' ghaoth 'n iar a' ghaoth 'n ear am bliadhna fhathast.—*The west wind will pay the east wind yet this year.*

Pàighidh am feaman am feurach.—*The tail will pay the grazing.*

Each beast will pay for its feeding with the manure it leaves.

Paisg mo chaibe, faigh mo ribe, chuala mi 'Gug-gùg' sa chuan.—*Put by my spade, get my snare, I heard the bird's cry out at sea.*

This is a Uist or Harris invention, supposed to be spoken by a St Kilda man on hearing the first indication of the coming of the birds on which his living chiefly depends.

Pathadh na caorach ort!—*The sheep's thirst to thee!*

This is a bad wish=death to thee! The sheep can exist without drink, man cannot.

Peata caillich, pigheid clachain is dalta spìocaid—triùir as còir a sheachnadh.—*An old wife's pet, a village magpie and a scrub's step-daughter—three to be avoided.*

Peileir a' ghunna bhig ga chur sa ghunna mhòr.—*The bullet of the little gun put into the big gun.*

> Phòs mi luid airson a cuid;
> Dh'fhalbh a' chuid, ach dh'fhan an luid.
>
> *—I married a trull for her gold so fine—*
> *The gold is gone, but the trull is mine.*

Piseach mhath ort!—*Good luck to thee!*

> *Al.*—Buaidh is piseach ort!—*Success and luck to thee!*
> The latter is a very favourite expression of good wishes.

Pìobair' an aon phuirt.—*The piper of the one tune.*

> *Al.*—Pìobair' an aona chuir—*The one-bar piper.*
> It appears that at one time there were professing pipers so miserably furnished that they could play only the first bar of a tune, the repetition of which was too much for the most patient human ears. When the ancient order of Bards fell into disrepute, they used to go about the country in bands, living as best they could. Once a band of them came to a farmer's house in Islay, where they were hospitably entertained for a week, got plenty of dry bread, and a piper to play to them his one tune. He happened to be of the one-bar species, and when the bardic company departed, their leader ('*Ceann-steòcaire*') made the following impromptu:—
>
> > Pìobaireachd is aran tur
> > 'S miosa leam na guin a' bhàis;
> > Fhir a bhodhair mo dhà chluais,
> > Na cuir pìob a suas gu bràth!
> >
> > *—Piping and dry bread to me*
> > *Are worse than agony of death;*
> > *Thou man who hast deafened me,*
> > *Never, never pipe again!*
>
> N.B.—The word *tur* here is noticeable, as now quite obsolete in the sense of 'dry'. The word *turadh* = 'dry weather' is derived from it.

Pògadh an leanaibh air sgàth na banaltraim.—*Kissing the child for the sake of the nurse.*

> See 'Air ghaol'.

Port ùr air an t-seann fhidhill.—*A new tune on the old fiddle.*

Pòsadh thar na h-innearach, is goisteachd thar muir.—*Marriage o'er the midden, sponsorship o'er sea.*

> Better marry ower the midden than ower the muir.—*Scot.*
> Better wed over the mixen than over the moor.—*Cheshire.*

R

Rachadh e tro tholl tora gu nì fhaotainn.—*He would go through an auger-hole to get anything.*

Rachainn a thaomadh na fairge dha nan iarradh e orm.—*I would go to drain the sea for him if he asked me.*

Rathad cam thun a' chaisteil.—*A roundabout way to the castle.*

Rathad Mhòr-innis do Chill Fhionnachain.—*Going by Morinish to Kilfinichen.*

> A roundabout way. This is a Mull saying. A Tiree saying is 'Rathad Hogh do Haoidhnis'; a Coll saying 'Rathad Feall do dh'Ameireaga'. An Ardnamurchan saying is 'Rathad nam Mealla Ruadh thun na Ranna' or 'Cuartachadh Iain Ruaidh thun na Ranna'; the Ranna being on the north of Ardnamurchan and the 'Mealla Ruadh' the precipitous red rocks on the south side.

Rathad muilinn Drongaidh.—*The way to the mill of Dron.*

> *Al.*—Rathad mòr leathann rèidh, rathad muilinn D.—*A broad level highway, &c.*

> There was no made road.

Reic e pheighinn-phisich.—*He sold his luck-penny.*

Reothadh an lodain làin.—*The freezing of the full pool.*

Reothairt na Fèill Moire, 's boile na Fèill Pàdraig.—*The Spring-tide of Lady Day; the fury of St. Patrick's Day.*

> High tides and winds occur about these times.

Ri fheuchainn bidh fios agad.—*You'll know when you try.*

> Ri fuachd Callainn, 's math clò ollainn;
> Ri fuachd Fèill Brìghde, fòghnaidh cìsfheart.
>
> *—For New Year cold, good is woollen cloth;*
> *For Candlemas cold, mixed stuff will do.*

Riaraich am pailteas gu math, is riaraichidh a' bhochdainn i fhèin.—*Divide the plenty well, and the scarce will divide itself.*

> When there is much, it requires to be carefully distributed, to prevent waste or inequality; where there is little, the division is more easy, and there is no danger of waste.

Rìghneas an laoigh fhirinn.—*The toughness of the bull-calf.*

Rinn e baothaire dheth.—*He made a fool of him.*

Rinn e coileach-dubh dheth.—*He made a blackcock of him.*

> He shot him dead.
> This suggests the saying of the bard Iain Lom, when he was shown a quantity of blackcocks' heads at Inveraray and asked if he had ever seen so many? 'Yes,' he said, 'I saw more of them at Inverlochy'—alluding to the slaughter of the Campbells at the battle there.
> *Al.*—Rinn e biadh eun deth—*He made birds' food of him.*
> *Al.*—Rinn e pasgadh na pìob air—*He doubled him up like a bagpipe.*

Rinn e faraiche den fharaiche.—*He made a plug out of the plug-driver.*

> Driving out a plug with another, and that other sticking in its place.

Rinn e luath is deargannan ann.—*He made ashes and fleas there.*

> I.e., he stayed there long enough.

Rinneadh airson toil na cuideachd e, mar chaidh an tàillear do Pheairt.—*It was done to please the company, as the tailor went to Perth.*

Roghainn den chuid as miosa.—*Choice of the worse part.*

Roghainn den chuid nach fhaigh e.—*Choice of what he will not get.*

Roinn a' mhic ri mhàthair.—*The son's sharing with his mother.*

Roinn mic is athar.—*The sharing of father and son.*

Roinn MhicCrùislig air na crùbain.—*MacCruslick's dividing of the crabs.*

> He put the contents of the best-looking ones into the worst-looking ones, which he afterwards got for himself.

Roinn na màthar ris an nighinn.—*The mother's sharing with her daughter.*

Ruaig coilich air dùnan.—*Putting a cock on a dunghill to flight.*

Rudeigin an àit' an earchaill.—*Something in place of loss.*

Rug bò laogh dha.—*A cow has borne him a calf.*

Rug iasg orm.—*A fish has caught me.*

> Said by a person when seized with a fit of sickness.—Note by Macintosh. This saying is unintelligible, and not in use.

Ruthadh an leanaibh Ilich, ruthadh an teine.—*The bloom of the Islay child, the bloom of the fire.*

> The *leanabh Ileach* was a remarkable boy, with a hard stepmother, who fed him badly and heated his face at the fire when she wished to pass him off as a well-fed ruddy child.—See *Cuairtear*, 1842, p. 79.

> Ruthadh shuas an àm laighe,
> Dh'èireadh Fionn moch sa mhadainn;
> Ruthadh shuas sa mhoch-mhadainn,
> Dhèanadh Fionn an ath chadal.

> *—With a rosy sky at bedtime,*
> *Fingal would rise early;*
> *With a rosy sky at dawn,*
> *He would take another sleep.*

> My ta 'n ghrian jiarg tra giree teh, foddee shin jerkal rish fliaghey—*If the sun rises hot and red, we may look for a wetting.*—Manx. When it is evening ye say; 'It will be fair weather, for the sky is red,' and in the morning, 'It will be foul weather today, for the sky is red and lowring.'—*Matth.* xvi, 2, 3.

Evening red and morning gray
Are sure signs of a fair day;
Evening gray and morning red
Sends the poor shepherd home wet to his bed.—*Eng.*

Eening red and morning gray,
The taikens o a bonny day;
Eening gray and morning red,
Put on yir hat or ye'll weet yir head.—*Scot.*

Ruigidh an ro-ghiullachd air an ro-ghalar.—*The best of nursing may overcome the worst disease.*

Ruigidh dàil doras.—*Delay will arrive at the door.*

Ruigidh each mall muileann, ach feumaidh fear fuireach a bhristeas a chas.—*A slow horse will reach the mill, but the horse that breaks his leg must lie still.*

Al.—ach bristidh each tuisleach a chas—*but a stumbling horse will break his leg.*

Rùisgidh brù bràghad.—*The belly will bare the breast.*

Y bol a bil y cefn.—*Welsh.* Your belly will never let your back be warm.—*Eng.* The back and the belly hauds ilka ane busy.—*Scot.*

Rùisgeadh e thaigh fhèin a thughadh taigh a choimhearsnaich.—*He would strip his own house to thatch his neighbour's.*

Ruith choin an dà fhèidh.—*The running of the dog that chases two deer.*

Losing both. See 'Cù an dà fhèidh'.

Ruith na caorach caoile le leathad.—*The lean sheep's run down the slope.*

Rhuthr enderig o'r allt—The run of the steer from the hill.—*Welsh.*

Ruithidh an taigeis fhèin le bruthaich.—*Even a haggis will run downhill.*

Strange to say, this does not occur in any of the collections of Scottish proverbs; but it is quoted, with his usual wonderful felicity, by Sir Walter Scott. On the eve of Prestonpans, Evan Dhu M'Combich (*Waverley*, ch. xlvi) is made to say, 'Even a haggis—God bless her!—could charge downhill.'

Ruithinn air bhàrr an uisge dha.—*I would run on the water for him.*

Rùn caillich gun trod i.—*A crone's secret (or delight) is to scold.*

> Rún caillighe an sciolláireacht (*scolding*).—Ir.

Rùn do chridhe air do chuisle!—*May your pulse beat as your heart would wish!*

> This is a very pretty saying.

S

Sac trom air a' chois chaoil.—*A heavy load on the slender leg.*

A burden imposed on a child.

Saighdearan a' chlobha.—*The tongs soldiers.*

Al.—Saighdear-sitig—*Dunghill-soldier.*
A term contemptuously applied to holiday soldiers.

> Sàil-chuaich is bainne ghobhar
> Suath ri d'aghaidh,
> 'S chan eil mac rìgh air domhan
> Nach bi air do dheaghaidh.

> *—Wash thy face with lotion*
> *Of goat-milk and sweet violets;*
> *There's not a king's son in the world*
> *But will then run after thee.*

This is a solitary specimen of Highland skill in cosmetics.

Salaichidh aon chaora chlaimheach an treud.—*One scabbed sheep's enough to spoil a flock.*—*Eng.*

Salaíonn aon chaora chlamhach sréad.—*Ir.* Ta un cheyrey screbbagh doghaney yn slane shioltane.—*Manx.* Ae scabbit sheep will smit a hail hirsel.—*Scot.* Eet skabbet Faar fordær ver en heel Flok.—*Dan.*

> Grex totus in agris
> Unius scabie cadit.—*Juv.*

Una pecora infetta n' ammorba una setta.—*Ital.* Il ne faut qu'une brebis galeuse pour gâter tout le troupeau.—*Fr.*

Sannt gun sonas, èiridh an donas dha.—*Luckless greed won't succeed.*

Sannt caillich sa chruaich mhòine.—*An old woman's greed at the peat-stack.*

Saoghal fada 'n deagh bheatha dhut!—*Length of good life to thee!*

Saoilidh am fear a bhios 'na thàmh gur e fhèin as fheàrr làmh air an stiùir.—*The looker-on thinks himself the best steersman.*

De beste stuur-lieden (*pilots*) zijn aan land.—*Dutch.*

Saoilidh an duin' air mhisg gum bi a h-uile duin' air mhisg ach e fhèin.—*The drunk man thinks all drunk but himself.*

Saoilidh bradaidh nam bruach gur gadaichean uile càch.—*The thief of the braes thinks all others thieves.*

Saoileann gadaí na gcruach gur slaididh an slua.—*Ir.* Piensa el ladron que todos son de su condicion.—*Span.* O ladraõ cuida que todos taes sao.—*Port.*

Sàr-dhubh do ghonaidh ort!—*The worst of bewitchment to thee!*

Al.—Seun do ghonaidh ort!

Sàth mòr ainmig do na leanaban fireann, sàth beag minig do na leanaban boireann.—*A large feed seldom for the male child, a small feed often for the female child.*

Seach gun tug mi 'n rèis, bheir mi 'n òirleach.—*As I have given the span, I'll give the inch.*

Seachain an t-àth far an do bhàthadh do charaid.—*Shun the ford where your friend was drowned.*

Seachain an t-olc is seachnaidh an t-olc thu.—*Avoid evil and it will avoid thee.*

Shaghyn dagh olk.—*Manx.*

Seachain mo chluas, 's cha bhuail m'adharc.—*Avoid my ear, and my horn will not hit.*

Seachd bliadhna an cuimhne na bà, 's gu là a bhàis an cuimhn' an eich.—*Seven years will the cow keep in mind, all his life the horse.*

The horse remembers his stable longer than the cow her byre.

Seachd bliadhna saoghal a' chait—
Sin gu h-èibhinn agus ait;
Seach sin cadal agus tur-chadal.

—*Seven years lives the cat,*
Joyfully and cheerfully,
All the rest is sleep, sound sleep.

Seachd bolla shneachda Gearrain,
Dol a-staigh thro aon toll torra.

—*Seven bolls of February snow*
Through an auger-hole to go.

Considered seasonable weather.
See 'Thèid cathadh'.

Seachd seachdainean bho aois gu bàs eadar Càisg is Inid.—*Seven weeks always between Pasch and Shrove-tide.*

Al.—eadar Càisg is Nollaig—*between Pasch and Christmas.*

Seachd sgadain, sàth bradain; seachd bradain, sàth ròin.—*Seven herring, a salmon's feed; seven salmon, a seal's feed.*

This saying is interesting, as showing that our ancestors were well acquainted with the fact that the salmon eats herring, which has in modern times been a matter of question and inquiry among ichthyologists.

Seachdain an t-sionnaich, 's bu mhath nach bu bhliadhn' i.—*The fox's week, and 'tis well that it is not a year.*

Wythnos y llwynog.—*Welsh.*
The first week in lambing-time—end of April.

Seachnaidh duin' a bhràthair, ach cha sheachain e choimhear-snach.—*A man may do without a brother, but not without a neighbour.*

Lit.—'may avoid.' See 'Is fheàrr coimhearsnach'.

Sealladh àrd na seana mhaighdinn.—*The high look of the old maid.*

Ye breed o auld maids, ye look heich!—*Scot.*

Seann sgeul Earraich.—*An old Spring story.*

    Told in the long nights.

Searrach na seann làrach, cha bhi tighinn-a-mach ann.—*An old mare's foal will never come to much.*

    See 'Mac bantraich'.

Searrach seann òigich, cha robh e riamh sgairteil.—*The foal of an old stallion was never vigorous.*

Seasadh gach soitheach air a mhàs fhèin.—*Let every vessel stand on its own bottom.*

    Let every tub stand on its own bottom.—*Eng., Scot.*

'S e do bheatha fuireach, ach 's e do bhuidheann falbh; chì thu doras do thaighe fhèin bho dhoras mo thaighe-sa.—*You are welcome to stay, but you had better go; you can see your own door from mine.*

Sgeul ga innse don ghearran, 's an gearran a' cur bhram às.—*Telling a story to the gelding, and the gelding breaking wind.*

Sgugairneach de dh'eun deireadh Foghair, 's mairg a dh'fheith ri d'bhreith sa Mhàrt.—*Useless bird at Harvest end, pity those who waited for your birth in March.*

    Al.—Gugarlach.
    Applied to clumsy workers, more in the way than helpful.

Sèid agus sèid an gual, ach sèid gu righinn cruaidh an sop—sin mar thèid an tein' a lasadh.—*Blow and blow again the coal, but a long, hard blow to the wisp—so the fire will lighted be.*

Sèididh aon sròn shalach an clachan.—*One snotty nose will set a whole church a-blowing.*

Seileach allt, calltainn chreag, feàrna bhog, beithe lag, uinnseann an deiseir.—*Willow of the brook, hazel of the rock, alder of the bog, birch of the hollow, ash of the sunny slope.*

    Al.—beithe a' chnuic—*the birch of the knoll.*

Seo mo chuid-sa 's do chuid fhèin; siud cuid Dhòmhnallain.—*This my share and yours; that for little Donald.*

> Once upon a time, when crofters lived at Druim Uachdair, in Badenoch, a poor widow at the end of a severe Spring was in great straits. She went to a neighbour and begged her, for the love of God, to give her as much meal as would make porridge for herself and her children. 'The Devil a grain have I,' said the other woman. 'God bless my share, mother,' said her little boy, who was sitting at the hearth. The poor woman went away sore-hearted; and presently there came in to the house she had left no less a visitor than the *Fear Mòr*, whose name had just been mentioned. He immediately went to the meal-chest, and proceeded to take it out in handfuls, two for himself and the mistress of the house, one for little Donald. The former he put into a sack, the latter he left; and having finished the work, went out, emptied the sack into the burn, and disappeared in a cloud of smoke!

Sgadan geàrr gun mhealg gun iuchair, 's mairg brù an tèid e.—*Short herring without milt or roe, pity him that eats.*

Sgal crèathaich is eubh caillich—dà nì nach mair fada.—*The noise of burning brushwood, and the cry of an old woman, don't last long.*

Sgaraidh aimbeairteas deagh chomann.—*Puirtith pairts guid company.—Scot.*

> Poverty parteth fellowship.—*Eng.*

Sgian an fhir ud shìos an truaill an fhir ud shuas—*This man's knife in that man's sheath.*

Sgiobair tòn-ri-creig, math air tìr 's dìblidh air muir.—*Shore-skipper, good on land, craven at sea.*

> A long-shore skipper makes a lubberly sailor.—*Eng.*

Sgoiltidh farmad na creagan.—*Envy will split rocks.*

Sgoiltidh sùil a' chlach.—*An eye can split a stone.*

> The evil eye. See note to 'Ceum air do cheum'.

Sgreuch na muice a' dol don iodhlainn.—*The screech of the sow on her way to the stackyard.*

Sgrìob liath an Earraich.—*The gray track of Spring.*

Al.—Bheir sgrìob ghlas Earraich cairt bharrach Foghair—*A green Spring will fill the cart in Autumn.*

Shaoil leis gum bu leis fhèin an cuan fo gheasaibh.—*He thought the ocean his own under his spells.*

Applied to persons with an overweening or insane idea of their own importance.

Shuidh mosag air a sasaig.—*The scrub sat on her easy-chair.*

Sasag, or *sunnag*, an easy-chair made of wickerwork and straw.

Sian fala mu d'shùilean!—*A shower of blood round thine eyes!*

Siud a' bhuille aig an stadadh m'athair, arsa nighean a' chùbair.— *That's the blow where my father would stop, said the cooper's daughter.*

A blow too many would set the hoop flying, instead of fixing it.

> Siud mar thaghadh Fionn a chù:
> Sùil mar àirneig, cluas mar dhuilleig,
> Uchd mar ghearran, speir mar chorran,
> 'S an t-alt-lùthaidh fad' on cheann.

> —*Thus would Fingal choose his hound:*
> *Eye like sloe, ear like leaf,*
> *Chest like horse, hough like sickle,*
> *And the pith-joint far from head.*

Al.—Gnos mar chuaille,
Cluas mar dhuilleach,
Earball mun speir
'S an speir mar chorran.

—*Muzzle like club, ear like leaf, tail to the hough, and hough like sickle.* This refers to the old Scottish deerhound. The English greyhound is thus described in a rhyme given by Ray:

> A head like a snake, a neck like a drake,
> A back like a beam, a belly like a bream,
> A foot like a cat, a tail like a rat.

Sìod' air cabar, 's bidh e brèagh'.—*Put silk on a stick, and it will look fine.*

Sìol nam pudharan.—*The seed of injuries.*

Sionnach ag iarraidh a ruagaidh.—*A fox asking to be chased.*

> Sireadh caimein an connlaich,
> Sanas a thoirt do chuaille—
> Duine toirt a chomhairle
> Far nach gabhar uaith' i.
>
> —*Searching for a mote in straw,*
> *Hinting to a fool,*
> *Is the giving of advice*
> *Where it is not taken.*

Sireadh sop an connalaich.—*Searching for a wisp in stubble.*

Sìth do d'anam, is clach air do chàrn!—*Peace to thy soul, and a stone on thy cairn!*

Siubhal a' chait a chaidh don eas dhut!—*The way of the cat that went to the waterfall to you!*

Siubhal Artair ort!—*Arthur's journey to you!*

Siubhal Mhurchaidh bhon bhothan ort!—*Murdoch's way from the bothy to you!*

Siubhal na Samhna dha!—*Let him go like Hallowmas!*

> Never to come back. The two preceding sayings have the same meaning. Can Arthur mean the king?

Slàn far an innsear e!—*May it be well where it is told!*

> The word *slàn*, 'healthy', 'whole', is here used elliptically, without a verb.

Slaodadh an arain anns a' bhrochan.—*Trailing the bread in the gruel.*

Slèibhte riabhach nam ban bòidheach.—*Russet Sleat of pretty women.*

> See 'Clachan an t-Srath'.

Sliochd nan sionnach, Clann Mhàrtainn.—*The race of the foxes, Clan Martin.*

> The fox is sometimes called *an gille-Màrtainn*.

Slìog am bodach is sgròbaidh e thu, buail am bodach 's thig e gu d'làimh.—*Stroke the churl, and he will scratch you; strike him, and he will come to your hand.*

> If you gently touch a nettle,
> It will sting you for your pains;
> Grasp it like a man of mettle,
> It as soft as silk remains.

Smeuran dubha san Fhaoilleach, is uighean fhaoileag as t-Earrach.—*Bramble-berries in February, and seagulls' eggs in Spring.*

> Things out of season.

Snìomhaidh tighearna feàrna tuathanach daraich.—*An alder lord will twist an oak tenant.*

> *Al.*—Toinnidh an t-uachdaran feàrna an t-ìochdaran daraich.
> Alder is soft wood, of comparatively small value. The story of the man who was encouraged by his wife to 'gang up and be hangit, to please the laird' may be taken as an illustration of this saying from the 'good old times'. Somewhat similar pressure is still exercised occasionally in modern times.

Socraichidh am pòsadh an gaol.—*Marrying sobers love.*

Sonas a chodach air a' bheul fharsaing.—*The wide mouth's happiness in its food.*

Sop às gach seid.—*A wisp from every truss.*

> Applied to any miscellaneous collection or farrago.

Soraidh leat fhèin, ach mallachd aig beul d'ionnsachaidh!—*Blessing on yourself, but curse be on your teacher!*

Spagada-gliog Chlann Dòmhnaill agus leòm Leathaineach.—*Mac-Donald swagger and MacLean airs.*

> *Al.*—Spagada-gliog Chlann IllEathain.
> See 'An t-uasal'.

Sradag a' ghobha, tha i duilich a bàthadh.—*The smith's spark is hard to quench.*

> The smith has aye a spark in his throat.—*Scot.*

Sròn cho biorach 's gun tugadh i biadh à faochag.—*A nose so sharp that it would pick a periwinkle.*

Sròn ri monadh.—*Nose hillward.*

> 'Nez retroussé.' Applied to persons easily offended—'nosey'.

Stiùbhartaich, cinne nan rìgh 's nan ceàrd.—*The Stewarts, the race of kings and of tinkers.*

> Stewart is a very common name among tinkers, often adopted for the sake of the supposed respectability it conferred.

Stoc suirghiche.—*A wooer's block.*

> In Lochaber a block of old bog-pine was sometimes kept, as a test of skill and patience in chopping wood, for young men coming a-courting.

Suas an luideag!—'s e 'n duine an t-aodach.—*Up with the rag!—the dress is the man.*

> Sé an t-éadach a ghní an duine.—*Ir.*
> See 'Ged nach e 'n duine'.

Suas leis a' chuigeil bharraich! 'S ioma latha fada gu Bealltainn.—*Up with the loaded distaff! There's many a long day till May Day.*

> Supposed to be the language of procrastination.

Suidh gu h-ìosal, is dìol gu h-uasal.—*Sit lowly, and pay nobly.*

Suidh' an dèidh èirigh, a' chuid as miosa den chèilidh.—*Sitting after rising, the worst part of gossiping.*

Suidhe a' gheòidh an doras taigh an t-sionnaich.—*The sitting of the goose at the fox's door.*

Suidhe bochd an taigh na h-airce.—*A poor seat in the house of want.*

Sùil a' chait air sìoman.—*A cat's gaze at a straw-rope.*

> This is applied to the bestowal of much attention on trifles.

Sùil mun t-sròin.—*Eye to nose.*

This is the ὑπόδρα ἰδών of Homer, describing a haughty disdainful look, eye downward to nose.

Suipear ghabhail soillse là Oidhch' Fhèill Brighde;
Dol a laighe soillse là Oidhch' Fhèill Pàdraig.

—*On St Bride's Eve, supper with daylight;*
On St Patrick's, bed by daylight.

Al.—Suipear an soillse là, mach o Là Fhèill Brighde;
Laighe 'n soillse là, mach o Là Fhèill Pàdraig.

Suirghe fada bhon taigh, 's pòsadh am bun an dorais.—*Courting far from home, and marrying next door.*

Al.—Suirghe air na h-aonaichean, is pòsadh aig a' bhaile—*Wooing o'er the moor, and marrying at home.*
See 'Pòsadh'.

Sùlairean sgìre na h-Aoidh, 's muinntir aoigheach nan Loch.—*The solan-geese of Eye, and the hospitable folks of Lochs.*

Two neighbouring parishes in the island of Lewis, the former of which is now called Stornoway, a great station for herring-fishery and fish-curing—hence the allusion to solan-geese.

Sult searraich air a leis.—*A foal's fat is on his quarter.*

Sùrd air Suaineart! Chaidh Aird nam Murchan a dholaidh.—*Stir thee, Sunart! Ardnamurchan is done for.*

Two neighbouring districts in Argyllshire. The saying is used as a spur to emulation in work.

T

Tachraidh d'fhiadh fhèin riut.—*Your own deer will come in your way.*

Tadhlaidh bò a h-ath-bhuaile mur h-olc an innis.—*A cow will revisit her fold, if the pasture be not bad.*

Tagh do bhean mar as math leat do chlann.—*Choose your wife as you wish your children to be.*

Tagh do bhean 's i 'na currac-oidhche.—*Choose your wife with her nightcap on.*

Tagh do chainnt.—*Choose your speech.*

> (Be civil.)

Tagh do choluadar mun tagh thu d'òl.—*Choose your company before you choose your drink.*

> *Al.*—Tagh do chuideachd mun tagh thu do dheoch.
> *Al.*—Tagh do chompanach mun suidh thu.—*Choose your companion before you sit down.*
> Choose thy company before thy drink.—*Eng.*

Tagh nighean na deagh mhàthar, ged a b'e 'n donas a b'athair dhi.—*Choose the good mother's daughter, were the devil her father.*

Tàillear a chronachadh tàilleir.—*Set a tailor to check a tailor.*

> Tàirneanach an dèidh nòine, tàirneanach an toraidh mhòir;
> Tàirneanach ro nòine, tàirneanach gorta 's fuachd.
>
> —*Thunder in the afternoon, the thunder of plenty;*
> *Thunder in the forenoon, the thunder of want and cold.*

Tàillear a' ghogain ime, 's figheadair na fuaraig.—*The tailor of the butter cog, the weaver of the crowdie.*

Tàirnidh gach neach ri choltas.—*Like draws to like.*

> See 'Druididh' and 'Is ionmhainn'.

Taisg bonn is cosg bonn, 's bidh tu sona; taisg bonn 's na cosg bonn, 's bidh tu dona.—*Save a coin and spend a coin, and you'll be happy; save a coin and spend none, and you'll be wretched.*

Talach a' ghille ghlic, ga ithe 's ga chàineadh.—*The wise lad's grumbling—eating it and abusing it.*

> *Al.*—Talach a' ghille ghlic—gabh na gheibh, is iarr an còrr.—*The wise lad's grumbling—take what you get, and ask for more.*

Talach air meud a chuibhrinn.—*Complaining of the greatness of his portion.*

> *Al.*—Talach uallaich—*Complaining of his load.*
> Not uncommon among people bloated with wealth.

Tàlaidhidh am biadh fiadh na beinne.—*Food will entice the mountain deer.*

> *Al.*—an t-eun adhair—*the bird from the sky.*
> See 'Càtaichidh' and 'Meallaidh'.

Taomadh na mara làine.—*Baling out the full tide.*

Tapan gòraig air cuigeal crìontaig.—*The silly one's tuft of wool on the thrifty one's distaff.*

Tarraing am bleidir' ort, 's bidh e oidhch' agad.—*Encourage the sorner, and you'll have a night of him.*

> *Al.*—Tadhladh am bleidire, 's bidh an oidhch' ann.—*The beggar takes care to call at evening.*

Tatha mhòr nan tonn, bheir i sgrìob lom air Peairt.—*Great billowy Tay will sweep Perth bare.*

> This was an old prophecy, fulfilled more than once.
> See 'Dh' fhalbh Peairt'.

Tàthadh goirid a' ghobha agus tàthadh leobhar an t-saoir.—*The short welding of the smith; the long joining of the carpenter.*

Tè gheal bho fhear gu fear; tè odhar an doras a sabhail.—*A fair one goes from man to man; a dun one stands at her own barn door.*

> This is a suggestion that the plain woman will make a better wife. See 'Na tagh'.

Teanga fhada 'n ceann Dhòmhnaill Fhìdhleir.—*A long tongue in Donald Fiddler's head.*

Teanga cho geur ri ealtainn.—*A tongue as sharp as a razor.*

Teannaich do chrios gus am faigh thu biadh.—*Tighten your belt till you get food.*

> This is a known practice of American Indians.

Teine chaoran is gaol ghiullan.—*Fire of peats and love of boys.*

> Not of long endurance.

Teirigidh Cruachan Beann, gun dad a dhol ri cheann.—*Ben Cruachan will waste away, if nothing be added to it.*

> *Al.*—Theirigeadh Cruachan Beann le bhith sìor thoirt às, gun dad idir ga chur ann.

Teirigidh gach nì ri chaitheamh.—*Everything will end with wasting.*

Teisteanas a' choimhearsnaich air gach neach.—*A neighbour's testimony is the test of everybody.*

> *Al.*—Teist a nàbaidh.

Teodhaidh feòil ri fine, ged nach deòin le duine.—*Flesh will warm to kin, against a man's will.*

> *Al.*—Teodhaidh an fhuil ris an fhuil—*Blood warms to blood.*
> See 'Is tighe'.
> The sentiment and the double rhyme here are equally pretty.

Tha àm air an achmhasan, is tràth air a' chèilidh.—*There's a time for rebuke, and a time for gossiping.*

> To everything there is a season.—*Eccl.* iii, 1. Amser i fwyd, amser i olychwyd—*A time for meat, and a time for prayer.* Pob peth yn ei amser—*Everything in its time.—Welsh.*

Tha aon chas na 's leòr don fhìrinn, ach tuitidh a' bhreug le 'trì.—*One foot is enough for truth, but a lie falls with three.*

> See 'Imridh breug'.

Tha aon saighead às a bhalg.—*There is one arrow out of his quiver.*

Tha beul gun fhàitheam draghail.—*A hemless mouth is troublesome.*

Tha bheul air a ghualainn.—*His tongue is on his shoulder.*

> Wearing his heart upon his sleeve; the opposite of 'teanga fo chrios,' tongue under belt.

Tha bhioran air a bharran daonnan.—*His stick is always on its point.*

> Always on the move, and fidgeting about.

Tha blàth do chodach ort.—*You look like your food.*

Tha bhlàth ort nach eil dad agad air.—*You look as if he owed you nothing.*

'Tha bhuil,' ars am breabadair, 's a bhean air a mhuin.—*'The effect is seen,' said the weaver, with his wife on the top of him.*

> He had apparently given in rather too much to his better half.

'Tha biadh is ceòl an seo,' mun dubhairt am madadh-ruadh, 's e ruith air falbh leis a' phìob.—*'There's meat and music here,' as the fox said when he ran away with the bagpipe.*

> If there were nothing else to show the humour of our Celtic ancestors, this saying would.

Tha caitheamh ann is caomhnadh, 's tha caomhnadh ann is caith-eamh.—*There is a spending and a saving; a saving and a spending.*

> There is that scattereth and yet increaseth.—*Prov.* xi. 24.
> *Al.*—Tha caitheamh sona agus caitheamh dona ann.—*There is a happy spending and an unhappy spending.*

Tha car eil' air ruidhl' a' bhodaich.—*There's another turn in the old man's reel.*

> Ta lane chyndaaghyn ayns carr y phoosee.—*There are as many turns in the marriage tune.—Manx.*

Tha car eile an adhairc an daimh.—*There's another twist in the ox's horn.*

> An imaginative traveller gave an account of a wonderful ox whose horns reached the sky when he lay down. On being asked 'What became of the horns when the ox stood up?', he gave this answer.

Tha cheann eadar a' chliath 's an ursainn.—*His head is between the door and the side-post.*

> 'In Chancery.' 'In a fix.'

Tha chomhachag ri bròn, thig tuiltean oirnn.—*The owl is mourning, rain is coming.*

Tha chomhairle 'na cheann fhèin.—*His counsel is in his own head.*

Tha chridhe mireag ris.—*His heart is merry-making.*

Tha claimh mo chaorach fhèin air.—*He has the scab of my own sheep.*

Tha cuibheas air a h-uile rud, gu ruig òl a' bhrochain.—*There's a measure for everything—to the drinking of gruel.*

> *Al.*—a' chàil—*of kail.*
> Mae dogn ar bob peth.—*Welsh.* When moderately used it our lives does prolong.—*The Kail Brose of Old Scotland.*

Tha currac air a' bheinn; siud an t-uisg' a' tighinn.—*The mountain has a cap on; that's the rain coming.*

> When Cheviot ye see put on his cap,
> Of rain ye'll have a wee bit drap.—*Eng., Scot.*

Tha dà bhall dubh air an adaig, 's earball fad' air a' chuiteig.—*The haddock has two black spots, and the whiting a long tail.*

Tha dà thaobh air bean a' bhaile.—*The farmer's wife has two sides.*

> *Al.*—Tha dà thaobh air bean a' bhàillidh, 's dà thaobh air bàt' an aisig.—*The factor's wife has two sides, and so has the ferry-boat.*
> *Al.*—Tha dà thaobh air a' mhaoil (*or* rubh' a' chuain).—*The headland has two sides.*
> *Al.*—Tha caoin is ascaoin air.—*He has a soft and a hard side.*

Tha deargann 'na osan.—*He has a flea in his stocking.*

> A flea in the ear.—*Eng.*

Tha dlùth glic ann, agus inneach gòrach.—*He has a wise warp but foolish woof.*

> Said of one who is wiser than he seems.

Tha do dhà chrann air do bhois.—*Your two lots are on your palm.*

Tha e air a ghearran guanach.—*He is on his flighty horse.*

> Said of a restless person.

Tha e cho fileanta ri bàrd.—*He is as fluent as a bard.*

Tha e gu math, ach na tarraing fheusag.—*He is well, but don't pull his beard.*

Tha e mar a bha cat MhicAoidh—fhathast san fheòil.—*He is like Mackay's cat—still in the flesh.*

Tha e mar chù an dèidh seilg.—*He is like a dog after the chase.*

Tha e 'n geall na 's fhiach e.—*He is pledged for what he's worth.*

> Said of one in great danger.

Tha e nis air fòid na fìrinne.—*He is now on the sod of truth.*

> He is dead.

Tha e nis air slighe na fìrinne.—*He is now on the way of truth.*

> Tá sé nois i staid na fírinne, agus sinne ar staid na bréige.—*He is now in the state of truth, and we of falsehood.—Ir.*
> He is dying.

Tha e ruith air an rud a gheibh e.—*He is running on what he'll get.*

> *Al.*—air aimhleas—*on his hurt*; air salchar—*on foul ground.*

Tha esan 'na Iain feadh an t-saoghail, mar a bha e riamh.—*He is John all over the world, as he ever was.*

> Iann eo, Iann e vo—*John he is, John he will be.—Breton.*

Tha fear ann a leigeas a mhaidean le sruth.—*There is one that lets his wood go with the stream.*

Tha fhàgail fhèin aig gach neach.—*Everyone has his fate.*

Lit.—'his abandonment'—left to himself.

Tha fhortan fhèin air MacGuaire, biodh e cruaidh no biodh e bog.—*MacQuarrie has his own luck, whether it be hard or soft.*

This refers to the ancient chiefs of Ulva's isle.

Tha fios aig an luch nach eil an cat a-staigh.—*Well knows the mouse that the cat's not in the house.*

Pei y gath fyddai gartref, gwaeth 'd fyddai—*Were the cat at home, it were worse for you.*—*Welsh.* An uair fhágas na cait an baile, bíonn na luchóga ag rince (*dancing*).—*Ir.* When the cat is away, the mice may play.—*Eng.* Absent le chat, les souris dansent.—*Fr.* Quando la gatta non è in casa, i topi ballano.—*Ital.* Vanse los gatos, y estienderse los ratos.—*Span.* Wenn die Katze ausser dem Hause ist, tanzen die Mäuse.—*Germ.* Als de kat slaapt, spelen de muizen.—*Dutch.* Naar Katten er borte, löbe Musene paa Bœnken.—*Dan.*

Tha fios aige càit a bheil na muca-mara breith.—*He knows where the whales breed.*

Said of one who pretends to knowledge of everything.

Tha fios aige cia meud a nì còig.—*He knows how many make five.*

Tá fios aige cé mhéad gráinne pónaire a ghní cúig—*He knows how many beans make five.*—*Ir.*

Tha fios fithich agad.—*You have a raven's knowledge.*

That is, knowledge more than is natural. The raven was believed to possess supernatural knowledge, and of coming events in particular. This was also the Norse belief. Odin was said to have two ravens which communicated everything to him.

Tha fuasgladh a cheiste aige fhèin.—*He has the solving of his own question.*

Tha fuil fèidh ort, 's cha tu fhèin a mharbh e.—*There is deer's blood on you, and you did not kill it yourself.*

Tha fuil ghointe 'na cheann.—*He has bewitched blood in his head.*

> Said of a person who seems infatuated.
> *Al.*—sùil ghointe—*a bewitched eye.*

Tha fuil mo mhuic-sa cheart cho mèith ri fuil do mhuic-sa.—*The blood of my pig is just as rich as the blood of yours.*

Tha gu leòr cho math ri cuilm.—*Enough is as good as a feast.*—*Eng., Scot.*

> Ni helaethrwydd heb ddigon.—*No abundance without enough.*—*Welsh.*
> Genoeg is even zoo goed als een feest—*Dutch.*

Tha h-uile duine còir gun fheuchainn.—*Every man is good till he's tried.*

> This was the ground taken on a remarkable occasion by the Enemy of Mankind.—See *Job* I.

Tha h-uile fear 'na leòmhann air a chuid fhèin.—*Every man is a lion over what's his own.*

> See 'Is dàna'.
> The word in Macintosh is not 'a chuid,' but 'a chèaird,' which was probably a mistake.

Tha i cho math air snìomhadh ris a' bhana-Ghreugaich.—*She is as good at spinning as the Greek woman.*

> This seems to refer to Penelope.

Tha iad air bhòrdaibh mòra, 's air thubhailtean geala.—*They are at big tables, with white tablecloths.*

> *Al.*—air bhòrd mòr, 's air àrd-onair, am broilleacha bùtha—*at big table and high honour, in the very centre of the booth.*
> Said of 'upsetting' little people getting among good company.

Tha iad cho mòr aig a chèile ri dà cheann eich.—*They are as thick as two horse heads.*

Tha iad fad' air roinne nach urrainn leanailt.—*They are far behind that cannot pursue.*

> *Air roinne* is an old phrase, equivalent to *air deireadh*, generally obsolete, but still used in Tiree.

Tha dà eun bheag sa choill ud thall, 's their an dara fear ris an fhear eile, "S toigh leam thu, 's toigh leam thu'; 's their am fear eile, 'Dearbh sin, dearbh sin.'—*There are two little birds in yonder wood, and the one says to the other, 'I like you, I like you'; and the other says, 'Prove it, prove it.'*

This is an imitation of the chirping of birds, but with a moral meaning.

Tha làrach buain-fhòid air an adhar—nì e latha math a-màireach.— *There's the mark of turf-clearing in the sky—'twill be fine tomorrow.*

This is a graphic description of a break among *cirro-stratus* clouds.

Tha losgadh a chorraig 'na chuimhne.—*He remembers the burning of his finger.*

Tha maragan is bantraichean rin gabhail anns an teas.—*Puddings and widows must be taken while they're hot.*

There are coarser English and Scottish versions of this saying.

Tha mheòir an dèidh na sgait.—*His fingers are after the skate.*

Said of a bad piper. The saying originated with a young piper who was being instructed at the Piper's College at Boreraig in Skye. Having got skate to dinner one day, which he did not approve of, and playing afterwards indifferently, he was asked what was wrong with him. 'The skate sticks to my fingers,' was his reply.

Tha mi nas eòlaiche air coille na bhith fo eagal na caillich-oidhche.— *I am more accustomed to a wood than to be afraid of an owl.*

I have lived too near a wood to be frightened by owls.—*Eng.*

Tha mise cho mòr às mo phoca 's a tha esan às a bhalg.—*I am as proud of my poke as he is of his bag.*

Tha 'n an-shoocair 's an t-an-fhacal aige.—*He bears the skaith and the scorn.*

Tha 'n cat san luath—thig frasan fuar.—*The cat's in the ashes—it's going to rain.*

Tha 'n clamhan gobhlach 'nam measg.—*The fork-tailed kite is among them.*

Tha 'n deala snàmh—thig frasan blàth ro fheasgar.—*The leech is swimming—warm showers will come ere evening.*

Tha 'n duine ionraic ionraic eadar bhun is bhàrr.—*The upright is upright from head to foot.*

Tha 'n eubh am chluais; gun gleidheadh Dia na 's caomh leam!—*The cry is in my ear; God keep all who are dear to me!*

> A plaintive sound ringing in one's ear was considered a presage of death or calamity.

Tha 'n seillean fo dhìon—thig gailleann is sian.—*The bee keeps close; a storm is at hand.*

Tha 'n t-àm cur anns na maidean.—*It is time to be starting.*

> *Lit.*—'It is time to put (motion) into the sticks', i.e., the oars. This is a Tiree phrase.

Tha 'n t-iasg sa chuan mar tha 'n sluagh air tìr.—*The fish in the sea like us mortals be.*

> Easily taken with bait, and generally going in shoals.

Tha 'n taigh dorcha, ach an cridhe soilleir.—*The house is dark, but the heart is bright.*

Tha 'n t-ìm gann san Olaind.—*Butter is scarce in Holland.*

> Said when anything is scarce where usually abundant. This saying probably originated with some Dugald Dalgetty.

Tha 'n t-òlach ann an cliabh.—*The mad fellow is in a creel (strait-jacket).*

> MacAlpine (*Dict.*) says this is applied to people who have bad Gaelic!

Tha 'n t-seamrag a' pasgadh a còmhdaich ro thuiltean dòirteach.—*The shamrock is folding its garments before heavy rain.*

Tha 'n uaill an aghaidh na tairbhe.—*Pride is opposed to profit.*

> The translation of this in the 2nd ed. of Macintosh is 'Pride is in the bull's front'!

Tha 'n uaill 'na bleidire cho mòr ris an easbhaidh, agus ro mhòran nas uaibhriche.—*Pride is as importunate as poverty, and much more arrogant.*

Tha 'n uaisle mar a chumar i.—*Nobility is as it's kept up.*

Tha 'n uchdach goirid ged tha 'n eallach trom.—*The brae is short, though the load be heavy.*

Tha na brògan an ceann shìos an taigh-mhòine.—*The shoes are in the far end of the peat-house.*

> When the peats are done, people must put on their shoes, as they can't warm their feet any more at the fire.

Tha rathad làimh ris an rathad mhòr.—*There's another road near the highway.*

Tha rionnach air an adhar—bidh latha math a-màireach ann.—*There's a mackerel sky—'twill be fine tomorrow.*

Tha sin aig coin a' bhaile.—*The town (or farm) dogs know that.*

> Aeth hynny ar gyrn a phibau—*That is gone upon horns and pipes.—Welsh.*
> It has become the talk of the town.

Tha sin sgrìobht' am bathais a' chait.—*That's written in that cat's forehead.*

Tha sinne mar a dh'fhaodas sinn, 's chan eil an rìgh fhèin mar bu mhath leis.—*We are as best we may, and the king himself is not as he would wish to be.*

Tha smùideag fhèin an ceann gach fòid.—*Every peat-end has its own smoke.*

> Tha smùdan fèin à ceann gach fòid,
> Is dòrainn ceangailt' ris gach math.—*D. Buchanan.* Ys id ar bawb ei bryder—*To every one is his care.—Welsh.*

Tha e sa chuideachd, mar bha cù luideach a' cheàird.—*He is in the company, like the tinker's shaggy dog.*

Tha taobh dubh 's taobh geal air, mar bha air bàta Mhic Iain Gheàrr.—*He has a white side and a black side, like the boat of Short John's son.*

> Mac Iain Gheàrr (or Ghiorr)'s proper name was Archibald Mac-Donell. See 'Ged is fhad'. He was a noted riever, and followed a known practice of pirates in having his boat and sails of different colours on each side. See *Teachdaire Ur,* Jan. 1836, p. 52.

Tha teas an teine 'na luirgnean.—*The heat of the fire is in his legs.*

> Said of a *cat griosaich,* one too fond of the fireside.
> *Al.*—Tha teas na luaithre 'nan lurgann *or* ad labhran.
> Said of people going hastily from the hearth on business.

Tha thapadh air teang' an Eireannaich, ach 's ann an dèidh làimh tha 'n Gàidheal glic.—*The Irishman's wit is on his tongue, but the Gael is wise after the time.*

> Cha vel y Vanninagh dy bragh creeney, dys y laa lurg y vargee—*The Manxman is never wise till the day after the fair.*—*Manx.* A Scotsman is aye wise ahint the hand.—*Scot.*

Tha thu cho lùrdanach ris a' bhalgaire bheag.—*You are as sly as the little fox.*

Tha thu cho sona 's ged an robh clach ad chàbaig.—*You are as happy as if your cheese weighed a stone.*

Tha thu ro mhear—b'fheàirrd' thu pòsadh.—*You are too merry—you ought to marry.*

> The alliteration in English was too good to be avoided, but it is right to say that *mear* in the original may mean more than merriness.

Tha thusa 'n sin fhathast, 's do bheul fo do shròin.—*You are still there, with your mouth under your nose.*

Tha thusa mar bha thu 'n-uiridh, 's ged bhiodh tu na b'fheàrr, cha b'fhuilear.—*You are as you were last year, and if you were better, it would be no more than was needed.*

Tha togail do bhothain fhèin ort.—*You have the upbringing of your bothy.*

> Said to an ill-mannered person.

Tha trì faobhair air lurga caillich, is bòrd-urchair air a taobh.—*An old woman's leg has three edges, and her side a gunwale.*

Tha trì latha Iuchair san Fhaoilleach, 's tri latha Faoillich san Iuchar.—*There are three of the Dog-days in February, and three February days in the Dog-days.*

Tha tuille 's a phaidir aige.—*He knows more than his pater-noster.*

> Tá níos mó ná a phaidreacha aige.—*Ir.*
> *Al.*—Tha chreideamh catharra (=*cathedra*) aige.—*He has his pater and creed.* It has been heard as an objection to a man's evidence being allowed that he hadn't his *creideamh catharra.*

Tha uaisle fo thuinn an Clann Lachainn.—*There is a hidden nobleness in the MacLachlans.*

Tha uiread de dh'ainmeannan air ris an naosg.—*He has as many names as the snipe.*

> The snipe is known under many names, e.g. *naosg, gobhar-adhair, meannan-adhair, croman-lòin, butagoc, eun-ghurag.*

Thachair a bhràthair mòr ris.—*He has met his big brother.*

Thachair an cat riut air bàrr na stairsnich.—*You met the cat on the threshold.*

> The cat was considered an ill-omened creature.

Thachair cleas tuath an droch thighearna dhaibh.—*The trick of the bad landlord's tenants befell them.*

Thachair ludh an uinnsinn fhiadhaich dha; cinnidh e gu math, ach millidh e chraobh a bhios an taice ris.—*The way of the wild ash befell him; it grows well, but kills the tree that's near it.*

Thàinig gille gu Mac-a-Leisg.—*MacLazy has got a servant.*

> Said when a lazy messenger is saved the trouble of going on an errand by the coming of another messenger.

Thàinig caoraich Gheansaidh a-raoir, 's dh'ith iad e.—*The Guernsey sheep came last night and ate it.*

> Said of anything that has mysteriously disappeared, or that never existed. 'Caoraich Gheansaidh' is applied to any imaginary creatures. The saying is Hebridean, but the origin of it is unknown. Guernsey potatoes used to be known in Skye.

Thàinig ialtag a-steach—bidh frasan a-mach air ball.—*A bat has come in—it's going to rain.*

Theab 's cha d'rinn—cù 's miosa bha riamh san Fhèinn.—*Almost, but didn't, the worst dog in the Fingalian pack.*

Theagamh gun tig do bhò gu m'bhuaile-sa fhathast.—*Perhaps your cow may come to my fold yet.*

> Wha wats wha may keep sheep anither day.—*Scot.*

Thèid an fhealla-dhà gu fealla-trì.—*The joke may end in earnest.*

> See 'Is tric a chaidh'.

Thèid an leanabh a dholaidh eadar a mhuime 's a mhàthair.—*Between his nurse and his mother, the child will be spoiled.*

Thèid an sannt os cionn na h-aithne.—*Greed will overcome acquaintanceship.*

Thèid an t-anfhann dìcheallach thar an làidir leisg.—*The diligent weak will beat the lazy strong.*

Thèid an t-eòlas thar a' chàirdeis.—*Acquaintance goes beyond relationship.*

> See 'Is fheàrr caraid'.

Thèid barail an duine ghlic faisg don fhìrinn.—*The wise man's opinion will go near the truth.*

Thèid cathadh Earraich tro bhòrd daraich.—*Spring snowdrift will go through an oaken door.*

Thèid dubhag ri dualchas.—*The swarthy girl takes after her blood.*

   Al.—Theid cuilean ri dualchas.

Thèid duine gu bàs air sgàth a nàire.—*A man will die to save his honour.*

   See 'Is beò duine'.

Thèid dùthchas an aghaidh nan creag.—*Nature will withstand the rocks.*

   This might be rendered 'Blood against everything,' an intensely Highland sentiment, expressive of the feeling known as 'clannishness'.

Thèid molt dhen fhear chadalach, is mart dhen fhear chèilidh-each.—*The sleepy man will lose a wedder, the gadabout a cow.*

   The loss of the lazy man is small compared with that of the trifler.

Thèid neart thar ceart.—*Might will prevail over right.*

Thèid seòltachd thar spionnadh.—*Cunning beats strength.*

   Oni byddi gryf, bydd gyfrwys—*If thou art not strong, be cunning.*— Welsh.

Thèid trian daltachd ri goistidheachd.—*A third of fostership goes to sponsorship.*

   This means that the bond to a foster-father is three times as strong as that to a godfather.

Their gach fear, 'Ochòin, mi fhèin!'—*Everyone cries, 'Alas for me!'*

Thig a' mharcachd sna h-eich mhòra leo fhèin.—*Riding comes naturally to full-grown horses.*

   Applied to hereditary tendencies.

Thig an fhìrinn a-mach le tubaist.—*Truth comes out by accident.*

Thig an itheadh air an imlich.—*Eating comes of licking.*

Thig an t-acras nas trice na aon uair.—*Hunger comes oftener than once.*

Thig an donas ri iomradh.—*Evil comes by talking of it.*

> *Al.*—Thig an t-olc ri iomradh.
> Speak o the Deil, and he'll appear.—*Scot.* Talk of the Devil, and see his horns.—*Eng.* Als men van den duivel spreekt, dan rammelt reeds zijn gebeente (*you hear his bones rattle*).—*Dutch.* When you speak of the wolf, prepare the stick for him.—*Arab.* Wann mann den Wolf nennt, so kömmt er gerennt.—*Germ.* Quand on parle du loup, on en voit la queue.—*Fr.*

Thig dànadas gu droch oilean.—*Boldness leads to bad manners.*

> Nimia familiaritas contemptum parit.—*Lat.* Too much familiarity breeds contempt.—*Eng.* La mucha familiaridad engendra menosprecio.—*Span.* A muita conversação he causa de menos preço.—*Port.*

Thig Dia rè airc, 's chan airc an uair a thig.—*God comes in distress, and distress goes when he comes.*

> Man's extremity is God's opportunity.

Thig eàirleigeadh air an rìgh.—*Exigencies come on kings.*

Thig fear an t-saoghail fhad' às gach càs.—*The man of long life will come out of every trouble.*

> See 'Fear an t-saoghail fhada'.

Thig fear na h-iarraidh gun sireadh, ach fear na fiach cha tig idir.—*The man that wants comes unasked; the man that owes comes not at all.*

Thig gach olc ri aois—thig baothachd, thig boile, thig bàs.—*Every ill comes with age—silliness, raving, death.*

> See 'Is ioma leannan'.

Thig innleachd ri aimbeart.—*Want breeds ingenuity.*

> Ἑυρέτις ἄρα ἐστὶ λογισμων ἡ ἀνάγκη.—*Gr. (Heliodorus).* Necessity is the mother of invention.—*Eng.* Nécessité est mère d'invention.—*Fr.* Need maks a man o craft.—*Scot.* Noth lehrt Künste.—*Germ.* De armoede is de moder van alle kunsten.—*Dutch.*

Thig iomadh olc à aon olc.—*Many ills flow from one.*

> Δίκη δίκην ἔτικτε, καὶ βλάβην βλάβη.—*Gr.* Litem parit lis, noxa item noxam serit.—*Lat.*

Thig là a' choin duibh fhathast.—*The black dog's day will yet come.*

In olden times, MacPhie of Colonsay had a great black hound, of which it was predicted that it would never do but one day's good service. It grew up an idle useless animal, but its master resisted all proposals to have it given away or killed. The day came when it did noble service for its master, though it could not save his life.

Thig Latha Nollaig.—*Christmas Day will come.*

Said of persons long of coming.

Thig math à mulad, 's thig sonas à suaimhneas.—*Good comes of sadness, and happiness from quietness.*

It is better to go to the house of mourning than to go to the house of feasting.—*Eccl.* vii, 2.

Thig nòs do mhàthar às do shròin.—*Your mother's first milk will come out of your nose.*

Al.—Thig sin às do shròin, 's thèid an cràdhadh innte.—*That will come out of your nose, and pain will go into it.*

These are threats or predictions of chastisement.

Thig ri latha nach tig ri linn.—*There will come in a day what won't in an age.*

Al.—Thig rud ri àm (*or* uine) nach tig ri aimsir.
Al.—Thig ri aon uair rud nach tig ri dhà dheug.
Accidit in puncto, quod non contingit in anno.—*Lat.* Accasca in un punto quel che non accasca in cento anni.—*Ital.* Τὰ φέρει ἡ ὥρα, χρόνος δὲν τὰ φέρει.—*Mod. Gr.* Il advient souvent en un jour ce qui n' advient en cent ans.—*Fr.* It happeth in one hour that happeth not in seven years.—*Eng.*

Thig sgrios air àlach na mallachd.—*Destruction shall come on the cursed brood.*

The seed of the wicked shall be cut off.—*Psalm* xxxvii, 28.

Thigeadh dha fhèin a bhith 'na oighre, an tì a shireas air gach aon neach.—*It would well become him to be an heir, who begs from everybody.*

Thiginn gu d'choimhead ged bhiodh tu a' còmhnaidh an còs creige.—*I would come to see you, though you lived in a rock-cave.*

Thilg e 'n cearcall-màis.—*He has cast the bottom-hoop.*

    He has thrown off all restraint.

Thoir bean à Ifrinn, 's bheir i dha taigh fhèin thu.—*If you take a wife from Hell, she'll take you home with her.*

    Al.—bheir i rithist ann thu—*she'll bring you back there.*

Thoir dhomh comaidh.—*Let me share your food.*

Thoir do 'ghu robh math' don choileach.—*Give your thanks to the cock.*

    A recommendation of early rising. 'Gu robh math agaibh'—*'Good be with you'* (=thank you) is the ordinary addition to a reply to 'How do you do?'

Thoir do phathadh don allt, mar a nì an cù.—*Quench your thirst from the stream, as the dog does.*

    An excellent motto for Temperance Societies.

Thoir eun à nead glan.—*Take a bird out of a clean nest.*

    Choose a wife of good parents. See 'Pòs nighean'.

Thoir leat a' bhò don chaisteal, 's thèid i dhachaigh don bhàthaich.—*Take the cow to the castle, and she'll go home to the byre.*

    Ca a cou to the haa, and she'll rin to the byre.—*Scot.*
    An ox remains an ox, even when driven to Vienna.—*Hungar.*

Thoir òirleach don bhalach, 's gabhaibh e 'n rèis.—*Give the impudent fellow an inch, and he'll take an ell.*

    Gie a carl yir finger, and he'll tak yir hail hand.—*Scot.*

Thoir spìd do d'charaid—'s ann air do mhuirichinn fhèin a laigheas e.—*Throw reproach on your kinsman; it will rest on your family.*

    A very good and wise advice: clannishness in its commendable phase.

Thoir tlachd don mhath, is math an t-olc.—*Love the good and forgive the bad.*

Thoir thusa nuas an rionnag sin, 's bheir mise nuas an rionnag eile, ars an duine beag ris an duine mhòr.—*Bring you down that star, and I'll bring down another, as the little man said to the big man.*

Thug e breab sa bhuaraich.—*He kicked in the shackles.*

> *Buarach* = cow-fetter.

Thug e cheann fon choille.—*He betook him to the wood.*

> *Al.*—Thug e choille fo cheann.
> A common thing in olden times for outlaws or men in peril.

Thug iad aghaidh am buill 's an caman air.—*They turned all their force against him.*

> *Lit.*—'turned their balls and shinty clubs on him'.

Thuigeadh mo sheanmhair sin, 's bha i dà linn air a h-ais.—*My grandmother could understand that, and she was two generations behind.*

Thuit a dhà làimh ri thaobh.—*Both his hands fell at his sides.*

> A case of total collapse.

Thuit an tarbh-coill' orra.—*The forest-bull fell on them.*

> Macintosh says this means that a misfortune befell them. The *tarbh-coille* was a dark cloud, which, if seen on New Year's Eve, portended a dark and stormy season. The ideas connected with this *Tarbh-coille* and with *Dàir na coille* (q.v.) remind of the *genitabilis aura* of Lucretius.

Thuit an tubaist air an Dùghlas.—*Mishap has fallen on the Douglas.*

> This saying applies to more than one of the great house of Douglas, as may be seen by those who read Home of Godscroft's delightful history.

Taigh a thughadh gun a shìomaineachadh, saothair dhìomhain.—*Thatching a house without roping it, vain labour.*

Taigh do sheanar dhut!—*Your grandfather's dwelling to you!*

Taigh Eòghainn mhic Iain Bhuidhe dhut!—*The house of Ewen son of Yellow John to you!*

Taigh gun chù, gun chat, gun leanabh beag, taigh gun ghean, gun ghàire.—*A house without dog, without cat, without child, a house without cheerfulness or laughter.*

> *Al.*—gun cheòl-gàire.
> This pretty proverb appears to be purely native.

Taigh-òsda, muileann is ceàrdach—na trì àitean as fheàrr airson naidheachd.—*An inn, a mill and a smithy—the three best places for news.*

Tinneas-feachd.—*Army-sickness.*

> Sickness on the day of battle = cowardice.

Tinneas nan Dòmhnallach.—*The MacDonald sickness.*

> Armstrong (*Dict.*, p. 297) says this was a kind of pulmonary affection called *glacach.* It is said that the family of the Lords of the Isles received a charm from some shipwrecked foreigner to whom they showed kindness by which they could heal this complaint. A *duan* was repeated over the patient, who was then touched with the right hand. In the following rhyme this healing gift is alluded to:
>
> > Mòr-Dhòmhnallaich Shlèibhte,
> > Dan gèilleadh an galar—
> > Teichidh Glacach an èig,
> > 'S thèid às da gu h-ealamh.

Tìodhlac na cloinne bige, ga thoirt 's ga ghrad-iarraidh.—*The little children's gift, given and soon asked back.*

> O bairns' gifts ne'er be fain; nae suner they gie but they seek it again.—*Scot.* Tabhartas Uí Néill, is a dhá shúil ina dhiaidh.—*O'Neill's gift, and his two eyes after it.*—Ir.

Tionailidh maoin maoin; agus tionailidh fiachan fiachan.—*Wealth draws wealth, and debt draws debt.*

Tìr nam Beann 's nan Gleann 's nan Gaisgeach.—*The Land of Mountains, Glens and Heroes.*

> This is a favourite motto and toast. Another version is 'Tìr nan Gleann 's nam Beann 's nam Breacan'.—*The land of Glens and Bens and Tartans.*

'Tiugainn,' ars an Rìgh; 'Fuirich, gus am faod,' ars a' Ghaoth.—*'Come away,' said the King; 'Wait till you may,' said the Wind.*

Tiugh no tana, 's math teth e.—*Thick or thin, it's good hot.*

Togaidh an obair an fhianais.—*The work will bear witness.*

Togar càrn mòr de chlachan beaga.—*A big cairn may be raised of small stones.*

Toiseach agus deireadh na sìne, clachan mìne meallain.—*The beginning and end of the rainstorm, small hailstones.*

Toiseach na coille, is deireadh na fèithe.—*Go first through the wood, and last through the bog.*

> Tosach coille is deireadh móna.—*Ir.*
> A wise practical advice.

Toiseach teachd is deireadh falbh.—*First to come, and last to go.*

> The motto of Gaul MacMorn. See Gillies's *Sean Dàna*, p. 311.

Toradh math sa chuid eile!—*I wish you good of the remainder!*

> An expression of thanks when one has received part of anything.

Toradh na feudalach gun am faicinn.—*The fruit of the cattle that have not been seen.*

Tràth bhios tuar a' dol às air na gobhair, cha bheir iad ach buic.—*When the goats die out, they bring forth only bucks.*

Treabhaidh na daoidhean, 's cha dèan na saoidhean ach treabhadh.—*The wicked till, and the good can but till.*

> He maketh His sun to rise on the evil and on the good, and sendeth rain on the just and the unjust.—*Matth.* v, 45.

Treabhaidh an treabhaiche math fearann an amhlair.—*The good ploughman will plough the land of the fool.*

> The wise and able will, in the natural course of things, take the place of the incapable.

Treas donas a' ghille-ghnothaich, a bhith fada muigh gun dad fhaotainn.—*The third vice of the message-lad, to be long away and bring back nothing.*

Treas sonas mhic an tuathanaich, nighean air a' chiad chloinn.—*The third good luck of the farmer's son, a daughter for his eldest child.*

Treubhach a-muigh agus meadhrach a-staigh.—*Brave abroad and cheery at home.*

> The Highland type of a man of the right sort.

Treubhantas an duine bhig—fead is fuaim.—*The small man's valour, a whistle and a noise.*

> Trì aois coin, aois eich;
> Trì aois eich, aois duine;
> Trì aois duine, aois fèidh;
> Trì aois fèidh, aois fìrein;
> Trì aois fìrein, aois craoibh dharaich.
>
> —*Thrice dog's age, age of horse;*
> *Thrice horse's age, age of man;*
> *Thrice man's age, age of deer;*
> *Thrice deer's age, age of eagle;*
> *Thrice eagle's age, age of oak.*

> There are stories told of deer attributing antediluvian age to them; but that here said of the eagle has not even such authority.

Trì coilceadha na Fèinne—bàrr gheal-chrann, còinneach is ùr-luachair.—*The three Fenian bed-stuffs— fresh tree-tops, moss and fresh rushes.*

> See Llhuyd's *Arch. s.v. coil ceadha.*

Trì mallachdan an tuathanaich—an Taoitear Sàileach, reothadh Cèitein is ceò Iuchair.—*The tenant's three curses—the Tutor of Kintail, May frost and July fog.*

> This is a Kintail saying, referring presumably to Sir Roderick Mac-kenzie, Tutor of Kintail during the minority of his nephew, the first Earl of Seaforth. He ruled with a rod of iron, and made himself detestable to the tenantry.

Trì rudan as mios' a rinn duine riamh—èirigh bho bhiadh gun altachadh; èirigh bho mhnaoi fhèin gu mnaoi fir eile; 's èirigh bho Aifrinn gun a h-èisdeachd.—*Three of the worst things man ever did—to rise from food without grace; to rise from his own wife to another man's; to rise from Mass without listening.*

Trì rudan cho fuar 's a th' ann—glùn fir, adharc mairt is sròn coin.—*Three of the coldest things—a man's knee, a cow's horn and a dog's nose.*

Trì subhailcean a' bhàird—ciocras coin gu làn a bhronn'; fios fithich a' ruith gu ròic; tart frithir gu òl a dhram.—*Three gifts of the bard—the dog's hunger for a feed; a raven's bidding to a feast; an impatient man's thirst for his dram.*

> This is not very ancient, nor very true. But it did apply, and does, to some men calling themselves bards, and passing for such with the ignorant.

Triùir a thig gun iarraidh—Gaol, Eud is Eagal.—*Three that come unbidden—Love, Jealousy and Fear.*

Trod a' bhodaich ris a' cheathairn.—*The old man's scolding of the caterans.*

> Very ineffectual—like some protests that have been seen in modern times against military invasions and grand spoliations.

Trod a' mheasain 's a chùl ri balla.—*The barking of the lapdog with his back to a wall.*

> Ye're like the dowgs o Dunragit—ye winna bark unless ye hae yir hinner end to the wa.—*Scot.*
> See 'Is dàna cuilean'.

Trod chàirdean is sìth nàimhdean—dà rud nach còir feairt a thoirt orra.—*The scolding of friends and the peace of enemies—two things not to be regarded.*

Trod nam ban mun sgarbh, 's an sgarbh a-muigh air an loch.—*The scolding of the wives about the scart, and the scart out on the loch.*

    Like disposing of the hare before it's caught.

Trodaidh na builg fhalamh.—*Empty bladders make a noise.*

    See 'Is labhar'.

Tromb gun teanga.—*A trump without a tongue.*

    'Trump' is Scotch for 'Jew's harp'.

Tuarasdal a' cheàird—pàigheadh ro-làimh.—*The tinker's wages—paid beforehand.*

    In other words, money thrown away.

Tuarasdal na circe, làn a sgròbain.—*The hen's wages, her crop-full.*

Tughadh na h-àtha air a' mhuilinn.—*The thatch of the kiln on the mill.*

    Tir the kiln to thack the mill.—*Scot.*
    Robbing Peter to pay Paul.

Tuig thus' an t-eathar, 's tuigidh an t-eathar thu.—*Understand the boat, and the boat will understand you.*

    An excellent Hebridean saying. A boat, a horse, a man or woman can be managed only by one who understands them, and whom they will understand accordingly.

Tuigidh bean bean eile.—*One woman understands another woman.*

    They generally do so better than men.

Tuigidh cù a chionta.—*A dog knows when he does wrong.*

Tuigidh e rud am broinn suip.—*He'll understand a thing hid in a wisp.*

    He'll understand a hint conveyed in some trivial shape.

Tuigidh fear-leughaidh leth-fhacal.—*A reading man will understand half a word.*

One word is enough for the wise.—*Arab.* Verbum sat sapienti.—*Lat.*

Tuigidh na bailbh a chèile.—*The dumb understand each other.*

Tuigidh na geòidh fhèin a chèile.—*Even the geese understand each other.*

Tuilleadh air a' chàrnan.—*More upon the little cairn.*

Tuireadh a rèir an fhuinn.—*Lament according to the tune.*

Tuislichidh an t-each ceithir-chasach.—*The four-footed horse may stumble.*

Gheibheann beathach cheithre cos tuisle.—*Ir.* A horse wi four feet may snapper by a time.—*Scot.* A horse stumbles that hath four legs.—*Eng.* Anco il cavallo si stanca, sebben ha quattro piedi.—*Ital.* Een paard met vier pooten struikelt wel.—*Dutch.* Il n'y a cheval si bon qui ne bronche.—*Fr.*

Tuiteam eadar long is laimrig.—*Falling between ship and landing-place.*

Tuitidh a' chraobh a bhithear a' sìor shnaidheadh.—*The tree that is constantly hewed at will fall.*

Tuitidh cliabh gun iris, 's thèid a' bhreug do h-ionad fhèin.—*A ropeless creel will fall, and the lie will go to its own place.*

Tuitidh tòn eadar dha chathair, agus tigheadas eadar dha mhuinntir.—*Seat comes down between two chairs, and house-keeping between two families.*

Turas nam ban thun a' bhaistidh.—*The wives' journey to the christening.*

U

Uaisle gun chuid, is maragan gun gheir.—*Birth without means, and puddings without suet.*

> *Al.*—Clag mu chuaille, bean-uasal fhalamh.—*A cudgel hung with bells, a lady without means.*

Ugh aig eireig, 's bean aig sgalaig.—*A young hen with an egg, and a farm-servant with a wife.*

> Creatures with a sense of their superior importance, in respect of what they have achieved.
> An addition sometimes given is 'Brèid air seann nighinn, 's i ga shìor chàradh'—*An old maid with a head-dress, continually getting mended.*

Ugh gun ìm gun salann, an ceann sheachd bliadhna thig a ghalar.—*An egg without butter or salt will breed a disease after seven years.*

> See 'Aran is uighean'.

Ugh na circe dol a shireadh ugh a' gheòidh.—*The hen-egg going to seek the goose-egg.*

> The hen's egg gaes to the haa to bring the guse's egg awa.—*Scot.*
> 'Spoken when poor people give small gifts to be doubly repaid.'—*Kelly.*
> *Al.*—Ugh na circe duinne dol don taigh-mhòr, gun ugh a' gheòidh a thoirt às.—*The brown hen's egg going to the big house, without bringing back the goose-egg.*

Uidh air n-uidh thig an t-slàinte, 's 'na tonna mòr' an euslainte.—*By degrees comes health, but in great waves comes sickness.*

> *Al.*—Muin air mhuin thig an euslainte, ach uidh air n-uidh thig an t-slàinte.

Uilleadh na bà a-mach 's a-steach—mur leighis sin an Gàidheal, chan eil a leigheas ann.—*The oil of the cow, without and within—if that won't heal the Gael, there's no cure for him.*

> *Al.*—Uraireachd na bà—*The fat of the cow.*
> Milk, cream, butter, neat-foot oil are all included.

Uir, ùir air sùil Odhrain, mun labhair e tuille còmhraidh!—*Earth, earth on Oran's eye, lest he talk more!*

The story to which this saying is supposed to refer is that at the time of founding his religious establishment at Iona, St Columba received divine intimation that one of his companions must be buried alive, as a sacrifice necessary to the success of the undertaking, and that St Oran offered himself, and was duly interred. On the third day St Columba went and opened the grave, to see how his friend fared. Presently Oran raised his eyes, and uttered these words:

> Chan eil am bàs 'na iongantas
> No Ifrinn mar a dh'aithrisear.

> —*Death is no wonder, nor is Hell as it is said.*

The story goes that St Columba, shocked by such sentiments, exclaimed in the words given above given, and covered up St Oran again as fast as possible.

The above is the substance of a quotation given by Macintosh in a note on this saying, but without naming the author. A better version of Oran's words, got from Tiree, is

> Chan eil an t-Eug 'na annas,
> 'S chan eil Ifrinn mar a dùbhrar;
> Cha tèid math am mugh',
> 'S cha bhi olc gun dìoladh.

> —*Death is nothing strange,*
> *Nor Hell as has been said;*
> *Good will not perish,*
> *Nor evil be unpunished.*

It was part of this tradition that Oran used to dispute with Columba about the torments of the future, and entertained laxer views.

The story of St Oran's burial appears first in the old Irish life of St Columba, of which Mr Skene gives a translation by Mr W. M. Hennessey at the end of Vol. II of his *Celtic Scotland*, and of which the original was printed for the first time by Mr Whitley Stokes in his *Three Middle Irish Homilies*. It is as follows: "Colum Cille then said to his people, 'It is well for us that our roots should go under ground here'; and he said to them, 'It is permitted to you that some one of you go under the earth of this island to consecrate it.' Odran rose up readily, and thus he said, 'If thou wouldst accept me,' he said, 'I am ready for that.' 'O Odran,' said Colum Cille, 'thereof thou shalt have the reward, viz., to none shall his request be granted at my grave unless from thee he seek it first.' Odran then went to heaven. He then founded the church of Hii.' " There is no mention here, or in any other writing, of the strange event of the third day.

Oran is not even named by Adamnan; nor is he included in the oldest list of the twelve companions of Columba. The Oran after whom *Reilig Odhrain*, Oran's burial-place, is named, is designated 'Abbot' by Angus the Culdee, and his death is recorded in the Annals of the Four Masters in the year 548, i.e., fifteen years before Columba came to Scotland. The result is that the above curious story and saying are left without a particle of historical foundation. As an invention, however, they are both interesting and instructive.

Uisge-beath' a' bhalaich mhòir, òlamaid gun taing e.—*The great churl's whisky, let us drink it, and no thanks to him.*

This is the only proverb in all the present collection in which whisky is mentioned; and it is not an old one.

Uisge donn na duilleig, uisge dubh nam freumh 's uisge glas a' Chèitein—trì uisgeachan as mios' a th' ann.—*The brown rain at the fall of the leaf, the black rain at the springing of roots and the gray rain of May—the three worst of waters.*

Of a quite different import is another similar saying, 'Uisge donn na duillich, tha e ro mhath do na fearaibh òg'—*The brown rain of the foliage is very good for young men.*

Uisge mòr a sgaoileas ceò.—*Heavy rain scatters mist.*

See 'Gaoth tuath'.

Uisge teth bhon bhuain, 's uisge fuar bhon àr.—*Hot water after reaping, cold water after ploughing.*

> *Al.*—bhon chrann.
> For washing: hot water in warm weather, cold water in Spring—very sensible advice.

Urchair a' mhaodail air a' bhrochan.—*The paunch's hit at the porridge.*

Urchair an doill mun dabhaich.—*The blind man's shot at the tub.*

> *Al.*—Mar thilg an dall a phloc—*As the blind man threw his cudgel.*
> Mal dall yn tawlu eiffon.—*Welsh.*
> According to a certain story, Dabhach was the name of Ossian's wife, and the blind old bard one day, provoked by something, threw a deer's bone at her, and missed.—See Campbell's *Leabhar na Féinne*, p. 38.

Urnaigh an-diugh, 's breugan a-màireach.—*Prayers today, and lies tomorrow.*

Urnaigh maraiche rè stoirm.—*A sailor's prayer in a storm.*

> Passato il pericolo, gabbato il santo.—*Ital.*
> See Rabelais, B. IV, c. 19, 'Of Panurge and Friar John in the storm'.

Urram a' bhleidire don t-stràcair.—*The sneak's deference to the swaggerer.*

SAYINGS IN VERSE

Here follow some sayings in verse which, for various reasons, were
not included in the body of this collection. Some of them can hardly
be reckoned as proverbs, but are worth preserving. Translations of
these, and of the didactic verses that follow, must be dispensed with.

> A mhic a' bhodachain lachdainn
> A bun Loch Abar nan craobh,
> Cleas a' chait a dh'òl an t-uachdar,
> Thèid a' chluas thoirt dhìot mun mhaoil.

> A mhic, ma thèid thu gan taghadh,
> Na tagh na dubha mòra, no na donna-mala;
> Na tagh Cinneagag, no Cruinneagag, no Snàthdag,
> No Leum-air-mheall, no Cnap-air-sluigean,
> No Luinneagag-liana, no Pìobaire-na-tobhta;
> Ach tagh bean dhonn, mar thonn air uisge glan;
> Ciarag bheag air dhath na luch, na sir 's na seachain.

This is one of the most complete versions of that already given at
p. 368.

> An Srath Fhionghaineach geal,
> San grinne beus gun smal;
> An Srath san cruaidhe clach,
> 'S an sgaitich' cu is bean!

This refers to the parish of Strath in Skye, the old territory of the
MacKinnons.

> Carson a bhithinn mar chroman-lòin,
> A' tional lòin air bhàrr gach pris?
> Carson nach caithinn-sa an saoghal,
> 'S gur cinnt gun caith an saoghal mis' ?

> Gaoth an iar air Rubh' na Feiste,
> Oidhche dhorcha, ceò is uisge,
> Clann Dòmhnaill air bhòrdaibh briste—
> Leam cha mhisde!
> Birlinn chaol chorrach,
> Siùil àrd bhinneach,
> Sgioba fhann fheargach
> Gun urram aon da chèile.

This expresses the bad wish of a MacLeod for the MacDonalds when these two great clans were at deadly feud, and nothing could be more terribly graphic. There is a genius in the imagination of the accumulated horrors. The *Feiste* is a wild black rocky point on the west of Skye, near the grand cliff of Waterstein, a place of dread for any distressed bark, in a dark night with west wind. The description of the galley, as 'slender and crank, with high peaked sails,' and that of the crew as 'weak, angry, none respecting his fellow,' is the beau-ideal of nautical risk and of anarchy.

A version somewhat similar was given to me as a MacDonald prayer for the MacLeods, but this is the better one.

> Is feàrr beagan na bhith gun nì,
> Is feàrr caraid na con-a-mhìr,
> Is feàrr a bhith sona na bhith glic,
> Ach coisnidh an t-aithneach an t-anam.

This is given by Macintosh, and the word 'con-amhir' is translated 'enemy', but it is to be found nowhere else.

> Is ioma fear buidhe
> 'Na shuidh' ann an Uibhist
> Nach itheadh na h-uighean sa Charghas
> A rachadh don aonach,
> 'S a ghoideadh na caoraich,
> Ged chrochte le taod no le cainb e.

This is a good specimen of Gaelic satire.

> Ma bhios mi beò, beiridh mi mac;
> Gheibh mi fear ged nach co-dheas;
> Bhon as i mo mhàthair nach beir mac,
> Is e mo bhràthair mo roghainn.

This is said to have been the answer of a matron, whose husband, son and only brother had been captured, and who got her choice, which of the three to have released. It is pleasant to know, on the authority of Macintosh's note, that the whole three were restored to the spirited matron.

> Mar an iadhshlat ri balla,
> No mac-talla ri creig,
> Leanaidh amhluadh gu daingeann
> Ri fear-tagraidh nam breug.

Good sentiment, but bad rhyme.

> Mèirle dhèanamh air a' mhèirleach,
> Gum b'e sin a' mhèirle bhorb;
> Chan eil taobh a thèid am mèirleach
> Nach eil mèirleach air a lorg.

> Mèirle salainn 's mèirle frois—
> Mèirl' o nach fhaigh anam clos;
> Gus an tèid an t-iasg air tìr,
> Chan fhaigh mèirleach an lìn clos.

This illustrates the great value attached to salt and lint-seed, especially among a fishing population, at a time when the duty on salt was excessive, and lint was cultivated in the Hebrides. Another version is:

> Mèirleach salainn is mèirleach lìn,
> Dà mhèirleach nach fhaigh fois;
> Ge b'e thig no nach tig a-nìos,
> Cha tig mèirleach an lìn ghlais.

> Mi 'm shuidhe air cnocan nan deur,
> Gun chraiceann air meur no air bonn;
> A Righ, 's a Pheadair, 's a Phòil,
> Is fada an Ròimh bho Loch Long!

This deep-felt utterance is ascribed to Muireadhach Albanach (*circa* 1180–1220), the first distinguished representative of a great Clan, *Clann Mhuirich*, commonly called Macpherson, as he sat down at the head of Loch Long in Argyleshire, on his return from a pilgrimage to Rome, having walked the whole way, save the ferries.

> Muileann Bhun Màigh—'Thèid agam air, thèid agam air';
> Muileann Choire Chuinnlidh—'Leig thugam e, leig thugam e.'

This is a pleasant imitation of the sound of a mill-happer. The two mills mentioned are or were in Lochaber, the one at Moy, the other at Coirachoilly.

> Na biodh ro-ghaol, 's na biodh fuath,
>   Agads' air sluagh Innis Threud;
> Na smaointich air na chaidh thoirt bhuat,
>   'S a' chuid nach deachaidh bhuat gun tèid.

This is from one of Dr. MacLeod's papers in the *Cuairtear*, Jan. 1842, p. 311. These words were said to have been heard by a man sitting at midnight on his wife's grave.

> Nic Gleosgair mhòr, 's a triùir nighean,
> 'S a beairt-fhighe, 's a fùcadair.

This refers to three remarkable stacks of rock, called MacLeod's Maidens, off the coast of Idrigill, on the west of Skye, compared by Sir Walter Scott to the Norse 'Choosers of the Slain' or 'Riders of the Storm'. One of the three smaller rocks and the *fùcadair* ('fuller') have disappeared; and the *beairt-fhighe* ('weaving-loom') is now scarcely visible.

> Seachd bliadhna ron bhràth,
> Thig muir air Eirinn rè aon tràth,
> 'S thar Ile ghuirm ghlais,
> Ach snàmhaidh I Chaluim Chlèirich.

An elegant but periphrastic translation of this by Dr. John Smith is given in his Life of St Columba.

> Seasaidh an fhìrinn
> Gu dìreach, daingeann, rèidh,
> Chan ann air a' ghaineamh
> Ach air creig mar stèidh.

This seems to be a paraphrase of *Matth.* vii, 24–27.

> 'S e 'm buileachadh nì 'n cruinneachadh,
> 'S e 'n cruinneachadh nì sguaban,
> Na sguaban nì na mulanan,
> 'S na mulanan na cruachan.

> Seinn-fèin riamh nì mholamar,
> Tha 'm balbh mar na linnte làna—
> An sruthan as eudoimhne
> Is e labhras gu dàna.

This is given in the first ed. of Macintosh, but not in the second.

> Siadar sin is Siadar,
> Cha do chinnich duine riamh ann;
> 'S ged is lìonmhor do chnocan,
> Leaghaidh do chuid mar am feur ann.

This saying, in reference to a farm near Uig in Skye, is attributed to Coinneach Odhar, the Brahan Seer.

'S mòr an dearmad mearachd focail,
'S ann tha 'n t-olc anns a' mhì-rùn;
'S feàrr fear foghainteach feargach
Na fear mìn cealgach 's e ciùin.

Tha 'n uaisle 'na h-eire throm
Air an fhonn nach faighear nì,
'S mo chreach! ma gheibhear an crodh sa bhuaile,
Chan fhaighear an uaisle leis a' mhnaoi.

Al.—Far am faighear an crodh chan fhaighear am modh.

This is part of the son's reply to the father's advice on marriage (p. 368) in one of the versions.

Teirgidh gach nì ri chaitheamh,
'S a bhith ga chaitheamh gu minig;
'S an nì sin nach caithear,
Ged nach caithear, gun teirig;

Bhon a theirgeas gach nì gun chaitheamh
Grathann mun tig am bràth,
Is còir gach nì a chaitheamh
Mun caith e fhèin às a thàmh.

Trì mìosan cù,
Còig caogad cat;
Is ionann bean is bò,
'S bliadhna mhòr don làir.

This refers to the time of going with young. The usual meaning of the word *caogad* is 'fifty', but here it is used to signify 'nine days.'

Triubhas air na luirgne loma,
Bonaid air na maolanaich,
Fèileadh air na daoine tapaidh,
Casag air na slaodairean.

Tùs mì-rath 'nam bheachd,
Ge b'e aca neach ga foirm,
An coileach a bhith 'na thàmh
Is a' chearc a bhith dha gairm.

VERSES FROM THE GILLIES COLLECTION

The following verses are from John Gillies's collection of Gaelic poetry, published at Perth in 1786, now a rare book. In the *Cuairtear* of June 1842, five verses are given, entitled 'Comhairlean an t-Sean Duine,' substantially the same as some of these, but with variations. Among the MSS of a Kintail poet, Duncan MacRae, dated 1688, in the possession of Mr Donald Mackinnon, Edinburgh, in a piece called 'Pairt de Chomhairle Mhic Eachain 'Ic Fhearachair do Mhac an Tòisich a Dhalta,' two verses occur which correspond nearly verbatim with two verses of Gillies's edition. Other two are in Macintosh's collection. In the collection of Irish proverbs appended to Canon Bourke's Grammar are still other two verses, headed 'Comhairle an t-Seanduine,' somewhat different, but apparently part of the same poem. An additional verse, appended to the ironical advice, was got by Mr A. A. Carmichael in Uist. It is evidently a part of the same poem. All these fragmentary relics illustrate how rhymed compositions are preserved, in whole or in part, from generation to generation. A few emendations of Gillies's text are given, the more important of which are noted. His grammar and spelling are not of the best. The wisdom, good feeling, humour and pithiness of these verses are remarkable.

COMHAIRLEAN DUINE GHLIC DO MHAC

Comhairle thug ormsa Brian:
Gun mo chiall a bhith gu tais,
Gun dol an cogadh no 'n sgleò
Mur saoilinn teachd beò às.

Thug e orm comhairl' eile,
'S ar leamsa nach i bu tàire:
Ge bu leam earras an domhain,
Gun a chur an coimheart ri m'nàire.

Cuimhnich sìor-thathaich an teampaill,
'S na cuir do theann-gheall san eucoir;
'S na tugadh ort òr no beatha
Mionnan eithich a thoirt air feudail.[1]

Ma chluinn thu faoin-sgeul air fann,
Na cuir do leth-làmh 'na lùib;

Na bi 'nad urrainn anns a' bhrèig—
Leig an sgeul ud seachad uait.

Bi ciatach macant' air d'eòlas,
'S na tog trògbhail air d'aineol;
Na abair gun diùlt thu chòir,
Na ob is na iarr onair.[2]

Bior 'nad dheàrn fhèin na fàisg;
D'easbhaidh ri d'nàmhaid na rùisg;
Rinn[3] sgeine ri d'fheòil na èisd;
Bèist nimhe ri d'bheò[4] na dùisg.

Na bi gu sracanta borb;
Na tadhail gun lorg an sruth;
'S na tigeadh a-mach às do bheul
Aon nì thoilleas duit fèin guth.[5]

Na dèan tàir air buirbe fir;
Na òl balgam garbh à goil;[6]
'N tràth chì thu 'n ealtainn ghlan gheur,
Saltair gu sèimh seach a saidh.[7]

Na bi ro mhòr is na bi beag;
Air fàl-ni[8] na caith do chuid;
Air ghràdh h-òinich na tog trod,
'S na h-ob i mas h-èiginn duit.

Na bi caithriseach air sràbh;
Na dèan cnàid air duine bochd;
Na mol 's na diomoil an daoi,
Na gum faighear saoi gun lochd.

A laoigh, o 's leòr d'òige,
Na còmhdaich cùis chonnspaid;
Na rùisg le rabhladh do bhladh;[9]
'S na tog adhbhar gun ùghdair.

---

[1]*eadail* in Gillies. [2]*Al. urram.* [3]*faobhar* in G. text in Macintosh. [4]*do d' dheoin* in G. text in M. [5]*which will earn you reproach.* [6]*Al. Na cuir fearg air fuirbidh fir,/'S na toir balgam à dian-ghoil. Al. Na buail dòrn* &c. [7] *Tread softly by its edge.* [8] *a trifle.* The *Cuairtear* version of the second and third lines of this verse is *'S an co-òil na cosd do chuid;/ A taigh mìlidh na tog greigh.* [9] *Don't expose your character by coarse jesting.*

COMHAIRLEAN CHORMAIG DO MHAC

These verses follow those above in Gillies's Collection; the first three ironical, the rest serious.

An tùs, ga fheuchainn, thubhairt e:

Nuair a thèid thu thaigh an òil,
Tionndaidh a' chòir bun-os-cionn;
Suidh gu somalt' air cuid chàich;
Diomoil is na pàigh an leann.

Smachdaich d'athair 'na àm,
Tuig nach fhèarr e na thu fèin;
Aon fhacal air am bi blas
Na leig a-mach às a' bheul.

Bi neo-shiobhalta ri mnaoi,
'S bi gu garbh ri duine bochd;
Bi gu dìochuimhneach air d'arm,
'S bi gu tlàth ri dol an troid.

The following verse, got in Uist by Mr Carmichael, plainly belongs to this composition, and may take the place of an omitted verse, coming second in Gillies's version, which is coarse, without any special merit.

Nuair a thèid a' chùis mun cuairt,
Seal mun togar duais a' bhùird,
Fear dhan fhèarr as lèir a chòir,
Buail do dhòrn air anns an t-sùil.

An Cormaig ceudna da-rìreadh:

Seachain caonnag dhìomhanach,[1]
Is nì e ciall a ghleidheadh dhuit.

Seachain a' mhuinntir mhì-rùnach,
Dam bi[2] an teanga bhaoth-ràdhach,
Leis an annsa[3] breug na fìreantachd,
Mun toill e nàire saoghail[4] duit.

Na bi struidheil friotalach,[5]
An taigh an òil ma thuiteas tu;
Glèidh teanga shàmhach[6] shicir ann,
Nach toill nàir an cuideachd dhuit.

Dèan tadhal beag nan companach,
O 's òl tha costail[7] millteach dhaibh;
Bi ceart air cùl gach aon duine,
'S chan fhaod iad aon lochd innseadh ort.

Na innis-sa do d'chompanach
An uaigneas d'uile inntinn,
Air eagal 's, ma thig àmhghar air,
Am feirg gun dèan e inns' ort.[8]

Thoir gaol do d'mhnaoi a-rithistich[9],
Mas àill leat gràdh[10] mu chomhair sin,
'S aon fhuil is fheòil 'nur dithis sibh
An fhad 's as beò air domhain sibh.

Na bi bruidhneach an taigh mòr,
'S na bi sòradh[11] air seann fhear.

An onair nach fhaigh thu do ghnàth,
Na bi ga h-iarraidh aon tràth;
An fhàilt bhruidhneach gun bhith buan
Mar rionnach an cuan a' snàmh.

Beannachd ort 's na cùm an fhearg,
'S na dèan cealg air duine bochd,
Na bi dian ged robh ort dìth,
Oir 's e Dia a bheir nì dhuit.

Thoir do chomhairle mu seach
Air gach neach a bhios 'na feum;
An rud a dhiomolas tu chàch,
A shamhail gu bràth na dèan fèin.

Comhairle de chomhairlean Phòil,
Na teirig an spàirn le d'dheòin;
Na dèan sùgradh riutha siud,
O 's tric friogh air an fhior bhrùid.

The words in Gillies altered above are here given:

[1] *dhiomhidis.* [2] *biodh.* [3] *ionnsa.* [4] *saoghalt.* [5] *frisealair.* This word is unknown. Gillies in a note gives 'doichiollach' as a gloss. *Friotalach* means 'fretful'. [6] *sheamhaidh.* [7] *costach.* [8] See *Sirach,* vii, 19. [9] Provin. for *rìs.* [10] *gras.* [11] *saoith'reach*; in Macintosh, *saraichte: sòradh,* 'grudging,' the *Cuairtear* version, is better in sound and sense.

DUNCAN LOTHIAN'S PROVERBS IN VERSE

This collection forms part of a tract of 36 pp, being the 2nd edition,
'Edinburgh, Menzies, Lawnmarket, 1834'. It contains 1. a Dialogue
in verse, 'Deasbaireachd eadar am Papa agus an t-Athleasacha,' a
Discussion between the Pope and the Reformation; 2. 'Sean Fhocail
agus Comhadan,' Proverbs and Similitudes; 3. 'Deoch an Doruis,'
The Door-Drink, already given on p. 183; 4. David Mackellar's
Hymn to the Creator; 5. an anonymous Hymn; 6. The Christian on
the Brink of Jordan, a Hymn by the Rev. John Macdonald of
Urquhart, afterwards Dr. Macdonald of Ferintosh. The first three
are by Lothian, a brief memoir of whom forms the Preface, signed
by John McLachlan, Elder in Fincastle. It states that Lothian,
'Donnacha Loudinn,' was a native of Glen Lyon; served for a time
as a turner under Dugald Buchanan at Kinloch Rannoch; came
thence to Struan; and finally to Fincastle, where he died about the
age of 80. The first edition of these verses was published at Edinburgh in 1797; the third at Edinburgh in 1844. MacLachlan says he
had great difficulty in finding a copy. In Reid's *Bibliotheca Celtica*, p.
76, this entry occurs—"COMH CHRUINNEACHHIDH Orainnigh
Gaedhaelach agus Bearla le Donacha Loudin. *Seria mixta jocis, Ovid.*
Aberrain Clo-bhuailt ann le Sheumais Chalmers Airson Wm. Sharp,
ann 'n Inverness. 1780. 12°, 6d." It is difficult to believe that there
were two Duncan Loudins; and yet the above title is very unlike the
character of this Duncan's muse; and the publication it refers to was
evidently unknown to MacLachlan or his publisher. He was inti-
mately acquainted with Duncan, of whom he says, 'Bha eòlas cridhe
agam air'; characterising him as a sober godly man, a good speaker,
deeply earnest in exhorting others, who spent his life in great esteem,
shunning every appearance of evil. The influence of Buchanan is
apparent in these verses, the composition of which was probably
suggested by his *Bruadar*. They are very good, and deserve to be
known and kept in mind wherever Gaelic is spoken.

SEAN FHOCAIL AGUS COMHADAN

Nuair a chailleas neach a mhaoin,
   'S gnothach faoin bhith 'g iarraidh meas;
Ge do labhair e le cèill,
   'S beag a gheibh e dh'èisdeas ris.

'S beag sgoinn de mhòintich am monadh;
   'S beag sgoinn de choille am fàsach;
'S lugha meas tha dhuine falamh
   Nuair tha earras an dèidh fhàgail.

'S ioma caraid th' aig fear saidhbhir,
   Tha daoine bochda gun phrìs;
'S gann a dh'aidicheas an càirdean
   Gum buin iad dhaibh, is iad bhith 'n dìth.

'S feàrr a bhith bochd na bhith breugach,
   'S feàrr fheuchainn na bhith san dùil;
'S feàrr am fear a chostas beagan
   Na 'm fear a theicheas ann an cùil.

Tha 'n fhìrinn gu cliùiteach sona,
   Cha chron air duine bhith fial;
'S feàrr beagan anns an onair
   Na 'n donas is ceithir cheud.

Is ainmig a dh'èireas fortan
   Le fear crosda bhios gun chèill;
'S feàrr do dhuine fuireach sàmhach
   Na droch dhàn a chur an cèill.

Eiridh tonn air uisge balbh;
   Gheibhear cearb air duine glic;
Eiridh gnothach le fear mall;
   Bristidh am fear tha call gu tric.

Tha ghaineamh fhèin anns gach sruthan;
   Chan eil tuil air nach tig tràghadh;
'S don' an càirdeas gun a chumail,
   'S chan fhaighear duine gun fhàiling.

Is coltach fear tha ris an fhoill,
   'S nach eil sgoinn aige den chòir,
Ris an duin' a thaisg an luaidhe
   Agus a thilg uaith' an t-òr.

'S dona thig maighdeann gun bhith beusach;
   Cha dèan fear gun ghèire dàn;
Cha dèan fear gun fhoghlam leughadh,
   'S cha tig lèigh gu duine slàn.

'S math bhith sìothchail anns gach ball;
   Caillidh duine dall an t-iùl;
Is sona neach a bhios gun bheud,
   Ach caillidh luchd nam breug an cliù.

Smuainich mun dèan thu labhairt,
   Mas àill leat do ghnothach bhith rèidh;
'S fearr dhut sealltainn beagan romhad
   Na sealltainn fad' air do dhèidh.

Is trom snigh' air taigh gun tughadh;
   'S trom tubaist air na dràicean;
'S duilich do mhnaoi beanas-taighe
   Dhèanamh air na fraighean fàsa.

Cha trom leis an loch an lach,
   Cha trom leis an each an t-srian,
Cha trom leis a' chaor' a h-olainn
   'S cha truimid a' cholainn a ciall.

Cha trom leis an fhiadh a chabar,
   Cha trom leis a' choileach a chìrean;
Nì mheasas aon neach mar leathtrom
   Chì neach eile mar thoil-inntinn.

Tha 'n neach tha gleidheadh seanchais dhìomhain,
   'S a leigeas diadhaidheachd fo bhonn,
Mar a bha 'n tè a thog a' chàth
   'S a dh'fhàg an cruithneachd air an tom.

Caillear mart an droch mhuthaich
   Seachd bliadhna ro a mithich;
Tha siud a' feuchainn 's a' dearbhadh
   Gun tig an t-earchall le mifheairt.

Chan fhuirich muir ri uallach,
   'S cha dèan bean luath maorach;
Cha dèan bean gun nàire cugann,[1]
   'S cha dèan bean gun fhuras aodach.

Far am bi bò, bidh bean;
  'S far am bi bean, bidh buaireadh;
Far am bi fearg, bidh bruidheann,
  Is às a' bhruidhinn thig tuasaid.

Am fear a bhrathas,'s e mharbhas;
  Cha dèanar dearbhadh gun deuchainn;
'S gann a dh'aithn'eas tu do charaid
  Gus an tachair dhut bhith d'èiginn.

Chan eil saoi gun choimeas,
  Chan eil coille gun chrìonaich;
'S feàrr beagan a mhathadh
  Na seann fhalachd a dhìoladh.

'S math caraid anns a' chùirt
  Ma thig neach gu trioblaid;
Ach 's feàrr aon eun[2] san làimh
  Na dhà dheug air iteig.

Leig d'eallach air làr mun lag thu,
  Ma dh'aithn'eas tu d'eallach trom;
Is mòr gur feàrr an cù a ruitheas
  Na 'n cù a shuidheas air tom.

Bean thlachdmhor, gun ghnìomh, gun ghleidheadh,
  Ged a thaitinn i ri d'shùil—
Ciod am feum a ta an lann
  Mur bi làmh air a cùl?

Pigheid chaileig air bheag cèill,
  Ged robh feudail aic' is stòr,
Chan fhaod a fear a bhith sona
  Ma bhios i gnogach anns an t-sròin.

Bean gun nàire gun ghliocas,
  Bean mhisgeach, gun bheusaibh,
B'fheàrr dhut cù a chur mu d'amhaich
  Na do cheangal ri tè dhiubh.

Bean àrdanach labhar,
  Bean ghabhannach[3] chèilidheach,
Is tùs trioblaid is aimbeairt
  Dol gu d'cheangal ri tè dhiubh.

Am fear a gheallas, 's e dh'ìocas,
  'S e 'm fear a dh'iarras a phàigheas;
Cha chòir do neach a bhith ullamh
  Gu dol an cunnart no 'n gàbhadh.

Am fear nach dèan àr ri latha fuar,
  Cha dèan e buain ri latha teth;
Am fear nach dèan obair no gnìomh,
  Chan fhaigh e biadh feadh nam preas.

'S fearr sìth à preas na strì ri glais;
  Bi faicilleach mu d'ghiùlan,
'S furas seasamh an gnothach ceart,
  Ged thèid gach cùis gu dùbhlan.

Is tùs a' ghliocais eagal Dè;
  Cha dèan eucoir do chur suas;
Co-dhiù as math no 's olc ad chrè,
  'S ann do rèir a gheibh thu duais.

'S feàrr an ceartas glan na 'n t-òr;
  Is beag air duine còir an fhoill;
An neach a mheallas tu o d'chùl,
  Chuir e dhùil an cuid an doill.

Is ciatach gnothach follaiseach,
  Ach 's dona comann cealgach;
An rud a gheibhear aig ceann an Deamhain,
  Caillear e aig earball.

Is olc an toiseach cogaidh geilt;
  Chan ionann sgeul don chreich 's don tòir;
Is searbh glòir an fhir a theich,
  'S am fear a dh'fhuirich, nì e bòsd.

Is feàrr bhith tais na bhith ro bhras,
  On 's e as lugha cùram;
Is feàrr suidh' an taigh a' bhròin
  Na 'n taigh a' cheòil 's an t-sùgraidh.

Cha toir neach air èiginn beairteas;
  'S duilich droch chleachd a chur fàs;
Bheir gach Dòmhnach leis an t-seachdain,
  'S bheir am peacadh leis am bàs.

Na bi ealamh air trodadh,
  'S na bi toileach air tuasaid;
Ach mas toigh leat do leanabh,
  Na bi leisg air a bhualadh.

Bi 'n còmhnaidh air taobh na sìochaint,[4]
  'S na bi dì-chaisg[5] air bheag adhbhair;
'S feàrr dhut amadan a bhreugadh
  Na dol ga fheuchainn ann an caonnaig.

Na bi talach air do chuibhrinn,
  Ged a robh i baileach[6] sòmhail;[7]
'S feàrr grèim tioram le sìochaint
  Na taigh làn iobairt le còmh-stri.

Dol a strì ri rud gun choslas,
  Chan eil ann ach gnothach faoin;
Cha tig feur tre na clochan,
  'S cha tig folt tre chlaigeann aosd'.

Tha e cruaidh air duine lag
  Dol ri bruthach cas 'na steud;
'S tha e tearc am measg an t-sluaigh
  An neach sin a gheibh buaidh air fhèin.

Na bi cur na ciont' air càch
  Ma tha 'n fhàiling agad fhèin;
Is duilich neach a rib' an slaod[8]
  Is ceann an taoid aige fhèin.

Neach tha gu math, is còir dha fuireach,
  Gun bhith strì ri rud nach iomchaidh;
Is tric bha call an dèidh an turais,
  Ach 's buidhe le amadan imrich.

Is feàrr cù beò na leòmhann marbh;
  'S feàrr min gharbh na bhith gun bhleith;
An rud a chì thu thogas fearg,
  Na dèan dearmad air a chleith.

Thoir aire ciamar ghluaiseas tu;
  Cha toir thu buaidh le farmad;
Is tric le gnothach mì-rùnach
  Gun crìochnaich e neo-shealbhmhor.

Bi eòlach mu dhuine an tùs
  Mun innis thu do rùn ga cheann;
Na cuir do chlàr air a thaobh
  Do neach nach saoil thu chuireadh[9] ann.

Na gabh farmad ri neach idir,
  Ged shaoil thu a staid bhith mòr;
A' bheann as àirde tha san tir,
  'S ann oirre 's trice chì thu 'n ceò.

'S math an gille-greasaidh 'n t-eagal;
  Tha rud air theagamh duilich innseadh;
'S fheàrr dhut teicheadh le onair
  Na dol thoirt oidhirp neo-chinnteach.

Nuair a thèid thu don tigh-leanna,
  Na iarr a bhith 'g amailt na pàirtidh;[10]
'S mithich druideadh chòir an dorais
  Nuair a theannas an sporan ri àicheadh.

Is dìomhain dut bhith toirt teagaisg
  Do neach a chuir cùl ri eòlas;
Mar thionndaidh's a' chòmhl' air a bannaibh,
  Pillidh an t-amadan ri ghòraich'.

Ged a robh thu dripeil,
  'S còir dhut a bhith air d'fhaicill;
'S iad na toimhsean trice
  Nì na toimhsean cearta.

Tha ar n-ùine ruith gun stad,
  Ceart cho luath 's thig clach le gleann;
Nì i stad nuair ruigear[11] lag,
  'S bidh a h-astar aig a cheann.

Ceart mar a thig gailleann nan sian
  Nuair nach miann leat a bhith ann,
Is amhlaidh sin a thig an t-aog,
  Ged a shaoil thu nach b'e 'n t-àm.

Ceart mar a sgaoileas an ceò
  Nuair a thig teas air on ghrèin,
Is amhlaidh sin a shiubhlas glòir
  Is ioma dòchas air bheag feum.

Cha b'e comann an dà ghamhna
    A bha shannt orm dhèanamh riut,
Ach rud bhiodh agad ghabhail uat,
    'S an rud bhiodh uat a thoirt dhut.

Nach b'e siud an comann saor,
    'S cha b'e comann nam maor mun chlàr?
B'e 'n comann-san bhith toirt a-null,
    'S cha chomann ach a-null 's a-nall.

Mas fìor gach seanfhacal
    A labhradh le luchd gèire,
Bheir fòid breithe agus bàis
    Duine air athadh 's air èiginn.

[1]*cugann*, milk set for cream. [2]*aon* and *dheug* are supplied here for better version and metre. [3]*gabhannach*, 'flattering'. [4]*siochaint*, subst. for *sìothchaidh*. [5]*di-chaisg*, 'uncontrollable'; not a dictionary word. [6]*baileach* more commonly *buileach*. [7] *sòmhail*, 'small,' opposite of *dòmhail*, 'bulky'; more generally *sùmhail* and *dùmhail*. [8]*rib' an slaod*, to entangle in a coil. [9] Subst. for *chuir rud ann*. [10]'Don't interrupt the party.' [11]*ruigear* subst. for *thig i 'n*, as preferable.

APPENDIX

I

1. 'Aireamh na h-Aoine' &c., p. 8.

Counting cattle on Friday was considered peculiarly unlucky. *Ruith na h-Aoine*, 'the Friday fate', was sure to follow. See, to the same effect, 'Ma mharbhas tu beathach Dihaoine,' p. 340.

Eòlas na h-Aoine, 'the Friday spell', was a name applied to the evil eye. If one possessing this unfortunate *eòlas* saw another bathing, the bather was sure to get drowned.

Friday has long been held an unlucky day in various Christian countries. This is generally supposed to be founded on the fact that it was the day of our Lord's Crucifixion. Accordingly, it is a fast day in the Church of Rome, whence the Gaelic name *Di-h-Aoine*, literally 'Fast-Day.' The belief in the unluckiness of Friday is not confined, however, to Christian countries. It prevails also among the Brahmins, who hold that no business of any importance should be commenced on Friday. *Asiat. Res.*, Vol. VI, p. 172; Chambers's *Book of Days*, Vol. I, p. 42.

The Scottish proverb 'Friday flit, short time sit,' and the English 'Friday's hair and Sunday's horn goes to the dool on Monday morn,' illustrate this superstition.

II

2. 'Am port as fheàrr' &c., p. 26.

Roderick Morrison, the most famed of Highland harpers, and a poet of no mean powers, was son of John Morrison of Bragar (see Note *ante*, p. 51), and born, according to MacKenzie (*The Beauties of Gaelic Poetry*, p. 85), in 1646. His father, who was a man of some mark, and of varied ability, had five sons, of whom three became clergymen. Rory was sent as a boy with two of his brothers to be educated at Inverness, and there he lost his eyesight from smallpox. Instead of theology, music became thenceforth his study, and his father is said to have declared that the education of Rory as a musician cost him more trouble and expense than that of the three ministers. On his return from a visit to Ireland, Rory met in Edinburgh the Chief of the MacLeods, Iain Breac, described by MacKenzie as 'that sterling model of a Highland Chieftain' and said to have been one of the last that had in his retinue 'a Bard, a Harper, a Piper, and a Fool—all of them excellently and well provided for'. This spirited Chief engaged Rory in the double capacity of Bard and Harper, in both which offices he earned a reputation that still lives. His Lament for his beloved patron, *Creach na Ciadain*, and his *Oran Mòr Mhic Leòid*, full of praise of the dead, combined with plain but dignified strictures addressed to the young Chief, are very creditable, and still worthy of remembrance in that ancient and hospitable house. Few families anywhere can boast of having had two such bards in their service as Mary MacLeod and Roderick Morrison; and no sentiment more appropriate could be addressed to a MacLeod Chief than this of Roderick:

> Bi gu fiùghantach smachdail,
> Rianail, reachdmhor, 'n Triath Leòdach,
> Na faic frìd an sùil brìdein—
> Cha chùis dìon do Mhac Leòid e!
>
> Cha chùis dìon do Mhac Leòid
> A bhith dòlam 's rud aige;
> Lean an dùthchas bu chòir dhut
> 'S biodh mòr-chuis 'nad aigne!

After the death of Iain Breac, change of days came to Dunvegan and to Rory: in his own pathetic words,

> Chaidh a' chuibhle mun cuairt,
> Gun do thionndaidh gu fuachd am blàths.

The Chief had given him the farm of Totamor in Glenelg rent-free, from which he appears to have been ejected by the new laird, Roderick, of whom he says:

> Dheagh mhic athar mo ghràidh,
> Bu tu m'aighear, is m'àgh, is m'olc.

After this he returned to Lewis, where he died at a good old age, and was buried in the old churchyard of Eye, near Stornoway.
The above facts are taken chiefly from MacKenzie's sketch, in which

a few mistakes occur. The poet's father is said to have been an Episcopal clergyman; he was a farmer. At the time of Rory's visit to Edinburgh it is said that the Scotch nobility and gentry were at the Court of King James in Holyrood House. James VII never was in Scotland after he became king. Macintosh says Rory was harper to MacLeod in the reign of Queen Anne, which is probable enough.

Sir Walter Scott thus alludes to Roderick in *Waverley* (ch. xvii.): "Two paces back stood Cathleen holding a small Scottish harp, the use of which had been taught to Flora by Rory Dall, one of the last harpers of the Western Highlands."

Macintosh in a note on the above proverb (2nd ed., p. 199), gives the following interesting reminiscence:

"Harps were in use in the Highlands and Isles of Scotland from time immemorial, till the beginning of last century, and even later; for Mr Robertson of Lude, General Robertson's great-grandfather, the gentleman whom the elegant poet Struan immortalises in his poems, was a famous performer upon that instrument, and I have heard my father relate the following anecdote of him:

"One night my father said to Lude that he would be happy to hear him play upon the harp, which at that time began to give place to the violin. After supper Lude and he retired to another room, in which there were a couple of harps, one of which belonged to Queen Mary. 'James,' says Lude, 'here are two harps, the largest one is the loudest, but the small one is the sweetest; which do you wish to hear played?' James answered, 'The small one,' which Lude took up, and played upon it till daylight.

"Upon a visit to my native country of Athole, about five years ago, I had the curiosity to enquire of General Robertson if the harps were still in the family. The General told me they were, and brought them upon the table, at the sight of which I was quite overjoyed in viewing the musical instruments of our ancestors, as well as those of the renowned heroes of Ossian.

"After my return to Edinburgh, I immediately gave notice of the harps to the Highland Society of Scotland, who wrote to General Robertson requesting a sight of the harps, which he was so obliging as to grant.

"Mr Gunn, teacher of music in Edinburgh, has since published an Essay upon the Harp, with representations taken from these very harps. I have the vanity to think the bringing these harps before the eyes of the public to be one of the most pleasant actions of my life, as in all probability they must either have been lost or destroyed by time, without ever having been known to the world; and those fastidious gentlemen who take pleasure in opposing everything respecting the antiquity of the Caledonians would have persisted in denying the use of the harp among these people, as they do many other things."

The two harps above mentioned are now in the Museum of the Society of Antiquaries of Scotland, to which they have been kindly lent by the owner, Mr Steuart of Dalguise.

Campbell, Macintosh's editor, adds to the above that when visiting the Western Highlands and Islands in 1815 collecting melodies for his *Albyn's Anthology*, he visited the grave of Rory Dall's pupil, the last of our Hebridean harpers, Murdoch MacDonald; and that Mrs MacKenzie of Dervaig in Mull remembered his playing on his harp in her father's house. This Mrs MacKenzie was the Miss MacLean specially mentioned by Boswell in his *Tour through the Hebrides*. She was the daughter of a Dr. MacLean who lived near Tobermory at that time, 1773. Dr. Johnson said of her, 'She is the most accomplished lady that I have found in the Highlands. She knows French, Music and Drawing, sews neatly, makes shell-work, and can milk cows; in short, she can do everything. She talks sensibly, and is the first person I have found that can translate Erse poetry literally.' She accompanied her singing on a spinnet, which Boswell said was well-toned, though made in 1667.—Carruthers' ed., p. 249.

III

'Cha ghluais bròg' &c., p. 111.

Eòghann a' Chinn Bhig, 'Ewen of the Little Head', was the eldest son of one of the first lairds of Lochbuie in Mull, and married a daughter of MacDougall of Lorn, a very ill-tempered and niggardly woman, who got the nickname of *Gortag*. He quarrelled violently with his father, and is said to have struck him. The old man complained to his relation MacLean of Duart, who was glad of a pretext for invading Lochbuie, and came down with an armed force against Ewen.

On the evening before the battle, Ewen consulted a witch, of whom he asked whether he was to win the fight. She said he would win, if on the morrow his wife would give him *butter without asking for it*, 'im gun iarraidh.' Next morning Ewen sat and waited long for the butter, rubbing his hands and stamping with his feet. At last his wife said, 'Chan fhàg breabadair na seana bhròig craiceann air deàrnaibh,' '*The kicker of the old shoe won't leave skin on palm*'; on which Ewen responded as above, '*Neither shoe nor speech will move the bad housewife.*' He went away in a rage, leaving his food untasted, turned his dogs into the milk-house, and hastened to the fight, from which he never returned alive. It took place in Glen Cainnir near Lochbuie, where a stroke from a broadsword swept off Ewen's little head. The horse then rushed from the fight with his rider on his back, and was so seen again for days, careering wildly through these glens, up and down passes and precipices fit only for goats or birds. For many generations thereafter this headless rider, still in full armour, continued to be seen or heard, a well-known and dreaded object, and always appearing when any important member of the Lochbuie family was in danger or near death. The name of Ewen of the Little Head is still a power to frighten children in Mull and the neighbouring islands. In the *Teachdaire Gaelach* of August 1830, there is a slightly different version of this legend, written with the usual vivid power of the Editor, Dr. Norman MacLeod. He gives it as if told at Iona, where a tombstone with the figure of a horseman in full armour was said to be that of Eòghann a' Chinn Bhig; and the last vision of him, racily described, was said to have been only 'twelve years ago'. The reason given for the restless activity of Ewen's spirit is admirable—'Thuit e 'na thrasg'—'*He fell fasting*'!

IV

The season of Spring was more specially a matter of observation and interest to our ancestors than any of the other seasons, on account of its importance as the time of year on the character of which their existence and comfort so much depended. Accordingly we find it divided into various periods, with fanciful names, founded, so far as their meaning can be guessed, on the imaginary causes of the various changes of weather. The longest of these is the *Faoilleach*, or *Faoilteach*, on the etymology of which Armstrong says, 'The original meaning was perhaps the wolf month (*faol*, a wolf), from the circumstances that wolves, with which the Highlands once abounded, became more daring and dangerous in the depth of winter. *Faoilteach* may also be derived from *faoile*, welcome, joy. The Highlanders regard stormy weather, towards the end of January, as prognostic of a fruitful season to follow, and *vice versa*.' The former of these etymologies is supported by the word *Wulfes-Mónaδ*, said to have been the Anglo-Saxon name given to the month of January, Old Style, for the reason above mentioned. The other etymology is supported by the rhyme given at p. 199, *ante*,

> Faoilleach, Faoilleach, làmh an crios,
> Faoilte mhòr bu chòir bhith ris.

The *Faoilleach* corresponded roughly to the present month of February, embracing the last two weeks of Winter, O.S., and the first two of Spring. Sometimes the first half was called the *Faoilleach Geamhraidh*, and the other half the *Faoilleach Earraich*.

Some time in this month three Summer days were supposed to come in exchange for three cold days lent to July, and the saying is 'Tha trì latha Iuchair san Fhaoilleach' &c.—see *ante*, p. 405. The occurrence of such mild days early in February is still a matter of common observation, and is never considered seasonable.—See 'Chan eil port' &c., *ante*, p. 126.

After this came a week called the *Feadag*, the Plover or Whistle, so called probably because of the piping winds then prevalent. The following rhyme refers to it:

> Thuirt an Fheadag ris an Fhaoilleach,
> 'Càit an d'fhàg thu 'n laoighean bochd?'
> 'Dh'fhàg mis' e aig cùl a' ghàrraidh,
> 'S a dhà shùil 'na cheann 'nam ploc.'

> —*Said the Plover to the Stormy,*
> '*Where did'st leave the poor wee calf?*'
> '*I left him behind the wall,*
> *With his eyes like lumps of turf.*'

Another rhyme makes the *Feadag* the *mother* of the Faoilleach and of course preceding it:

> Feadag, Feadag, màthair Faoillich fhuair.

For this, however, there is no other authority.

After the *Feadag* came the *Gearran*, the Horse or Gelding, a period as to the duration of which authorities differ very considerably. The

Highland Society's *Dictionary*, MacLeod and Dewar, and MacAlpine, all make it 'the days from March 15th to April 11th inclusive'—four weeks. Armstrong says, more vaguely than usual, that it is 'the latter end of February,' and no more. The saying given on p. 353, *ante*, 'Mìos Faoillich' &c., makes it two weeks, while several living authorities make it one week. The presumption is in favour of a short period, which is supported by the only suggested meaning of the name *Gearran* (*geàrr-shian*—H. S. Dict., MacLeod and Dewar), and the words *an gearran geàrr* in the rhyme given below.

The *Feadag* is severe, but the *Gearran* is no better, as the rhyme says:

> Is mis' an Fheadag lom, luirgneach, luath—
> Marbham caora, marbham uan;
> Is mis' an Gearran bacach bàn,
> Is cha mhi aon bhonn as fheàrr;
> Cuiream a' bhò anns an toll
> Gus an tig an tonn thar a ceann.

> *—I'm the bare swift leggy Plover—*
> *I can kill both sheep and lamb;[1]*
> *I'm the white lame Gelding,*
> *And not one bit better;*
> *I'll put the cow into the hole*
> *Till the wave comes o'er her head.*

or otherwise

> An sin thuirt an Gearran geàrr,
> Ni mi farran ort nach fheàrr,
> Cuiridh mi bhò mhòr sa pholl &c.

After the *Gearran* came the *Cailleach* or *Old Woman*, which lasted a week—12th to 18th April. The grass had by this time begun to grow, and the Cailleach, representing a hostile and withering influence,

---

[1] If this is to be taken as with any approximate accuracy characterising the Seasons, it follows that lambing was earlier in those days than now. There are various indications in these old sayings that Spring and warm weather came sooner in former days than now.

[2] A *slacan* is a beetle; but a more poetical version makes it *slacan-druidheachd*, magic wand.

sits down and tries hard with her *slacan*[2] to beat down the grass, and keep it from growing. Finding her efforts vain, she flings away her mallet in wrath, and vanishes with a shriek into the realm of Night, exclaiming,

> Dh'fhàg e shìos mi, dh'fhàg e shuas mi,
> Dh'fhàg e eadar mo dhà chluais mi;
> Dh'fhàg e thall mi, dh'fhàg e bhos mi,
> Dh'fhàg e eadar mo dhà chois mi;
> Tilgeam seo am bun preas cuilinn,
> Far nach fàs feur no duilleach!

> —*It escapes me up and down,*
> *'Twixt my very ears has flown;*
> *It escapes me here and there,*
> *'Twixt my feet and everywhere;*
> *This 'neath holly tree I'll throw,*
> *Where no grass nor leaf shall grow!*

This is a lively description, and the selection of the holly in particular shows felicitous accuracy.

After the abortive attempt of the *Cailleach*, the time came to sow, and that *quamprimum*:

> Ge b'e 'r bith mar bhios an t-sian,
> Cuir do shìol anns a' Mhàrt.

The *Màrt* corresponded probably to the month of March, but it was used as a term for the sowing-season, more than for any definite period. The term *Gibleann* in like manner was applied to the month of April. See 'Am feur' &c., p. 25.

Another period not so commonly mentioned is the *Gobag*, Little-Gab, or Dog-fish, sometimes called a week, sometimes three days, and coming in apparently between the *Feadag* and the *Gearran*. A saying that refers to it is

> Feadagan is Gobagan e, tuilleadh gu Fèill Pàraig,

which may be rendered,

> *Whistling and biting winds on to St Patrick's Day,*

i.e., 30th March, O.S., when the equinoctial gales and worst weather should have passed.

Neòil dhubha na Càisge, 'the dark clouds of Easter', came in the fourth week of March, followed by *Glasadh na Cuthaig,* 'the cuckoo's greening', or preparation time.

The *Oisgean* or Ewes, called *Trì Là nan Oisgean,* 'the three days of the Ewes', or *Là nan Trì Oisgean,* 'the Day of the Three Ewes', were three days immediately following the *Cailleach,* which would bring them into the third week of April, O.S. The name suggests the 'three borrowing days' of the Lowlands, but the period and character of the *Oisgean* is quite different. According to the Lowland tradition (Chambers's *Pop. Rhymes of Scotland,* pp 143-4; *Book of Days,* I, 448), these three days were the last of March, and said to be borrowed from April. According to the English version, referred to by Sir Thomas Browne, and thus given by Ray,

> April borrows three days from March, and they are ill.

The Stirlingshire version quoted by Chambers gives, as he says, the most dramatic account of this tradition, and seems to throw light on the Gaelic name, substituting 'hogs' for 'ewes', though otherwise not satisfactory:—

> March said to Averill,
> 'I see three hogs on yonder hill,
> And if you'll lend me dayis three,
> I'll find a way to gar them dee!'
> The first o them was wind and weet,
> The second o them was snaw and sleet,
> The third o them was sic a freeze,
> It froze the birds' feet to the trees;
> When the three days were past and gane,
> The silly poor hogs cam hirplin hame.

In point of fact, the few days in March that might with any propriety be called 'borrowed' are warm and summery, and not the opposite. The idea of April lending cold days to March seems rather absurd.

Be that as it may, the three days of the *Oisgean* are more probably to be considered mild days borrowed from Summer than killing days borrowed from April. There is a Highland tradition to that effect, which ascribes the origin of the borrowing to the three days allowed to the children of Israel for their journey into the wilderness to eat the Passover. That the name was derived from the idea that a few mild days are given in lambing time, for the sake of the ewes and lambs, is at once more probable and more pleasant than the opposite version.

After the withering *Cailleach* comes the lively *Sguabag*, the Brushlet or Little Blast, and thenceforth the Spring goes on merrily—*Suas e, 'n t-Earrach!*—'Up with the Spring!' Last of all came the pleasant *Cèitean*, foretaste of Summer, supposed to include the three weeks up to 12th May; followed by the cheery note of the cuckoo on yellow May Day, *Latha Buidhe Bealltainn*, when the powers of Cold and Darkness have been overcome once more, and the world is gladdened by the returning reign of Light and Warmth.

V

'Gach dàn gu Dàn an Deirg' &c., p. 211.

(1) *Dàn an Deirg* has always been one of the most popular of Ossianic Ballads, though, in the various forms in which it has been handed down to us, its merits seem scarcely equal to its reputation. One verse, in one of the shorter versions, is singularly beautiful. The wife of the Dearg, whose love for her husband had been so silent and restrained that he felt doubtful of it, was thus expressed when the concocted story was brought to her of his having been killed, which killed her:

> Chì mi 'n t-seabhag, chì mi 'n cù
> Leis an dèanadh mo rùn an t-sealg,
> 'S on a b'ionnmhainn leis an triùir,
> Càirear sinn san ùir le Dearg.

> —*I see the hawk, I see the hound*
> *With which my love was wont to chase;*
> *And as the three to him were dear,*
> *Let us with Dearg be laid in earth.*

See Campbell's *Leabhar na Féinne*, pp 107–113, for the various versions, in which, however, the above will not be found *verbatim*.

(2) *Laoidh an Amadain Mhòir* has always been held in great esteem as a suitable piece for recitation, the story being interesting. Mr Campbell in his *West Highland Tales*, III, 154, gives the best version of it hitherto printed, the text of which, however, is in some places very unsatisfactory.

(3) *Sgeul Chonail*, 'the Tale of Connal'. There are several tales of

this name: the most elaborate is the story of Conall Gulban, given by Mr Campbell in Vol III, p. 188.

(4) *Cliù Eòghainn*. For an account of this poem see Note to 'B'fhasa Eòghann a chur air each,' *ante*, p. 59.

(5) 'Loch Cé,' Lough Key, is described by Dr. O'Donovan, in his Notes to O'Daly's *Tribes of Ireland* (p. 38), as 'a beautiful lake, with several islands, in the barony of Boyle, County of Roscommon, near the margin of which stands Rockingham, the magnificent residence of Lord Lorton.'

VI

'Is fheàrr leum-iochd' &c., p. 277.

A different interpretation of this saying has been received from Aberdeenshire, viz., that in lands allotted on the 'run-rig' system, the crofter who got a 'balk' attached to his rig was considered luckier than his neighbour with a somewhat larger rig, but without the balk, the grass of which was of more than compensating value. The Rev. Mr Michie of Dinnet has heard the above saying used in the Highlands of Aberdeenshire in this sense.

The customs as to the *Cailleach* and *Maighdeann-bhuana* seem to have varied somewhat. Two reapers were usually set to each rig, and according to one account, the man who was first done got the *Maighdeann-Bhuana* or 'Reaping-Maiden,' while the man who was last got the *Cailleach*, or 'Old Woman'. The latter term is used in Argyllshire; the term *Gobhar Bhacach*, 'Lame Goat', is used in Skye.

According to what appears to be the better version, the competition to avoid the *Cailleach* was not between reapers but between neighbouring crofters, and the man who got his harvest done first sent a handful of corn called the *Cailleach* to his neighbour, who passed it on, till it landed with him who was latest. That man's penalty was to provide for the dearth of the township, *gort a' bhaile*, in the ensuing season.

The *Maighdeann-Bhuana*, again, was the last cut handful of oats on a croft or farm, and was an object of lively competition among the reapers. It was tastefully tied up with ribbons, generally dressed like a doll, and then hung up on a nail till Spring. On the first day of ploughing, it was solemnly taken down, and given as a *sainnseal* or handsel for luck to the horses. It was meant as a symbol that the harvest had been secured, and to ward off the fairies, representatives of the ethereal and unsubstantial, till the time came to provide for a new crop.

Jamieson in his *Scot. Dict. s.v.* 'Maiden,' 'Carlin,' 'Rapegyrne,' 'Kirn' and 'Claaick,' gives some interesting information regarding this ancient custom, which was not peculiar to Scotland. He says the harvest-home, when early finished, was called in Aberdeenshire the 'Maiden Claaick', when as late as Hallowmas, the 'Carlin Claaick' (=*Cailleach*). Additional particulars regarding the Aberdeenshire customs will be found in Mr Walter Gregor's forthcoming work on the folklore of the North-East of Scotland.

VII

THE REV. DONALD MACINTOSH

The good man to whom we are indebted for the first collection of Celtic Proverbs ever made was born in 1743, at Orchilmore, near Killiecrankie, on the north side of the Garry. His father was originally a cooper, married early in life, retired to his native Orchilmore, and there spent the rest of his days as a small farmer or crofter. According to Campbell, he was 'descended from the ancient Thanes of Glentilt,' a claim which need not be called in question. These Thanes, formerly Stewarts, and before that Macdonalds, appear to have used the name of 'Toshach' (sounded long: *Tòiseach*=First) as a surname in 1501 (Skene's *Celtic Scotland*, Vol. III, p. 273), and that of 'Mac Toschy' as early as 1382 (*Id.*, p. 358). Macintosh, in Gaelic *Mac an Tòisich*, means the Son of the *Tòiseach*, or Captain. After attending the parish school, and acting for some time as teacher to the younger members of his father's family, and such of the neighbouring children as were committed to his care, Donald removed to Edinburgh, in the hope of bettering his fortune. He probably found some difficulty in getting any congenial occupation there, and Campbell says he remembers seeing him, in 1774 or 1775, as one of Peter Williamson's Penny Post men, 'with his bell in his hand, and uniform cap on his head, on which were painted in gilt letters WILLIAMSON'S PENNY POST, alternately collecting and delivering letters in his useful though humble vocation'. He next found employment as a copying clerk, and after that for some time as tutor in the family of Stewart of Gairntully. There was at that time some wakening of literary activity in the direction of Gaelic poetry and antiquities, stimulated no doubt by the success of Macpherson's Ossianic labours. Macintosh appears to have done something in the way of collecting old poetry, but being of a very modest disposition, he preferred to assist others than to attempt anything in that line on his own responsibility. One piece got by him in Lochaber in 1784 from a namesake of his own, John Macintosh, 'Ceardach Mhic Luin,' appears in Gillies's *Sean Dana*, p. 233. The idea of making a collection of proverbs and old sayings was a happy one, and the merit of it appears to be entirely due to Macintosh himself. His design, as expressed in the 'Advertisement' prefixed to his collection, was 'to preserve the language, and a few remains of the ancient customs of Scotland, by bringing so many of the proverbial sayings of the people into one point of view'. In this laudable undertaking he received sufficient encouragement and assistance. He returns special thanks to Sir James Foulis of Colinton, for the use of 'some valuable Gaelic MSS,' to Professor Ferguson, 'a gentleman to whom this country is much indebted,' and to Neil Ferguson, Esq. of Pitcullo. Others to whom he renders his thanks are the Rev. John Stewart of Luss, Rev. James Maclagan, Blair Atholl, Rev. Joseph Macgregor, Edinburgh, Mr William Morrison, writer in Edinburgh, and Mr Robert Macfarlane, school-master, 'all of whom were particularly obliging, having procured him the perusal of many curious manuscripts, which considerably augmented this collection'. Nor does he omit a special paragraph of thanks 'to John Macintosh from Lochaber, formerly a tenant under Macdonald of Keppoch, a worthy, honest man, well versed in old Gaelic sayings.' Campbell says that a considerable proportion of the collection was got from this man in 1784, and that previous to this the collector had got a valuable and extensive portion of his materials from John Wallace, residing at Lettoch, near Moulin. In addition to those above-mentioned as having assisted the collector, Campbell mentions the venerable Henry Mackenzie, the 'Man of Feeling,' as one of those who gave him the benefit of their literary judgment and advice.

The following is the title-page of the book:

A COLLECTION of GAELIC PROVERBS and FAMILIAR PHRASES; Accompanied with an ENGLISH TRANSLATION, Intended to facilitate the Study of the LANGUAGE; illustrated with NOTES. To which is added, the WAY TO WEALTH, by DR. FRANKLIN, translated into GAELIC. By DONALD MACINTOSH. *Ge d' dh' èignichear an sean-fhocal, cha bhreugaichear e.* Edinburgh: Printed for the Author, and sold by Messrs. DONALDSON, CREECH, ELLIOT, and SIBBALD, Booksellers, Edinburgh; JOHN GILLIES, Perth; JAMES GILLIES, Glasgow, and by all the Booksellers in Town and Country. MDCCLXXXV. The modest little book was dedicated 'to the Right Honourable David, Earl of Buchan, Lord Cardross, Founder and President of the Society of Scots Antiquaries' &c., in appropriately warm and complimentary terms. The proverbs, with translation on the opposite page, occupied 142 pp. The translation of Franklin's *Way to Wealth* was done by R. Macfarlane above-mentioned, by desire of the Earl of Buchan. In a short address in Gaelic prefixed to it, from the Earl to the Highlanders of Scotland, he says he was the first man who donned their manly dress in the Lowlands after the prohibition of it was revoked, and that in time of snow and storm.

Soon after the publication of the book, Macintosh obtained employment in the office of Mr Davidson, Deputy-Keeper of the Signet and Crown-Agent, in which he continued for several years. A more distinguished but less substantial acknowledgement of his merits was his appointment on 30th Nov., 1785, as 'Clerk for the Gaelic Language' to the Society of Antiquaries of Scotland. There was no salary attached to the office, which Macintosh held till 1789, when it was reported that there was a vacancy in it 'by the removal from Edinburgh of Mr. Donald Mackintosh,' and the Rev. Joseph Robertson Macgregor was chosen 'Secretary for the Gaelic Language'. The office was abolished long ago. Macintosh presented a number of things, chiefly coins, to the Society. Among others were 'A piece of Prince Charles Edward's brogues, which he left with Mr. M'Donald of Kingsburgh in 1746, now in the possession of Mr. Oliphant of Gask,' and 'A parcel of that Prince's hair'.

The death of Prince Charles Edward in 1788 led to a curious result in the Scottish Episcopal Church, and an important change in the career of Donald Macintosh. In the lofty language of his biographer, it 'paved the way for a more exalted station in society,' that, viz., of a priest of the Scottish Episcopal Church.

"Well do I remember," says Campbell, "the day on which the name of GEORGE was mentioned in the morning service for the first time—such blowing of noses—such significant hems—such half-suppressed sighs—such smothered groans, and universal confusion, can hardly be conceived! But the deed was done—and those who had participated could not retract." Some staunch Jacobites, however, who held that the person to be prayed for, as King of Great Britain and Ireland, was not GEORGE but HENRY (Cardinal York), protested against what they called a 'schism' on the part of their weaker brethren, and forthwith formed themselves into a separate body, claiming to be the true old Scots Episcopal Church as by law established after the Restoration. How many clergymen remained true to the White Cockade cannot be ascertained. The number must have been very small, but it included one prelate, Bishop Rose, now far advanced in life, and described by Campbell, himself a warm Jacobite, as "almost in his dotage". He resided at Doune (called by Campbell 'Down'), and there a Mr Brown, of the same persuasion, was consecrated as his coadjutor and successor. On the death of Bishop Rose, Bishop Brown, says Campbell, "had to look about him for a successor, and who should fall in his way but the subject of this memoir." From this it would appear that Brown was now the sole representative of the nonjurant Episcopal clergy of Scotland, as Macintosh became after his death. In June 1789, Macintosh was ordained Deacon by Bishop Brown, and thereafter, in due time, Priest. This, doubtless, was the cause of his removal from Edinburgh in 1789. "Here then," says Campbell, "we hail our worthy countryman placed in a relatively higher position in society than even his predecessors the Thanes of Glentilt." In touching contrast with this elevation is Macintosh's simple statement in his Petition to the Court of Session, that he officiated at first with a salary of £5, thereafter £8, from a Fund raised in 1739 for the relief of poor Scottish Episcopal clergymen, with the addition of £1 from the interest of £100 bequeathed by a Mrs Buntine to that Fund. Campbell gives no information as to Macintosh's residence from 1789 to 1794. The probability is that he had no fixed residence, but moved from place to place, as a missionary or untitled bishop of Jacobite Episcopacy, till he finally settled in Edinburgh. Even after that it appears, so far as anything definite can be gathered from

Campbell, that he made an annual tour through the Perthshire Highlands, by Loch Katrine and Glenfinlas, on to Glen Tilt, up to Glenshee, and as far north as Banff, administering the sacraments and religious instruction among the scattered remnant who owned his pastoral authority. Campbell, with characteristic grandeur, says, "The destinies willed it not that he should enjoy his exalted station long with dignified ease and honour; for his reverend brethren, who had 'bowed the knee to Baal', questioned the validity of his ordination, which embittered his life in secret, and caused other embarrassments, particularly to those well-meaning individuals who considered him as the only spiritual pastor left of *the true Church*, against which 'the gates of hell should not prevail'. Meanwhile, our compiler pursued his path of duty as a clergyman, but did not forget those secular pursuits which went hand in hand with his more serious avocations." In 1794 Macintosh distinguished himself by raising an action in the Court of Session against the Managers of the Fund above-mentioned, to which he claimed sole right, as the only representative of the true Scottish Episcopal Church. In the Petition he is described as 'Episcopal Minister in Bailie Fyfe's Close'. The action was dismissed with a somewhat unnecessary display of wit and loyalty on the part of the Court, the Lord President, Sir Ilay Campbell, remarking that he was "at a loss whether to frown at the audaciousness of the pursuer, or to smile at the high pitch of folly of his witless advisers, in wantonly thrusting a plea of so extraordinary a nature into His Majesty's Supreme Court of Justice. What! a person claiming a right in virtue of his refractory adherence to obsolete opinion, long since exploded—nay, glorying in his disloyalty to the best of kings and existing governments."

From the 'Session Papers' (Campbell's Coll., 103) containing some of the Prints in this case, the following additional facts have been got. The Petition, with which the case commenced, sets forth that the Petitioner is "a minister of the Scots Episcopal Church, and Pastor of a congregation of that persuasion, which, though respectable, is far from being numerous; that the income he derives from them is, and always has been, altogether insufficient to raise him above indigence, from which he was for many years saved almost entirely by a small pension of £9 a-year, paid him from a fund held by Trustees for the relief of Scots Episcopal Clergymen in his situation; that of this salary he has been deprived by the present defenders" &c. The prayer of the petition was to ordain the defenders to pay him this £9 per annum from 1795 onwards, "or such salary as to the Court seems proper". The ground for refusing the petition seems to have been that the Petitioner declined to take the oaths to the existing government, and to pray by name for King George, which an Act passed in 1792, repealing all penal statutes against the Episcopal Clergy, and restoring the privileges formerly conferred on them, prescribed as a condition of such restoration.

In 1801 Macintosh was appointed Gaelic Translator and Keeper of Gaelic Records to the Highland Society of Scotland, in succession to Mr Robert Macfarlane, which office he held till his death. A salary of £10 a year was attached to it. That it was not a sinecure is indicated by the Catalogues of Gaelic MSS, belonging to the Highland Society and others, given in Vol. III of the London Highland Society's *Ossian*, pp 566–573. These were compiled by Macintosh, who also transcribed some of the MSS. The office of Gaelic Translator and Keeper of MSS to the Highland Society was conferred after Macintosh's death on the Rev. John Campbell, who held it till 1814, after which it was not again filled up.

Macintosh's circumstances were somewhat improved in his later years, though his income was but small. Campbell mentions two legacies left to him by kindly members of his scattered but faithful flock, one of £100 by Mrs Eagle, Edinburgh, another of £150 by Mrs Paterson, Banff. "These sums," says Campbell, "together with his annual savings, enabled him to leave behind him a property, which he apportioned in several small legacies, as specified in his will." In that will, which Campbell had before him, but of which, with all his other MSS, no other trace can be found, he thus designated himself: "I, the Reverend Donald Macintosh, a priest of the Old Scots Episcopal Church, and last of the nonjurant clergy in Scotland."

In 1808 his health rapidly failed; he was unable to undertake his annual journey to the Highlands; he made his will, set his house in order, called in the Rev. Mr Adam, of Blackfriars' Wynd Episcopal Chapel, received the Sacrament from his hands, and soon after, on 22nd November 1808, breathed his last. He was respectably buried in the Greyfriars' Churchyard, but no stone marks the spot where he was laid.

Macintosh never married. "He had a taste," says Campbell, "for his

native melodies, and performed them not unskillfully on the violin."
He even extended his musical accomplishments so far as to play
upon the spinet. He purchased an old one for a few shillings, took
lessons from a lady, and in less than two months "he could thrum
nicely 'I'll mak' ye fain to follow me'."

The chief part of the "property" above-mentioned consisted of his
library, which, considering the smallness of his income, did much
credit to his literary taste. This collection, numbering about 2000
volumes, he bequeathed, after the worthy example of a greater man,
the saintly Leighton, "for the purpose of establishing a library in the
town of Dunkeld, under such regulations for the preservation of my
books and manuscripts, and for promoting the access of the public
thereto, as to the said trustees shall seem good." The books were
chiefly connected with Scottish history, political and ecclesiastical,
and included a considerable collection of pamphlets, about 60 vols.
The bequest was accepted and carried out, and the library is still
maintained in Dunkeld, under the name of "The Mackintosh Library," to which numerous additions have from time to time been
made. None of Macintosh's MSS, however, appear to have found
their way to Dunkeld. At any rate, they are not there now, nor can
they be traced to any other quarter, with the exception of some
unimportant documents, believed to be in his handwriting, among
the Gaelic MSS in the Advocates' Library. Their value may not have
been great, but it is to be regretted that the wish of the estimable
testator in regard to them was not respected. In the Edinburgh
University Library what appears to be his handwriting will be found,
in a copy of the Gaelic 'Blessing of the Ship,' appended to the old
copy of Carswell's Prayer-Book.

There is no authority for spelling the name of 'Donald Macintosh'
otherwise than as it appears in the only authentic specimen of it
under his own hand, in the first edition of his book. In the second
edition, and in various other notices of him, the 'k' is introduced,
which some people think of importance. The 'k' is harmless, but
quite superfluous, as much so to MacIntosh as to MacIndoe,
MacInroy or MacIntyre. Its omission has the authority, so far as any
is required, of two such Celtic scholars and historians as Gregory
and Skene.

Index

whistling, 202, 203, 220, 372
white, 117, 315, 404
whiting, 397
Whit Sunday, 265, 285
wickedness, 2, 350
widow, 401
wife, 348
wife, 15, 16, 25, 75, 128, 179, 181, 209,
    217, 218, 227, 260, 263, 272, 305,
    307, 354, 362, 369, 393, 397, 410
will, 23, 33, 119, 200, 201, 210, 304
willow, 386
wily, 151
win, 21, 24, 106
wind, 5, 28, 29, 34, 40, 43, 81, 89, 100,
    108, 111, 137, 145, 154, 175, 193,
    214, 215, 242, 287, 307, 316, 346,
    375, 413
windpipe, 31
wine, 220, 233
winner, 7
winnowing-cloth, 306
winter, 11, 138, 144, 164, 180, 189, 222,
    257, 258, 288, 367
wisdom, 103
wise, 26, 27, 63, 86, 90, 93, 111, 113,
    124, 125, 151, 170, 174, 226, 284,
    305, 349, 370, 394, 406
wit, 41, 257
withe, 30, 90, 100, 312

wives, 72, 284
wood, 53, 113, 136, 147, 179, 193,
    212, 263, 289, 355, 398, 401, 411,
    413
woof, 61, 195, 226, 398
wooing, 40, 95, 254
word, 8, 24, 79, 113, 134, 238, 276, 284,
    314, 319, 349
work, 35, 278, 279, 281, 296, 296, 315,
    318, 373, 413
world, 8, 83, 207, 218, 223, 269, 288
worm, 39
worthless, 256, 355
worthy, 25, 66, 256, 324
wound, 33, 127, 266, 292
wren, 82, 109, 263, 313
wring, 35
wrong, 93, 243

Y

yard, 127, 334
yawn, 347, 349
year, 72, 263, 288
yearling, 95
Yellow John, 411
yellow, 26
yesterday, 363
youth, 71, 99, 140, 147, 225, 246, 311

Also available from

BIRLINN

THE DROVE ROADS OF SCOTLAND
A.R.B. Haldane

ISBN: 1 874744 76 9   Price: £9.99 pbk
Publication: October 1996
268pp • 216 x 138mm • 16 b/w plates and
maps • First paperback edition

One of the great classics of Scottish history, Haldane's work interweaves folklore, social comment and economic history in this fascinating account of Scotland's droving trade and the routes by which cattle and sheep were brought from every corner of the land to markets in central Scotland. An engrossing tour of Scottish history.

SCOTTISH PLACENAMES
Iain Taylor

1 874744 52 1   £5.99 pbk   now Oct
Format: 160pp • 198 x 129mm

A dictionary of over 5000 Scottish placenames including the meaning and origin of each name. This is the only book available to emphasise and detail the Gaelic origins of many Scottish placenames.

MOIDART *Among The Clanranalds*
Rev. Charles MacDonald
Editor: John Watt

1 874744 65 3   £9.99 pbk   256pp
Format: 220 x 140mm   8pp b/w plates   now Sept

Previous editions of this classic family history sold out almost immediately on publication. This, the first paperback edition, includes illustrations plus an introduction and notes for the modern reader.

SCOTTISH FOLKLORE
Raymond Lamont-Brown

1 874744 58 0   £5.99 pbk   154pp

Scotland has some of the richest and most varied folklore in the world, influenced by the Celts, Picts, the Scots, the Vikings and the Anglo-Saxons. This book provides an A-Z of locations throughout Scotland and the folklore associated with each place.

SCOTTISH CUSTOMS
Sheila Livingstone

1 874744 41 6   £6.99pbk   160 pp

A compendium of customs observed by our forefathers and the origins of these customs where known.

'a mine of information... well researched and supported by illustrative quotations from contemporary sources...'
The Scotsman

SCOTTISH DATES
Brian D. Osborne and Ronald Armstrong

1 874744 40 8   £6.99pbk   160 pp

Brian Osborne and Ronald Armstrong have researched the key dates in Scottish history – historical, literary, artistic, scientific – providing a fascinating and essential reference book to Scotland's past.

SCOTCH OBSESSIONS
Brian D. Osborne & Ronald Armstrong

1 874744 68 8   £6.99pbk   208pp

An original, witty and occasionally controversial investigation into the beliefs, passions and phobias which have formed and influenced the Scottish character throughout the centuries.

ISLAND GOING   Robert Atkinson
1 874744 31 9   £9.99 pbk   384pp   35 b/w photos

In 1935 John Ainslie and Robert Atkinson set out on an ornithological search for the *Leach's Fork-tailed Petrel*. Their search was to last for twelve years and to take them to many remote and often deserted Scottish islands.

GÀIR NAN CLÀRSACH / THE HARP'S CRY
Edited by Colm Ó Baoill
Translated by Meg Bateman

1 874744 13 0   £10.99 pbk   245 pp

The first published anthology of Gaelic poetry and song from the 17th century, including melodies where known. It represents the last great artistic flowering of a heroic warrior society soon to vanish in wars and defeat.

THE CELTIC PLACENAMES OF SCOTLAND
W.J. Watson

1 874744 06 8   £14.99 pbk   558pp

First published in 1926, this remains the greatest source book ever written on the placenames of Scotland.

THE HEBRIDES: VOLUMES 1, 2 AND 3
J.M. Boyd and I.L. Boyd

Vols 1&3 136pp   Vol 2: 244pp   f/c &b/w photos

An outstanding trilogy of books spanning the complete natural and human history of the Hebrides, and forming the only work available on the subject.

A Habitable Land surveys the geology, climate and variety of habitats in the Hebrides, and discusses how life is sustained on the very edge of the Atlantic Ocean.

A Natural Tapestry is an ecological profile covering the environment from the sea-bed to the mountain tops.

A Mosaic of Islands highlights the wildlife and geology of the Hebrides in island groups and looks in depth at the two most famous of Scotland's nature reserves – Rum and St Kilda.

1: **A Habitable Land**   1 874744 55 6   **£8.99**
2: **A Natural Tapestry** 1 874744 56 4   **£9.99**
3: **A Mosaic of Islands** 1 874744 57 2   **£8.99**

A HUNDRED YEARS IN THE HIGHLANDS
Osgood Hanbury MacKenzie

1 874744 29 7   £5.99 pbk   221pp

Born in 1842, Osgood Hanbury Mackenzie, son of the twelfth Laird of Gairloch, offers an insight into the harsh social and economic climate of the period, at one of the bleakest points in modern Highland history. His memory lives on in the great gardens he founded at Inverewe, now cared for by the National Trust

A DESCRIPTION OF THE WESTERN ISLES
Martin Martin

1 874744 19 X   *£8.99 pbk*   *540pp*

Three of the earliest accounts known of the Hebrides: *A Description of the Western Islands of Scotland*, circa 1695, *A Voyage to St Kilda* – almost unique among accounts of Hebridean travel in being written by a native, Martin Martin, and *A Description of the Western Isles of Scotland* by Sir Donald Monro, written in 1549.

From J.F. CAMPBELL
POPULAR TALES OF THE WEST HIGHLANDS

Vol 1 ISBN: 1 874744 15 7   *£12.99 pbk*   *554pp*
Vol 2 ISBN: 1 874744 16 5   *£12.99 pbk*   *598pp*

MORE WEST HIGHLAND TALES VOLS 1 & 2

Vol 1 ISBN: 1 874744 22 X   *£12.99 pbk*   *522pp*
Vol 2 ISBN: 1 874744 23 8   *£12.99 pbk*   *384pp*

The finest treasure-house of Scottish tales ever published.

These tales, ranging from simple fairy stories, to epic legend, represent only a small part of the collections built up by John Francis Campbell of Islay. His death interrupted further work, and it was only in 1940 and 1960 that some of the leading scholars in the Gaelic world combined to continue the process of publication.

An Isle Called Hirte
The History and Culture of St Kilda to 1930
Mary Harman

ISBN: 1 899272 03 8   Price: £25.00 hbk
Publication date: October 1996
Format: 360pp • 260 x 190mm •
50 b/w photos & over 100 diagrams

Although much has been written about the Isle of St Kilda, this is by far the most exhaustive and comprehensive account yet to appear. The author looks closely at the people and their way of life, their homes, their farming, fowling and fishing, their customs and their contact with the outside world.

Mary Harman's extensive research has uncovered new historical detail and also provides, for the first time, a comparison of all the known maps of the island.

Skye: A Postcard Tour
Bob Charnley & Roger Miket

0 9516022 2 5   £6.95 pbk
b/w illus throughout   96pp

A journey around the Isle of Skye as it was seen by the visitor two and more generations ago.

The Summer of '89
Bob Charnley

0 9516022 1 7   £14.95 hbk
b/w illus throughout   120pp

Following the chance discovery of a faded photograph album, Bob Charnley set out to recover information about the people and places portrayed in the highly evocative images it contained. His painstaking research, together with the photographs themselves, offers a glorious insight into Victorian Scotland.

THE PERTHSHIRE BOOK
Donald Omand

ISBN: 1 874744 84 X   *Price: £16.99 hbk*
Publication: Spring 1997
Format: 272pp • 234 x 156mm
Illus: 2 x 16pp plates & line drawings
throughout

A comprehensive collection of essays creating the definitive story of Perthshire, and covering all aspects of the area's history, landscape and culture.

With contributions from experts in each subject, the contents include:

Geology and Landscape	Dr R. Duck
Early Peoples	Dr Jack Stevenson
The Romans	Gordon Maxwell
The Dark Ages	Alan Small
The Middle Ages	Derek Hall
Early Modern Times	Jonathan Eagles
Modern Times	Jeremy Duncan
The Rural Economy	Prof. Jimmy Caird
Strathearn	John Foster
The Tay	Prof. Jimmy Caird
The Trossachs	Louis Stott
The City of Perth	Prof. Jimmy Caird
Castles and Mansions	Bruce Walker
Vernacular Buildings	Bruce Walker
Commerce & Industry	Tony Cooke
Place Names	Ian Fraser
Some Famous Local People	Prof. Jimmy Caird
The Travelling People	Dr Sheila Douglas
Dialect	Dr Sheila Douglas
Tales & Legends	Dr Sheila Douglas

Full of fascinating facts, *The Perthshire Book* is essential reading for all those, locals and visitors alike, who love the area. It is also an excellent introduction for those who have yet to discover the delights of this region.